E-COMMERCE
E-BUSINESS

E-COMMERCE
E-BUSINESS

DR. C.S. RAYUDU

B.Com. (Hons), M.Com., L.L.B., M.A. (Economics), Ph.D., CIC., FUWAI

Professor of Commerce and Head

S. K. University,

Anantapur,

ANDHRA PRADESH.

Himalaya Publishing House

ISO 9001:2015 CERTIFIED

First Edition : 2004
Reprint : 2007, 2008, 2009, 2012
2013, 2014, 2015, 2017
Reprint : 2018
Reprint : 2022

Published by : Mrs. Meena Pandey for **Himalaya Publishing House Pvt. Ltd.**,
"Ramdoot", Dr. Bhalerao Marg, Girgaon, Mumbai - 400 004.
Phone: 022-23860170, 23863863; **Fax:** 022-23877178
E-mail: himpub@bharatmail.co.in; **Website:** www.himpub.com

Branch Offices :

New Delhi : "Pooja Apartments", 4-B, Murari Lal Street, Ansari Road, Darya Ganj, New Delhi - 110 002. Phone: 011-23270392, 23278631; Fax: 011-23256286

Nagpur : Kundanlal Chandak Industrial Estate, Ghat Road, Nagpur - 440 018. Phone: 0712-2721215, 2721216

Bengaluru : Plot No. 91-33, 2nd Main Road, Seshadripuram, Behind Nataraja Theatre, Bengaluru - 560 020. Phone: 080-41138821; Mobile: 09379847017, 09379847005

Hyderabad : No. 3-4-184, Lingampally, Besides Raghavendra Swamy Matham, Kachiguda, Hyderabad - 500 027. Phone: 040-27560041, 27550139

Chennai : No. 34/44, Motilal Street, T. Nagar, Chennai - 600 017. Mobile: 09380460419

Pune : "Laksha" Apartment, First Floor, No. 527, Mehunpura, Shaniwarpeth (Near Prabhat Theatre), Pune - 411 030. Phone: 020-24496323, 24496333; Mobile: 09370579333

Cuttack : Plot No 5F-755/4, Sector-9, CDA Market Nagar, Cuttack - 753 014, Odisha. Mobile: 09338746007

Kolkata : 3, S.M. Bose Road, Near Gate No. 5, Agarpara Railway Station, North 24 Parganas, West Bengal - 700109. Mobile: 9674536325

Printed at : M/s Sri Sai Art Printer Hyderabad. On behalf of HPH.

PREFACE

What is Commerce? What is the potential of e-commerce? What is exactly new in e-commerce? These are frequently asked questions which have been answered to a great extent in this book. It is a process of buying and selling products and services over the Internet at any time from anywhere to anywhere without geographical limitations, time zone etc. As a new medium of business accompanied with the system of elecronic payments e-commerce enables meeting trading parties globally via the Net.

The Internet connection is becoming a strategic necessity for modern businesses. The most easy to use and cost effective way of doing business over the Internet is e-commerce. Its unique feature is that the Internet presents enormous opportunities to simultaneous business dealings, has unique value in terms of reduction in transaction costs, giving value-added services while communicating with customers, suppliers and financial institutions. It is a synergy of both physical and virtual business. It is the fastest and economically feasible way of communication between business establishments and the Net users.

E-commerce is a set of integrated software components that provide solutions for various businesses through merchant accounts, shopping carts, storefront, cybercash and the electronic wallet system. The new business system has potential, resulting in better business transactions, wide market coverage, speed, access to even small businesses, high profit margins, instant customer-relations and disintermediation. Today in global trading, there is a complex web of trading relationship in which each business matters and the customer means potential business for corporate houses and firms catering to the needs and demands of consumers.

E-commerce includes online promotion, online ordering, electronic shopping and cyber payment of financial transactions for the business being conducted electronically. It is a cutting-edge technology of business, a new paradigm which developed in 1997. As a buzzword, it has emerged as the most potential aspect of the electronic marvel known as the Internet Revolution. It basically uses electronically networked information system to carry out commercial activities crisscrossing boundaries around the globe through information highways and super highways.

E-commerce is a generic name for a range of technologies that allow the easy and maximum exchange of business information. Commercial activities have evolved through differnet stages of economic development. E-commerce is the present generation medium ensuring easy accessibility to information and the global way to potential business opportunities

Prof. Dr. C. S. Rayudu

28/489-E-4,
Saradanagar,
Anantapur-515 001.
Andhra Pradesh.

CONTENTS

Fundamentals of E-commerce

What is commerce?

The word 'commerce' is the basic concept for electronic commerce or e-commerce, pertaining to the buying and selling of goods while 'commercial' denotes business practice and activities intended to make profit. Electronic commerce, like any other business, deals with the exchange of money for soft or hard goods and services.

In other words, substantial commerce is a process of distribution of goods from a place where they are produced and found in plenty to a place where the goods are in short supply or scarce and hence in demand. The concept of commerce is a very comprehensive and complex organism and includes all the necessary functions involved in buying and selling. It consists of all persons, organisations and institutions engaged in the distribution of goods. They include railways, road transport, shipping, merchants, banks, insurance, companies, brokers, wholesalers, retailers, stock market, distributors, agents, service providers etc.

E-commerce is a selling and transfer process requiring several institutes. It is a systematic and organised network for the exchange of goods between producers and consumers. The Net establishes the interconnections between producers and consumers directly and in this, the Net embraces all those related activities which are indispensable for maintaining a continuous, free and uninterrupted distribution and transfer of goods.

Limitations of Conventional Commerce

- Traditionally, commercial transactions have been carried out mainly through paperwork. They are manually transmitted and forwarded by postal services. The process is called paper-based system of commerce.
- Delay in finalising transitions: There are many associated delays like transportation delay, manual processing delay and ordering delay etc.
- It is known for higher labour cost due to manual processing and related paperworks. Other costs include data typing, retyping, document storage, handling, maintenance etc.
- The conventional commerce system is error prone.
- Yet another limitation of conventional commerce system is relating to the uncertainty of events. These uncertainties mainly pertain to transportation. There is uncertainty about whether the transaction is received at the other end, and there are uncertainties of cheque clearance.
- The entire process of business is time consuming and a costly affair.
- Timely analysis update and the current position cannot be a ascertained instantly.
- In the traditional business communications, orders cannot be raised to reflect both the demand and no stock availability. Immediate instructions cannot be sent to the distributors in time with the other to ensure fast delivery of the services.

- The advantages of the potential market cannot be obtained quickly, thereby losing customers.
- Offline processing will never increase sales and nor will it provide the means for immediate payment.
- There is no place in the old practice for impulse buying.
- The absence of round the clock buying and level playing field are great drawbacks of conventional commerce.
- In many respects, conventional commerce fails to benefit modern consumers who want and appreciate on-line transactions.
- Enhancing market size is a long time consuming process not advantageous to the remote merchants and customers. This fails to generate substantial business.
- It is not cost effective and does not permit lowest transaction cost in a traditional commercial practice
- The traditional method of doing business involves middlemen like distributors, resellers, agents etc. There is no direct contact between the producer and the consumer. Consumers would get goods through several market intermediaries. This subsequently increases the price of goods which consumers finally pay.

Origin of E-commerce

From EDI to E-commerce: Though Electronic Data Interchange (EDI) is a technology which is about 20 years old, it has not been successful. E-commerce maybe dominated by the Internet rather than the EDI. The explosive and unprecedented growth of the Internet during the late 1990s has created the vision of e-commerce.

Everything business partners do, whether traditional business or EDI, it is now outdated and this is the harsh truth. The future belongs to e-commerce, which is a whole new way of working and thinking for good business prospects and becoming market savvy.

Evolution of E-commerce

E-commerce as a revolution started in the year 1997, when people started conceptualizing the opportunities of e-business. The term e-business was first used by IBM in 1997, when it launched a themalic campaign built around the term. E-business i.e. electronic business is derived from such terms as e-mail and e-commerce. The year 1998 was the year of hype and 1999 was the year of consolidation of the concept of e-commerce. Thus, e-business is a goose that can lay golden eggs, and it would be of benefit to allow the goose to reach the egg laying stage.

Now it is e-commerce that is most associated with the Net. In that respect, therefore, 1999 was some sort of watershed. It was a year, which in view of the critics, was the year in which e-commerce came of age. It emerged at the end of the old century and entered in to enable the new millennium to prosper.

Electronic commerce has been one of the most exciting developments following the Internet revolution. E-commerce basically uses the electronically networked information systems to carry out potential commercial activity across the globe enabling times to generate business in a big way.

Information technology has amply exhibited its potential to revitalize and revolutionize the business process on a global phenomena. It has the means to provide basic infrastructure for an efficient global business.

Nothing New

A new word has appeared, changing the way of business and by now people are accessing and doing potential business on-line.

E-commerce is nothing new because:

- Credit cards have been processed by computers since the 1960s.
- ATMs have been common since the early 1980s.
- Banks have not needed to move money on paper for many years.
- Large corporations, stock brokers and the government rarely write cheques in their day-to-day activities any more.

What is new is that today e-commerce permits small business houses too to participate and generate more business through the Internet. It means the new electronic media is not exclusively confined to large companies alone to be called a genuine e-commerce. The internet is a global community wherein both private, public, small and large companies anywhere in the globe can trade over the Net. They can exchange products, services and payment. This is the new meaning of e-commerce.

Terminology

E-business offers two types of electronic commerce : online e-business and offline e-business.

Online commerce is known as e-commerce which strategically pertains to online shopping. The buzzword of electronic commerce is written as e-commerce.

The expression may be spelled as extra-net, e-commerce, e-business, e-service and e-trading .

'E' is just like any automation. E-commerce is synonymous with e-business and e-trading.

E-business and E-commerce

E-business is comprehensive in essence, with the entire business being run using the Internet. It includes buying, manufacturing, selling and managing both internal and external information required to run a particular (potential) business.

While e-commerce is only a subset and branch of e-business, it is only a form of trading using electronic means to connect buyers and sellers who give a boost to any business category. The Internet provides the connectivity required for e-commerce. It is only the trading aspect of e-business. E-commerce is a generic name for a range of technologies that allow the exchange of information related to business transactions electronically. Internet commerce is the new terrain of e-business.

Definitions of E-commerce and E-business

E-commerce is a revolutionary form of industry that enables organisations to interact electronically with their customers. It allows companies to be more flexible and efficient in their operations and also leads to enhancing closer relationships with both the customers and suppliers. But most importantly, e-commerce is the only tool which can extend a company's reach to a global level. The Internet is a global business platform for companies all over the world.

An organisation that connects critical business systems directly to their critical constituencies (e.g. customers, employees, vendors and suppliers) via intranet, extranet and the 'world wide web' means e-business. The Internet technologies such as extranet and intranet are changing the way organisations operate. An intranet can enable employees to collaborate and coordinate with each other in addition to regular communication, which is facilitated by the existing office network (E-Mail). *"The Intranet is becoming the leading platform for developing and deploying strategic business applications, enabling people to communicate with colleagues, collaborate in teams and coordinate strategic business processes".**

E-business is all about cycle time, speed, globalisation, enhanced productivity, reaching new customers and sharing knowledge across institutions for competitive advantage in business.*

1. World Trade Organisation Committee on Trade and Development: There is no universally agreed definition of electronic commerce. However, in the World Trade Organisation work programme on E-commerce, it is understood to pertain to production, distribution, marketing, sale or delivery of goods and services by electronic means.

A commercial transaction can be divided into three main stages :

— the advertising and searching stage

— the ordering and payment stage and

— the delivery stage.

Any or all of these stages may be carried out electronically and may therefore be covered by the concept of "electronic commerce".

2. The International Trade Administration: E-commerce is any activity that utilises some form of electronic communication for exchange, advertisement, distribution and the payment for goods and services. Electronic payment systems for e-commerce are still evolving. They are far cheaper than mailing out paper invoices and processing received payments. Customers are appreciating the convenience of electronic payment and saves the company a lot of money.

3. Ashis Mahadwar, Vice President (Business Development) Planetasia.com: E-commerce is the means to complete online transaction and integrate the supply chain into the transaction management process such as receiving orders, making payments and tracking down the deliveries of orders.

4. Work Programme of the World Trade Organisation (WTO): E-commerce as a commercial process includes production, distribution, marketing, sale or delivery of goods and services electronically.

5. Arnaud Dufour: Electronic commerce encompasses all kinds of commercial transactions that are concluded electronically mostly via the Internet.

6. Mile Dunn, Chief Technology Officer at Dell Online: E-commerce is a telephone order placed by an individual who has used a website to gather product information pertaining to his/her requirement.

---

* *Arunesh Sharan, IBM Consulting Room.*

E-market and E-commerce

E-commerce in simple terms, consists of e-market and e-commerce whereas marketing refers to using the Net to market products and services. E-commerce refers to commercial transactions on the Internet. In e-marketing, billions of rupees of commercial transactions are done every year.

Commerce-Generation

The Concept of Commerce at different stages of Economic Development : Commercial life has evolved through the different stages of economic development. Chronologically, it is difficult to state how long one stage lasted. For convenience, commercial history can be divided into the following visible stages. The concept of commerce in each stage is different depending upon the generations and technology designed by various generations.

1. ***Barter System:*** In this stage, those in possession of surplus bartered their goods. This is personal selling practice organised at the stage of barter. The barter system was a result of exchanging commodities which two parties did not posses. So the barter system was one way of meeting their individual requirements.

A long time ago, people found the need to trade. One person had something another wanted, so they traded fur pelts.

2. ***Money Economy:*** The barter system proved defective to scalable commercial difficulties. The economic goods offered for exchange were not always of equal value. The difficulties of the barter systems were difficulty of storage, transportability, double coincidence and lack of common measure of value. This led to a more effective measure to ensure successful barter or trade the currency. Money represented value and allowed parties to buy things without carrying the fur pelts.-

3. ***Face to Face:*** E-Generation finds and designs a variant and new ways of business to sell, buy products and services including new methods of payment. Conducting business face to face has been the business practice for centuries.

4. ***Mail Order Business:*** Later generations introduced mail order business and the catalogue method.

5. ***Super Market:*** Departmental stores, consumer cooperative stores and super markets came into existence that put a roof over goods. These developments drove some of the small shops out of business.

6. ***Telephone Ordering:*** Another significant event is telephone ordering, which is nothing but a process of buying from a catalogue but without orders in writing.

7. ***Television:*** Television brought the sales pitch into our living rooms and creating an impact on our buying behaviour.

E-commerce is a present generation's new medium and the fastest and simplest global way of selling and buying products and services by electronic means and payment on-line. It encompasses a wide management of transactions from private e-mail sales to real time on-line stock trading. But as in the past with new technology, smart people with products and services can reach new markets and succeed. E-commerce is second nature to nearly everyone in terms of business with access to computers. Technology created by the new generator will remain new till the next generation technology emerges.

E-commerce is just a new way to do business. Customers are still customers and they need businessmen and corporate houses to cater to their needs and demands.

Frequently Asked Questions (FAQ) about E-commerce

- What is e-commerce ?
- What do people mean by e-commerce ?
- What is the big deal ?
- What is exactly new in e-commerce ?
- How is it emerging recently ?
- What do we understand about e-commerce ?
- How much does the services cost ?
- How to get current website or business listed ?
- What is smart credit card ?
- What is digital signature, digital certificate and digital payment?
- Is it possible to buy more than one item ?
- What is on-line shopping and on-line transmission ?
- What is and how should one ensure security and privacy ?
- What is hot on the Internet?
- What is not hot on the Internet?

Recently there has been a substantial hype created regarding e-business /e-commerce. The trend seems to be that everyone wants to add/prefix 'e' to all business activities on the Net. We in India are still in the infancy stage of developing e-commerce applications and deriving the benefit of extended global reach by setting up virtual business using the Internet.

E-commerce — A New Concept

E-commerce is one such concept that is used to apply business logic and to capitalize the potential global market through Internet. This in turn has made every small scale industry to work out strategies of generating business through the Net and thus having a global presence.

To many people, E-commerce is just a lot of hype. To understand what it is, it is better to do a piece of business through the Net to understand the real meaning of e-commerce, its knowledge is to be financially better by reasonable investment and experience a global presence as mentioned earlier.

E-commerce is a buzzword many businessmen are not still aware of the difference between the web server and an application service. The concept is still evolving. It is a job that is to be defined systematically. If the popularity of e-commerce has taught us something in recent years, it is that more and more people are increasingly getting used to and depending upon the Internet.

Traditionally, shopping or buying has been a very personalized behaviour of the consumer and the relationship developed between the retailer and seller. From the days of trading by bartering till today, the typical buying and selling mode was on a shopping plank, basically on the floor of the store. The information technology revolution is changing all this, the advent of e-commerce or the buying and selling through the electronic medium of the Internet is creating waves and it is here to stay.

It is both for wholesale and retail business and more and more people are shopping online. It is evolved from traditional business, combined with the emerging power of the Internet.

E-commerce is a unique and potential opportunity for business of any size, particularly for those who automate their supply chain.

The expression e-commerce is missed word or you can say inappropriate. The suitable word is I-Commerce.

It is a new medium of business with new technology allowing not just to exhibit or selling products/service over the internet, but payment as well as potential small and big business needs.

It is a two edged sword, because the merchants benefit out of it, as what he wants, and customers also benefit out of it, as they decide their choice of product. Thus it has grown as a multi-trillion dollar industry.

E-commerce does not mean online shopping. Shopping on the web is a small part of the e-commerce industry. But it includes online stock, bond transactions. downloading and software. The hottest news is that it has come and is here to stay. As a system, it integrates seamlessly into the structure of a web site and ensures a smooth flow of information from the company to the individual.

In recent years, there seems to be a lot of confusion in the minds of many Indian business persons and others pertaining to business transactions (commerce) on the Net. To help clear the idea, we start with the following beginning.

This is the digital age where most of the business transactions, particularly in India, are done in a traditional way.

Most people in the industry business field have encountered the term e-commerce, which has become a buzzword in all cross sections of the industry and trade, to name a few, IT vendors, software designers, users, financial markets, government departments and professionals.

E-commerce is buying and selling on the Internet. It is true in major part. But this is only a limited perception. Online stores are actually a small part of it. Companies also provide sales promotion and technical data and customer support are all online activities that facilitate the exchange of goods and services between businesses and individuals and business to business for financial and monetary gains. Online sales is indeed where most of the companies hope to prosper. No small wonder that every one is keenly interested in getting a share of a pie.

Start own business and be a part of the emerging giant wave–that is e-commerce on the Internet.

Most people think e-commerce means online shopping. The term also refers to online stock and bond transactions and buying and downloading software without even going near a store. In addition, e-commerce includes business-to-business links between business houses and the customer that makes purchasing easier for large organisations.

As far as the potential areas of e-commerce go, there are tangible goods sold via the Internet and other electronic media. The sellers include computer products, consumer products, books and magazines and music and entertainment products.

E-commerce simply means a process of conducting business through the Internet i.e. form of trade using the Internet to connect buyers and sellers to effect commercial transactions. It is opposed to conventional means of doing commerce. It also includes business to business connections that make purchasing easier. It is online shopping which means buying and selling and payment electronically.

It is direct buying and selling process. E-commerce is about selling products and services on the Internet any time, anywhere without limitations of geography, time zone or working hours. E-commerce has emerged as potential business frontier, with potential electronic business transactions in the supply chain of business communities.

As a new media of business, the technology permits trading partners to transfer critical business data and information integrating with back office systems.

In other words, it meant exchange of goods and services for payment using electronic technologies. Physical delivery may occur once the business transaction has been finalised on the Internet. This encompasses both business-to-business and business-to-customer activity.

The Internet is used as potential area of business concept covering any business transaction executed electronically between trading parties.

Ferrester Research defines e-commerce from the user's perspective as using the Internet to —

- Identity suppliers.
- Sell its products and services.
- Make purchase commitments.
- Complete financial transactions.
- Obtain services.

E-commerce opens up a new communication path to the consumers for promoting their brands, supports sale process and generates potential response. Interaction through selling and marketing products online also provides a potential opportunity for merchants to collect information and credit ie. 1:1 relationship with customers who are potential prospects for any authentic business deal. So, what matters most is authenticity and clear dealing with whom communication is underway even today.

Nature of E-commerce

In the fast changing world of dot coms, global business is the order. The business people who are hesitant to board the Internet to do e-commerce would find themselves outside the new growth matrix.

Internet is becoming a strategic necessity for modern business. Even as the old brick and mortar models collapse into smaller kiosks or retail outlets, the Internet has destroyed all geographical advantages enjoyed by them. This is a call for newer, economically feasible and more customer friendly technologies. The Internet has emerged as the ultimate answer to survival in the new world order. In short, e-commerce is a new paradigm of business. E-commerce is the most easy to use and cost effective web hosting service on the Net.

The Internet is literally a whole new world for various businesses to explore and capitalize.

- Electronic business is no longer an alternative. It is an imperative for corporate houses.
- E-commerce is way for a business to use the power and tools of Internet.

The cyber web offers a full service of e-commerce solutions for small businesses too.

E-commerce has many dimensions as mentioned below:

- E-commerce concentrates on Internet solutions of securing global business. It is developing businesses in a big way. Internet marketing is easier with information in e-commerce and offers an interactive sales medium.
- Whatever spin is put to this emerging business term, there is no denying of the clearer trend towards electronic transactions of all sorts.
- It is a potential business tool which has made it possible for business firms to compete in a global environment, that is it is a cutting edge technology.
- The e-commerce revolution started in India more than a decade ago. With the advent of technological infrastructure facilities, there is likely to be exponential growth in the usage of Internet for e-commerce in India.
- Whether it may be called as e-commerce, e-business, entranet or e-services, the core fact is that the Internet presents enormous opportunities to simultaneously add unique value and reduce transaction costs when communicating with customers, suppliers and partners.
- E-commerce has the potential to revolutionize the business done and improves comprehensiveness of Indian business. In it, the whole world is the market, to buy and sell cyber goods. Around 1997, the term e-commerce came as buzzword. So much has been said about e-commerce in recent years but necessary strategies have not been worked for its growth and success.
- E-commerce today is a synergy of physical and virtual business. In tune with the changing medium of business, a business firm chalks out strategies to do e-business, otherwise the firm may be out of business.
- By using data that is collected, merchants can generate web pages, send e-mail notifications informing customers of sales and special promotions or evaluate the effectiveness of marketing programmes.

Convergence

E-commerce is a potential ocean enabling firms and individuals to ride on the waves of profit and global presence. A few big Indian concerns and many small and big concerns outside India planned to foray into e-commerce and other web-based applications. Diversification into e-commerce will enable to provide a greater range of solutions to its customers, solidifying relationships with customers and partners.

E-commerce focusses on the selling and buying of products and services through the Internet as a stand-alone complete application. It includes a complete sales process including marketing, sales, customer support and communication with suppliers as a front end to enterprise resource planning. It is a new media of business bringing about a paradigm shift in underlying economics of business.

Features of E-commerce

What does e-commerce mean to business? Electronic trade means better business communication and data interchange information is essential for every and any business. The quality and quantity of information which a business delivers to customers or use this information to make decisions can determine just how competitive the business is.

A company already may be using a number of electronic based tools to help acquire and extend information and communication needs. These may include personal computers, word processors, courier, facsimile machines, telex services, cellular phones, pagers and more. Unfortunately, many of today's communication tools are not really upto the speed of today's business needs, and can actually create barriers to achieving the goals set on the basis of strategies formulated by a company.

For instance, postal facilities can keep business waiting for information for days or even weeks. Overnight couriers may save time but can be an expensive proportion. Traditional telex and fax is quick but costly and communicating by telephone can become an endless game of tag.

Now a business can avoid these problems by using e-commerce which is fast, cost efficient, time saying and easy to use — i.e., economic transibility and good business generation.

Electronic business can result in better transactions, wide market coverage by offering the benefits of speed, convenience, being cost effective, timeliness, high profit margins, instant customer relations, no loss of customers, impact and control — all are a fraction of the past traditional business methods. A concern can do everything it can to run its business efficiently and profitably.

Application of electronic operations to commercia! activities means better business solutions. It greatly facilitates a firm to make better decisions, sale forecasts, prices and other valuable information can be sent and received instantaneously. A business will always have the information it needs faster, easier and more completely in the new system of communication than ever before.

This enables firms to have an edge over competitors by informing, following up and requesting information faster and easier to customers.

Another feature is that it helps to maintain greater control, at work, home or while travelling, communicate with any business partner or firm, anywhere instantly.

1. Improve Responsiveness: How does e-commerce help business? It helps by improving responsiveness to market conditions and customer preferences. Every business must know how important timing is to marketing and selling products. Timing is important to cater to the demands of customers.

If distributors, dealers and sales force do not get the right information at the right time, there will be a financial crisis as well as losing valuable customers.

E-commerce network enables a company to implement marketing programmes with greater precision such as :

- Pre-empt competitiveness with a change in marketing tactics before they can react.
- Improve responsiveness by revising price change and marketing programmes as and when required.

2. *Expedites and Streamlines Reporting:* It has been an experience in conventional commercial practices with factors like delays and ineffectiveness in reporting systems crippling effectiveness. Responsive, timely information flows from sound management systems. Electronic commerce improves delivery and distribution both within and outside organisations. The benefits are:

- Stored lists of key recipients facilitate distribution.
- Electronic delivery time.

3. *Coordinates Sales Efforts:* Some marketing studies reveal that most sales people spend nearly 75 per cent of their time on the roads, relying heavily on telephone calls for contact with their head officers and customers. Telephone tag makes an endless frustrating game out of tracking down leads and following up to authenticate sales calls. In addition, misplaced or undelivered information results in low sales records. Other benefits of electronic business are :

- Eliminating telephone tag.
- Sending and receiving message at convenience.
- Linking sales team numbers to gather, including international representatives, and
- Closing sales without delays.

4. *Effectiveness and Efficiency:* Electronic commerce can increase the efficiency and effectiveness of public relation programmes, broadcast press releases, financial updates and other corporate communications. Copy reviews and approvals are expedited by circulating instant messages to key internal and external contacts.

5. *Close Contact with Clients:* In any business where maintaining close contact with customers is a priority consideration, electronic business can increase responsiveness of the company and ensure customer satisfaction. Appointment confirmations, requests for information, follow-up reports and electronic data interchange can be effected with greater efficiency using instant messages.

6. *Planning and Execution of Meetings:* The mechanism of electronic operations in business facilitates planning and execution of meetings. Executive management meetings, seminars, workshops, symposia and conventions take a great deal of time and effort to manage. Arrangements must be coordinated among a variety of diverse groups in different locations e.g., hotels, speakers, exhibitors, attendees, the media etc. Reports and surveys need to be distributed before and or after the event. And there are always the headaches of late breaking events and last minute announcement. In an electronic business environment, video-conferences, document conference, computer-based conference, which offer companies the flexibility of both electronic and paper distribution, can make these jobs easier and more effective.

Need for E-commerce

The global business environment is moving faster than ever before. Increased competition at home and abroad means quality as well as profitability must be preserved by corporate houses. This pressure has led to a reappraisal of the accepted existing business practice in the search for greater efficiently.

Traditionally, the response in the face of competitive threat has been to reduce costs by rationalizing production, shedding labour and restructuring business, coupled with investments in technology to improve productivity and generate profit.

Revolutionary changes have taken place in the area of commerce in recent years with the advent of information technology. But still, the huge bulk of commercial activities are taking place in conventional mode, dealings and settlements still remain locked in slow, antiquated, outdated, time consuming, paper bound and postal service processes.

Business documents produced by one computer are printed and posted only to be entered in the recipient's computer. The entire process of commercial activities are time consuming, error prone and a costly exercise. It is estimated at between four percent and seven percent of the value of goods traded.

Today in global trading to be more specific, in a complex web of trading relationship, each business house is itself a customer of another business house. You can see conventional slow paper based trading all too easily becomes a barrier to the trade.

It is this area on which attention is now focussed because it offers tremendous potential to switch over for electronic commerce instead of traditional commerce.

Imagine an electronic and paperless commerce having a direct line from one business computer system to the computer of all trading partners like customers, suppliers, buyers etc.

In electronic commerce, every transaction is done electronically.

The good news is that e-commerce is already happening, thus transforming the way business is conducted.

E-commerce is the lifeline of any successful business in today's complex and competitive business environment. With the globalization of trade and commerce and growing interdependence in the world's economy, it has become evident that the life line of all successful corporations is due to switching over to e-commerce from conventional commerce. The power to establish business relationships, contact with customers, suppliers, dealers etc. with speed and ease, the buying and trading have reached its destination with minimum time loss and cost, by electronic means, is an asset that every corporation ought to have a line of electronic commerce. An efficient electronic trade net is imperative if one wants to stay ahead in the business world that is driven by competition.

Large corporate bodies and multi national organisations are becoming increasingly aware of the fact that home grown, conventional, paper based postal services systems soon prove to be absolute both in terms of cost and management efficiency.

In order to stay abreast of global hags in commerce and technology, it is therefore essential to have at every business organisation new solutions that are integrated, flexible and user friendly, enabling quality, time to be utilised in the core business. And to be able to do this means choosing a modern electronic commerce on which a business can trust implicity.

The emerging IT based e-commerce will not give you 'out of a box' solutions but a corporation will understand new development in foreign market potential and customize a solution to suit the needs of a business customer for whom efficiency, reliability, timeliness and cost considerations are the very important principles.

Increasingly business potential, timely and accurately captured and efficiently electronic business data interchange, is the key to any business success. In today's competitive world, corporations both large and small, need to be able to respond quickly to emerging new opportunities and threads and the needs of mass customenrs customers.

Efficient, fast and cost effective methods of business activities are essential for every business today. Unfortunately, till recent years, the conventional commercial practices fell short of their requirements in terms of speed, distance, potential, value addition and cost effectiveness. It is the e-commerce that offers and combines all of the above features.

E-commerce is changing the way the companies do business today. What began as a simple and fast way for corporations to electronic data interchange has evolved vitally into a business tool.

The need is emphasized :

- Sales returns could be analysed and fed into the ordering process, orders could be raised to reflect both demand and known stock availability.
- Instructions could be sent to distributors in parallel with the order to ensure fast delivery.
- Carriage by road, rail, sea or air services could be booked simultaneously.
- Customs clearance documentation could be available in advance of goods arriving, avoiding hold-ups and payment, instructions could be issued to banks to ensure prompt payment. This will be possible without the immense paperwork surrounding today's business transactions.

Objectives of E-commerce

- Stimulating supply of new and competitive information age products and services.
- Stimulating use and demand for information age products and services.
- Developing a competitive market with an effective regulatory framework.
- In information society, one stop shop for information, promotion and advice is desirable.
- Designing information security programmes.
- Legal recognition of electronic signature.
- Voluntary licensing system for providers of cryptographic services.

Categories of E-commerce

E-commerce can be divided into the following categories :

- E-tailing or virtual store front on websites with online catalogue, sometimes gather.
- A virtual mall.

The gatherings and use of demographic data through web contracts.

- Electronic data interchange, the business to business exchange of data.
- E-mail and fax and their use as media for reaching potential prospects and established customers.
- Business to business buying and selling.

Types of E-commerce

The term *e-commerce*, however, can mean different things to different people, depending on how it is defined. For our purpose, however, e-commerce consists of the following three types :

1. Online Promotion: Here the site can take the user through the purchasing decisions by allowing them to choose a colour and size of the product and then find out how much the total purchase with cost. However, the actual purchase needs to be made offline. For instance, car company sites. In this case, the website automatically informs the nearest dealer of the enquiry including the purchasing decision date recovered from the web site interaction.

2. *Online Ordering:* The client registers on the site and is given a secure user name and password. A website can now be used to initiate product delivery which is unique to that user (a dynamic website). The most common use of this special information delivery is in giving price information over the Internet. Depending upon the address of the registered website user, a different price currency appears on site.

3. *Electronic Shopping:* For some categories of retail products, Internet shopping is now very easy. It allows customers to browse a website, choose the product they would like to and enter a credit card to order the product information of minute. Customers choose the delivery service they would like and the deal is done.

The latest shopping cart technology means the store can be opened for business 24 hours a day, 365 days a year. Naturally, payment security is of paramount importance for both the vendor and the customer. It is possible to arrange secure payment systems that allow the use of credit cards across the Net. The system also provides to integrate the Internet sales date with traditional accounts stock and management systems, so that Internet sales data and distribution are handled seamlessly.

Essential Requirements for E-commerce

There are several roads to promote and sell products and services online without having regular Internet access. But strictly it is not really e-commerce. It is old an style of commerce and is only another way of advertisement.

An essential element to constitute e-commerce is that the customer should be able to perform an entire transaction having products and services delivered online, either on a web or e-mail. Therefore, for a genuine e-commerce, the customer should atleast have an internet e-mail account and a website or atleast minimum single web page.

Telephones and faxes are mostly used in conventional commerce, while e-mail is essential for internet business and is the easiest device for those appreciating the benefits of internet access.

The top six essential requirements are listed below :

- Identification of business areas, most suitable for completion of e-commerce such as supply chain, front end, back end, computing, business-to-business or business-to-customers.
- Re-engineering the entire business process in order to make it applicable feasibly in terms of e-commerce.
- To asses the size or scale of e-commerce application and development.
- Post Implementation, analysis and surveillance.
- Concentration and developing system for the business-to-business segment as it has major business opportunities.
- Supply chain management optimization is one of the strongest drivers of global e-commerce solutions market, as it spurs potential business-to-business transactions.

Factors to get on E-commerce

- *Pricing:* Pricing of services is determined by the needs of each business and the levels that makes the most business sense.
- *Contacting:* Contacting a representative is another factor. The fastest way to contact and be connected by representative is through online.
- *Getting a website:* The user has to necessarily get his current website or business listed on the Net. The best method is to fill in the online form and this will give the company global presence.
- *Selection of web developer:* Best available local web developers may be selected to design and help business to develop and implement e-commerce solutions.
- *Account:* Business has to reach the website and establish a business account.
- *Loss of credit card:* In case of loss of credit card or stolen, alternative steps are to be taken. The measure is to change the payment option in electronic payment account to use a new credit card.
- *Buying more than one item:* The customers can buy large quantities of a particular product by changing quantity on the order form.
- *Cancellation of purchase:* The mechanism facilitates cancellation of any purchase order made. The credit card will not be charged until after the order form is processed. If the customers want to cancel the order before completing the order form, it can be done.
- *Summary statement:* An abstract of all purchase made can be obtained, in the form of a summary statement. It provides access to the online receipts of all purchases made in each store of electronic commerce service.

Getting started on E-commerce

- Launching a website is only the first step. Getting started with e-commerce is much more than establishing a website.
- To carry on transactions under e-commerce technology, it requires a completely new business strategy.
- To determine how to develop an infrastructure that works with the existing business system.
- To build up e-commerce solutions that scales with future business needs.
- Every business has to necessarily re-engineer its strategy to exploit the benefits provided by e-commerce technology.
- Build deeper ties with business partners on a global canvas.
- To design solutions that work with a broad range of customers.
- To start with, it is necessary to focus to automate order management system merchant accounts, credit card, cheque payment and security etc.
- E-commerce system is designed to work within existing constraints. It is necessary to have standard web technique while remaining compatible to with the existing system and expertise resource applications.
- It is always desirable to adopt a strong 128 bit encryption for all transactions.
- To set up webstore front and e-commerce catalogue easily and affordably.

- To buy a special suitable software package along with services to use the e-commerce system.
- To have the most easy to use and cost effective web hosting services on the Internet.
- Shopping cart system for servicing e-commerce transactions to accept secure payments and secure transactions.
- Providers of comprehensive open e-commerce solution environment comprising enterprise applications, internet applications and services technology to enable businesses to participate in the internet economy.
- The mechanism needs a real time e-commerce transaction processing services for payment, tax calculation, risk management, fulfilment, management and distribution control.
- Adoption and development of reliable secure, e-commerce solutions that rapidly deliver business value and competitive advantage to customers globally.

How to Sell Online — Basic Elements

There are a few basic elements you need to follow before to begin selling online:

1. Business: If a business person has a great idea to venture into e-commerce to promote products or services and desirous to sell online through Internet, he must first fulfil all legal procedural requirements for doing business locally or internationally. It includes license, permission and demonstration etc.

The other elements are domain name, website design, website hosting and merchant account. These elements are discussed in detail in forthcoming chapters.

A merchant account is essential to do business on the Internet. If a person does not have a merchant account, he has to set up business strategies before going for trading over the Net. There is no need to have a ready merchant account and online credit card processor to take orders online. However, a merchant account is imperative to accept credit cards.

2. Secure Certificate: Another important element is to have a secure certificate or secure socket layer (SSL) which makes online orders secure. Once a business person sets off a great idea, product or service, the partner must apply for SSL certificate. Verisign or Thawte are the popular secure certificate service providers.

3. Server: After obtaining SSL certificate, the partner should set up an e-commerce server account. It is the server account where the website will be hosted.

4. Online Credit Card Processor: In an e-commerce environment, the credit card is to be processed online. There are several merchant account providers who offer credit card processing solutions like cyber cash, authorize net payment. These organisations process credit card transactions online.

5. Shopping Cart: A business person has to set up online shopping carts. There are shopping cart solutions providers. They are shop sites and open markets which are powerful shopping cart software which offer, businesses to easily set up online shopping.

Parties to E-commerce Transactions

An e-commerce transaction is concerned with and passes through different parties involved in the payment process. The parties involved for the completion of e-commerce transactions may include :

1. *The User:* He is a card holder and party in the e-commerce transaction, who plans to purchase goods or services online.

2. *The Merchant:* The merchant is the company or business house wishing to sell goods or services to enable customers to buy online.

3. *The Issuer:* It is a credit card company that issues cards to the users to initiate online buying.

4. *The Acquirer:* He is usually the banker of the merchant-to be specific, the merchant's financial institution.

5. *The Certificate Authority:* It is an independent and neutral third party authority that issues certificates to the merchant, t.he issuer and in some cases, the card holder.

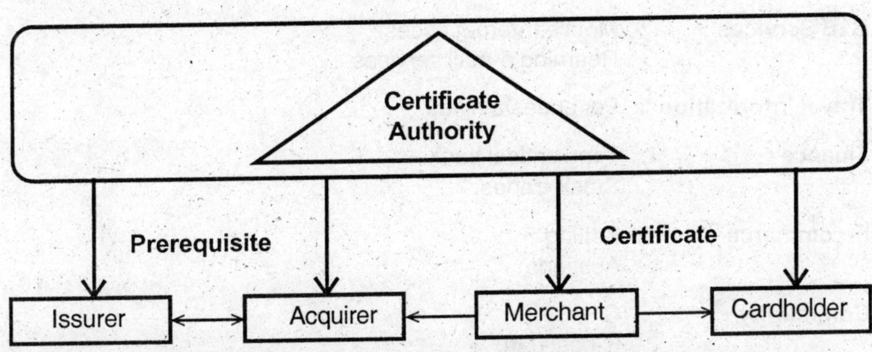

Fig. 1.01 Parties in E-commerce Transactions

M-Commerce (Mobile Commerce)

Buying and selling of goods or services by phone is called phone is called M-commerce or mobile commerce. Phones used are more distinct than others. In this, Wireless Access Protocol (WAP) brings web content to handsets independent of the various network layers and device characteristics.

There are three sets of devices presently available. They are:

- WAP Platforms (cell phones)
- PDA (Personal Digital Assistants palmpalot) and
- Dedicated Services- digital cameras and walkman radios.

WAP enabled mobile phones are rapidly emerging for online commerce.

M-Commerce Or Mobile Commerce

Today, the world is wireless and M-commerce a parallel universal commerce almost as large as the Net. M-commerce is an entirely different paradigm in which *the emphasis is more on location specific and activity specific products and services.*

M-commerce solutions are also available. For instance, Inktomi, is offering 'shopping dial tone' solutions via the WAP directory and catalogue services for cell phone users. By this, online commerce is accessible irrespective of the platform used. According to some research studies, it is working with over 400 merchants in Europe to offer 5 million products via WAP. The Internet users worldwide can access the Net via mobile devices. Advertisements in the form of text links. micro-banners and audio jingles on mobile networks are also available to benefit consumers from M-commerce.

Merchants in many advanced countries are poised to reap the benefit of M-commerce. Therefore, M-commerce is opposed to proprietary platforms which can spur impulse buying for certain items like music albums etc.

It maybe noted that commerce companies regionalize M-commerce as a potentially unique service.

Phone.com is a company which specialized in WAP gateways, micro browsers and wireless mark-up language (WML) content tool. M-commerce players have been providing generally unique compelling services rather than just trying to excite the market.

Applications well suited for WAP domain include:

B2B Services	:	Mobile Internet access Roaming e-mail services
Travel Information	:	For buses/airlines
Finance	:	Time critical banking Stock trades.
E-commerce	:	Betting Auctions
Community	:	Chat E-post card

The mobile phone and WAP markets will always be there as a mass market.

Wireless Access Protocol (WAP)

WAP is simply a protocol. It is a standardized way wherein a mobile phone user talks to a server installed in the mobile phone network. It is a distinctive development in the wireless industry which revolves around wireless mark-up language, which is built upon existing net standards as XML and Internet Protocol (IP). WAP is not based on HTML but WML.

WAP is the gateway to a new world of mobile which permits to access web based interactive information services and applications from the screens of their mobile phones. These include both consumer and corporate solutions like e-mail, corporate data, news, sports, information services, entertainment, television, movies, travel, leisure, culture, medical care, electronic commerce transactions and banking services.

Nokia has already introduced in India its product—the Nokia 6210, which offers high speed data and WAP capabilities. Motorola and Ericsson etc. or other major handset vendors are planning and gearing up to launch their WAP compliant handsets to cater to the technology- savvy customers.

Bottle Necks

Though M-commerce is a development worth praising, there remain some challenges:

- Limited size of handset screen.
- Limited bandwidth.
- Restricted cursor movement.
- Smaller key pad options.
- Small has better life in hand held devices.
- Difficulties in upgrading handsets to newer versions of WAP.
- Incompatibility of many gateways.
- High traffic latencies.
- It is very difficult to configure WAP phones for new WAP services, because different parameters are required to gain access.
- Commercial quantities of WAP phones are not available as required.
- Accessing web content via mobile telephones is a bit too complicated, requiring too much thought and a number of key pad punches.

Features and Uses

- WAP provides a standardized way for accessing the internet on mobile phones. The user can remotely access his corporate intranet and pick up e-mail through the mobile handset.
- Permits to quickly browse internet content while riding a taxi.
- It is a transparent platform that permits handsets to access content on standardized web servers.
- User friendly terminals equipped with internet micro-browsers.
- Operators have a greater chance of increasing air time usage.
- Open standards and economies of scale.
- It enables easy access to the net content.
- It is a useful tool for businesses who need reliable and convenient access to vital information while on the move.
- It facilitates easy integration as part of an enterprise's information management infrastructure and
- Enables access to critical company information such as database, intranet and e-mail.

Other features assist companies to configure a large number of phones with the company specific WAP access points, dictionaries and other information: They are :

- WAP is a fast emerging way to rectify bottlenecks of mobile information services, a key application for wireless communications which have not been successful.
- The payment process can be simplified in mobile e-commerce by providing server applications.
- WAP transmits payment data securely over wireless networks to financial institutions.
- The mobile user browses the internet on a PC and finds an e-commerce site which is nothing but mobile enabled and
- Greater chance of driving up average revenue per user.

E-Services

What is e-service? *E-service is an asset that is made available via the Net to either drive a new revenue stream or create new efficiencies.**

The concept of e-service needs to get recognition and be popularised. E-services communicate with each other, fulfilling requests and or triggering other e-services which in turn carry out their complex work flow of transactions.

Intelligence service is necessary which supports the e-business services offering and providing comprehensive IT support to customers worldwide. IT services are required to support clients who cater to customers across the world. There is a potential business link between client and customers.

What is needed is to ensure global comprehensive customer support and leading edge technology services. Merchants can sell online services and offer products immediately. Various businesses and customers are getting more and more connected to e-services. Volumes of new data will be arriving from unimaginable sources and across multiple platforms. The e-selling retailers have to fortify their sites against potential crashes.

There is difference between web-based services and e-services. Under e-services, the user need not access the Net. Any application running on any device can request an e-service. E-services are self-contained, they act as resources to other applications and can be performed, initiated, scheduled or committed by software with or without intervention. E-services is a part of the internet business unit which provides strategic infrastructure to enable e-business solutions. E-services Include the software environment and extends from servers to clients to appliances. These are services that would allow you to do business in the e-business, e-commerce world without too much expense by paying on transaction basis. Infact, e-service is the next generation of Internet business which is fast expanding.

Potentials are very vast for e-commerce services. The demand for Internet and e-commerce related software and services are increasing exponentially. Some of the e-commerce services are:

- Legacy application
- Internet Application Integration
- Electronic Data Interchange (EID)
- Migration to web based models
- Strategic IT consulting
- E-commerce training services
- Business website development and maintenance
- Software solutions and services
- Establishment of a national digital certification authority
- Providing a global level telecom infrastructure for communication services and
- Availability of free use of atleast 56 bit encryption technology leading to 128 bit technology.

Examples of E-services

Issuing of driving licenses is presently based on paperwork. In a net based transaction, all sorts of verifications can be done and finally one take the real test. It saves time, money and energy. E-services can make this possible because some of these transactions cut across ministers.

---

* *Stacy Plemmons, Vice president, Hewlett Packard, India, Computer Today, 16-31, Aug.1999.*

Take the passport office. This demands end to end transactions where you apply and verifications get done and ultimately the applicant can be called in just for an interview and then the passport may be issued. The police can offer verification services on the Net. The applicant can apply for passport electronically. It requires a web service through which these are extended to the customers.

E-services Technologies

The concept of e-services included a host of new technologies which form the basic building blocks for delivering e-sevices. These include e-speak, chat and web qos. A brief description of these services is as follows:

1. *E-speaking:* This technology is used to automate business transactions on the Net. This technology is designed to enable e-services to interact with each other, which is basic e-services, i.e., spontaneously to meet heads, complete a task and conduct transactions across the Net.

It is a counter piece of IT efforts to benefit from the growth of the Internet. The Net is the biggest change to benefit in the years to come as many are approaching Internet to connect buyers and sellers. Connections of these computers require a standard way for application to talk to each other. This speaking technology is e-speak, helps to engage in several multi million deals with potential companies. E-services will make money off net transactions.

E-speak helps greatly in B2B transactions. A business transaction between two companies is essentially about developing a relationship between the two:

- Either developed in the past, or
- A fresh relationship based on business needs.

The parties have to agree on delivery time frames and contracts. The contract means what happens when the shipment of goods takes place.

The concept of e-speak permits the whole process to be a technology based interaction which is standardized. As it is Internet-based, the system can be tracked to check on the status of the shipment, as is done by courier or shipping agencies. The important aspect is that being a computer to computer transaction, the entire business can be done dynamically and the participants can come in and out of the contract easily. The technology also allows matching automatically and allows a lot of brokers managing the services on the Internet.

E-speak is for services. It can be used for supply chain integration. Like enterprise resource management integrated the transaction, sales and services of fixed companies in pre-agreed relationships, here an entire network of services from suppliers to distributors and financiers can be plugged into transaction in non-contractual partnership.

By its nature, e-speak expands the scope for online business. This technology empowers to offer end users and business customers access to rich, functional online resources that go far beyond the traditional fact finding and procurement capabilities of today's Internet sites.

From the relations point of view, one can discover and build partners who one does not even know of. The big B2B players can standardise things on e-speak for which technology is already show-cased and widespread.

E-speak opens services software that allows e-services to communicate freely and dynamically with each other.

E-speak components can be used in a modular or stand-alone basis to perform basis functions such as even aggregation and billing authentication, authorization and more.

2. *Chat:* This is a set of technology designed for links and interactions. It is an integrated software suitable for information applications and devices to various services.

3. *Web Qos:* It helps to stabilize web service and optimize resources by prioritizing uses and applications.

4. *E-Speak Broker:* The key enabler of e-speak technology is the e-speak broker who discovers, composes, brokers and completes a series of transactions, from a dynamic and infinite universe of service providers and suppliers. The anchor point for e-services, the e-speak broker cascades services in response to complex requests, paying dividends to broker providers of these services at every turn.

5. *Internet Broker (E-service broker):* The e-services broker allows companies to become the central point or the broker, in delivering e-services to consumers and business. An e-services broker can be anyone from a traditional service provider to a corporation interested in hosting a brokered service on a community of interest online.

E-service brokers earn on every one of these services, rich rewards including benefitting customers. The lingua franca for e-services, e-speak will help to find gold in this explosive opportunity.

An e-services broker can begin with a single component, such as a translation application. For example, he may generate a more complex, specialised offering by combining procurement capabilities with the translation module.

An e-services broker holds the key to the exciting new world of e-speak, creating and maintaining the central point where buyers and sellers, previously unknown to one another, come together in productive new ways. One can earn revenues from these transactions, all along the line as brokered relationship and mediating complex e-services transactions.

Levels of E-commerce

Electronic commerce is the process of conducting commercial transactions electronically over the Internet. This process is carried out primarily in five levels, and the main aspect of e-commerce is a merchant selling products or service to the consumers.

There are five major segments under the broader category of e-business. However, the following are some popular e-commerce models used by companies engaged in e-commerce :

- Business to business e-commerce (B2B)
- Business to consumers e-commerce (B2C)
- Consumers to consumers e-commerce (C2C)
- Business to employees e-commerce (B2E) and
- Consumer to business e-commerce (C2B)

A brief description of these levels and their nature is given below.

1. *Business to Business E-commerce (B2B):* E-business is the process of conducting business on the Internet. Its scope includes not only buying and selling but also services, fulfilling the needs of customers and collaborating with business partners.

Business to business e-commerce is smart business. The opportunity for business to business e-commerce is even greater.

A wholesaler may sell products to the retailer. There are advanced e-commerce softwares which support multi-tier pricing. This helps to set up online stores to offer preferred pricing to some vendors and shared price to others. Such a software is Fast Card 2000.

This includes internet-enabled initiatives of an enterprise to form commercial linkages with another enterprise, dealer, warehouse or manufacturer. In this form of e-commerce, paperwork and time-to-market get vastly reduced. Network Solutions of Bangalore is a role model of business-to-business e-commerce in India. Throughout the world, this e-commerce mode is the biggest. (A.K. Mohanty)

In a B2B transaction, the interaction is between businesses. For example, a website that is catching for the steel industry might have facility for buyers and sellers to list their requirements and post their products. It helps them in quickly closing the transactions and the buyer can get quality material and can choose from different suppliers.

B2B commerce is a growing business in the e-commerce arena- with the increasing use of the internet, more and more business are realising the commercial advantage of giving business clients a streamlined and easy manner to order products or service online. It facilitates access to the ordering process to only those with whom a concern has a commercial relationship.

Business to Business e-commerce provides small and medium enterprises (SMES) with an excellent opportunity to access new markets, improve customer service and reduce costs. And while hurdles exist, they should be viewed more as speed breakers rather than road barriers. As a medium of information storage and dissemination, the internet has and is emerging a clear winner. Its rate of penetration has far outpaced the growth of other popular media such as newspaper, radio and television.

B2B transactions are however relatively high value in nature, and organisations are slow to change their traditional systems for the supply chain management. The reasons for the growth in B2B e-commerce are many. In an increasing competitive scenario, e-commerce offers highly attractive cost saving options. The shift to this process is often driven by the needs of buyers. Suppliers have little untrative to move up the e-commerce value chain.

Innovative methods of enhancing B2B and B2C levels of e-commerce include :

- CD-ROM catalogues that are linked to the user's online catalogue, enabling him to browse offline and order online.
- Kiosks placed at physical store locations or in shopping malls to introduce users to the easy online ordering options.
- Extranets to link businesses together that conduct regular business to business transactions and

- Affiliate programmes to drive business to your commerce site from other content related sites.*

B2B e-commerce is expected to be the largest mode of transacting e-business and is a global phenomenon. It involves taking internet enabled initiatives to form commercial links with other enterprises, dealers or manufacturers. In this form of e-commerce, a business firm places orders for supplies with another business firms directly over the Internet. Paperwork and time required for processing the order and delivery of the goods are thus reduced to a great extent.

2. *Business to Consumers E-commerce (B2C):* It is for the customers to buy stores from the web. The problem to be recognized in this is to secure payment, using encryption, transaction integrity, quick response, time and reliability.

B2C e-commerce involves selling of goods and services to consumers or end users. It allows them to browse the product catalogue, select products or services and complete the order online.

In a B2C transaction, the interaction is between a consumer and the preferred business. For example, the most popular site is amazon.com, which is the first online bookseller which has proved a potential competitor to the traditional bricks and mortar booksellers such as Barrens and Noble.

In this category of e-commerce, businesses use the internet to offer to consumers sales and services around the world 24 hours a day, seven days a week and 365 days a year, The sites Amazon, Rediff and Uphar are among those belonging to this category. These websites are meant for selling goods directly to consumers through the internet. The two-way accessibility of the internet enables operating companies to directly ascertain customer preference and buying trends. Businesses are using these consumer insights to formulate marketing strategies and offer to the customers what they want and when they want. E-busuness in this mode significantly reduces the costs associated with intermediaries, service centres and mass marketing campaigns. Since e-commerce makes just in time delivery possible, the supplier does not have to store the goods. He can procure them from the suppliers as and when he gets the order from the buyer through the internet (A.K. Mohanty).

What is business to consumer e-commerce? Electronic commerce of e-tailing is formally known as business to consumer e-commerce. It is a process of selling of retail goods on the Internet.

A small portion of e-commerce is business to consumers as opposed to business to business.

B2C is the most popular form of e-commerce, wherein the individuals are directly involved in B2C e-commerce, and businesses use the internet for offering their products or services 24 hours a day through global access. The sites Amazon.com and Rediff are among these. These websites spell goods directly to consumers over the Internet. The two way accessibility feature of the internet enables operating companies to ascertain consumer preferences and buying trends directly.

3. Consumer to Consumer E-commerce (C2C): Here interaction is between consumer to consumer. For example, in sites like e-Buy Bid or Buy.com, Baazi.com which are auction sites, one can virtually sell and buy any goods (either used or new ones).

This form of e-commerce is nothing but the cyber version of the good old auction houses. If anyone wants to sell anything, all one has to do is post a message on the site, giving details of the product and the expected price and wait for an interested customer to turn up and buy it. The buyer gets in touch with the seller through the Internet and the deal is crosed once the amount is finalised (A. K. Mohanty). Online message boards and barters are also examples of C2C e-commerce.

---

* *Website http: WWW.infocomcorpo.com/e.eommerce p.1 of 2.*

4. Consumer-to-Business E-commerce (C2B) : E-commerce, by empowering the customer, has been strategically redefining business. An example of C2B model of e-commerce is the site Price line.Com, which allows prospective airline travellers, tourists in need of hotel reservations etc. to visit its websites and indicate their preferred price for travel between any two cities. If an airline is willing to issue a ticket on the customers offered price, the consumer can then travel to the mentioned destination at his terms. (A. K. Mohanty).

5. Business to Employees E-commerce (B2E) : This is concerned more with marketing a corporation's internal processes more efficiently. Customer care and support activities also hold ground. The requirement is that are all self-service with applications on the web that the employees can use themselves.

E-commerce Communities

With the web growing at the rate of one site every six seconds, it is becoming much harder to find information through the search engines. As a consequence, Internet users are grouping together in like minded communities.

These communities are being seen as the forum for commercial success. Communities are emerging in certain business sectors such as professionals, lifestyle or medical patient groups and national and international trading. Business analysts predict a rosy future for the community concepts based around their success in attracting millions of members and recording success in signing up high profile retailers.

Infact, without the focus of an online community, successful e-commerce becomes an uphill battle. Communities are full of people and people service by things. However, communities contribute far more to the commercial landscape than just bringing people together. They provide structure and definition of a potential market place. Communities need commerce and commerce needs communities. When e-commerce is linked to a community site, it stands a much better chance of success. The mechanics can either be a link to a specific vendor's catalogue from a bank or shared commercial e-commerce facilities.

E-commerce Procedure

1. Filling form Online: This is selling online and customers place their order by e-mail. When a customer visits a e-commerce site, he has to fill out an online form to enquire about products or services. The supplier or merchant has to read the data of enquiry about products and services including name, address, credit card number, instructions and so on. They should get them encrypted, compressed, encoded and sent to by e-mail. The response is effected quickly because the web users are accustomed to fast turnaround times.

2. Selecting Product Service : The first step to be followed in the e-commerce process is the product service. The customer browses the merchant's websites, decides and selects products/service item. In this connection, the shopping cart software package is to be used. The shopping cart helps to add, delete and accumulate the total with regards to the product/service.

3. Web Server : Online processor's web server is a key factor in the e-commerce process. As soon as the customer has finished shopping, item selection and viewing shopping cart, they are linked to a secure form on the merchant's web server.

4. Encryption: Cryptography provides a tool of e-commerce security. As there is no formal exchange of signed document or legitimacy of trading partner, with the possibility of illicit modification

—these are the various aspects to be examined as security aspects. Cryptography provides effective security for e-commerce super structures.

5. Forwarding: The encrypted data is then forwarded to the online processor, which provides payment services. Today, there are many real time online payment systems services. They are Authorise.net, Future cash, Banesto (Called service international) Credit Card Network, Net Bank etc. They keep the details of customer's orders and in turn forward only the relevant credit card information to the banking system.

6. Leased Lines: The bank or other financial institutions have been receiving thousands of transactions everyday. The online processor maintains a dedicated or leased line connection to the banks or institutions. The arrangement facilitates to process any number of transactions received everyday.

7. E-mail Receipt: The facility of e-mail receipt is available for e-commerce over the Internet. The optional e-mail receipt method helps the merchant and the customer to notify by e-mail of the purchase approval and purchase details. It is only optional. Irrespective of e-mail receipt, the order particulars are transferred to the merchant's sites for timely processing of the order.

8. Merchant Account: A merchant account is necessary for accepting credit cards. The banks process merchant account transactions besides contacting the customer credit card company. It may accept or decline the amount of the credit card purchase. When the merchant has opened a merchant account, he specifies the name of the bank and account to which funds are to be transferred. Once the bank has occupied the credit card transaction, the funds are transferred to the bank account specified by the merchants.

9. Credit Card Processing: Payment processing system plays a critical role in e-business. The whole concept of frauds related to credit card is a bigger risk to merchants than customers. The internet merchants have to take the same precautions as in mail or phone orders. Generally, merchants are at risk of fraudulent orders. Credit cards are the most popular way for paying for goods and services on the Net.

10. Verification: The transaction information is sent via leased lines to the credit card network, where the validity of the card is checked and the availability of funds on that account is verified. An authorization code is written via leased lines to a secure server.

11. Merchant Getting Money: The banker of the merchant will collect money from the merchant account.

12. Shipment of Goods: Dispatching the goods is the final step in the process of online shopping. The goods are finally shipped which is done outside the Internet facility.

Retail Store Front

The world wide web (www) has an array of sites that offer merchandise songs, full audio CDs and MP3 software necessary for encoding.

1. Retail Sites: There are retail music sellers like cdnow.com, amazon.com and samgoody.com

These sites offer digital song files to customers. The record makers partner with e-commerce sites to sell music in proprietary formats or via the approved codecs.

2. *Portal Sites:* Sites like audible.com, broadcasts.com, altavista.com, listen.com, eatsleepmusic.com gather top selling audios and videos from different sources including music television and feature films for both downloading and streamlining content. Other sites in the fray are luma.com, riffage.com, emusic.com, mp3.com, world wide bands.com, content.ubl.com/cca/rio and many others.

3. *Hardware Manufactures:* Hardware developers are Diamond, Sony, LG, Saehan and, Samsung. They produce portable audio and video players that connect customers directly to those on the Net.

4. *Record Company Sites:* Big names like polygram.com, bmg.com and virginrecords.com. offer memberships for a fee. Surfers can download the songs for playback on a PC or portable device or to be turned onto a CD. Audio files are distributed in codecs than include water marketing to track piracy and encryption to limit the number of times a song can be copied and played.

5. *Artist Sites:* Artists, with their sites like beastieboys.com, acrosmith.com and therollingstones.com sell compact discs and singles as digital files directly to consumers, who can download music in several formats, including MP3, Liquid Audio, a2b, MS Audio or G2. Copyright protections are built in with water marking, and songs can be played on several new hardware devices. Customers can also listen to samples in streaming audio before buying.*

The Internet retail shopping network may range several store fronts: Toys–A Kids paradise, Cool summer cloth, Automobiles, Transport, Classified, Clothes, Software, Speciality Shop, Stores and Malls, Entertainment, Groceries, Hobbies, Services, Luggage and Ladies speciality shops.

Others in the list are :

Featured products (automotive, gifts, clothes, health, sports gear and Speciality shops)

Finance and insurance (Financial services, News/Media)

Computers and Internet (Software, Consulting, Hardware)

Government and Public administration (Consulting, Real estate, Engineering)

Home and Garden (Children, Audio, Plumbing, Security)

Resource industries (Energy, Chemicals, Agriculture, Utilities)

Telecommunications and Media (News/Media, Electronics, Internet)

Wholesalers (Apparel, Flowers, Food)

Business services (Advertising, Consulting, Office equipment)

Education and Training (Career Training, Books, Games, Music)

Food and Drinks (Restaurants, Directories, Retailers)

Health and Fitness (Health and Beauty, Books, Retailers, Food)

Manufactures and Construction (Architecture, Industrial suppliers, Storage)

Retailers (Apparel, Books, Gifts, Toys and Auctions)

Travel services and Lodging (Transportation, Hospitality, Outdoors)

---

* *Computers Today, 16-30, Sep. 1999, p. 49.*

Arts, Business Services, Catalog Favorites, Electronics, Flowers and Gifts International, Parenting, Pets, Telecommunications, Auction, Career, Computer services, Fashion and Apparel, Food and Beverages, Kids, Personal care, Small and Home Office Travel, Books and Magazines, Cars and Motorcycles and Food Products.

Food processing, packaging and milling machinery and equipment.

Dairy and confectionery equipment.

Air conditioning, refrigeration and cold storage systems.

Air and Water Pollution Control equipment and accessories. Hotel, Kitchen equipment and tableware.

Consultancy services and miscellaneous products related Food industry and Hospitality, Fashion Accessories, General Services, Home and Garden, Music and Movies, Personal Finance, Sports and Recreation,

Music under the categories of –

Hindustani, Carnatic, Bhajans, Ghazals, Folk songs, Western (international) Pop, Jazz, Rock and Country Music.

Cyber Music Sites

Like retail cyber stores for products and service sites, there are many music related sites on the Internet. These musical sites are useful for the musicians and many other music lovers. These sites are in format called Musical Instrument Digital Interface (MIDI). With the help of synthesizers, MIDI can be played and this is in addition to the mere conventional recorded sounds. There are several virtual bands from where a piece of music is downloaded and uploaded.

Internet is fast moving even to music. A file can be downloaded and then played one's own machine to produce sounds. This is called sound byte. Music cannot easily be played directly from another computer. The user has to necessarily download the file in silence, store it on your own machine and play from it. The meteoric rise of the online music industry and its producer customer-direct link business model is one of the thrilling developments of the Net. Within a short span, the online music industry has grown enormously and altered the music industry's power structure. The origin of the online music saga is the invention of the MP3 compression format developed by Moving Picture Experts Group (MPEG). It is a popular online music seivice site. The MP3 format permits to convert large music files usually to manageable MP3 files. It can be played by MP3 enabled music programmes such as Winamp.

It is a free software that can be downloaded from the site. The introduction of music file sharing services like Napster has been another thread of this existing cyber saga. Thus, immense popularity has been gained by online music through these various developments.

Harsha Media Private Limited has launched a separate e-commerce music site catering to music lovers. The website address is www. Indiafilmmusic.com. The site is accessible by the world community. People can order cassettes and CDs from anywhere in the world. It is a musical global phenomena. The online music store has more than 10,000 collections of cassettes in all Indian languages.

The exhaustive collection covers all categories of music like devotional instrumental, classical, pop music, golden collections, popular film music, remixes etc. This music store will allow music lovers access to the best and latest of indian music. The website is updated everyday with details about the latest releases. The site caters to those who have preference for international stars in various music catergories.

Payment for purchases of cassettes and CDs are being currently accepted by international credit cards. Plans to put the music store on the Web is emerging as the latest technology.

Three Rules of E-business

"Enabling your organization for e-commerce calls for much more than merely establishing a web presence. In a comprehensive e-commerce scenario, all elements of the supply chain need to get interconnected." Every successful e-business should take care of the following three rules : customer relationship management, supply chain management and e-commerce customer relationship management.

This means identifying, selecting, acquiring, developing and retaining your most profitable customer. Supply chain management requires to deliver the right product to the right place at the right time and at the lowest cost. E-commerce is about delivering a more personalized and higher-quality experience to suppliers, distributors and customers.

Supply Chain Management

The concept of Supply Chain Management (SCM) has undergone a drastic change exponentially in order to deal with the new dynamics that is evolving in e-commerce.

The traditional supply chain management includes: matching of demand and supply, managing physical distribution of goods and build to order management.

In tune with the new technology which emerged as a medium of business, the global supply chain management needs to be redesigned as one stop e-commerce solutions on priority basis.

A comprehensive e-business solutions environment has been developed comprising of industry specific, internet-based applications and services and suitable technology, which enable companies to effectively participate and succeed in the net economy.

In supply chain management, there is a fixed set of supplies who are linked at the back end.

The growing popularity of Customer Relationship Management (CRM) is based on need-toknow customer profiles and buying patterns. There is still a basic need for users to manage their identities as they deal with different parties over the Net. From a corporate customer profiles.

E-commerce Areas: These areas need to be potentially analysed To understand what is e-commerce, nature, scope, implications etc, e-commerce software, Legacy application integration, e-commerce solutions, Internet application integration, e-commerce websites and Electronic data interchange, Migration to web-based models, e-commerce security, privacy and safety, New IT frameworks and integration with business strategy (strategic IT consultance) E-commerce training services, Business site development, Maintenance, Internet and e-commerce related software.

Who is Concerned with E-commerce

- Women
- Family
- More affluent online shoppers

- Better educational items
- Artists
- Musicians
- Advertiser
- Business people

E-commerce Opportunities in India

1. *Higher commerce potentials*

- Computer Hardware
- Computer Components
- Computer Software
- Auto parts
- Apparel with brand authority

2. *Medium e-commerce potential*

- Sports goods
- Toys
- Specialty stores
- High ticket furniture
- Jewelry
- White goods
- Auctions

3. *Limited e-commerce potential*

- Department stores
- Low ticket furniture
- Discount apparels
- Perishable goods
- Perfumes
- Low ticket immediate needs

Reseller Program

The reseller scheme functions more like a partnership arrangement of trading. Reselling with reference to e-commerce is nothing but reselling goods or services which one has bought from another person at a profit. Information Technology (IT) providers have developed a reseller program or partner program, which for them is a network of value added partner (VAP). This program helps companies to develop their own potential profitable Internet business. Having entered into such a partnership, the resellers have access to existing industry trends with multi-solutions providers, and to work with professionals who want to position themselves as a single reliable source of IT. The differential reseller discounts are more competitive incentives of a given percentage on the total monthly client's invoices.

It establishes a link to the company on the website when a Net user clicks on it, and a cookie is placed on the computer that identifies as a reseller. He will be credited with the order and the company receives a commission cheque.

The company will take the responsibility of ordering, billing of the customer and pays the commission. The ordering system automatically checks for the reseller cookie. On finding the cookie, the system automatically records as the reseller and he is paid commission at the fixed rate for each sale generally.

The reseller is subsequently referred to IT providers, clients for web programming, data base design, systems integrations and network engineering.

Benefits and Features of Reseller

They read as follows :

- Reseller program is easy to understand, easy to deploy and operate.
- The reseller will not be charged any membership fee.
- There is no need to invest in high-end equipment and technical support staff. It requires no additional hardware and the existing FTP is sufficient to support the programme.
- It is an excellent choice for every professional or company who provides IT.
- The scheme offers some of the most competitive incentives in the industry.
- Reseller program helps to increase revenues and expand customer base.
- There will be no channel conflict. It means resellers' customers are resellers' customers only. The provider will only manage /host the account only.
- The reseller and the client will receive professional and technical support free of charge.
- The resellers can earn profits by receiving a prescribed percentage.
- Provider receives commission cheques based on the collected total amount of monthly invoice from the clients.
- To the provider, it increases web hosting revenue and attracts new merchants.
- World wide web market for their products and services can be quickly accessed. Value added services and preferred pricing are other features of the reseller program.
- There is a benefit of bundling i.e. additional web hosting, scanning services, domain registration and counselling services can be availed. Cooperative promotion and technical support are important aspects of the program.
- There is no need to hire consulting firms or designers due to the availability of existing professionals.
- Another benefit of a reseller program is that it adds value to the existing business. It also permits to reach the potential global audience and enhances its value to existing clients.
- When clients are more, it increases the periodical residual income. It eliminates overheads on maintaining an advanced internet architecture, technical support, staff and administrative support.

E-commerce Strategy

It is necessary to develop a dynamic business strategy based on business opportunities to provide value to various firms. This requires an understanding of the company, the industry and the unique attributes of current internet technologies. The salient objectives of the strategy are:

- Focus on the customer and provision of improved services and interaction
- Increase mind share and brand awareness.
- Expand geographic reach.
- Increase revenue and market share.
- Review and streamline both internal and existing back office applications.
- Deliver accurate, current and appropriate personalized content using two way communication capability of the web.

The strategy defined above, should have objectives that are sustainable, hold high barriers to entry for competitors and have high switching costs for users besides being difficult to copy.

While developing an e-commerce strategy, it is pertinent to consider the internet's potential to further the business objectives of various firms. Selecting products and services to be offered and delivered on the Net is one of the key decisions of this strategy.

Some of the other areas that demand attention include :

- The incorporation of the Internet into the existing line of business and existing channels of distribution.
- Making the websites dynamic and interesting to attract visitors and retaining the loyalty.
- Introducing incentives to convert visitors to the site into potential buyers.
- Improving customer service and satisfaction by keeping back room operations under control to honour all commitments.
- Reducing design and development cost and improving employee productivity.
- Ensuring that company data such as knowledge of customer, suppliers and partners remains secure. Ensuring security is important in e-commerce transactions.
- Accessing the e-commerce developer to create e-commerce infrastructure.
- Issuing automatic authorization to the customer and ensuring thus the ease of passage of the website.*

The strategy for conducting potential e-commerce are as follows:

- Select a product line that has potential to sell well over the internet.
- Plan to operate on a very low inventory management overhead from staffing and office space.

---

* *Goldman Sachs, 16-30, Nov. 1999, Computers today, p. 60.*

- Select the supplier with the least cost. shortest delivery time and the most suitable stock.
- Organize shipping of the product from the supplier to the customer through a reliable third party delivery channel.
- Establish effective communication channel with other e-brokers to find the best deal for brokerage and the client.
- Make your site fast and easy to use. Customers prefer easy and quick accessibility to the websites.
- Use graphics that don't take long to load and make site navigation easy.
- Create methods to measure customer satisfaction levels through focus groups, anonymous responses and third party feedback.*

Critical Factors for E-commerce Success

1. *Target the Right Customers:* American Airlines and National Semiconductor Corporation are great examples of companies that have carefully worked out and targeted their web initiatives to the right customer: the one who makes a difference to the bottom line. American Airlines targets its websites at its most loyal customers: its 32 million gain advantage as frequent fliers. National Semiconductor targets people who have the greatest influence on the decision to purchase its product design engineers.

2. *Own the Customer's Total Experience:* Whether online or offline, you need to deliver a consistent "branded" experience to customers by saving their time and by giving them control over their experience of doing their business with you. The Hertz Corporation's number one gold club provides a great example of the kind of business process redesign required to own the customer's total experience, both on the road and in cyberspace. Amazon.com has mastered the customer's total experience for online retailing. Their business strategy is customer satisfaction and retaining their loyalty.

3. *Streamline Business Processes that Impact the Customer:* Both Babson College and the NSF understood clearly who their end customers were (students and researchers, respectively). Yet both organisations discovered that to do business and ensure that process design is right, they had to involve a variety of other key stakeholders in the redesign effort.

4. *Provide a 360-Degree View of the Customer Relationship:* Organisations dealing with customers need to have a complete view of that customer's relationship with them in terms of products, accounts and past interactions. Whether the customer helps himself to information over the web or the phone, that information must be accessible. Both Bell Atlantic Corp. and Wells Cargo have worked long and hard to provide this 360-degree view access a variety of potential interactive channels. These companies have used the Net to expand their business canvas and bring convenience and access to services at the doorsteps of the consumers. These companies are thus known to be 'customer-focussed.'

5. *Let Customers Help them Selves:* Dell Computer Corporations Bell Online and I Print Inc., the online print shop provide great examples of how far you actually have to take and benefit from self-services when you do business on the Web. Customers want to be able to do everything

---

* *RGS Asthana, information Systems, Computer World, Dec. 1-15, 1999, pp. 82-84.*

themselves: researching, configuration and ordering products, trouble shooting problems, checking on the status of a repair or print job, and tracking delivery of the works.

6. Help Customers do their Jobs: When your customers are business people, you as an organisation need to understand exactly how they do their job and where your company fits in. That's what Boeing Co. did when it designed its web-based spare part ordering system for airline maintenance professionals. That's what Photo Disc. undertook when it began to offer digital photography to graphic design professionals. The key: *save the customer time and let them play " what-if" games with your inventory.*

7. Deliver Personalized Service: In this era of one-to-one marketing, how will you know what customers really value in the way of personalization? Take your cues from the Wall Street Journal-interactive edition in the cyberworld and from GM's onstar division in the physical world. Both companies discovered that what customers value is the depth of the interactive experience. If you can provide a level of personalized service that isn't possible any other way, as an successful organisation, you because a part of their lives. This should be a hassle free experience for the customers.

8. Foster Community: Both business to business player Cisco Systems Inc. and business to customers player Tripod Inc. have mastered what it takes to build online committees that generate value. Cisco's customers answer on another's most technical questions. Tripod's members vie with one another to create the most interesting consent.*

The other deciding factors for e-commerce and its successful operation are read as:

- Range of products provided
- Services
- Marketing
- Security
- Credit card processing
- Shopping cart
- Certification authority
- Website and its promotion
- Digital signature
- Computer density
- Context
- Cost control
- Connectivity
- Cyber laws
- Commonsense

Minor Issues contributing towards potential e-commerce include:

- Guidance to information security.
- Understanding the business information risk.

---

* *Patricia Seybold, information Systems, Coputer World, March 1-15, 1999.*

- Keeping confidentiality of business information
- Information security and internet.
- Consideration of Information via the Net as an asset.
- Computer assurance guidelines.
- IT technology programme.
- Legal measures.
- E-commerce, education and training.
- Solutions, technologies and support.

Surefire ways for E-commerce

1. *Ignore What Already Exists:* Most experts agree that e-commerce as a business tool on the Net is doomed to failure if no one carefully considers how it fits in with the existing business model. It is important to analyse and know how e-commerce will affect your overall business, including sales channels, marketing, order fulfilment, inventory and accounting procedures. Without this information, you run the risk of developing a site with little business relevance and technical flaws.

2. Think Psychedelic Design: Despite the proliferation of advice, even from staidly gray outfits such as the wall street Journal, many sites look like drug-induced marvels of flashing lights and confusion. Providing too much information on the opening page deters net users from acknowledging the site with appreciation.

3. *Build it to Run Slowly:* Sites run slowly as a side effect of cluttered designs and flashy stuff. They also creep along if they are overburdened by too much unpredicted traffic. Take a hint from Zona Research, a market research film in Redwood City, Calif., wherein a recent study called "shop until you drop", Zona found that customers are less likely to use a site if it takes more than eight seconds to load.

4. *Don't bother Offering a Search Function:* Many companies require users to go through a confounding number of twists and turns to find a product on the websites of companies. In the above mentioned Zona study, two-thirds of the survey participants indicated a marked degree of difficulty, in finding products on e-commerce sites. Refer back to item 2: there is no formula for simple and intuitive design, However, everyone knows what the search button means. The worst drawback in building an e-commerce site is not providing a solid search capability to enable easy accessibility to information to the Net users.

5. *Confuse them at the Point of Purchase:* Once customers find the perfect product, they are often tripped up by the buying routine. Take the case of a travel site that was successful in providing information, but failed to get customers to work through the confusing 12 click process it took to book reservations. "By applying cognitive design principles to the purchase process, we got it down it three clicks. The result was a 15 percent increase in the number of visitors who booked reservations through the site", says Dick Loveland, principal at Neoglyphics Media, a consulting firm in Chicago, US.

6. *Don't Acknowledge Receipt of an Order:* This may not kill your site, but it will annoy customers When a project depends on the fulfilment of a product order, as it is likely with any business-to-business transaction, the site must be accountable. Always confirm the order receipt to avoid the aggressiveness of the customers.

7. Don't bother with Back-end-systems: "Most e-commerce sites fail because their back-end-accounting and inventory systems are not integrated with ordering" says David Gibson, Vice President of IXL, an internet firm in Boston. Companies not attempting integration must implement a supplementary back-end process, which usually requires that data be re-entered into different systems. Volume sales quickly overwhelm these manual processes and cause a myriad of mistakes.

Mannhein Auctions, which inflates the sales of used cars between consignors and leaders, is developing a system that will provide real-time inventory information to customers who want to track where their cars are the sales process. "We spend too much time trying to integrate a legacy accounting system. In the end, we had to build a new accounting system from scratch. Had we made that decision on Day one, the project would be further along, and we would have spent on operations for the Atlanta firm.

8. Charge Higher Prices on the Site than through other Outlets : Inconsistent pricing is another side-effect of the insufficient integrations back-end systems. The unique pricing strategies, worked out with each business partner, are rarely evident on the e-commerce site. Why would a partner use a site that charges a higher price for a product price for product than the one-available over the phone? Asks Mitch Ruud, manager of e-commerce for Great Plains Software in Fargo, N.D.

9. Don't Provide a Feedback Mechanism: By omitting simple, e-mail feedback, you cut yourself off from important information. First, you will never know whether your site meets your customer's needs because they won't be able to tell you. Second, you can't gather suggestions for improvement. And finally, you will fail to provide good service which is an important facet in the faceless world of e-commerce.

10. Build something your Partners will Refuse to Use: Self-evident perhaps, but an inordinate number of businesses overlook the following fact. Its easier to phone in an order, safer to fax it on paper or less expensive to maintain the status, than it is to use your e-commerce site-that site will always go unused. *

What not to do for E-commerce

1. Over Engineering: Do not attempt developing a site that is too complex. It will turn out to be an implementation nightmare. Often unrealistic and convoluted plans lead to projects getting grounded forever. More importantly, challenges posed by new and unfamiliar technology tend to prove costly, to the extent of having to abandon the attempt at setting up an online store altogether as technical costs mount. Therefore, first identify the most basic goals of your online store and then implement these. When the basic system is in place, you can always add on all the bells and whistles to make the site more customer oriented.

2. Taking on More than You Can: Be smart and choose hosting services that provide turnkey solutions instead of doing it all by yourself when setting up shop. Why? Because, e-commerce can involve a highly complex combination of equipment choices, website building and hosting issues, as well as security and billing technologies ...and the list goes on. So, let any high quality store hosting service or web hosting service worry about fending off internet hackers, as well as hardware and software issues that only the top computer networking gurus can handle. In this way, you can concentrate on selling your product while delegating much of the technical chores to others.

---

* *Downe Shand, Information Systems, Computer World, July, 16-31, 1999pp. 52-53.*

3. *Forcing a Square Peg into a Round Hole:* Remember, products that sell well in retail stores need not sell well online. Infact, it is proved otherwise, thanks to factors like high shipping costs, need for personal salesmanship etc. So. evaluate the product's suitability for online sales. Start with asking questions such as :

- Are the prices attractive to entice shoppers to buy online than from a retail store?
- What will be the cost of shipping and handling ?
- Will the consumer trust your online service guarantees ?
- A simple exercise such as this will save you much time and expense in the long run proving profitable to your business.

4. *Ignoring Security Issues:* Ensure network before your e-commerce site goes live, else it could prove disastrous. There are two options here: You can retain the services of network security consultants besides installing specialised security software or let a hosting service take care of the security service.

5. *Going it Alone:* Considering the vast complexity of e-commerce issues, it would be a mistake not to outsource some of the e-commerce set-up tasks as needed. Infact, desipte using turnkey hosting services, many e-commerce stores in the US have been known to fall due to lack of professional design and marketing know-how. So, intead of undertaking a long and difficult process of planning, only to stumble on the final design and presentation of the store, retain an e-commerce oriented web development agency.

6. *Complex Webpage Design:* Remember, it doesn't matter what sophisticated technologies are installed on the host webserver for the prospective shopper. What matters is what is displayed in the shopper's web browser, that is the front.end. So make sure that you have a well designed interface, which is easy to download and navigate and ensure easy accessibility to the consumers. Without professional, marketing oriented and easy -to-use page lay-out, even the most sophisticated back-end technologies will be of no use in ensuring potential sales.

Likewise, cluttered web pages that either make it difficult to navigate your site, or make it difficult for the shopper to know how to place an order can cause an online store to fail. If you are serious about building a successful e-commerce site, make sure that your site works to your advantage rather than emerge a cause of lost sales opportunities.

7. *Neglecting the Telephone Number:* Now, for the winner : In most online stores, the point-of-sale is not online. What usually happens is that a shopper browses through a site, compares values with other sites and then places an order over the phone. Despite customer behaviour, many sites fail to make a phone number available for ordering. In order to make it easy for the shopper, phone numbers should be listed prominently on every page of the site.*

How to Build an E-commerce System

The establishment of an e-commerce system involves some basic steps to be followed. What steps should to be taken in order to establish an e-commerce system? It is a frequently asked question. Following are the important steps which will give you a general idea what constitutes an efficient e-commerce system.

---

* *Dataquest, Feb. 28th, 1999. 158-159*

1. Identifying Business: Identifying potential business opportunities is the first step. First determine the company's line of business which will determine these opportunities. The kinds of technology and business partners are also to be identified to achieve e-commerce goals.

2. Selection of Technology Infrastructure: Infact, e-business encompasses several activities which uses contemporary technologies. The infrastructure facilities like access to PCs, Internet, credit cards, telecommunication networks, Internet Services Providers (ISP) etc. are essential for the growth of e-commerce, more particularly in of developing country like India. India will need a robust and world-class information technology and telecom infraskucture with substantial Internet penetration. The Internet market of India is under served. The telecom and ISP market is working out strategies to adapt to changes in the global environment and meet the expectations and demands of the market to accelerate Internet penetration which is synonymous with the e-broking business in India.

3. Imlementation of E-business Solutions: Implementing e-business solutions is the most complex and challenging issue because it involves complex technology and organisational issues. E-commerce will not work in a vacuum and solutions should be integrated with other systems. It is also necessary to consider managing the system inhouse, work with partners or outsource the solutions. This challenge extends to increasing awareness of the benefits of e-business to customers.

4. Shopping Cart: It is a shopping cart catalogue, is an appalet that allows customers to order online. Configuring a shopping cart is an important step, consisting of a number of parameters and data which are displayed for each item purchased. It describes options, size, colour etc. of the product. A shopping cart allows you to add, remove, alter, calculate etc. before ordering a product online.

5. Selection of Language: Different countries have their own national languages. Internet facilitates many world languages, enabling Net customers to shop online. The Net user can choose from a list of languages available in which the shopping cart text can be displayed. This will ensure satisfaction of customers who access sites their preferred online purchasing.

6. Selection of Currencies: Like choosing language, the selection of currency is also crucial and it needs to be taken in order to establish an effective e-commerce system. There is a possibility to accept more than one type of currency. For instance, one may be able to choose payment either in dollars or in rupees.

7. Shipping Costs: Calculating shipping costs is yet another step in setting up e-commerce. The rate of the product, price of either total or each individual item etc. are popular methods to calculate shipping costs. In most of the e-commerce transactions, these two systems are used.

8. Designing Storefront: A storefront for business over the Internet is facilitated by the e-commerce software which helps the users in designing an effective storefront. The instructions are included in the software package. The purpose of designing a storefront is to welcome the visitors to the store. It also contains logo of the storefront and is professional looking. In the storefront, various other features attract customers and business partners who can easily navigate a site. This pertains to an effective liaison between business partners and customers.

9. Data Paths: To set up an effective e-commerce system, demands to configure data paths are to be given priority. The e-commece software captures the order information from the shopping cart. Fulfilment of customer's orders is the ultimate goal.

10. Database: The entire system of e-commerce is based on building a database, which the shopping cart will access to obtain information which is displayed to the customers. The type of database server is in use which designs the format of the database. Generally, the database contains full information about the products or services offered for sale such as product numbers, sizes, colours, prices, description etc.

11. Software: E-commerce software is designed to serve as a device to create a storefront , and the catalogue that will provide customers with description and pictures of the products or services available online. The advantages of the Internet infrastructure cannot be obtained without the e-commerce software. An organisation can develop and run an e-commerce website only with the help of e-commerce software. E-commerce software also helps to conduct B2B transactions through Electronic Data Interchange (EDI).

12. Security: Above all, security, privacy and authentication are essential for successful e-commerce. Theft, hackers, intrusion and other internet crimes are common problems in recent years. Unless security is available, an effective e-commerce system cannot be built up. Today, e-commerce software enables secure transactions through secure socket layer and secure electronic transactions which are internet security protocol. It is the most serious problem affecting e-commerce. It is important to make customers confident of the service and deliver the services the as per the promise made when acquiring new customers.

Tips to Launch a Perfect Online Store

Having mentioned the don'ts, now here is what constitutes a *perfect* online store. On the world wide web, glitzy graphics shown on online stores do not necessarily guarantee potential sales. On the other hand, a well designed site, both in terms of content as well as presentation, can give your online store the edge you need to succeed by retaining and consider the following tips:

1. Clarity and Ease of Navigation: Mega selling websites such as those of Amazon.Com, Dell Computers and Cisco make clear to the shopper which categories of products are available and provide easy site navigation links. From anywhere in these sites, the shopper can easily proceed to browse more products without having to waste time searching. This makes it clear that a good navigation system is required for successful e-commerce site, but ironically, many sites on the Internet are sorely lacking in this regard, thus failing to ensure customer loyalty.

2. Privacy of Shoppers: When purchasing online, shoppers are often required to provide an entire host of personal information, including mailing address, phone number, e-mail ID and billing information. In general, requiring these disclosures can discourage many shopper from purchasing directly online in terms of security. To alleviate shoppers' privacy concerns, the better- designed sites provide guarantees than this personal information will not sold as leaked to other companies for mailing lists and other solicitations purposes. Boosting consumer confidence is essential for a perfect online store. In the Internet world, the fact remains that customers are discerning to a great extent, with few loyalties and that they are extremely demanding in terms of online services. So the organisation must be geared up to this fact and surpass the expectations of customers giving the shopper the opinion of clicking on the thumbnail for a larger graphic.

3. Fast loading Pages: Many consumers connect to the internet from their homes with relatively slow modems. For this reason, the perfect online store would be fast loading, not bogged down by overly long content or graphics. One strategy which has become more commonplace, is to show small product description, and then 'thumbnails with an initial product description and then giving the shopper the opinion of clicking on the thumbnail for a larger graphic.

4. Technical Support: Often, online shoppers are wary of poor customer support, showing hesitancy if the merchant will respond to issues that may arise after the desired purchase has been made. The concern is whether the online merchant has the expertise or personnel required to resolve technical issues relating to the set-up or use of the product. The perfect store would post its technical policies clearly to address the shoppers' potential concerns.

5. Return and Exchange Policies: Another factor affecting consumer confidence is a concern that they will be dissatisfied with the product purchased without the benefit of examining the product physically before purchase. Remember that the colours displayed on the computer monitor are sure to vary from their actual colour. For example, the elegant royal blue shirt you just purchased online might turn out to be purplish when it is delivered at your doorstep or might turn out to be lighter in weight, or smaller than anticipated. The perfect online store would post an unconditional exchange or refund policy If the customer remains deoxidised and thus boost consumer confidence.

6. The Right Look and Feel: Marketing is crucial part of any sales process. Ultimately, the online store must entice potential shoppers to make substantial online purchase. To a great extent, sites accomplish this with well planned graphic design. A perfect site would feature a pleasant colour scheme and attractive design elements which serve to highlight the products being offered without overshadowing or conflicting with them. Remember, graphics do not have to be large in file size or be flashy, to be effective and attract customers. As we mentioned earlier, a quick loading site is a must.*

Taleshopping

Meaning and Concept: Teleshopping network is an electronic commercial or advertising and an ideal marketing option for small manufacturers with innovative new products. The object of this network is to enable the customer to see the product first, and then have easy access to the product and make strategic decisions to buy. Though teleshopping networks are still in the infant stage in India, small manufacturers with new products work out strategies to introduce them into the market with low advertisement budget, through teleshopping networks which are entering into the market to get visibility at the national level and reaching the mass audience at cheaper costs. The chief aim of teleshopping network is to educate and guide the potential consumers by demonstration of product's potential usage and application.

A teleshopping network is an economic and chief means of providing an alternative root to reach the customers. The main reasons for the small manufacturers going for the teleshopping network are high marketing, manufacturers and special features of the products. Teleshopping network, however, does not remain an exclusive marketing option for long. It is only about product awareness among the Net users reaching threshold manufacturers of potential business. Once a product awarenes reaches a threshold, manufacturers had invested in the mainstream marketing to boost sales volumes. Some of the products of new concepts introduced in this marketing have turned to attract consumers by resorting to teleshopping networks which have dual advantges of product visibility and marketing responsibility.

In the present day, competitive market conditions with a wide range of substitute products are available for new manufacturers to enter the market and compete with rival products to get visibility

---

* *Data Quest, Feb. 28, 1999 p.159.*

at national level, and it costs heavy promotional investments. But through networks and with little amount, the manufacturer can ensure national recognition among the cunsumers.

Teleshopping network thus establishes a commercial relationship between customers and the manufacturers. Teleshopping networks have entered the marketing world with the sole aim of providing cosumers guidance information and their usage and application with special charactestic features. The manufucturers are going for potential networks where sales are ensured to be reasonably as high as expected. As far as awareness generation by teleshopping networks is concerned, they are more than equal to the task, given their high reach capacity of converting viewership into sales. The audience for teleshopping networks also constitutes a considerable proportion of the total viewership.

Franchise Outlets

The problem of returning and replacing products is a common feature because of their unsatisfactory quality standards. Credibility related to product quality still assumes greater importance. As such, teleshopping networks usually give some sort of a guarantee for the product they sell. There have been numerous instances of lack of consistency in quality, failure to deliver products as per the screened promises of the products. In order to solve this major common problem, some of the renewed teleshopping networks have opened franchise outlets in selected areas to give the consumer an opportunity to see and examine the product and see its demonstration after they see it on the screen channel. Franchise outlets also facilitate to enhance the speed of delivery of the products ordered by consumers.

Some Teleshopping Networks

Only a beginning has been made in India in the field of teleshopping. Following are some of the existing and operating teleshopping networks. The business canvas of teleshopping networks needs to be painted with the colours of substantial financial returns and much remains to be done in this direction:

- Zee TV's Asian Sky Shop.
- Teleshopping Network (TSN)
- United Teleshopping (UTS)
- In Teleshopping.

Foreign Teleshopping Networks

American Teleshopping majors are :

- Home Shopping Network (HSN)
- Perhaps Quality Value Convenience (QVC)

They are reportedly entering the Indian market in a big way through potential tie-ups.

Timings and Cost of Teleshopping Networks

The main reason for choosing teleshopping is the high cost of marketing and as an *alternate* to the existing mainstream marketing. The question often arises as to whether teleshopping network is cheaper or not to reach customer's mind with its presence in the market. But usually, air time rates of television are very high. It is true but the concept of teleshopping networks can utilise the zero revenue hours of channels. The zero revenue hours are usually midnight hours, twelve noon and from 3.P.M. to 6 P. M. The cost for the network through television is much higher.

Products for Teleshopping Network

The networks have been working on improving different market related aspects. Teleshopping products are generally not sold on visibility but on the quality of salesmanship. The networks have turned out well for viewership and have been very successful in terms of consumer guidance in product usage and applications but not in terms of generating sales.

Pertaining to certain products, the concepts are highly functional though innovative, not aspinational or image related and consumers need to be guided in their usage. Experiences also show that the criterion for product selection is their unique penetration into the market and the capability of rendering themselves to demonstration. So, the products like households, kitchen appliances, health products, jewelry, toys, games etc. have relatively better prospects by teleshopping. Its coverage may also expand, covering categories of products such as electronic apparel, beauty products and services including travel, financial services and insurance. For the movement of product, the site mainly caters to housewives who are more prominent due to timing schedules of the capsules. Some other products turned to teleshopping are the ready to carry mat with attached pillows, Suzi, a manual food processor, roti chef, a plug-on instant chapati making product etc.

New products require marketing inputs which teleshopping networks add to their packages of services.

Working Features of Teleshopping Networks

- The teleshopping networks relieve small manufacturers offering new product concepts from the complex and difficult task of reaching the minds of the consumers and targetting the market.
- The networks provide and extend a direct attractive and cheap root to the consumers and manufacturers.
- Teleshopping networks themselves offer dual advantage of product visibility and potential marketing responsibility.
- The networks make it easy for the product to benefit from national expansion to attract mass consumers, mass audience or the mass market.
- Teleshopping provides an alternative to mainstream marketing because of the high cost of advertising and special characteristics of products to sell.
- Teleshopping networks greatly help consumers to be educated and they guide the prospective customers by demonstrating the product's usage and applications.
- When the product concept itself is very new, teleshopping networks are useful to educate potential customers and ensure their preference to the choice product.
- Teleshoppig networks urers are more useful to those concerns, particularly small manufacturers which have a low advertising budget and need to build awareness and acceptance of the new product concept.
- These networks act as a launching pad for new products having features of a low cost, high level of reach, delivery to and feedback from customers and all other things that small manufacturers need to have.

- They give an opportunity to consumers to see, examine the product and see a demonstration after they see it on the television channel.
- Teleshopping networks are most suitable for small producers introducing a new product concept which also ensures the speed of response from consumers.
- Young small concerns offering new products cannot undertake activities of specialized nature requiring concentration on consumer preferences and marketing because of their financial problems.
- Teleshopping networks can remove all artificial entry barriers emerging in the market place due to high volumes of advertising and growing competition in the market.
- The networks also provide package of services. For instance, advising them as how to write a user's manual and in which language free of cost at all levels.
- Networks undertake after sales services by establishing a special customer service cell which checks up on delivery related qulality complaints and requests for demonstration.

Because of these special features and advantages along with some problems being faced by the networks and manufacturers, teleshopping has a bright future in the country, particularly in respect of certain products of innovative and image related products on which consumers need to be guided in their usage and applications to benefit from the same in the long run.

Telemarketing

The use of telephone for Telemarketing is of recent origin. It is still in the infant stage in India, but widespread to some extent in other countries. The expression 'telemarketing' is a potential arrangement for ordering of products and services by communicating with business houses and it is a two-way process. The reasons for increasing use of telephones for business is a cultural evolutionary and revolutionary mechanism and strategy. As evident today, people have been using phone for a wide variety of purposes relating to business and marketing, personal, social, political aspects etc.

The modern marketing strategy depends increasingly upon customer awareness, customer orientation and customer satisfaction. These segments require allowing services to the consumers and for the suppliers to maintain a continuous and satisfactory relation with them. Telephone itself is a sophisticated tool, having potential powers and is being used for telemarketing. It helps to get calls, for services and products, contacting decision makers and securing appointments. These activities secure substantial revenues for the organisation. The use of telephone also improves sales performance and these are the days of teleculture. There are some studies which indicate that the business use of free phone calls would increase fivefold by the end of the century.

The technique helps to build a digital network for more customers nationwide and world wide. There are various networks like wireless networks, broadband networks and public career networks. The teleshopping networks have emerged in recent years as one of the most high profile disciplines in the marketing of products into other countries. In India also, large telebusinesses have emerged. The power behind phone for marketing has been recognized, it is finally earning its marketing potential.

The system is designed to improve customer service and relationship sophisticated to provide free sale information by telephone with computing electronic and computer related sophisticated technology. The customers who are wishing to contact with the suppliers can do so directly.

In India, business houses are becoming increasingly aware of the importance of telemarketing in recent years as a valuable addition to the sales process. It is an effective means to ensure ongoing high quality customer service. Telemarketing is one of the marketing mixes and is the most modern and attractive sales strategy.

That there is need to recongnize the individual needs of each and everyone of our customers cannot be denied or refused. In order to do this, we must interact regularly with our customers and we must capture and analyze responses so that we can perdict changes in their behaviour and attiude, thus allowing us to stay ahead of the same. Telemarketing allows us to have this controlled interaction and can, therefore, provide invaluable research back to our customers or into our own marketing and development process.

Telemarketing units are involved in many internal and external activities like customer care, customer response, lead generation and database clearing, selling, research, customer retention and debt changing.**

Objectives and Advantages of Telemarketing

They pertain to:

- Ordering of goods and services.
- To render services required for the product or service thereby.
- To establish long marketing relationship.
- To retain customers and acquire new potential customers.
- The cost of retention of customers or client is cheaper.
- To ensure electronic-based system of control.
- The system enables telemarketing organisations to access and refine the effectiveness of their plans, sales campaign etc.
- To improve business by strategic telemarketing systems to support sales efforts.
- Establish a complaint procedure with cable line number on their packages.
- Telemarketing system is supportive for assistance in the marketing campaigns.
- To establish contacts with customers to secure appointments.
- Increasing awareness of the product with the customers who are contacted by telephone.

New Marketing Technology

Advancement in sophisticated communication techniques have led to the use of relatively new technologies in marketing and customers' services. Voice recognition, caller line identification, customers' telephone and integration etc. are relatively new technologies in marketing and customer service. Even live telephone operator systems have been replaced with the automated system. The information technology can be linked to telephones with the power of information. It has been a boon in recent years and will continue to do in the forthcoming years.

The new technologies in this direction are interactive voice response, computer telephone integration and caller line integration etc. which constitute the various systems for telemarketing.

The system calls for the automatic entering of caller details into business database. The details of the product or products as contained in brochures or other literature will be forwarded to the

* Michael Hammer, Sales and Marketing Management, 1965, Aug., p.19.

caller. The details of callers are also supplied to the sales force or local representatives so as to enable them to be proactively reconnected by phone or mail.

Point of Sales System

People prefer to undergo pain and tolerate and wait in endless queues while on a pilgrimage but quite honestly if a businessman or a trader expect the same of them while shopping at their stores, it would be a sorry state of affairs for the businessmen or traders. Customers need information pertaining to the services required by them around the world in stores and super stores with a variety of products and impeccable service. Giving the customer comfort, convenience, prompt attention and quick settlement of bills are the important considerations that every trader should keep at the back of his mind.

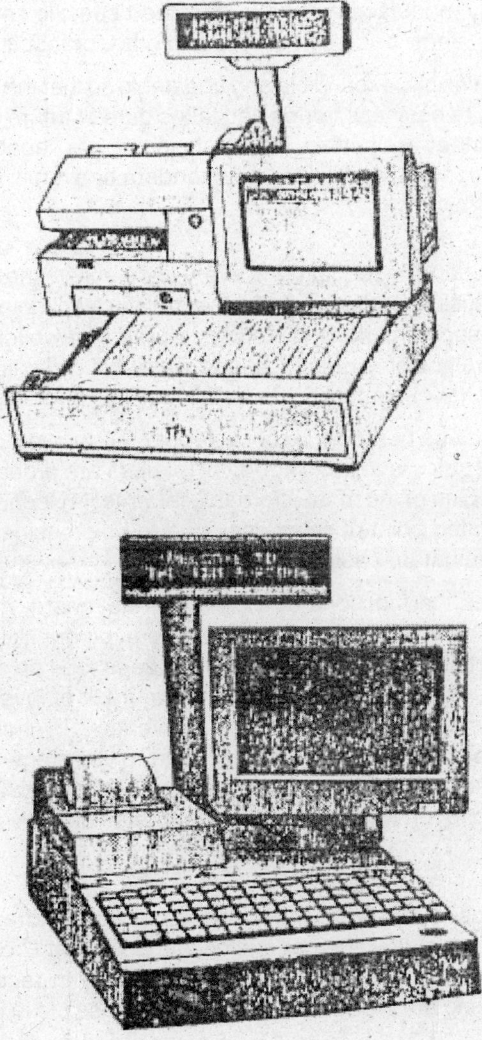

Fig. 1.02 Point of Sale Terminals

Today, all these services require complete automation of information handling right from the front yard register control, inventory, sales support, backyard-incoming -outgoing order control etc. These are to name just a few. It all depends upon the size of the shop, the nature of products or services offered and the extent of automation available with the business house. So the bigger the store, the more will it need solutions that match upto the expectations of consumers that grow with the times.

Automation of information handling gives the traders or businessmen many spin-off benefits, because with proper information, they will be able to monitor and plan inventory control, sales strategies etc. which will subsequently help them to achieve a quantum leap in profit earning because we are aware that time is money.

To solve all these problems and to maximize profits and ensure satisfaction to clients, there are available in the market a few computers and point of sale (POS) products.

Many information technology manufacturers have designed specific space saving devices such as strategic application and systems and point of sale and other products.

These equipments are highly flexible, expandible and updateble so that the information network built in a business survives with future business trends and takes care of future needs. Also what is important in these products are that they are perfectly compatible and are capable of fitting into any existing information network of the concern, individual, or in tandem or even in clustens.

Application

In short, with new information handling equipment, every shop enjoys the advantage of being able to build and generate potential business in an cost effective step by step method. These products are used in departmental stores, super markets, hotels/restaurants, jewellery stores, hospital, distribution, transport, gifts and novelty stores, electrical and water bill collection centres, grocery stores, apparel stores, shoe shops, travel agents, canteen, auto stores and electronic stores.

To get a retail outlet the best sales person cum book keeper, cum-inventory controller, cum-stores manager in a box, the point of sales is a great friend. All retailers are probably looking for new ways to boost their business profits. One of the most affordable information technologies is the point of sales terminal which is an integrated point of sales designed to help business people to make more money, do the things of routine nature easily and in an cost effective way.

On the one hand, it combines the functions of a computer keyboard, monitor, credit card reader and receipt or voucher printing in one space saving unit equipment like this. On the other hand, the system guides you as a trusted personal assistant. It keeps tabs on cash flows, lets the businessman know which products are selling best and also keep track of inventory. In short, the system helps to manage business better and also keep track of inventory. In short the system helps to manage business better, improves profits, saves time and cost, gives plenty of time to do what would prove to be the best services for the Net users. The system uses a range of off-the-shelf and custom software applications to help to run the business even more efficiently.

Point of Sales Terminals

These terminals are mostly used today to identify goods in retail stores. It is a business practice by the manufacturer to print a code. The code is called Universal Product Code (UPC). It is a machine readable code of parallel bars. with widespread usage in recent years in super markets and grocery stores for labelling the products. The code is accessible in parallel bars.

The optical character reader is a device which performs the functions of the decoding of scanned bars. Point of sales terminals are used a read bar codes as well as the printed information. The terminal is controlled by the computer and displays the information scanned. It produces the total amount of value of purchases including taxes as well as itemized particulars.

Functions

The point of sale equipment prints receipts and bills containing vital information. This is information that can keep the customer's loyalty and satisfaction.

They are used for, Register controls, Inventory control, Incoming- outgoing offer control, Delivery control, Sales support, Printers - réceipts, Journals, Sales slips Coupon, Tickets, cables, credits, debits cheque, invoices, daily reports etc.

Advantages

They read as follows:

- The point of sale information handling equipment at stores disperses the queue quickly and will not take longer time as it is to take otherwise.
- It is new way to boost business profits.
- This integrated POS device is designed to help to make more money.
- On the one hand, it sometimes combines the functions of a computer.
- Keyboard, monitor, credit card reader receipt printer in one space saving unit.
- It doubles up as trader's trusted assistant.
- It keeps tabs on cash flows, tells which products are selling best and also keeps track of inventory.
- It helps to manage business better, improves profits and gives load of time to do what is best service for the customer.
- To add to this list, the technology uses a range of off-the-shelf and custom software applications to help to run business even more efficiently.
- Helps to get the retail outlet the best sales person-cum-book keeper, cum-inventor, controller and cum-store, manage in-a-box.

The point of sales terminal is a special card reading cell register in case of smart card transactions, a cardholder puts the card in the point of sales terminal. It receives its power supply from the terminal and communicates with the cardholder. These terminals are used to read even the bar codes in addition to printing information and displaying strategically scanned data.

Uses and Applications

- POS terminals reduce customer's waiting time and check out counters.
- Directly update the online files, receivables, inventory control etc.
- Quick sales analysis and reporting.

Bar Codes

A bar code is a machine readable code. The code consists of vertical bars of different widths which are used to represent the data. The codes are written in the form of bars or strips and are

Fig. 1.03 Bar Codes

Fig. 1.04 A Variant Bar Code

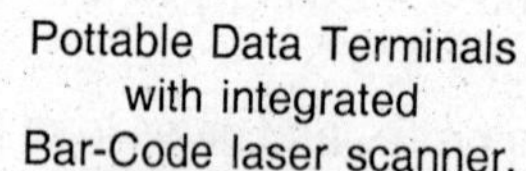

Pottable Data Terminals
with integrated
Bar-Code laser scanner.

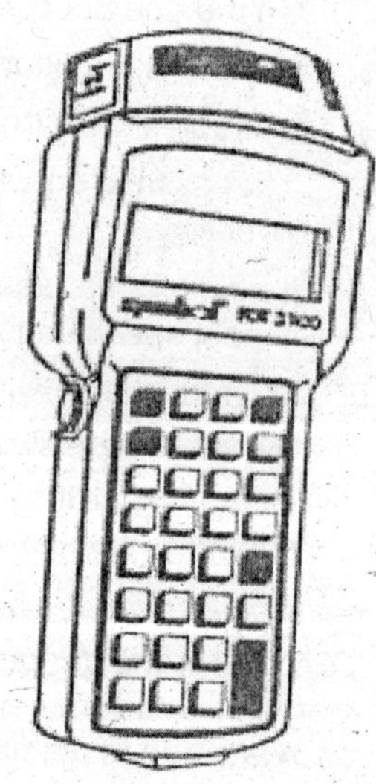

Fig.1.05

mostly used to identify a particular product on which bars or strips are written. They are often seen on books, packages etc. The universal product code consists of a 11 digit computer readable code that is used in labelling retail products. The data is coded in the form of light and dark bars. In retail stores, these bar codes are commonly used to identity a particular product. Usually, the manufacturers print a Universal Product Code (UPC) on most items sold in grocery stores.

When bar coded products are received at the retail store or the super market's check out stand, they are pulled across a fixed scanning window. There is a separate device called an optical character reader which decodes the bars. The patterns are converted into electrical pulses which are transmitted to the recognition logic service. A reader head is moved across the bar lines to read the information contained on the bars.

Electronic Mailing List

Business houses can use computers to their maximum advantage to print names and addresses from the lists of customers, dealers, wholesalers, agents etc. on to the gummed labels. This eases the mailing work of a routine day to day big job. Application of computer in the preparation of a mailing list is a basic application not only in business but also in government departments, hospitals, banks, insurance, universites etc. The process of computerized production of labels or mailing list attracts potential customers, clients etc. The end user can use the personal computer to enter the details like names, addresses, description, area, phone number etc. on a floppy disk. So, the input data of business houses and their mailing lists are contained in a file of dealers, customers, wholesalers, agents, suppliers etc. Each data record consists of a dealer's name, address, city, number, description, etc. in the case of dealer's file. Each data record consists of the agent's name, address, number, area, description etc. in case of the agent's file. So, it is possible to write and store the program to process the labels on the same disk at any given time.

There are available file or database management software packages to create and maintain a file. These packages are easy for users of specific data items, arranging into records and consolidating these records into integrated files. The menu options of the program facilitates to add new records to the stored file, delete existing records from a file which are not required, calling new files to print labels specific to the business concerned.

All these activities of adding, changes, in data and deleting file records is a fundamental data processing task. The process is called file management or file updating. So, it is the file or database management software package which makes this process an easy task.

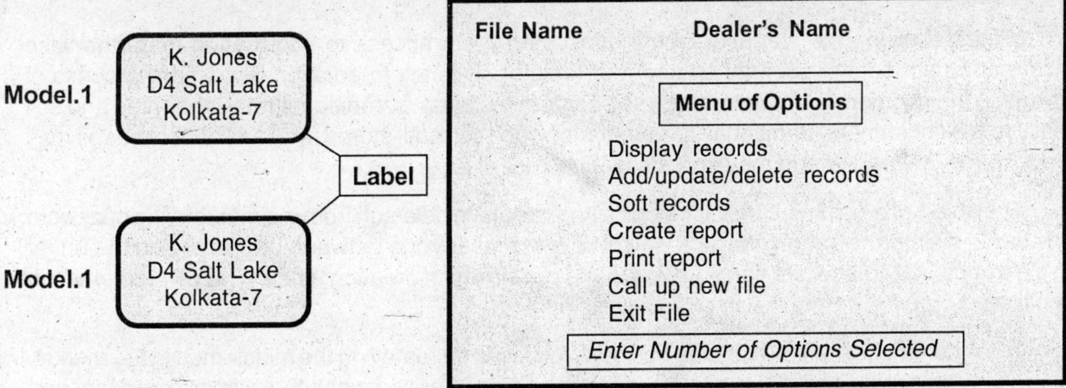

Fig.1.06 Mailing list

Computer application pertaining to the preparation of address list and mailing list is widespread and most popular. Separate software packages are available for this area of office administrating. These two lists are strategically beneficial in an office and are very suitable for packages. The process of this application is simple and self contained. Machine readable mailing lists are very much available. The data handling package is very easy. The task involved is such a package is that it should cover the following :

- Creation of file containing : Name, Occupation, Job description, Regional code, Consumer code.
- Print labels containing names and addresses.
- Print list of names and
- Selection according to job description, consumer code and areawise address.

With personal computers proliferating in various levels in our lives in a major way, most of the organisations operate their mailing list inhouse. But there are still plenty who are outsourced today to do the preparation of the mailing list. The market is flooded with hundreds trained in the field of electronic typing in all major cities in the country. Today, electronic typing particularly word processing is the most earning and competitive preparation of mailing lists and the services are booming. The service of mailing list takes a list of names and performs contact mailing for companies, government agencies and individuals. This service also takes the form of handwritten mailing lists and puts them into the computer system.

It is a process of creation of database for sorting names, address, occupation, cities, states and pincodes. It can generate lists of lables and letters on the magnetic media.

E-commerce and Disintermediation

In any market system in any country, whether developed or developing, the prevalence of middlemen is a common features. Middlemen are traders who pass products or services from producers to the final buyers. They are market intermediaries. Agents, brokers, wholesalers and distributors are the conventional middlemen. In the pre-internet period, the only way consumers, could get goods, was through several tiers of distributors and resellers.

The emergence of the internet has to a great extent resulted in eliminating the role of intermediaries from the market and establishing a direct contact between merchants and consumers. Short circuiting market intermediaries and buyers have direct online business with the merchants. This is called as disintermediation.

It means giving the Net user or the consumer direct access to information that otherwise would require a mediator such as an agent or reseller. This intermediation is the sure process of eliminating the middlemen. When web-based companies bypass traditional retail channels and sell directly to the consumers, traditional intermediaries such as retail stores and mail order houses may have to leave the market and may find themselves out of job.

The object of e-commerce is to strategically eliminate middlemen from the market. The buzzword of the day is disintermediation, that is a way of saying that anyone between the seller and the buyer is in big trouble. Of course, we cannot rule out the possibility of creating a new kind of middlemen in e-commerce.

The e-commerce method of doing business focusses on removing the middlemen in the market. Online commerce avoids products or services falling somewhere between the ultimate producer and the end user. The advancement in sophisticated information technology related innovations made it possible for manufacturers to sell directly to the end users, resulting in the elimination of distributors, resellers and agents etc. The present generation technology appreciates the application of disintermediation because it has created efficient ways to customize products and provide just-in-time inventory. It results in downsizing the cost of transaction and distribution. It reshapes the relationship of customers and companies which would be compatible to both.

Advertising Over the Net

Having and hosting a website whithout an effective plan is like designing a flyer and not mailing it out. The business may have a cheque needed for timely products or services.

Advertising online gives access to a global market and can be more cost effective than advertising in traditional media such as newspapers, radio, yellow pages or the direct mail. An effective solution to e-commerce requires a system to create a customized online campaign which covers strategic analysis and planning banner design and creation, selection and booking. The right venues, assessing traffic results and proactive ways to reach additional audience and draw them back to the site calls for strategic decision making and planning .

Advertising business on the web pertains to build eye-catching banner ads that generate sales. There are many reasons why business needs advertising on various sites — to reach a global audience.

Advertising e-solutions are available and newspapers and other media companies, retail mechants and advertisers can avail of them. They provide the fastest, easiest and most cost effective way for media organisations to protect and expand their advertising base. New online advertising opportunities are available to the marketers. A new marketing venue is available allowing advertisers to market and sell their products nationally, internationally and locally through the increased usage of advertising on newspaper websites.

There are two types fo banner ads on the Internet. They are exposure-based or enabled advertising and transaction-based or enabled banner advertising.

The approach of information technology on internet banner advertising is transaction enabled ads. In this, innovative online marketing schemes are more. Most of the banner ads are consumer brands. Next important is the technology brand. In India, consumer ralated products or services have not taken to internet marketing in a big way. Most of advertisments seen partly related to information technology, financial services and real estates as the internet became more affordable and cheap.

Today, we see on cyber valley the presence of brands like Ariel, Bajaj Auto, ICICI, and Citi Bank which are more popular on the online advertising arena.

Toady, corporate marketing strategies are now talking about transaction enabled advertising, site sponsorship and web ad is more popular on the Net. You might have witnessed clicking on any website and many websites most probably are welcomed with bright and animated banner advertisements.

There are many such advertisements i.e. from call home to click here for all grocery items needed. Browsing the internet offers you a whole lot of enticing and interesting but distraction advertisments for various products.

Global spending on online ads has been increasing and are likely to increase to more than triple and further over the next few years.

In India, considering the online ads, the market is very slow but surely making its presence felt. All related to ads, either individuals or organisations are seriously approaching the Net for ads. For instance, advertising agencies, marketing wizkids and companies are fast realising the potentiality and importance of wide area approach of the internet.

The important factors responsible for this increasing trend are:

- Marked increase in internet connections.
- Increasing awareness.
- Growing number of online dealers and customers.
- Specific information seeking surfers.
- Banner ads are a more popular means of advertising.
- Many business persons are getting more techno-savvy and innovative.
- Wider coverage.
- Online completion of transactions.

Hyper Banner

Hyper banner is the largest global banner exchange on the Web. Hyper banner's international sites use hyper banner's powerful, free tools to advertise, enhance and e-commerce their small and medium business websites. Hyper banner membership is rocketing.

That online banner advertising services will be in the first decade of the 21st century, a revolutionary change is now an accepted truth.

Features of Banner Advertisement

- Different advertisers appreciate banner ads for different puposes on the Internet. Some of them are geared strategically to make banner ads which are seen by the potential net users.
- To make users to actually click on the ads and visit the advertiser's site called 'Click Through'.
- To permit the user for accessing product enquiries and sales.
- Some banners are designed in such a way that they do not require the user to visit the site.
- To permit the users just to fill in some information on a form included in the banner ad and complete the transaction on the advertisement itself.
- Internet ads more interactive.
- It is economically feasible to go for banner ads.
- It is a borderless and worldwide coverage.
- It is an advertising dream with less costs.
- Banner ads are a popular means of advertising.
- Ads can be rotated and customized for maximum viewership and approach the targeted audience.

A full range of advertising and marketing services are available for online commerce. E-commerce advertising solutions consider a company's position in today's cyberspace market and carefully develop strategies to optimize rapid and potential business on the Web. But a web strategy for a particular company should be tailored to fit its needs and budget.

Today, diverse media approaches are available, from conventional basic print campaigns to campaigns carrying the full impact of sound, video, animation as well as interactive shopping with online secure buying and selling.

Ideapro's advertising services incude the following:

- Corporate unique selling proposition or USP development;
- Logos for print, multi-media and web use;
- Copywriting;
- Graphic design and lay-out;
- Corporate identify development and integration into marketing material, web presence,print and electronic advertising campaigns and
- Competitive product positioning and brand mangement services are available to companies planning to invest in electronic advertising campaigns.

Vitalosoft

A service provider can create online marketing goods through compelling and creative advertisements in many online formats including the animated banner ads, HTML banner ads, streaming audio (vide enhanced advertising) and Java banners.

Major companies are availing of opportunities of advertising on the internet. They are being challenged to find more effective and potential ways of conducting business at a faster pace, with lower costs and higher level of quality with fewer people. One area which is the focus of attention is Internet advertising with many companies taking to this kind of advertising as a part of re-engineering efforts to facilitate fast paced and cost effective communication. By taking to advertising over the Net, these companies experience much cost saving.

The Web has grown at an exponential rate over the past few years. Today, the Internet has become not only a vast information resource, but a powerful marketing tool for businesses looking for exposure to a large global audience at an economical cost.

Advantages of Internet Advertising

Companies increasingly prefer and appreciate the Net as an effective marketing tool for advertising. The reasons for the shift to advertise on the internet are that the world wide web offers the following advantages:

1. Simplicity: The important factor for preferring internet advertising is of its simplicity. The shift in opting for new technology as a powerful marketing tool for businesses is that the direction of advertising is easy and simple. Many companies are turning to the Net for advertising on account of this.

2. Less Advertising Cost: The value of advertisements on the internet in an online marketing place is the lower advertising cost. It is not only fast, easy but also convenient. Merchants are driving customers to their banners to avoid overhead expenses and geographical limitations imposed by conventional brick and mortar facilities. It is comparatively less expensive to provide products or services on the worldwide web than to print and distribute and redistribute by mail or broadcasting by radio or television.

3. *Fast and Easy:* Without any question, advertising on the Internet is in tune with new technology. The majority of online advertisers particularly in advanced countries are preferring net advertising as they provide a secure, fast, easy and interesting way of advertising both for merchants and customers. For this reason, preferring the Net for advertising is crucial for success in booming internet commerce market.

4. *Use of Multimedia:* The Net has become a powerful marketing tool for various businesses looking for exposure to a large audience at an economical cost because it lets the advertisers to have multimedia presentation. The cost effective technology permits to incorporate in a web advertising copy a mix of several features like rich text, audio, video, colour graphics, animation etc. all in one place. Consumers who are visiting web pages will be interested and attract them to read about the company, its mission, philosophy, view products, send e-mail, enquiries and place online orders and online payment process. All these can be operated without even having to leave the comforts of their home or office..

5. *Avoids Time Delays:* Many companies opting for internet advertising is in the direction of eliminating time delays. Direct advertising is crucial for success in the booming internet commerce market. The time delays associated with traditional advertising is emerging as deterrant to online marketing. The time it takes to print, reprint, distribute and redistribute etc. adds to the time it takes to deliver products or service information to a customer. It reduces incentive purchase online. Net advertising allows consumers to see advertising of products online and order online with instant payment.

6. *Direct Marketing:* Advertisers increasingly prefer online advertising because the world wide web is a direct potential marketing environment. E-commerce has grown at an exponential rate over the past few years, consumers also increasingly accessing the internet by using search engines to look for companies supplying specific products or services.

7. *Global Exposure:* The World Wide Web (WWW) is a potential marketing tool for businesses looking for exposure to a large audience at an economical cost. The shift in advertising patterns in the online market place is in the direction of global exposure. Banners by major organisations are driving customers to their websites and there are no geographical limitations as imposed by traditional advertising. It is estimated that WWW is accessed by millions of people world wide. To give an idea of who is an internet user today, let us give you some figures. The number of people who have accessed the Net have reached over 75 million users today. Information is available from anywhere to anywhere at any time 24 hours a day, 7 days a week. Thus, the principle of mass market and mass audience coverage is achieved through online advertising. Internet is reaching today a large proportion of PC owned householders, consumers, women and children etc.

8. *Corporate Appearance:* Many corporations are being challenged to find more effective ways of conducting business by appearance. A corporate web on the internet is a corporate headquarter. An attractive and well designed website permits to level the playing field with potential competing companies.

9. *Up-to-date Information:* Up-to-date information is available on the internetit-is not rigid but dynamic and flexible. This permits up-to-date information at any time. A change in price adding a new product of various services withdrawing a new product or running a special programme etc.

can be incorporated in the website in a contemparary fashion. Any new, additional alteration or modification of websites in minutes can be done and can be updated with new information regarding products and services to benefit the Net users.

10. No Running Around: The development of advertising in conventional methods is a long one in the entire process. It maybe in the case of print media i.e. via printing and reprinting, distribution and redistribution etc. In the past, all the functions involved in making an advertisement world wide web had to be done by different people, causing a lot of running around. World wide web advertising consultants and solutions are available who can and will handle all the needs of advertisers from the beginning. They will consult and analyse strategically the company's specific needs and wants, designs for the advertisement and create relevant graphics, animations, multimedia presentations, take any pictures needed for the products being advertised and convert them to the digital format, design and create brochures and work on magazine advertisements. Consultants now provide all services needed for web advertising making the website experience, profitable, enjoyable and free of hassles for the Net users.

E-commerce Education and Training

Commerce education is undergoing a drastic change, with the Internet having established itself and computer education in the country is undergoing a paradigm shift by placing more emphasis on online skills rather than theoretical knowledge. E-commerce related knowledge is ranked as one of the most wanted and appreciated internet skills. Teleshopping, e-commerce and web-based activities are demanding new skills. The e-era is changing various dimensions of our life. It is also revolutionising the way businesses are managed. Today, strategies have global associates, suppliers, financiers, regulators, employees, investors, competitors and customers from any corner of the world.

Today, we see radical change in the way businesses function for survival in the market, manage finance purchase, budget and managing logistics etc.

The courses on e-commerce can be introduced in which issues like electronic data interchange and networking can be included. This will give an opportunity and exposure to such aspects which enable the commerce student to expand their horizon by becoming successful IT professionals.

Thus, educational universities, college and other educational institutions are gearing themselves to invest their resources in terms of time, manpower and money to mould themselves to groom these students and those eager to join the bandwagon to survive in the potential e-commerce era.

In the e-business millennium, each new information technology is an e-business technology. The success of transformation depends on how well the personnel understand and implement e-commerce. Training students in the e-business concept and skills is thus critical to make a smooth transition to e-business. The post industrial societies are called information/knowledge societies and these are characterized chiefly by the denaturalization of information that is voice, text and images. They are geared to service in the competitive business environment.

Some studies have shown that developed countries are unable to produce more professionals nor are enough young people coming forward to take up this new profession. This area has reached a stagnant point, especially abroad. The world wide demand for computer professionals is increasing.

The topic of education and training on e-commerce is a very important dimension of commerce education.

E-commerce has changed the conventional business transaction in an ever increasing internet world, having given rise to new technologies and a new species of professionals namely web technologists. This profession requires training and education in the e-commerce industry. The demand for trained and skilled web technologies is already on the increase. To meet this demand, e-commerce courses have been necessitated. There are potential placement prospects in the field on both national and intermission levels.

The solution to each and every problem in the internet industry is education. It is sufficiently apt to have that e-commerce education is potential investment in terms of growth prospects for the emerging professionals in the field of e-commerce.

Running training programs for skill development in e-commerce would also be useful in promoting its widespread adoption. Even something as simple as creating a website is a step in the right direction, followed by the ability to respond to customer queries and take orders. They are the potential steps towards development and growth in the area of information technology.

Success in e-commerce venture depends on skills and knowledge. To develop potential business successfully in the competitive world of global e-commerce, the user needs education, knowledge of e-commerce processing, solutions, software, technology, website developing, merchant account, payment technology, credit card processing, smart card, application and usage.

One should have the benefit of diverse fields of experience required for e-commerce. There are a number of e-commerce training providers which train and impart knowledge on various disciplines relating to e-commerce. The courses educate potentially up coming net users and generate successful trade online, which are essential for the success of e-commerce.

IT education in relation to e-commerce has become a big business now and major players are competing on national and international levels in devicing courses, setting up more centres, slicing the course fee and affecting many people to become experts in this field. Even as specialised institutions have come up exclusively for training in e-commerce the need for hi-tech training institutes with the state of the art facility is important. There is a need for such institutes to gear up and know the latest technology relating to e-commerce and the information technology at large. If not, they will end up teaching something which would be not suitable with the present business requirements.

These institutes have already trained a large chunk of the population across the country in this field, specially in urban areas. The rural areas need to be targeted in this regard which will be possible by government information. They cover the basics of e-commerce, process technologies, websites, security aspects, payment solutions, HTML, programming languages etc. The e-commerce course is not just the usual basics of computing that are being taught.

On the official front, most of the state governments and specialised institutes are seriously considering to take infotech to commercial applications. They have formed task forces and committees to suggest courses for effectively implementing IT related e-commerce education.

Further, training institutes are mushrooming all across the country with the aim to impart education in the field of information technology and help the aspirants who want join the bandwagon of IT professionals. Their special courses are full of technical and operational knowledge, helping these aspirants to become familiar with the latest technology and its application.

The most important tool adopted for imparting computer-based e-commerce education is language, programming, scriptwriting, HTML, networking, transactions, payments etc. Technology and the various dimensions of e-commerce as of now, are basically being imported from abroad. Little efforts have been made to develop indigenous packages, technologies etc. at the national level. But the trends are changing. The general problem about imparting imported knowledge is that they often have characters that are out of context in India. Indian e-commerce education requires a great deal of customization.

The E-revolution has changed the way in which the IT industry is hunting for software professionals. It is looking out for horizontally specialized software professionals rather than the vertically specialized. There are several diverse specialized areas of e-commerce, calling for trained personnel in this area, unfortunately there is acute shortage of trained people in this area. The shortage is felt particularly in recent years on account of the sudden emergence of e-commerce use of Internet. It is not possible to appoint the persons to man various areas of internet related business jobs from the labour markets. Either the organisation has to develop and utilise the talented employees in such a way suitable to manage several technical, legal, artistic and administrative wings relating to e-commerce activities or to recruit such personal from outside.

Unsuitability and obsolescence of skills of personnel in the context of this new media of business is another factor which calls for continuous updating and development of human resources. E-commerce training and education is not a one shot affair, it must continue throughout the career graph of the trained personnel by regularly updating changes, developments, improvements and subsequent technological advancements. Otherwise, the business personnel of yesterday will not be suitable or will not be good enough for the future. Therefore, in order to be dynamic and to change according to the changes in business technology and emerging market demands, the people must continuously update themselves to successfully meet new challenges as they occur.

National Institute for e-commerce in association with the Institute of Business Management and Technology, Bangalore, has been imparting e-commerce education. The Manipal Centre for Information Science (MCIS) in collaboration with IBM has been offering e-business solutions training. IBM is an authorized training expert in e-commerce. It is the first IT global company to bring a comprehensive e-commerce training and education programme. The IBM training program is gaining significant relevance in this context. In India, IBM learning services are addressing individual training schedules as well as in the corporate sector.

A number of universities in the country have started post graduate course in commerce, both in formal and distance education stream. Besides, a number of private training institutes have been imparting e-commerce education and training people more than the Government because they are faster to introduce courses on new commercial technologies. On the other hand, they are quick to identify new emerging user segments like home users and they take advantage of the first birds to reap the benefits.

With the worldwide shortage of trained IT professionals with particular reference to e-commerce, the street corner institutes have sprung up all over the country. Some institutes are even promising to make their training into e-commerce professions over a short period and even giving guarantee for well established placements outside.

A number of IT training institutes have designed software and programming training to provide with the cutting edge in the field of e-commerce. There are specially designed modules for employing these trained personnel and executives in e-commerce.

The Government needs to drive the growth of e-commerce skills in the country following awareness of the several factors influencing the adoption and wide use of e-commerce. Fiscal encouragement, incentives and recognition are the most frequently discussed forms of the role of the Government towards e-commerce. However, the government can make several other significant contributions towards promoting e-commerce education and imparting skills among the potential young professionals. E-market place is the shopping mall of the 21 st century.

Any student seeking a career in e-commerce would go to any length to learn these technologies. The curriculum has been designed exhaustively taking into account the existing trends or complexion of the IT industry. It necessitates professionals to develop the skills of self learning and update themselves with all emerging technology.

Certificate professionals in e-commerce are given priority in the multinational corporations and major national companies. There is a vast scope for consultancy and contracting. The overall demand in other countries for e-commerce trained web internet professionals is very high. The demand in India too is picking up and the demand would exceed the supply and demand of these professionals in the years to come.

A Sea of Opportunities in Leading Edge

E-business consulting all over the world is being invested in by major corporations and individuals. In the Internet-based business, you are valued for your imagination, intelligence, positive attitudes and ability to think and function on a wide canvas. It is no coincidence that today's world of e-business needs the same qualities in the people driving it. Joining the net-based business will help to discover exciting and rewarding opportunities for hi-tech. professionals who are serious about developing innovative e-business solutions, integrating best of the breed software applications and shaping the evolution of business on the Internet. This field is an emerging exceptional opportunity for the new generation of IT professionals to develop their career in e-business.

Fields of Study

The fields of study pertaining to the Internet and computer applications include the following:

↳ Unix	↳ Web sever	↳ APS site server
↳ Linux	↳ Ariba	↳ Java servelets-
↳ Microsoft Internet Explorer	↳ Clarus	↳ SSL
↳ Net ascape communicator	↳ Sibel	↳ Unixplatforms
↳ Internet applications and operations	↳ Microstrategy	↳ Web logic tool
↳ HTML	↳ ERP	↳ CGI
↳ Front page 98	↳ Business objects	↳ Perl
↳ Java script	↳ Informations	↳ RMI
↳ Paint shop 5.0	↳ RDBMS	↳ Web server
↳ Java	↳ ASP	↳ VC++
↳ Javabeans	↳ Cold fusion	↳ C++
↳ Servelets	↳ VB	↳ SQL server
↳ Distributed computing	↳ Commerce one	↳ Data warehouse
↳ RMI	↳ EJB, DCOM	↳ Data Mining
↳ CORBA	↳ COM+	↳ Sybase
↳ Windows NT server	↳ Broad vision	↳ DB2
↳ NT enterprise server	↳ Interworld	↳ XML
↳ TCP/IP	↳ DHTML	↳ Crystal

Career Opportunities

They include the following:

Inside sales	Enterprise Messaging
Software development	Systems integration
Encryption techniques	Network infrastructure
Channel partnership account manager	Program management
Executive assistant	System Analyst
Office manager	Web Design
Sales professionals	Systems architecture
Sales support representative	Java web application development
Security software developers	Database administration
Technical support technicians	Systems administration
Sales employees	Java server application development
Telesales	Software engineering and methodologies
Marketing internship	Networking and communication
Credit cards management	Computer graphics
Merchant accounts	Image processing
Digital signature field	Database technologies
Awareness	Distrabuted networking
Counselling	Web technologies
Business reprocessing engineering	Office automation
Electronic interchange	Multimedia technologies
	PKI.

Potential E-commerce Companies

The following are the companies involved in e-commerce:

Amazon.com : It is the world's largest online book store. It is the cyber book shop which has also set up a physical book store to back up its legendary online ordering, a model success along other cyber book sellers.

CDNOW: It is the number one online music store.

It Bean: It is popular for sporting, sports gear and apparel stores.

General Electric: It is the world's company which has been processing the needs of customers with strong emphasis on e-commerce.

Wat-Mart: It is a retail leader gearing up the web net to enable customers to adjust to the showrooms without inventories as the store front to attract purchasers.

E-commerce — A Science and A art

As a Science: Science may be defined as an organised and systematized body of knowledge based on proper findings and exact principles, pertaining to a specific study and contain some general truths explaining past events and phenomenon. The body of knowledge has been systematized through the application of scientific methods. Thus, we may speak of the science of Astronomy, Physical Science, Biological Science, Chemistry and Social Sciences like sociology, political science, economics etc.

Therefore, it cannot be denied that e-commerce is a systematized body of knowledge. However, e-commerce management is not an exact science as other physical sciences like physics and chemistry.

As an Art: Art is the ability or skill which is more due to practice than learning. It is the bringing about of a desired result through the application of skills and knowledge. A science is learned, to seek knowledge and art is practised. In other words, science is concerned with the application or utilisation of knowledge. The characteristic features of an art related to personal skills and practical knowledge applied to achieve desired results and it is highly in nature.

An e-commerce professional is an artist because he strategically applies the acquired knowledge and skills obtained from the study of the subject to generate good financial results.

Both Science and an Art: It is clear from the above discussion that e-commerce contains both the elements of science and an art. So, e-commerce is both a science an an art. As a science, it provides principles because the subject is an organised and systematised body of knowledge. Like any art, it is also creative. It is applied to each time, to each situation and new situations which demand new principles, new technology, new designs and computer programs needed for changing circumstances. One has to acquire certain electronic, software and mechanical skills which are personal, efforts and remain with the individual, using computers on an individual approach. Every user, programmer, software developer, approach script writers and persons involved in website design, hosting, promotion, site selections by using skills art, imagination, innovations and techniques in dealing with different commercial transactions is appreciated by those IT companies where they are working. So, e-commerce as a science gives a systematized body of knowledge and an art applies both knowledge and skills.

The knowledge of e-commerce can be important to learners and newcomers also through formal training and education. It is not an inborn quality and the skills but acquired in a formal way. One has to learn and acquire the knowledge before applying for specific e-commerce . E-commerce cannot be effective without acquiring this science and applying it as an art. So, e-commerce is both a science and an art.

To illustrate, a doctor possesses the knowledge of the science of anatomy, acquires the knowledge in chemistry, biology etc. Just acquiring knowledge does not makes him a good physician. For this, he also practices by applying the principles of science. He has to apply his knowledge skilfully, diligently and intelligently. How and when to use his knowledge to situations makes him a good physician. Similarly, the skills of e-commerce operations should theoretically be acquired and practised as an art. So a person applying the technicalities and principles is considered as an applied scientist. The art deals with the application of skills acquired and efforts for producing desirable results. So, one should possess specialised knowledge one e-commece and the skills to put his knowledge into practice like the doctor getting trained to cure patients. So, as a conclusion, we can say that e-commerce is a science as well as an art.

E-commerce — A Profession: A profession is an occupation or job that needs special knowledge like medical engineering, law etc. Accordingly, e-commerce as a profession requires special body of knowlege on the subject. Profession of any discipline may require such activities for earning liveliood which required strategic knowlege application and intellectual skills to survive in the potential market today.

Features of a Profession: They read as follows :

- It requires advanced specialised application, formal education and training
- It demands the consistent exercise of discretion and independent judgement
- It has a sense of ethics and public responsibility.

Further, a profession should satisfy the following conditions:

- A systematic body of knowledge
- Code of ethics
- Responsibility of the society and
- Suitable remuneration
- These conditions are briefly dealt below.

A Systematic Body of Knowledge: Since 1997, there has been a rapid and constant growth of e-commerce techniques, principles and applications, making available specific literature about the theory programmes, technologies and practice of e-commerce. It satisfied the basics of a systematic body of knowledge to call it as a *profession*.

Code of Ethics: The profession has to follow certain standards and code of conduct and any violation of professional ethics will make organisations/individuals liable to punishment following crimes like cyber crimes, breaking, interceptions, hacking etc.

Social Responsibility: A revolution has been taking place to a large extent in the practice of business and social responsibility is being emphasized everywhere.

Suitable Remuneration: There is provision for payment of suitable fee for rendering their services which are attractive particularly in other countries.

Advantages/Benefits of E-commerce

1. Increases Sales: Secure real time processing increases sales on the website by providing a means for immediate payment that provides closure for sale. E-commerce solutions have been delivering down to earth selling strategies to enterprises who wish to profit from this emerging explosive new technology.

E-commerce increases sales by making it easy for customers to do comparison shopping based on their specific situations and to choose an insurance carrier. Sales are enhanced by making it much faster and simpler for customers to evaluate their levels of need.

2. Impulse Buying: Another reason you need to go for internet business is that it has potential for impulse buying, thereby making it easy for customers to buy from merchants online when impulse strikes.

3. Round the Clock Business: Internet commerce is made easy because you can money conveniently. With his distinct mechanism of commerce enabled website, the merchant can sell round the clock, everyday of the week, 24 hours a day and 365 days a year. There is no need to hire a clerk to run the store. This makes potential business for the merchants and organisations.

4. Level Playing Field: Can a business of small size get on to the Internet? It is a frequently asked question. Yes. Well, that is the best part of doing online business. It does not matter whether yours is a small, medium or large business. E-commerce is open to one and all regardless of size potential and shape. On the internet, no one knows you are a small business. As long as you have a product to sell or buy, you are on the Net. You will be online. All you need is an e-mail identity where millions of those potential buyers and suppliers can reach and be ready to do business with you. You can compete with the big guys in business.

5. Improves Networth: Putting business on the internet can improve its networth. It is evidenced as a phenomenal savings to gain and the equally phenomenal profits the company stands to make because of complete lack of physical barriers and collapsing of time frames. It permits to make tons and tons of profit

6. New Way of Business: Everything is online over the Net in today's competitive business market. Businesses do away with selling products and buying supplies in a traditional way. The new method of doing business does away with tenders, does away with middlemen and with the conventional media of communication. For that matter, there is no need to spend money on postage and on phone calls, faxes, etc.

There is no question of losing precious time waiting for buyers to contact. Instead, all that is necessary to do is to host a website and online store. Thousands of interested buyers or suppliers will contact you via e-mail or put on website terms and conditions, the manner of payment, reseller program etc. and virtually shake hands on the deal. This calls for long term business plans for the organisation.

7. Customer Convenience: Economy and convenience are the important reasons for investing and going on net transactions. Trading online makes it easy for people to buy from merchants online. The convenience of shopping from anywhere and at any time, from home or office is the major reason for consumers to buy online. Internet processing, credit card processing software, point of sales, terminal equipment etc. made it more convenient for the consumer to buy online. From the customer's point of view, online business means greater convenience and better fund management.

8. Increase Market Size: Look around you. The internet is everywhere. It is changing the business environment in a great way. Small businesses are using it to reach wider sections of consumers. Retailers on the internet are doing potential businesses on groceries, books, toys, music, electronic goods and sending e-greetings to the customers. Customers are accessing websites over the world, all at the click of a button. So, the Net is also changing and widering the way globally. Business people do business. It increases market size and has become electronically enabled. The commerce enabled website gives access to credit card users across the country and around the world. Business people are taking advantage of selling, buying and paying on the world wide web. The physical market place has become a virtual market place. Today, with the click of a button, one can find buyers and suppliers all across the world. One can also sell products or services online globally, buy online at a better rate across global shop sites.

9. *Instant Payment:* In recent years, markets do not like to accept cash or cheques. The problem with a cheque is that it is sometimes bounced. The merchants have to wait before goods are shipping in case cheques are used. In a credit card (smart card) and Automatic Teller Machine (ATM) the merchants can get nearly instant approval and goods can be sent out immediately. In the instant payment technology in this new media of business, both the merchant and the customers are benefited. Today, credit cards are commerce currency and help to do business over the Internet.

10. *Reaching New Customers:* Online stores offer capability to reacher wider sections of customers by offering a product or service worldwide. When a shop is opened online, the store is opened 24 hours a day, 7 days a week, and 365 days in a year, permitting to do business from anywhere to anywhere and at anytime. The website hosted will be visited by several people, and a presence on the web promotes a company's image and product, improves customer service, encourages new customers, service, acquisition and provides a new vehicle for sales and information. Business people are more concerned about e-commerce with accessing new markets particularly international markets. It is closely associated with the web business environment and new methods to acquire customers.

Online stores expand markets outside the local geographical area and lengthens seasons. An e-commerce merchant deals with people on a global canvas, most of whom he does not know. It is quite opposite to a local businessman who may satisfy himself with customers in his immediate surroundings. Thus, e-commerce caters to a much wider global audience than the neighbourhood.

11. *Small Business Too:* Small businesses may not have to look beyond their local Internet Service Providers. (ISPs). However, most e-commerce development tools targeted at small and medium sized businesses. The individual strength solutions are available for big concerns which cost a lot and are costing low for small and medium sized concerns. A smaller company will better its products and customer services can use virtual communities to challenge larger competitors.

Virtual communities erode existing marketing trends. Small businesses are already successful and are eroding territories. Internet commerce is not meant only for larger organisations, even small businesses can become potential players in online businesses. From cheap, simple to expensive, services, there is a wide range of products.

E-commerce enables businesses to compete with big guns in online business. It is only gearing into action which is delayed. It is possible to get one's own life time e-commerce internet, server and generate internet profit.

Another great commercial advantage of electronic commerce is that it often eliminates the need for intermediating institutions. It is a direct link with the Net users.

12. *Easy to Use:* For the Internet business, the ease of use means more than simplicity. The internet payment services including security features make the management of e-business easier. By using the services of website providers, one can set up in little as 15 to 20 minutes nearly and transact thousands of online business throughout the world. It drastically reduces time-taking decisions, lenghy procedures, thus streamlining the order process entirely.

This service is easy to use and operate. The things are made as easy and simple as possible through web interface.

13. *A Promising New Medium:* Merchants, customers, service providers, certification authorities and banks etc. practically consider this new medium as a promising one. The IT industry is optimistic about fast emerging e-commerce and seeks potential in the years to come. Things are changing fast and becoming dynamic for the better. Sales, marketing, advertising, retail operations, finance, computers, manufacturing, consumer products, media, IT etc. are the focus of e-business areas and private organisations are good and excellent users. In addition, services and distributions, HRD administration, Research & Development and production are among the other uses. Travel, transport, music, education, entertainment and other areas used for communication purposes is great besides facilites liks e-mail, FTP and website monitoring.

14. Cost Effective: As a new medium of business, the Net affords the lowest transaction costs among all other methods of doing, The world wide web (WWW) helps to promote services and ideas for a fraction of the cost of traditional advertising and marketing. There is no printing cost and no postage cost. It is cost effective because there is no maintenance cost, stationery cost and other costs.

The advantage of lower costs of building brands and the cost of acquiring customers is low.

15. Simplicity: The advancement in sophisticated communication technology has revolutionized the designing of internet technology. It is easy to use and the credit order can be processed on the spot. It is easy for customers to buy and sell products online with fast applications. Web pages can easily be updated. The process of e-commerce is simplified by adding products or services, product information, viewing orders, downloading orders and other administrative tasks are made easy.

16. Improved Customer Service: With the emergence of electronic commerce, the supply chain is shortened. It improves services given to customers, increases productivity, efficiency, access to international markets and cost reduction. Doing commerce over the Internet also helps companies to render improved services to their customers.

17. Direct Contact: It establishes business to customer (b2c) contact, but not business to business (b2b). This eliminates the intermediaries between various businesses and customers. The competitive advantage of e-commerce from this point of view is significant. Online business through the internet puts business in direct contact with a multitude of competitive suppliers and services and millions of customers. The survival of business will depend on how to set up shop along the information superhigways. i.e. the internet.

18. Saving Money: The entire process of e-commerce routine saves a lot of money. The average cost for a mail order phone call is higher. The cost of setting up of shop online compared to the cost of setting up of shop on land is cheaper. The land store is higher several times than online. As such, online stores can be set up or just a few thousands and hosted for the financial security of Net users.

19. Competitive Weapon: The experience of e-commerce since 1997 indicates that online consumers appreciate choosing the internet merchant who accepts secure payments compared to the one who does not.

20. Security and Privacy: Today, secure encryption technology is availbale following episodes of cyber crime. For instance, the secure socket layer (SSL) and secure electronic transactions offer security. The public key and private key mechanisms protect sensitive payment information. Protocol securities are now available that customers are assured that their personal sensitive financial data is protected by most sophisticated systems.

21. Serving Customers Better: Another reason why enterprises are moving towards e-commerce is to offer better service levels to their customers. E-commerce can support this business need through different ways. Starting with an online catalogue for ordering goods or a simple ordering system that allows the customer to fill in an online order form for services, businesses can bring in more reliability in their operations, since errors can be weeded out at the point of data captured itself. After an error free order has been logged and is in the process of being executed the customer might want to constantly be aware of the status of the order.*

22. Advertising: Yet another reason why it would be of essence to go for internet trading is that it enhances advertising . Accepting credit cards online increases the credibility of the business.

23. Lower Transaction Cost: If an e-commerce site is developed well, the web can significantly lower, both order-taking costs upfront and customer service costs after the sale by the automating processes.

24. Larger Purchases per Transaction: For instance, Amazon.com offers a feature that no other book store does. When you read the description of the book on the site, you can see what other books on related subjects, have other people who ordered this book also purchased the book. Because of features like this, people ended up buying more books.

25. Intergration into Business Cycle: A website that is well integrated into the business cycle can offer customers more informatin than was previously available. For example, if Dell tracks each computer through the manufacturing and shipping processes, customers can see exactly where their order is at any time. E-commerce offers the same luxury as traditional mail order companies, who introducted the concept of multiple vendors easily, and search large catalogues of various business.

26. Larger Catalogues: A company can build a catalogue on the web that could never fit in an ordinary mail box.

27. Improved Customer Interactions: With automated tools, it is possible to interact with a customer in many ways, at virtually no cost. And once you invest in and make personal connection, a happy customer is more likely to purchase something, again from the company.

28. Creating New Business Models: With e-commerce, you can create completely new business models. In mail order companies, there is a high cost of printing and mailing catalogues that often end up in the trash. There is also a high cost of staffing including the order taking department that answers the phone. In e-commerce, both the catalogue cost and office costs are nil. That means that it be possible to offer products at a lower price or products that could not be offered before the change in cost dynamics.* This calls for making products available or at lower costs and this is done by investing in the IT industry.

29. Online Purchasing: By organising their products or services offering into the interactive catalogue, e-stores allow customers to shop at a time *i.e.* convenient for them, they compare different brands and pricing outside the high pressure sales environment and by direct dealing from the home or office.

---

* *Gaurav Patra and Pankaj Mulick, Information Systems, Computer World, July 16-31, 1999.*

** *Tippoo, Advertisers Announcement, March 8, 2000.*

In all forms of direct marketing, success is geared to ensure effective collection and manipulation of customer information. E-commerce extends these capabalities allowing electronic merchants to create a genuine, one to one relationship with every customer, thus encouraging them to return to the existing e-commerce sites.

30. Customer Loyalty: Trading on the internet with security promotes customer loyalty. Online buyers tend to return to sites once they have visited before. Sales are increasing on websites which have been increasing sevral times during the last three years. This has been a result of extending security to the customers in relation to information given by them to the website developers.

31. Future: There is a potentially secure future for e-commerce. The entire business world is getting reshaped and re-engineered. The major growth of Information technology, quickly getting together and the emergence of ad hoc interest groups online promises to shift the balance of economic power to business to business, business to consumers and consumers to consumers. Virtual communities are already making their presence felt as they to a large extent erode the marketing and sales advantages of large companies.

32. Others: It is possible to make changes to virtual stores like items, prices and promotions etc. directly from two points of communication on the global business canvas.

Orders are fulfilled automatically. It is possible to obtain transactional reports daily, weekly monthly or however as frequently desired. It is possible to enhance the existing website by adding the capability of gathering information about prospective customers by ensuring them of online security.

Drawbacks/Disadvantages of E-commerce

1. Lack of Awareness: The biggest challenge before successful e-commerce over the Net is that of changing the minds and attitudes of the merchants in tune with the emerging information technology. Further, optimism and strategic business projections are required. If e-commerce has to be an alternate means of doing business in India, a new awareness is needed, something that would cut through the hype and u.s. look alikes.

Most of the business people do not understand the significance and implications of the electronic business medium or are unsure of the quallity and delivery schedule, physical delivery of goods and mode of payment. Lack of awareness of the technology and its potential benefits are also equally responsible for the poor growth of e-commerce. Lack of interest and willingness to make a paradigm shift has become a crucial issue. Many companies are not willing to accept that their businesses need a revolutionary change to subsist in the potentially digital world. In short, information technology should not be looked upon as an end but as a means to achieve overall development. The IT sector is people intensive, ensuring vast employment opportunities.

The single most important challenge today pertains to increasing awareness of the benefits of e-commerce to potential customers, educate the market and the customers will themselves opt for these services. So, the e-commerce fraternity should accept the fact that the customers are extremely demanding and that they should be geared up towards this end and surpass the expectations of customers.

2. *Lack of Infrastructure:* E-commerce infrastructure development is at its infancy stage in India. This unsatisfactory development is yet another major bottleneck for successful net business in India. The lack of infrastructure, if made available as required, will ensure that the investment in e-commerce starts flowing in because the business is happening and infrastructure will grow. To improve the country's wide infrastructure, major players must come forward to contribute their pie of technology. All the infrastructure framework needed for virtual e-commerce has not been there from the very beginning when it was started, there was a cry for the real shape of the virtual infrastructure for initiating successful e-commerce. This high cost of infrastructure development for e-business is also including the cost of leased lines.

3. *Lack of Confidence:* The people in India still show hesitancy in buying through the Net. Lack of quality products, timely delivery of products as some of them tend to go out of stock, lack of solutions security are the potential reasons for not developing e-commerce. People do not understand this new way of buying and selling products, i.e. the services in a digital environment which are available online.

4. *Skeptic Attitude:* Though the Internet is continuing to grow at a rapid rate, along with e-commerce transactions, the shoppers are still skeptical about safety and have not been quick to trust sending personal infomation such as credit card numbers or address over the Net. Lack of adequate imagination and understanding of what web-based technologies can do to markets and competition only adds to the delay in economic development. The old business habits are demanding and controlling the business. The risk averse attitude of the people is conspicuous and waiting for others to lead is also another attitude.

5. *Credit Cards Frauds:* In India, distribution channels are just one part of the problem related to e-payments. The bigger problem is that of security. All credit card related transactions are approved offline and given the high incidence of frauds, the banks are extremely wary of approving them. Infact, there are some unconfirmed reports of a multi-national bank refusing to approve credit card transactions carried out by a large Indian portal.

Other drawbacks may include that the buyers are quite prepared to boot the real mail for e-mail. The e-tailers themselves are not yet ready to keep pace with the potential e-commerce and this brings us to another point. Although e-commerce has the ingredients of being successful, it may have come slightly ahead of its time. The e-commerce mechanism eliminates the need for intermediaries. Unfortunately, this also has negative effects. So, security needs to be extended to customers to gain their loyalty including substantial business.

6. *Absence of Tax Laws:* E-commerce over the Net has effectively eliminated national borders. This has posed an important question as to tax on the transactions over the internet. Net business posed many peculiar technological and legal problems making it difficult to impose tax and formulate a sound taxation policy. The following are the various tax implications of e-commerce:

- There is no fixed physical location for the internet.
- It is difficult to monitor or prevent transmissions of information or electronic cash across the Net.
- Neither the users, adminstrators nor intermediaries have any control on the type of information, either transactions or cybercash and travelling through their networks.
- There is no emphasis on national boundaries, and messages travel across the boundaries of several countries globally. So, it means no difference, whether the information or electronic money sought to be transmitted are within one jurisdiction or between several.

- A person's location and identity is necessary for tax purposes. Since these two are difficult, the anonymity on the Net would pose a big problem for taxations.
- Electronic commerce eliminates intermediaries or middlemen. Though it is an advantageous feature, it also has negative effects because they could have served as leverage points for collection of tax also as information sources for transactions entered by the customers.
- In addition to technology problems, certain legal hurdles may also be encountered with reference to international taxation laws.
- The difficulties in defining service incomes as distinguished from sale of products, income or royalties cannot be ignored.

So, it is desirable that the Net be turned as a potential free trade zone.

7. Cyber Laws: Another important problem is lack of comprehensive cyber laws so as to ensure safety and protection. There should not be any legal regulations,or barriers to faster and increased development of e-commerce. The crying need of the hour is urgent action to be taken by the Government to enact cyber laws including electronic fund transfer, and amendments of Offical Secrets Act.

Cyber laws are not in place. In other countries, the business community is moving fast ahead, and stringent government regulations are there. The technology is changing the business paradigm so fast, govenment's ability to proactively change the law is a very diffficult task in India.

In addition to them, the fear regarding the security aspects of online transactions without proper government directives and the existing policy machinery contribute to cyber criminality. Adding to them, separate cyber laws and amendments are also required to many existing laws like Companies Act, Evidence Act, Copyright Act, Bankers Book Evidence Act, Indian Penal Code, Contract Act etc. The country entered into a cyber space and documents through the computers should be made acceptable in a court of law. This is actually a big hurdle on the way which would solve one big hurdle for the business-to-business and business- to-customers e-commerce segment.

8. Stock Dilemma: Many people are not too happy with e-commerce trends. Though online shopping may be growing but so is frustration with it. A key source of dissatisfaction is the out of stock dilemma. In most cases, advertised products or services are not available. The options of feedback and not receiving suggestions are also reasons for annoyance. Many online consumers want more detailed information on their purchases but are not available. The Net is becoming more mainstream and the expectations are also becoming more mainstream.

9. Lack of True Strength: The presence on the web alone will not always ensure successful e-commerce. Having a website or dot com is no longer a novelty and merely setting up a website will not help companies in increasing the volume of business. They must accept the true strength of this new electronic medium of business and its potential for improving efficiency in extending services to the consumers.

There are many people who are connected to the internet but cannot browse the web and they are only availing the e-mail facility for communication.

10. Lack of Skills and Expertise: Lack of skilled and trained personnel impedes the growth of implementation of IT related e-commerce. The use of the Net for trade requires a complex introduction of servers, browser software and knowledge of web design, hosting, promotion and many more skills. It requires understanding many new things. Many Indian businesses are not prepared to approach electronic commerce. For many business houses for which commerce over internet may not work, would take a lot of efforts for every little return.

11. Internet Outrage: Failures in networks and the Net itself can play havoc. We read of frequent press reports of internet outrages. The IT industry is not yet attempting to improve network reliability to prevent these outrages. Reliability is a major issue in net business that needs to be attended.

Though worldwide, many business people looking at e-commerce as a blessing, many people also perceived the cyber space as a threat. There are also reported evidences of enforcing new censorship regimes to prevent cyber crimes.

12. Absence of Cyber Brand Image: Another problem is that advertising on the Net tends to focus on e-commerce rather than on brands found in the real world. This would prove to be a deterrent in ensuring consumer loyalty.

The biggest thing going for it is a brand image and power. Though the already existing name is known and trusted, the issue is how to extend it into the new cyber reality. A concern should be to preserve the old values of trust and dependability of the brand, and at the same time, keep it upon on the Net. At the same time, the whole business structure will have to undergo a change re-engineered.

13. Inadequate Government Role: The government is not taking a serious view of e-commerce related information technology in terms of its promotion. Spreading awareness, imparting education, of the benefits of e-commerce, enacting new cyber laws, amendments to existing commercial laws, developing strong, communication infrastructure are the key domestic roles for the government to play. A very small portion of PC owners, non-owners who are aware of e-commerce perception and about the Internet is there which is being identified as the source of information, communication, learning and entertainment, but relatively few amongst them feel that it is a source of purchasing products or services. Government is not playing an active role by enacting different comprehensive cyber laws, bringing amendments to the existing business laws, not formulating a favourable IT policy and not making positive intervention when needed and ensuring adequate infrastructure.

The existing negative business environment for development of new IT and telecom technologies cannot be ignored. Technology/solutions providers, special bodies and organisations are not taking suitable steps to educate Indian traditional business persons and customers in the area of e-commerce.

14. No Emphasis on Commercial Exploration: E-commerce is not so popular and widespread in India rapidly because of several bottlenecks like content migration. Most of the PC users surf the Net for information rather than potential commercial transactions. This means that the market for this migrated content is very large. Many owners use the Net for learning, education, games and entertainment. To convince e-consumers, e-merchants will have to do a lot of education. Many business houses evidently do not come forward to leverage on some projects in the electronic commerce spectrum as it has already done at high speed overseas.

15. No Encouragement from Business Community: The business community is extremely an important sector to be targeted for the introduction of any technological innovations in business.

It means it is the business community that sustains e-commerce and greatly influences the thinking and adoption process of various segments of the society to move forward in the field of information technology. It motivates the people who share the courage and conviction to move the new business paradigm.

16. Preferring Foreign Sites: Online shoppers in India are not preferring Indian websites to a large extent and prefer US and other foreign websites. There are many reasons for this as they provide better selection, prices, stock, quality products, shipping, payment process security, customer service and wide variety of sites among other things.

17. Inactive Indian Software Houses: Software houses particularly in India are not devoted to ensuring strong expertise in the supply chain and distribution management solutions. Efforts are lacking to ensure strategic working on development of systems which will provide a comprehensive open-e-business solutions environment, comprising of enterprise applications, internet applications and service and a special technology to enable companies to participate in the emerging online economy.

Technology is in abundance. The hardware and software makers are yet to work out strategies to ensure e-business privacy and security solutions to Net users in India. The technologists who are out of touch with the market, customers and competition need to work out options and set business strategies.

18. Cyber Competition: It is becoming clearer that cyber structure is not enough to support cyber growth. Such a growth rate needs proper planning and world class global supply chain parameters. The profit strapped, not-struck cyber entrepreneurs have no vision and invest money on this. One should not forget about low entry barriers, and as a result, cyber competition is perhaps more fierce. Cyber competition needs improvement in better contents, faster delivery of services and online support. It is a great task to pacifying angry live customers and then think how difficult it is to e-reassure a lost one. This means again more investment and more capitalization which is further from break-even.

19. Difficulty of Reengineering: The web business structure will have to undergo a drastic change and be reengineered. It is not just about having a website or about sticking a web address on conventional advertising or transferring a few people to a new division and designation. It is about breaking free and creating new web services to satisfy the existing customers.

20. Skepticism: Skepticism pertaining to credit card usage is the killing factor, as it is embedded in the information psyche and would not change overnight even if credit payments over the Net are made accountable.

There is the lack of payment solutions. We do not have a wide range of payment instruments available on the Net. Payment instruments are very important to enable one to take up internet business with confidence.

21. Internet for Small Business: Another problem is that for major project, a large consumer product company needs profiling of customers who undertake transaction through e-commerce.

E-commerce is still being dominated by large corporations. Small and medium sized business houses have to take advantage of everything on the Net. Online shopping is clearly catching on with consumers and retailers need to keep pace with growing demands.

22. *Blocking and Censorship:* People worldwide are under virtual slavery. It has been reported in some media that many countries are blocking their citizens from accessing the Net, either partially or wholly. Censorship is enforced by some countries by stopping either a total ban on the Net or controlling the access traffic or installing filters blocking access to websites. Indian citizens enjoy unprecedented degree of freedom of speech and therefore may constitute a threat to the government. Development in any field may prove detrimental if it does not appreciate the code of ethics.

23. *Infant Stages:* Electronic commerce is still in its infant stage. Indian commerce is establishing itself in the area of internet business. The concept of e-commerce is still in evolutionary stage, it is a job that still needs to be defined. The IT function has not grown beyond the marketing department and credit cards, merchant accounts, digital signatures and prompt payment and one has to realize that the e-commerce role is more about harnessing technological resources to deliver profits to the Net users. Only a few Indian big houses have gone online to explore the potentials of e-commerce.

E-commerce has yet to take off in India, because Indian consumers are wary of leaving their credit card numbers on the Net. They eye the neghbourhood shopkeeper with suspicion and drive a hard bargain. So, e-commerce websites are losing thousands of customers.

24. *Barriers-Survey Findings:* According to a survery conducted by promoters of e-commerce, shoppers don't trust e-commerce, they cannot find what they are looking for, and there's no easy way to pay for things being ordered online. Other than that, it is smooth sailing.

Customers are worried about credit card theft, the privacy of their personal information and unacceptable network performance, Most shoppers still are not convinced that it is worthwhile to hook onto the Internet, search for shopping sites, wait for the images to download, try to figure out the ordering process, and then worry about whether their credit card numbers would be filched by a hacker.

As for business-to-business systems, the issues are less emotional but still serious. Businesses do not yet have good models for setting up their e-commerce sites, and they have trouble sharing the orders and information collected online with the rest of their business applications, Many companies continue to grapple with the idea of sharing proprietary business information with customers and suppliers which is an important component of many business e-commerce systems.

Sum Up

Thus, e-commerce is still commerce and still about human beings. Customers are still customers and merchants want people at their end. They send confidential, personal and financial information only by e-mail or can cash on the phone or might just prefer to visit.in person. E-commerce is just only a new way of doing business or an additional method of doing business. It is a new generation technology, a new method of doing business with new generation technology. Still, there are many drawbacks which fail to benefit the users of technology to a great extent.

E-commerce is to be viewed as business but not as a technology issue. It must be business driven but not IT driven and initiatives must be integrated thoroughly into the existing commerce structure and strategy.

□□□

Electronic Data Interchange (EDI)

Introduction

Getting and sending orders, bills collections, payables, receivables, orders, invoices, freight bills, shipment instructions, trading reports, enquiries, payment instructions, status reports and other information vital to various business operations are the routine business transactions. There are only two popular conventional systems which have been prevailing for a long period to perform these activities. They are postal services by postal authorities and telephone telegrams by the department of telecommunications. These two communication services are available for business transactions are traditional methods known for their cost, ineffectiveness and slack levels of performance. In order to solve the above problems, a new development has emerged in this area called electronic business data communication. Postal and telephone service under the conventional system are unable to perform with such a speed, accuracy and message load handling as electronic devices render data interchange service. These are broadly known as bottlenecks. Delay in decision making, failure to solve problems quickly, effective monitoring and evaluation are not possible under the conventional business data interchange system. In addition, the system is associated with errors human error in data transfer, loss in transfer, transcription problems etc.

In this complex, competitive global business environment with a huge database, it is found that typing, printing, retyping of all the available information is no longer feasible and useful. Imagine how difficult it is to manage a business organization, receiving and sending hundreds and thousands of standard forms like invoices. purchase orders, acknowledgements, payments, enquiry schedules etc. In a paper-based business data interchange system, all these forms should be entered in the computer, processed and transferred to trading partners by postal service. At the destination, the receiving trading partner again has to retype the information received. The entire double process is time consuming, costly, prone to human errors and losses etc.

Types of Business Data Transfer Systems

Traditionally, the transfer of business data by the trading partner has been by paper documents. There are two systems for business data interchange between trading partners. They are: paper-based system and electronic-based system.

1. Paper-Based System: Traditionally, data transfer from one business house to another has been carried out through paper-based documents. The documents have to be manually forwarded by postal services and entered into the destination computer. Hence it is called paper-based systems.

In the early days, transaction data has been interchanged through processor file transfer which is associated with problems like unwieldy, erroneous, error-prone and inefficient transactions etc.

Disadvantages of Paper-based System

There are several direct and indirect problems associated with the paper-based information system. The potential problems have been discussed below:

1. *Time Delays:* In the paper-based transaction system (exchange of business data), a number of delays occur along the time line. The following areas related to delays are:

(a) **Transportation Delay :** The primary source is transportation delay which is caused by the mail system or by any other system required to physically move paper documents between trading partners.

(b) **Manual Processing Delay :** This delay is caused by the need to key in, type or make an entry and re-key, re-type and re-enter information along the time line.

(c) **Ordering Delay :** Delays in transporting and keying in business information result in ordering delays. These delays may include payment delay, billing delays, poor customer services and inadequate management information.

2. *Labour Costs:* In the paper-based system, the whole process involves recurring labour costs. The main reason for high labour costs is due to the manual processing of business data through papers. Manual processing is required for data keying, re-keying, document storage, handling, maintenance and retrieval of data and document matching. When information is keyed in and re-keyed at each phase, then labour costs are increased.

3. *Errors:* The paper-based system is error prone because the same information is re-keyed multiple times, resulting in errors.

4. *Inventory:* As pointed out earlier, delay and uncertainties are associated in paper-based processing. Subsequently, inventories may be kept at a higher level than they need be. It means unnecessary blocking of scarce financial resources on inventory items alone, thus affecting the working capital.

5. *Uncertainty:* This is yet another problem with the paper-based system. There are three important areas where uncertainties exist:

- Transportation and keying in delays. It means that the timing is uncertain.
- The sender neither knows whether the transaction is received at all nor whether the firm agrees with what was sent in for the proposed transaction.
- In the payment areas, it is difficult to tell when a cheque will clear back to the disbursing bank.

6. *Paper Bound Process:* The major problem of data communication hitherto is that the huge bulk of commercial documents generated between companies in business transactions still remain locked in the slow, antiquated, paper-bound process.

7. *Time Consuming Process:* Paper documents produced by one computer system of an organization are printed, posted and entered into the other trading partner's computer system.

The above process is time consuming, error prone and costly. Its cost is estimated between 4% and 7% of the value of goods traded.

8. Untimely Analysis: Paper-baAed data exchange is a barrier to the trade. The analysis of sales returns will be delayed into the ordering process.

9. Demand doesn't Reflect Stock: In traditional data, communication order, cannot be raised to reflect both demand and know-stock availability. Immediate instructions cannot be sent to the distributors in parallel with the other to ensure the fast delivery of orders.

10. Loosing Customers: The trading partners have established electronic data interchange. The business firms which are not moving rapidly to implement electronic data interchange in tune with trading partners face the loss of trading relationships, resulting in the loss of potential markets.

11. Paper Standards: Common business transactions such as purchase orders and invoices are often printed as standard paper forms.

The conventional paper documents cannot transmit data directly to the other party. The electronic data interchange facilitates this transmission, thus ensuring potential business.

12. Other Problems: They include the following :

- Only a paper document on a form is generated.
- Documents are transferred to the trading partners through postal services.
- Office copies are reserved in paper-based office files.
- At the destinations, the receiving trading partners after receiving documents, have necessarily to re-key or re-type business data in their computers.
- Again a paper document alone is to be sent as acknowledgement to the originating trading partner.
- The repeated and routine re-keying of identical data in paper-based system creates a number of problems like lack of accuracy and increased uncertainty. Re-typing increases the chances of errors.
- Paper-based data exchange cannot handle large volume of repetitive standard work.
- Handling, filing, space, maintenance and transportation of data necessitated by this system is an herculean task.

Electronic Data Interchange (EDI)

In order to solve problems associated with the paper-based business data interchange system, the alternate mechanism came in the form of Electronic Data Interchange (EDI). The term, in non-technical usage, simply means electronic interchange of data between computer systems of the various participants. More technically, EDI is defined as *"the transfer of structured data for processing from computer to computer using agreed formats and protocol"*.

Electronic Data Interchange is the inter- organizational exchange of business documentation in both structured and processable form. EDI is actually a way of replacing manual data entry with the electronic data entry. The purpose of EDI is to eliminate delay in processing and data re-entry, thus generating more business transactions.

Common business transactions such as purchase orders and invoices are often printed as standard paper forms. When business information is available in a standard format, it can directly be transmitted to your trading partner's computer system for processing.

The structured and business information accessed by machines is electronically exchanged in standard formats between the computers of trading partners. EDI establishes a link between potential business houses. Business information is electronically interchaged between companies over a network.

This avoids the need for the information to be read, re-typed, re-keyed or printed. In this, the structure in which business data is to be interchanged must have a specified and defined structure agreed by the trading partners. Any type of business document can be exchanged or interchanged, but it should be a mutually agreed structure conforming to the current, national and international format standards followed within an industry. Before sending the data, it is to be converted into an agreed standard format. But the trading partners must have a computer to work with the EDI. They must negotiate trading agreements and formalize the data transfer systems.

EDI can be used to electronically transmit documents such as purchase orders, invoices, shipping notices, advice and other standard business correspondence between trading partners. EDI can also be used to transmit financial information and payments in electronic form. When used in this manner, EDI is usually referred to as Electronic Fund Transfer (EFT).

Therefore, EDI may be defined as computer to computer transfer of business and commercial data in structured and electronically readable and processable form. Thus, the advancement in sophisticated information technology and particularly the fast emerging EDI set of technology which has been revolutionizing the business throughout the globe, has come to stay, occupying a vital role-particularly in other countries, corporations are increasingly adopting EDI as a major trade facilitating mechanism. Thus, the EDI lets the business to replace conventional paper-based documents with the formatted, standardized business documents transmitted as electronic data.

EDI standardises the process of trading and tracks business documents like purchase orders, payments, invoices, shipping and delivery systems.

EDI translates these documents into a globally understood business language and transnits them between trading partners via secure telecommunication links.

The crux of EDI is the standard which contains predefined format called a *transaction set* for each document. It also contains a predetemined location for each piece of data that is necessary to conduct business.

Electronic data interchange has been around for a while. Infact, it was developed nearly more than 30 years ago and was first used by the US Government. According to the Data Interchange Standards Association, some one lakh US organisations now use EDI to conduct business.

Electronic Data Interchange has been the traditional means of transmitting data between businesses and trading partners. Despite the transmission, business due to increase of internet users still heavily rely on EDI for conducting trading and financial transaction with partners. One of the most daunting challenges that the company faces is expanding trading partner's options by installing a business- to-business solutions to work in conjunction with an EDI system.

Definition of EDI

The Accredited Standards Committee for EDI of the American National Standards Institute defines it as:

"Electronic data interchange is transmission in a standard syntax, of unambiguous information of business or strategic significance between the computers of independent organisations".

UN/EDI Fact Training Guide

"EDI is the interchange of standard formatted data between computer application systems of trading partners with minimal manual intervention".

The Birth and Advent of EDI

It is not that data has not been interchanged between the organisations in the past but in the absence of an effective integration of computers between the two business partners, such a data exchange was conducted without a network in place. That meant that either the data was exchanged on paper or was exchanged in ASCII format on a back-up device, that is the data was first offloaded from the databases of host computers and then loaded onto the databases of the client computers again. This led to not only time delays but also creeping in of a number of errors. However, with the Internet, it became feasible to rid this process of information and data interchange between computers of human intervention. This led to the advent of EDI.*

Before e-commerce came into existence and became the buzzword of potential business generation, corporate houses adopted EDI. The National Informatics Centre (NIC) was given the charge of boosting EDI within the country. The Videsh Sanchar Nigam Limited (VSNL) was given the responsibility for such transactions worldwide. EDI is yet in its infancy. Only 7 per cent of the business in the US uses EDI effectively.

Simply put, B2B e-commerce pertains to the smooth flow of information between an enterprise and all its business partners. The last decade saw the complete automation of flow of data and information between different processes within a company, thus enabling the Enterprises Resource Planning (ERP) revolution. In the absence of high bandwidth and availability of smart networks, it was not possible to seamlessly expand this information flow to include partners, i.e. the suppliers and the distributors.

Meanwhile (Very Small Aperture Terminals) cellular technology, ISDN, cable and other media offered rapid connectivity between computers across geographical locations. Thus, it became possible to get rid of human intervention in the voluminous data and information that needs to flow between business partners to make any big enterprises cost-competitive in the market place with EDI coming in the picture.

Features of EDI

The fundamental differences between EDI and electronic mail and fax is that the data exchanged through the EDI is meant for direct use by the destination recipient computer.

The following special features of EDI remove the drawbacks in conventional paper-based business data interchange :

- There is no need in EDI that the information received should be read by the other side of the trading partner and then interpreted and acted upon accordingly.
- The information so transferred through EDI can directly be used by the recipient computer.
- The formats of various business documents like invoices, purchase orders, acknowledgement and other documents are agreed upon by the trading partners availing the facility of EDI.

---

* *Computers Today, 16-31 April, 2000, p. 59.*

- Under EDI, data transfer from one business house to another is done through electronic documents which have to be electronically forwarded and entered into the destination trading partner's computer.
- In this system of electronic exchange of structured business information, the information should be in standard formats conforming to the current industry, national or international format standards.
- The EDI establishes an electronic link between companies.
- Its special feature is that it has reduced data entry links, avoids paper-based systems and improves business cycle time.
- In EDI, the concept of trading partners is very wide which may include intra company business links or external companies, Internal means the groups of departments and external companies are referred to as suppliers, customers and subsidiaries.
- It pertains to the fact that the information transferred through EDI will not have to be re-typed, re-keyed or printed. But the condition is that the information should be in pre-determined and pre-defined structure agreed by the trading partners who send and receive business data.
- It pertains to communicate with the trading partners by exchange of data with several trading partners directly and interactive with multiple companies through central information clearing houses.
- The third party's computer systems under EDI allows the sender to communicate with an unlimited number of trading partners.
- The translation service of the EDI translates the data into standard formats for transmission and for reverse translation in the data it receives.
- The application services, translation services and communication services of the EDI put together make the working EDI complete and give essence to online business.
- The mechanism is to pull down the forms, documents, process description and capture noting etc. into predefined and agreed standard formats.
- It may be noted that the aim of EDI is not completely to eliminate paper work, but rather to eliminate processing delays, data re-entry, re-typing and errors and discrepancies.
- In EDI, the data is transferred electroniclally in machine readable form and the message is mechanically processed by the receiving computer without any human intervention, interpretation or re-keying delay.

User Groups

Many organization groups have been using the global electronic trading. The major user groups are Trade, Transport, Customs, Finance, Banking, Construction, Statistics, Insurance, Travel and Tourism etc.

The establishment of links with trading partners' computer systems and the trade net facilitates exchange of many different types of business communication. They are mentioned below :

Business Documents

They include purchase orders, invoices, payment orders, memos, shipment notice, letter, receiving, advance, acknowledgements, payments, price or sales catalogues, listing of parts, enquiries, bills of lading, instructions to distributors, customs clearance documents, payment instructions to banks, online updating and request for quotation.

All these modes of business communication are done without paper, efficiently and effectively with quality.

Transaction Sets

The basic feature of EDI is to standardize, electronic message formats as these documents are directly used by the trading partners. Therefore, these documents should be predetermined, predefined and structured in computer readable and processable form. The formats should be in a common agreed structure by the trading partners.

EDI is concerned with the standardization of electronic message formats. When an electronic message is in structured format, it is called 'transaction set' for common business documents. The common business documents which can be predetermined in structured and standard format, capable of machine readable and processable format may include, among others the following : purchase orders, invoices, shipping notice, advice, request for quotation, purchase change order, bill of lading etc.

When these documents are structured and standardized they enable the computer of one trading partner to communicate with the computer at the destination trading partner without actually producing the paper documents. These transaction sets so electronically produced are interchanged and they eleminate the need of human efforts to read, sort and physically transport such documents. The transaction sets transferred through EDI are designed for direct use by both the sender computer and the recipient computer.

The common business documents (transaction sets) as identified above are to be converted into EDI formats. They may constitute bulk of the official communication under the paper document system.

EDI in India

In order to systematically promote and propagate EDI in India, various administrative structures have been created by the Ministry of Commerce. They Include:

- The establishment of the EC/EDI Council of India, which is the apex body consisting of the heads of all the key government departments and organisations connected with international trade as well as representatives of both trade and industry.
- The establishment of the India EDI FACT Committee which is responsible for formulating standards, streamlining procedures in line with UN/EDI FACT and maintaining a liaison with UN/EDI FACT bodies and
- The setting of a working group for motivating various functionaries in government organisations.

In order to meet the forthcoming demands and needs of the business community, two major organisations of India, viz., National Informatics Centre (NIC) and Videsh Sanchar Nigam Limited (VSNL) have established EDI-VAN services. Other VAN service providers include Satyam Online and Global Telecom services. Other orgaisarions that have been active in developing and promoting various aspects of e-commerce in India include the Federation of Indian Export Organisations (FIEO), the All India Management Association (AIMA) and NASSCOM. Some of the projects already underway are :

- The Indian Customs EDI system (ICES), a project for customs clearance.
- A pilot project for the Indian Bank Association for inter-bank EDI. IBA is also participating in an auto pilot electronic commerce project for the development of a bank-customer interface.
- EDI based systems at ports, involving customs, shipping agents and freight forwarders.
- An EDI project at various offices of the Directorate General of Foreign Trade (DGFT). A pilot project for the automobile industry initiated by the Union Ministry of Commerce.

But, inspite of all these efforts, the e-commerce market in India is way behind in terms of development and growth when compared to the OBCD countries. The fact is that we need to increase the velocity of e-commerce implementation in India. A quick look at the e-commerce scenario in USA shows a marked upswing in e-commerce transactions.

EDI and Wide Area Network (WAN)

The concept network means anything in the form of a net which may have many lines crossing each other. A network in connection with the computer environment means a link of many computers within the organization and outside. It is an interconnection between computers for the interchange of data by strategic communication links.

To work with EDI, it is necessary to establish the networking infrastructure. The EDI mechanism demands the availability of Wide Area Network (WAN) to which trading partners can subscribe. All the trading partners willing to use the services of EDI have necessarily to subscribe to the networking infrastructure in WAN, a number of autonomous computers are located over a wide or remote geographical area, and WANs are used to interchange business data over a long distance through the EDI.

The main objective of WAN in EDI is to provide an effective business data interchange between computers located in geographically scattered areas. There are two types of WANs, such as private network and public network. In a private network, leased circuits are used for installing a WAN, which has normally a limited capacity. Government networks are public WANs designed, and built by the Government, its departments like DOT, VSNL, Railways etc.

Gateway Electronic Data Interchange Service (GEDIS) and Videsh Sanchar Nigam Limited (VSNL)

The acronym GEDIS, popularly called so, stands for Gateway Electronic Data Interchange Service-provides GEDIS trade net. GEDIS is a revolutionary concept. The Videsh Sanchar Nigam Limited (VSNL) opened GEDIS in 1994 as a trading net to provide international and domestic electronic data exchange services.

It provides customers with a necessary infrastructure and an environment for electronic trading, paperless transactions and essential fund transfers. It is one of the value added services that has been fast growing with services available to the business houses in India and outside. The global trade net can facilitate to transmit information directly to other side trading partner's computer system for processing. This type of infomation transmission is known as Electronic Data Interchange (EDI).

GEDIS is the common link, a data clearing house. Every trading partner is required to have a link to the GEDIS to facilitate communication. In turn, GEDIS has interconnections with all world's major EDI networks.

Working Features of GEDIS

- GEDIS trade net offers substantial opportunities for improvements in effectiveness and efficency throughout business.
- GEDIS trade net permits trading partners to extend the use of those same automation and support systems to include the process of doing business with other partners electronically.

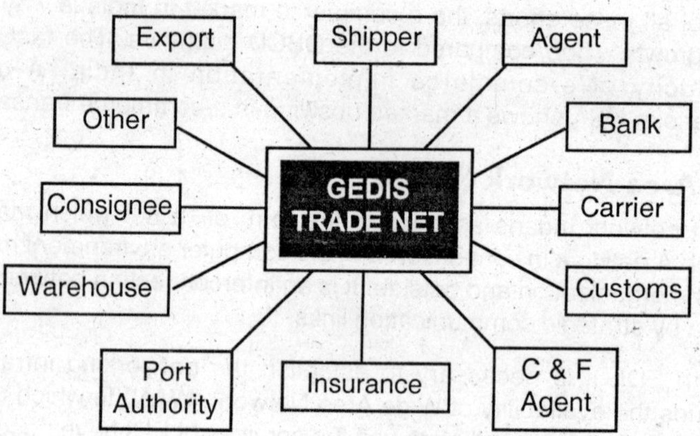

Fig. 2.01 Gateway Electronic Data Intercharge Service Network

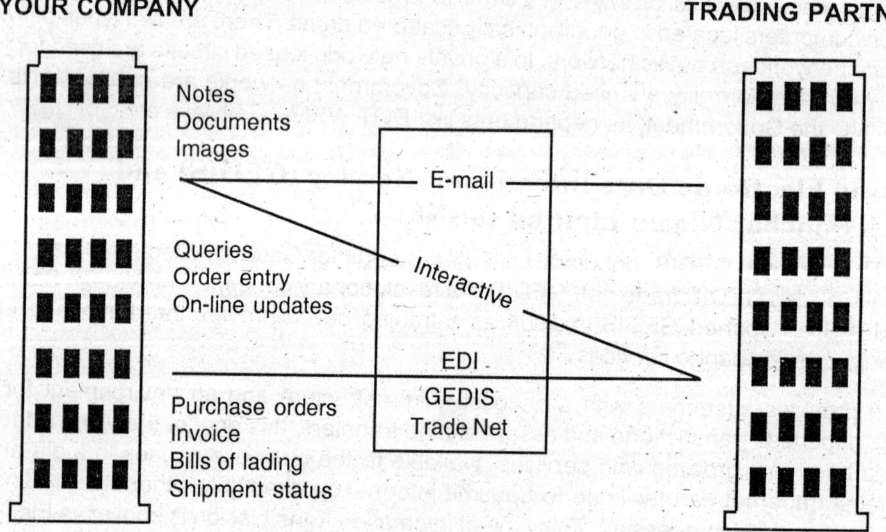

Fig. 2.02 GEDIS Trade List

- The trading partners can set up communication links between your own computer system and our trading partners' computer systems.
- When links are established with the trading partners' computer systems, GEDIS Trade Net permits the exchange of many different types of business communications such as orders, invoices, memos, letters, catalogues, parts listings, enquiries and much more.
- GEDIS extends network sevices which act as a data clearing houses. As such, only one link is needed for each company i.e. the link to GEDIS.
- The network also overcomes differences in the origin of computers. It caters services for all the popular computer brands manufactured in different countries.
- The network access is through wide ranging options such as PSTN, leased lines, GPSS, I Net, RABMN, NIC Net, INDO-Net etc.
- A GEDIS access point will not be far away, whenever a customer is in India.
- GEDIS is interconnected to all the world's major EDI networks.
- Connections are established with GEDIS and not with trading partners themselves.
- The partners don't need to be available before the computer and at the time of transmission.
- Another feature is that the GEDIS service is available 24 hours a day and 365 days a year.
- Its mechanism is that GEDIS simply stores the trading data received from companies and forward it electronically to the correct point on the network.
- The user of GEDIS can send all the data for all its trading partners in one operation if it suits and is feasible. It is the responsibility of GEDIS to sort out all the data and send it to the right address every time.
- GEDIS in its service doesn't alllow the sending of unsolicited mail. The business data of the user is protected by the password system, preventing unauthorised people from reading such data.

NIC Net and EDI

National Informatics Centre (NIC) has been offering messaging services to its corporate customers. These include electronic mail service over NIC Net. In order to meet the new demand from the business community, NIC has established an EDI/E-mail Value Added Network (VAN) Server over NIC Net. Along with some sort of hard ware for communications, the basic requirement is a software capable of handling and controlling both incoming or outgoing EDI messages to any number or a combination of trading partners.

NIC provides an EDI converter software, based on DOS, to be used as RUA for the EDI message class. This package operates both as stand- alone work stations as well as an unattended, front-end processor.

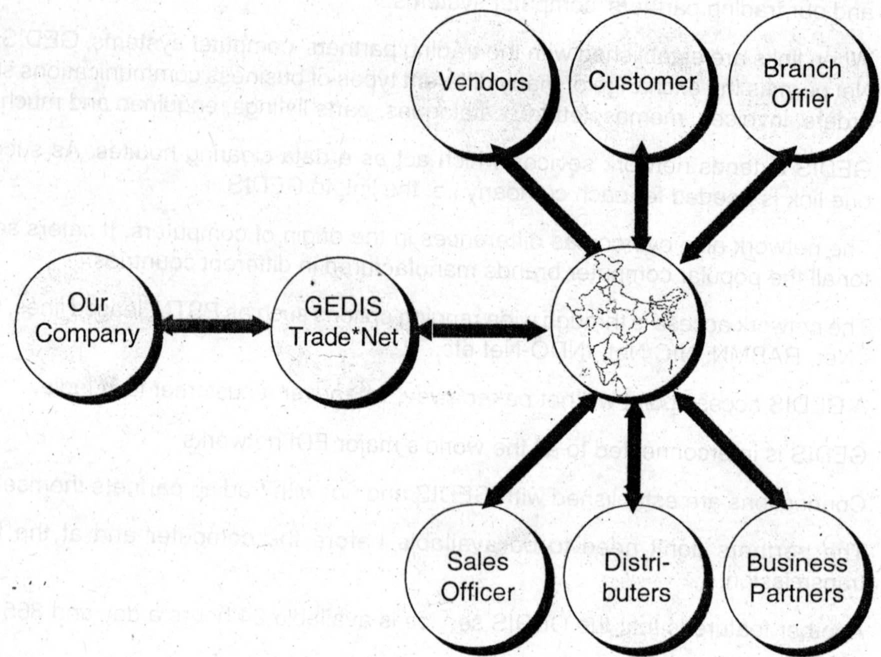

FIG. 2.03 GEDIS Trade Net.

It comes with a built-in and user friendly development tool kit for the customization of EDI message templates, screens, print outs and flat files for uploading and downloading. The package supports all versions of EDI-FACT fact and X12 standard and it is upgradable to any other industry standard including proprietary messages.

Trading Partners

In EDI, the term trading partner is frequently used. The expression trading partners means two companies or groups which exchange business data through EDI. The computers which trading partners use need not be from the same manufacturers. This term also includes document destinations which can be either intra-company or belonging to external companies. The EDI is business data interchange between business houses or companies which are involved in EDI are simply trading partners. It may include two or more organizations or parts of an organization exchanging business information with each other in a common mutually agreed structured format. In the electronic interchange of structured business documents, the concept of trading partners may include an organization internally among various functional departments or groups of departments or externally with its suppliers, customers and subsidiaries etc.

Partners in EDI may include official communications associated with commercial transations between the business, government, institutions, voluntary organizations, non-profit establishments in private, public, co-operative and joint sectors and most of the multi-national corporations. But usually trading partners normally consist of a company's principal suppliers and wholesale customers. In addition, large retail stores are among the early supporters and active participants in EDI.

Getting started with EDI-Steps

They Include the following :

- The EDI demands full cooperation and active participation of trading partners.
- To standardize electronic message formats for common business documents agreed by the trading partners.
- To reap the benefits and services of EDI, the basic requirement is first to computerise all the basic accounting records.
- The trading partners must agree to interchange transaction sets through EDI.
- To install EDI software that translates the information from unstructured format to the structured EDI format. The software also receives the message and translates from the standard format to the specific format. The software performs major functions like data conservation, data formatting, application and message communication.
- It is necessary to formulate EDI standards to provide guidelines on the communication of electronic message. The understandings or protocols between the users of EDI on how the business data are to be formatted and communicated is called EDI standards.
- Standards are guidelines or rules as how to use EDI. X.400 is an EDI communication standard for the transmission of messages electronically. There are separate retail industry standards and international standards.
- Three important components required to operate EDI are EDI standards, EDI software and direct links.
- The users must select a data standard to use GEDIS.
- Necessary advice and guidance should be obtained from the experienced VSNL consultants.
- The next step is to connect GEDIS. Only one link is needed for each company.
- The two trading partners/companies have necessarily to exchange business data electronically in the standard formats.
- The interested parties to use EDI, must specify the application in the EDI standard which they want to implement once companies/partners have established standardized data interchange procedure, and they are now in a position to use EDI to reap its benefits.

EDI Standards

The individual computers of trading partners or networking computers, through EDI have to follow EDI standards in order to achieve the objective of electronic data interchange between trading partners. This standard is the practice under EDI working, following a set of rules formulated and agreed upon by the users is called EDI standard. The EDI standards define and set a series of operational procedures which the computers of both the trading partners, have to follow. It is EDI protocols, which enable sending and receiving computers to interchange business data in standard, structured formats in a computer readable and processable form. Thus, EDI standards let the participant computers in EDI for the exchange of data from one computer to another computer. This is normally referred to as application to application EDI.

EDI standards are pre-determined, pre-defined agreements between the users of EDI. These rules permit users as how the data are to be formatted and communicated. Without formatting, rules and syntax electronic messages cannot be transmitted. EDI standards are guidelines which are called formatting standards and communication standards.

The following are the various EDI standards :

- X.400 is a popular EDI communication standard. It greatly facilitates the transmission of message electronically.
- Industry groups can adopt EDI standards, or they can develop their own EDI standards. International standards are established based on X12 standards. The Accredited Standards Committee (ASC) has formulated X12 under the American National Standard Institute (ANSI) for US business. These guidelines are called EDI for Administration Commerce and Trade (EDIFACT). The object of ASC X12 is to develop uniform standards for inter-industry electronic interchange of business transactions.

The following are the three X12 data interchange standards :

- Transaction Set Standards.
- Data Dictionary and Segment Dictionary and
- Transaction Control Standards.

- Retail industry standards have been formulated to serve large segments of the retail industry. The Uniform Communication Standards (UCS) are designed and used by groceries and other retail stores.
- EDIFACT is an international EDI standards for administration, commerce and trade, The International Standard Organization (ISO) is mainly concerned for developing syntax rules and data dictionary for EDIFACT. On the other hand, the United Nations Economic Commission Document Standards are used by all US-based business.
- Variable length EDI standards have also been developed for certain industry and service groups.

There are two variable length EDI standards :

- EDI standards for transportation industries which consist of four segments like air, motor, ocean and rail. The EDI standards for the transportation industry have been developed by a separate committee, known as the Transportation Data Coordinating Committee (TDCC). It is also called the Electronic Data Interchange Association (EDIA) and
- The Uniform Code Council (UCC) is concerned with the creation and ongoing maintenance of the Uniform Communication Standard (UCS). It is meant for the warehousing industry.

GEDIS- Standards Supported

GEDIS Trade Net is based on the HP 9000/827 System and the INSTRADANET Software. This provides a Store and Retrieve EDI service that accepts data formatted to the UN/EDIFACT (EDI For Administration Commerce and Transport) UNTDI (United Nations Trade Data Interchange) including TRADACOMS and ODETTE, and ANSI.X12 (American National Standards Institute). Syntax, thus restricting the user to send or receive incorrectly formatted data.

The Central service can accept any document conforming to EDI-FACT, UNTDI or ANSI.X12 Suntax. This includes over 150 different messages in commercial use today. Moreover new documents to any extent can be added to the central service without any change to the system.

Translation is carried out by the end user translation package-Intercept. Translation tables for any EDIFACT or UNTDI or ANSI. X12 document can be added or deleted from the Intercept. The Central service can also handle any free format on flat files attached an EDIFACT or UNTDI or ANSI.X12 envelope.

Importance of EDI

- The importance of EDI can be examined by observing the reasons why companies are interested in paperless transactions today.
- The paper-based system for handling business to business information exchange presents several problems in the existing business environment.
- A number of large firms are moving rapidly to implement EDI and are sending the message that trading partners should be prepared to do EDI or face the loss of business relationships.
- Many companies have already made dramatic changes in their internal operations by using office automation systems and decision-support systems.
- It is feasible to adopt EDI to reap potential advantages in business retain customers, maintain relationships with customers and do quick business.
- The pervasive effects of EDI cannot be ignored by business of any size. Today as we stand on the threshold of a world soon to be united by open systems, architecture and common EDI provides, an attractive strategic advantage.
- Within the coming decade, EDI will no longer be just a strategic option for companies with vision, but it will become a necessary function of business and reliance on computers can be avoided to a certain extent.
- Increasing numbers of business in the 1990s will be faced with an ultimatum i.e. adopt electronic data interchange or suffer the effects of a disorgainised and ineffectual environment. So, it will be EDI or 'DIE' in the business environment.

Types of EDI Files

The files which pass through the system are called documents. As such, EDI creates three types of files. They are Transmission Files (TF), Internal Format Files (IFF) and External Format Files (EFF).

The meaning and nature of these files are described in brief as follows :

1. Transmission Files: These files deal with documents for the same trading partner. These files contain one or more documents which are classified into functional groups. The same type of documents are packaged together in one functional group. It is the interchange set in which functional groups going ro one trading partner are packed together.

2. Internal Format Files: The file is basically meant for EDI's own use. This file contains a single document for a single trading partner. When the document is in the EDI system, it is called the internet format file.

3. External Format File: This file mainly relates to translation services. The EFF contains the same information as contained in the internal format file but it is translated into a pre defined standard document format.

Electronic Data Interchange Services

The EDI mechanism extends three types of services to the users which are different from each other. The services are: application service, translation service and communication service.

1. *Application Service:* The purpose of this service is to establish link between EDI and business application. The trading partners can avail of this service to transmit data to the choice destination and receive the same from an electronic data interchange system. To transfer documents, a set of callable routines is used. This allows the transfer of documents from the business application to EDI. The function of application service is to hold incoming and outgoing document as a single internal format file. In the EDI system, first the documents should be converted to a standard format before sending them to the trading partners. It is EDI mechanism that converts documents and sends them to the destination,

Apllication Services includes the following:

Incoming Documents : They do the following :

- It receives an internal format file from the translation service and
- It keeps the data in the internal format file stored in the database. The application service can access the document from EDI.

Outgoing Documents : A business application uses callable routines to send documents from the business application to the application service. Each document must pass through the translation service. It is the function of the application service to forward documents in the internal format file to the translation service.

2. *Translation Service:* The objective of EDI is the electronic interchange of pre determined and structured business information in standard formats between the computers of trading partners. Translation services basically perform the following two important translation services :

- In case of incoming documents from the trading partner in an external format, translation service translates to the EDI internal format file and
- In case of outgoing document from an internal format file, the translation service concerts outgoing documents into an agreed extenal format.

3. *Communication Service:* The mechanism of EDI converts documents to the standard format and transfers it to the trading partner. For sending document, EDI uses communication services and communication protocol. There are different standards and communication protocols available to the EDI users. The communication service of EDI extends services of sending and receiving transmission files to and from the trading partners. This service is available either direclty or by using a third party service called Value Added Networks (VAN).

Communication service includes the following:

Incoming Documents

- The function of this service is to receive a transmission file from the trading partners and
- The service also forwards the transmission file to the translation services.

Outgoing Documents

- The service forwards the transmission file also to the trading partners and
- It receives a transmission file from the translation service.

EDI and Internet

E-commerce is mostly facilitated by EDI and the Internet. Historically, the main mode of e-commerce has been EDI, which is a form of communication programme that allows business organisations to automatically exchange information pertaining to business transactions. EDI transactions involve predefined relationship among trading partners, suppliers and customers and are typically carried over specialised networks known as Value Added Networks (VAN) as mentioned earlier. These relationships and the use of private EDI networks allow EDI service providers to offer a degree of security, performance and reliability that is more difficult to achieve in ad hoc relationships and internet-based communications that characterise web-based commerce.

Direct application exchange of information, business-to-business interactions, well-and strategically defined specified message format, batch-oriented (that is asynchronous) operations. interactions based on pre-existing contractual relations etc. are some of the important functions possible through EDI (*A.K. Mohanty*).

Objectives of Electronic Data Interchange

- To establish trade net, a gateway to global electronic trading by way of communication links between a company and trading partners' computer system in India and abroad.
- To replace conventional paper documents by way of simplification with formatted and standardised business documents transmitted as electronic data.
- To solve the problem of unreasonable time consumption, error-prone activity and the costly exercise of information transmission.
- To establish a direct link by a corporate computer system to the computers of all its customers and suppliers to do business transactions and information exchange electronically.
- To eliminate the tedious practice of conventionally maintaining loads of paperwork surrounding today's environment of business transactions.
- To facilitate data transmission directly to the trading partners' computer systems for processing.
- To solve several problems virtually associated with today's paperbound system for processing.
- To solve several problems of loss of relationship with customers, suppliers and clients etc. by not having installed the latest EDI system.
- To bring improvement, efficiency and effectiveness in business houses.
- To replace paper-based processing.
- To introduce tremendous and potential improvements in tune with fast global business changes.
- To remove several known serious barriers of paperwork to potential trade.
- To free the business environment suffering the effects of a disorganised ineffective environment (DIE).

Electronic Trading Options

There are three Intercept — Plus electronic trading options for the user. They are :

1. ***Electronic Mail:*** The systems mail provides a powerful electronic messaging service to complement the use of electronic data interchange. It provides the facility to send messages to a facsimile number.

2. ***Interactive Access:*** The software incorporates a communications system manager to give access to a growing number of interactive services including database enquiry and information retrieval.

3. ***Electronic Fund Transfer:*** It supports electronic fund transfer transactions (EFT) and the specific authentication procedures necessary for EFT.

4. ***Connectivity Software:*** The user-end software product is to be used. The Intercept software packages are required to be used by customers to connect trade net or gateway to global electronic trading (GEDIS). There are many user-end software products of them, Intercept Plus is the key to electronic trading.

Uses and Applications

Intercept — Plus has the following uses and applications :

1. ***Man Machine Interface:*** It is known for simplicity and hence as easy to use as possible.

2. ***Data Tracking :*** It is the only software product with data tracking updated online. It is a command generation.

3. ***Document Data Entry:*** There are two important facilities available: Standard data entry schemes and secondly to select customised formats for particular document types.

4. ***Document Printing:*** In this software product, standard routines are available. Alternatively, customised print formats for special documents can be included.

5. ***Multiple Standards:*** In this, translation softwares are inbuilt to facilitate the conversion of data from accepted electronic data interchange, data standards to inhouse data formats and vice versa.

6. ***Unattended Operations:*** There is a facility that a person need not necessarily be present at the time of an operation. The user can present instructions to establish a service connection automatically at the time of selection. Similarly, one can send or extract specified data and process it, making it ready for internal use.

7. ***Security:*** The system has been designed to meet the increasing need for privacy and security of data. The user data is protected by a password system, preventing unauthorised people from reading personal data. Passwords so set can be used to limit access for specified individuals or to prevent unauthorised access to such information.

8. Multiple EDI Services: GEDIS software holds details of all trading partners and their network addresses and can automatically make the connection to other electronic data interchange services.

9. Application Interface: The application interface is the vital gateway from application to intercept Plussoftware. It permits to transfer documents in a flat sequential file format between internal application like order, invoice processing systems and the specific software.

Advantages of EDI

The electronic data interchange service trade net offers substantial opportunities for improvement in effectiveness and efficiency through the years of potential business. There are many major user groups of EDI — their experiences revealed that the concept has brought dramatic changes in their internal operations by using office automation systems and strategic decision support systems.

The advantages of GEDIS can be broadly classified into four broad categories: (i) operational officiency, (ii) logistical benefits, (iii) cost reduction and (iv) strategic benefits. The following are the brief and summarised benefits emerging from these four categories:

1. Operational Efficiency

- Faster information flow and instant availability.
- Improved accuracy by eliminating re-keying of data and
- Handling of paperwork and or media work eliminated.

2. Logistical Benefits

- Reduced order lead time.
- Improved delivery cycle.
- Better production scheduling
- Reduced stockholding
- Minimised stock-outs.
- Improved planning and forecasting and
- Increased sales.

3. Cost Reduction

- Reduced administrative overheads
- Reduced costs of stationery and printing and
- Elimination of redundant and or duplicated processes.

4. Strategic Benefits

- Access to new markets.
- Closer relationships with key business partners.
- Enhanced business opportunities.

- Competitive advantage and
- Opportunities to redefine the scope of business.

Other Benefits

1. Automation and Support Systems: The companies which are already using automation and support systems can be used in trade net to inculde the process of doing business with other companies electronically.

2. Standardisation: Common business transactions such as purchase orders and invoice documents are standardised, formatted and transmitted as electronic data. It permits to transmit data directly to the trading partner's computer system for its processing.

Facilitating Benefits

- EDI enables to make available custom clearance documents in advance of the goods arriving.
- It avoids hold-ups.
- To ensure prompt payments, payment instructions can be issued.
- Avoid the mountain of paperwork surrounding today's business environment.
- Orders could be raised to reflect both demand and know stock availability.
- Instructions can be issued to the distributor in parallel lines with the order to ensure fast service delivery.

4. Issue and Receive Orders Faster: In all business houses, buying and selling transactions are routine work. EDI helps to handle such work automatically and fast besides relieving the staff from routine work for both more demanding and less routine tasks.

5. Easy Sales: EDI helps to make sales more easily. Various businesses like quotes, estimates, order entry and invoicing will be executed more smoothly, effectively and efficiently. In a global electronic non paper-based system, orders are received electronically and this ensures that information is available virtually immediately. On the other hand, the trading partners can respond faster to various businesses and become more competitive in the global business environment.

6. Easy Collection: Invoices received electronically can be reconciled automatically, which means that they are earmarked for payment in trading partner's accounting department sooner. On the other hand, a concern's purchasing department is in a position to negotiate better turns for faster payments.

7. Avoids Blocking up of Capital: Yet another help that EDI extends is that it minimises the capital tied up in inventory. Every organisation which has implemented EDI will get benefits from reducing the order lead time. Maintenance of optimum and economic lot size or the right balance is crucial particularly in the case of manufacturing organisations with a just-in-time strategy.

8. Letters and Memos: Common business letters and memos are often printed as standard paper forms and the traditional system of communication. But under the electronic system, letters and memos are exchanged by an electronic mail system. Under EDI, they are electronically transmitted directly to the trading partners' computer system.

9. Enquiries: The benefits of the EDI implementation system is dramatic in its result. The system permits customers or suppliers to make direct online enquiries on product availability or other non-sensitive information.

10. Updating: The EDI facilitates bulk updation to catalogues and part listings. The business houses can provide updates of data files, such as calatogues to customers or part listings to franchisees.

11. General Benefits: Time delays are greatly reduced. Mail and processing delays are eliminated.

Uncertainty in timings is eliminated in some cases and reduced in others. This enables a firm to more accurate business transactions.

Content acknowledgement providbves the buyer a fast feedback on whether the order will be filled or whether the buyer must look at other options. This lessens the need for safety stock.

One-time keying means that labour costs can be reduced.

Payment can be processed through the settlement system the day after initiation.

Bottlenecks

They read as follows:

- Adequate and necessary communication infrastructure is not existing.
- The participating companies are not allowed to or refused to adhere strictly to the EDI standards.
- The absence of the value added network.
- The market for all commodities is increasingly becoming global.
- Multinational corporations have been arriving in India and other countries in a big way.
- Integration of business over the internet using e-commerce software have made waves in the US and Europe.
- Internet business particularly B2C presents itself as a big business opportunity.

All these reasons and various other factors resulted in the failure or insignificant use of initial EDI attempts in the country. As a result, the use of the Internet had become necessary and popular in a big way.

❑❑❑

E-commerce over the Internet

Nature and Evolution

Internet is the most efficient platform for accessing information and the potential marketplace today. It allows the customers to place an order simply by logging on to buy and sell things and placing the items they need in an electronic based medium without leaving their chair. E-commerce has opened up new communication pathways for promoting brands, supporting sales of products processing and generating responses from users.

Since the cost of selling up in an e-commerce e-store is considerably less than the real world equivalents, small and medium-sized companies are in a position to compete effectively with larger organisations. The Internet has relatively low cost of information delivery and can be revised and updated with new pricing and enabling users to access information within minutes with the click of the mouse.

Customers are appreciating the security of the Internet which ensures further increase in the growth of sales. The Web is at the erossroads in its evolution, moving towards making the world a global village, spreading information like lighting. Web merchants who experiment with contemporary and new technologies have the opportunity to grow with the web and become business giants with a global presence. Web information technology (WIT) offers a variety of e-commerce sites for small businesses all the way to the large retailers. It provides facilities like shopping cart, security, cybercash processing, on-line catalogue and customer database.

Internet is the borderless medium, offering awesome potential to organisations and individuals to do business on-line. Technology has allowed companies to automate many day-to-day business practices. Strategies to use the new technology should be exploited on the website for substantial financial returns.

A significant change is being initiated in the global business arena, with the Internet as the catalyst for various domains ranging from various internet applications to multimedia and in the process, unearthing tremendous potential for development services for the *'forces'* of the information age.

The global canvas of the Internet and the growing speed and importance of computers have developed a global village comprising of customers and the business fraternity. Today, the most revolutionary development is of the world wide web and the Internet, enabling millions around the world to access the Internet. The growth statistics show extension of the Internet at school, at work as well as in the home where the personal computers reign supreme.

The number of Internet users are multiplying and mushrooming at a fast pace. The total number of internet users is roughly doubling every year. The trend shows that the rate of growth seems to be actually increasing exponentially. There is almost a gold rush environment as far as the internet application is concerned.

Towards the end of the 1990s, the Internet was dominated by academics, students and other university subjects, especially science and engineering.

Things have fast changed, and as late as 1994, the word Internet drew blank stares from most people. By 1997, business people are investing substantially in the application world wide web.

Thus, the Internet is a worldwide mega network of smaller and larger interconnected computer networks.

The Internet represents a genuine revolution in global communication and substantial data exchange. The new revolution has opened unique and exciting opportunities to maximise marketing efforts of business firms and merchants both internally and externally. It provides an access to the vast wealth of information and services available online. It has left an impact on all industrial companies, products or services. Though the technology may be new, the fundamental goals remain the same — that is to effectively expand the marketing and customer areas profitably and in a cost effective way. Today's interactive technologies permit various businesses to achieve goals and objectives in the global business environment.

According to NASSCOM, the number of Internet connections in India stands at 2,80,000 as in the year 1999. The number of people using it stands at 8,00,000.

The Internet economy is creating new sets of dynamic design points yielding new challenges and potential opportunities. In tune with the changes, IT has also been evolving new digital business designs which go beyond the image of selling products on the Net. Businesses are making money with potential online business.

The Net is emerging as a leading business information channel. The number of worldwide web users is fast approaching the 200 million mark.

Today, major corporations are rethinking their business strategies in terms of the Net and its new culture and capabilities. Companies are using the Web by buying parts and supplies from other companies to collaborate on sales promotions and to do joint research. Exploiting commerce, availability and appreciation of the Net by global business has enabled many companies to discover potential strategies to use the Net successfully.

The emergence of new technological innovations in industry and trade usually occurs first in developed countries and moves to the developing countries. The technology transfer continues to be from the first world to the third world countries. Some technologies move fast and some others move slowly. Thus, if we consider the trends in e-commerce development and the predictions of these developments in the advanced countries, we can expect its arrival in the third world country only later. E-commerce developments are expected to be only evolutionary and not revolutionary in nature. This means that no path-breaking or potential innovations that will revolutionise the economic world are likely to take place. To enable such innovations, companies will have to work out potential business strategies.

E-commerce activities have made more progress in the recent years. Trade net, EDI, Nicnet and many other networking organisations have been established. The national economic and telecommunication agencies like VSNL are offering access to the international community by dedicated lines. More and more advanced facilities are equipped to identify the potential foreign markets and interchange appropriate business data electronically. In the beginning of electronic trade, the existing communication network, fax telegram, telephone, e-mail and WAN are widely used. The Net has become the fastest growing communication and advertising method in the recent years.

Concept of Network-Meaning and Nature

The word *'Network'* means anything in the form of a Net which may have many lines crossing each other. A network in connection with the computer environment means 'link' between a number of computers within the organisation and outside. Computer network is a series of interconnected points or channels communicating with each other. An interconnection of a number of computers and/or peripheral devices at distributed locations that transmit information necessarily to perform the functions of the network are potential business standards.

The interconnections are the sum total of various channels and is known as the computer communication network. Thus, a well knitted computer network envisages multi-channels. So, it represents an integrated operating system. A modern complex organisation may have many disseminating centres interconnected by various centres and reflects a potential network.

Computer Networking

Computer network is a mechanism of a collection of a set of computers and network components which are interconnected by communication lines. When they are connected, the system permits network computers and components to communicate and work together. The individual computers in a network system may be distributed within a small office, building, premises or distributed over large a geographical area. There are two separate systems of networking depending upon the location of computers. When the computers are located in a private and limited compact area, it is a local area network (LAN) and when computers are located over a wide geographical area, it is a case of wide area network (WAN).

In recent years, networking has increasingly become common. A computer network is a complex process having two or more computers interconnected. A networking is the capability of the computer which permits to link computers together. The object of this linking is to facilitate communication between computers and information can be exchanged between this interlinking. This interlinking of computers is more useful when the information is to be altered and updated for strategic decision making, control etc.,

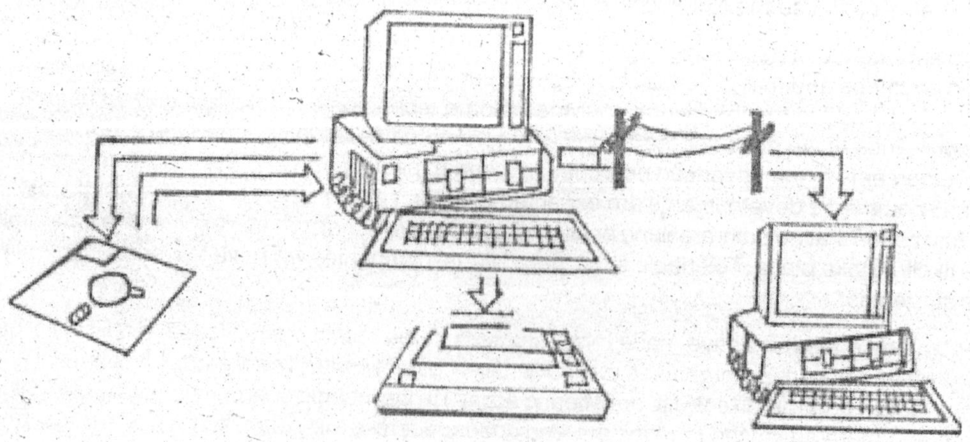

Fig. 3.01 A Network with Communication Links

where the computers are at separate locations and they can be interconnected and used simultaneously. The electronic means help the data being sent to and from between the computers and this is known as networking system. In other words, it is also called as point to point data transmission. Thus, any number of computers can be interconnected to constitute a processing complex in such a way that they can exchange messages or relevant business data. Thus, the linked computers in a network function by sending and receiving messages to each other. Thus, a set of two or more computers interconnected strategically work together as a single unit. From the viewpoint of the users, it is only a single computer unit but not a set of more computers, though there is more than one individual computer in the network. It is a sort of interconnected and interrelated set of independent and individual computers.

It is a system having sub-systems linked with several computers. It is an interface between the computers which are linked. The network facility gives an opportunity to get the computer to talk to another computer. It is the cable with the help of which computers are interconnected.

Modern communication technology permits building up local, national and international networks for effective information communication. The network has great capacity of storing, processing and transmitting information electronically, and any one having access to the network can receive any information from anywhere in the network.

Origin of Networking

It was approximately in the 1960s that intensive research works were undertaken with linking computers to one another and to people through telephone hook-ups. As a result, computers in different locations can be linked using new technology known as *packet switching.*

In the 1970s, a number of developments took place, witnessed the development of rules or protocol for transmitting data between computers and networks. These facilitated the development of the world wide web. Thus, all computers have links in terms of LAN and WAN. By the end of 1970s, these links were developed between counterparts throughout the world. Today, the world is tied together in a worldwide web.

In the 1980s, the group of networks collectively became to be known as the Internet. As a result, a number of individuals, organisations, companies, research institutes, universities and other educational institutions, government departments, agencies, consultants etc., started investing to have a presence on the world wide net. Under this system, any one with a computer and a modem can tap into the potential online business opportunities.

The 1980s is said to be the decade of networking in the history of information technology with both LANs as well WANs working successfully. Thus, there are two types of industries namely LAN manufacturers and WAN manufacturers. In the 1990s, it witnessed a period of progress, a generic marketplace and overlapping product sets. It is a decade of enterprise-wise management.

Features of Networking

- It facilitates to have external communication with outside organisations.
- Frees the executives from the need to change data or churning out business reports.
- Redefines the role of management and transforms the manager's role altogether.
- Permits the user to employ the same type of servers and browsers used for the worldwide web for intranet applications distributed over the local area network of organisations.
- Employees can interact with the business applications and co-workers of any department.

- There is no need to use the same brand of software and hardware before they can share information.
- The ultimate object of developing networking is achieved by making employees more productive.
- The networking system permits the distribution of information quickly, efficiently and particularly in the case of multi-national corporations to a global work-force in several countries.
- Web-based intranet helps to reach the goal of simplification of information sharing.
- Makes global work-force of transnational organisations more cohesive.
- The information is always online, it is real time and constantly improving the quality of data.
- It connects more computers or terminals and makes communication possible between the groups of networks and individual networks.

Advantages of Networking

They read as follows :

- File transfer between computers is easy and convenient.
- Mail transfer by electronic data means eliminating delay and permits quick decision by potential business organisations.
- It performs functions of web browsing as it performs by the Net.
- Easy and quick access, immediate availability information of permits increased production.
- It reduces the labour cost of doing paperwork. The maintenance of paper as used in the conventional organisations can be saved in terms of cost.
- It will enable the company to process the internal telephone listing by all relevant users.
- It saves lot of time and efforts of the employees as the technology permits face to face interaction.
- All the employees within the organisation have access to network and can exchange data easily among themselves.
- The electronic document, text, audio, video, graphics, animation at any one site of the Net can be circulated over the entire organisation.
- The products used on the Net like the web server and power browsers can equally be used on the Net too.
- Quick transactions across its manufacturing units.
- Business concerns and other institutions which are still using paper-based forms can benefit themselves by making transactions through the Internet.
- The system can ultimately reduce paper, printing and distribution cost.

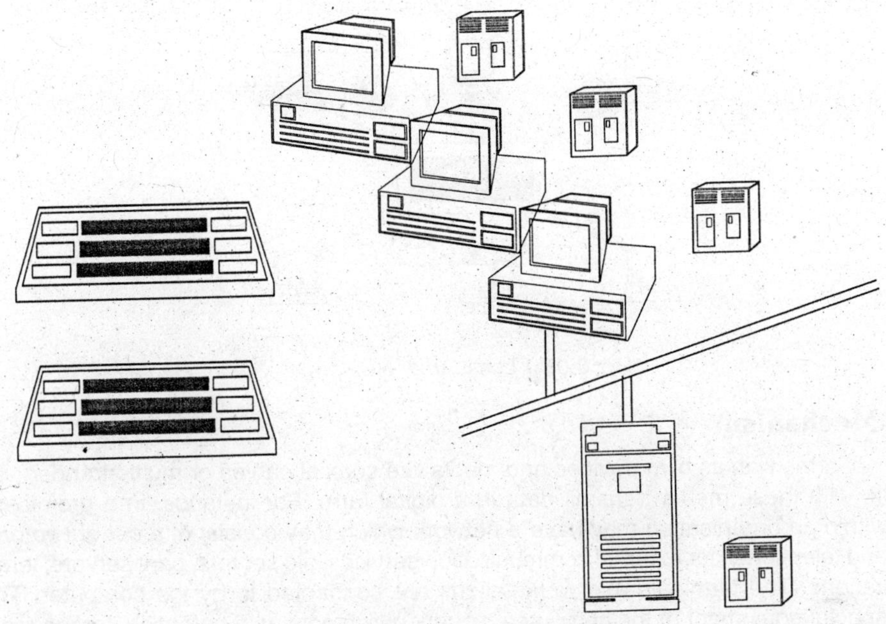

Fig. 3.02 Network Connections

Classification of Networks

The entire computer network can be classified into the following five broad categories. They are LAN, WAN, Internet, Extranet and the Intranet.

The nature and working of these categories is discussed in the following paragraphs :

Local Area Network (LAN)

Local Area Network (LAN) means communication system designed to link neighbouring computers that are located within a compact area such as an office, building or a campus. LAN is an independent and privately owned and organised communication system most effective within a particular premises.

The individual computers or group of computers may be located within the same building or in several closed or individual buildings owned by a private organisation, department, company or university etc.

When a set of two or more computers are interconnected in a single room or rooms within a building or buildings on a premises or a site, the system is usually known as the LAN.

A single PC is a stand alone set on a desktop with the facility to share the data stored in one or more. The individual PC is a work station, which lets several users to use the same computer programs, equipment and share relevant information. LAN is designed as a multi-user environment to facilitate the sharing of vast computer resources like printer, disk, central processing unit etc.

For instance, an organisation having several mini-computers located far apart can be interconnected. But it is to be noted that the LAN system is different from the mainframe computer system. LAN may cover a limited geographical area and maybe ranging about 8 to 10 kms or more.

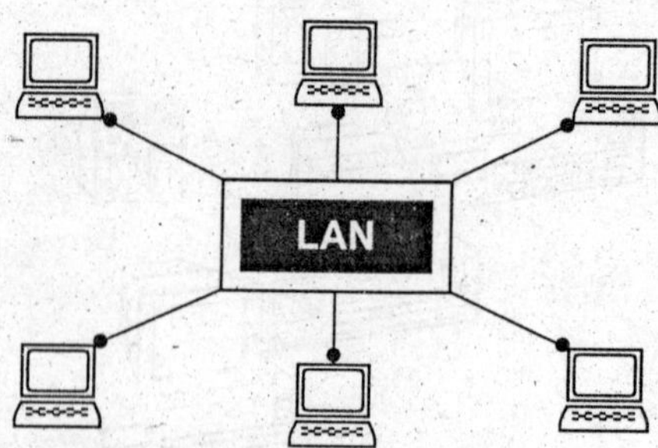

Fig. 3.03 A Local Area Network

Working Mechanism

LAN operates with its own devices and media like coaxial cables or multi-stranded cables. LAN network with these media transmit data in a digital farm. For instance, in a premises or a single site within an organisation may have a network which may consist of a set of two or more computers and telephones for external communication services, file servers, print servers, terminals and work stations. The terminals and workstations are connected to by the computer. The file server is a special equipment of the computer network which acts as a potential storage medium.

Any independent computer in the network can use stored data from the file server of the network. Similarly, the print server also is a similar one which functions to print it. The network may have an external communications server having a set of two or more telephones on the LANs. LAN with the help of the external communication server can communicate between equipments on the networks and receiving system outside LAN. In the local area network, the electronic mail is a popular facility available. In some LANs however, one computer may be shared in handling the electronic mail called the mail server. So, on a LAN, the user can communicate with *the mail server* when dealing with the mail.

It is basically a digital communication network which interconnects various computers located in a well described locality. A LAN is known for high speed data transmission rates. The rate may range from a few hundred kilobytes per second to a few megabytes per second.

Network Speed

Based on the rate of speed, the networks have been categorised into the following types :

High Speed Networks: Local area networks have designed to provide links between large main frames. They permit over twenty million bytes per second (MBps) to be transmitted.

Medium Speed Networks: The networks have been designed to link with smaller mainframe and mini computers. The rate of speed of these LANs ranges from one MBps and 20 MBps.

Low Speed Networks: The bytes that can be transferred in case of low speed personal computer network is very much restricted. About one MBps can be transmitted over the low speed personal computer networks. They are developed to provide a link between personal computers and various brands of personal computers grouped together.

Factors for Designing LAN

The following are the various reasons for designing LAN. Until the introduction of LAN, computing facilities were mostly contrasted, and each computing place was independent of other computers working in the same organisation. They have become isolated and individual sets and are not shared by others. With the recent advancement in the field of electronic technology, hardware and software, digital electronics has substantially contributed for designing the LAN system. However, there are a number of factors necessitated for developing such a networking. The following factors underline the importance of interconnection of various computer system in locality and bring the local area networks into the picture.

1. ***Centralised System:*** Until the advent of LAN, computing facilities in all organisations were mostly centralised. Recently, the computing requirements of an organisation have increased significantly between the computers and accordingly, interconnecting has become, necessitated.

2. ***Many Small Computers:*** It is also increasingly recognised that the utility of a large number of small computing facilities throughout the organisation can be increased in many ways, if there can be an interconnection between the computers. The important consideration is that the effective communication between computers is indispensable for management information systems, decision making etc.

3. ***Recognising Capability:*** Many organisations and institutions and other end users greatly recognised that the microcomputers have much or more capabilities than the most commonly used mainframes.

4. ***Non-Sharing PCs:*** One of the primary reasons for personal computers having a significant appeal is that they are a personal, individual tool and not shared by many others. Thus, PCs have become individual, and to a certain extent, underutilised.

5. ***Individual Productive Tool:*** It is the objective of any organisation to make their staff more productive. One of the best ways is to make the human resources in any organisation more productive and provide them with computers, particularly for managerial, personnel and other levels. One of the major machines providing information and communication of the present·day is the personal computer.

6. ***Unlinked Individual Computer:*** The driving force behind the use of the PC is to give each user an independent computing power. Thus, each centre has become unconcerned and unlinked with other computers. This prevents equal distribution of resources and access to all types of information.

7. ***No Communication Between Computers:*** Decision making on sound lines requires information from different computing centres. If different functional departmental computers are interconnected, then there is an easy access to varied information. Thus, the lack of communication between computers has led to developing a networking system. Computers need to communicate to reach the users in the organisations. A communication implies the generic process of transferring information from one individual to another.

Today, micro-computers or personal computers have as much as capability than the most commonly used mainframe computers. This is the reason why large organisations acquired and installed large number of small computers. Thus, all these factors underline the importance of interconnection of various computer systems in a premises and thus bring the local area network into the picture.

LAN Hardware

The hardware components of LAN may include the following :

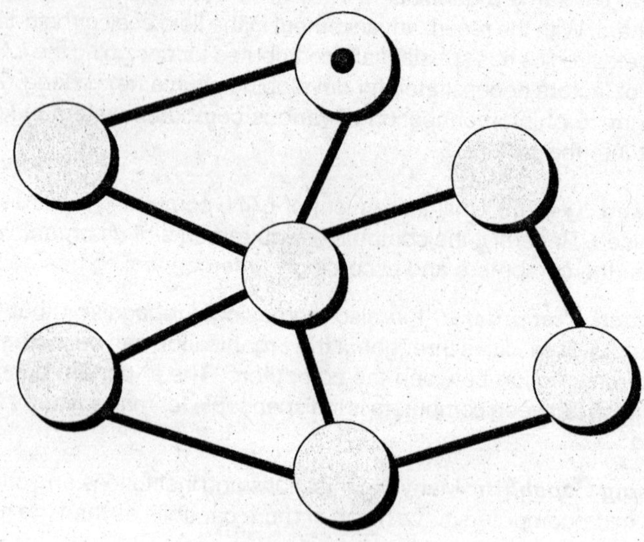

Fig. 3.04 Multi-LAN Links

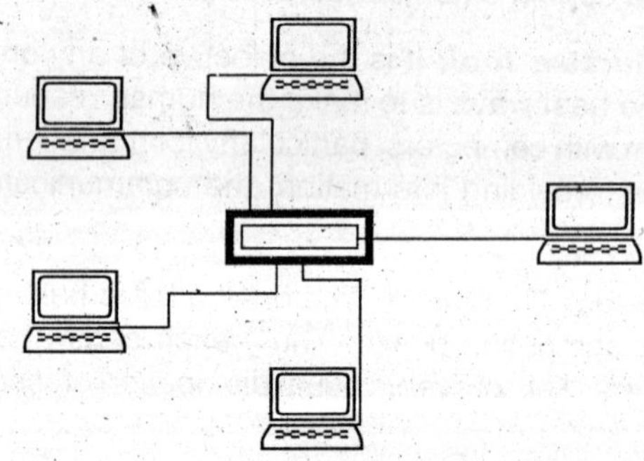

Fig. 3.05 Multi-LAN

Transmission Channel

LAN uses the following types of channels for data communication :

1. Twisted Pair Cable: It is made up of two insulate copper wires, twisted together. They are protected from spurious noise signals. This type of cable is used for short distance and the cable of transferring one-two megabytes per second.

2. *Coaxial Cables:* These cables are used for data transfer over a long distance. They are solid cables. Lower transfer loss and higher transfer are the features of the larger cable diameter. There are two types of coaxial cables namely 75 ohm and 50 ohm.

3. *Fibre Optic Cable:* A glass or plastic fibre is used in the fibre optics cable. They carry signals in the form of fluctuating light. The glass or plastic is thick as human hair. The data is transferred through the cable as pulses of light.

4. *Radio Waves:* Radio waves are used for voice communication. Waves cover a large area, are inexpensive and permits portable workstations but its drawbacks are insecurity and low rate of transfer.

5. *Network Interface Unit (NIU):* It is used to implement LAN protocol. All devices in the LAN are connected by network interface units.

6. *Servers:* The types of servers used in LAN include print server, file server and modem server.

LAN Software

LAN has a separate operating system which permits the sharing of resources like the printer, storage space etc. There are various types of operating systems-namely Novell Netware, LAN Server, Omninet, PC Net, IBM PC LAN and Etherlink Plus.

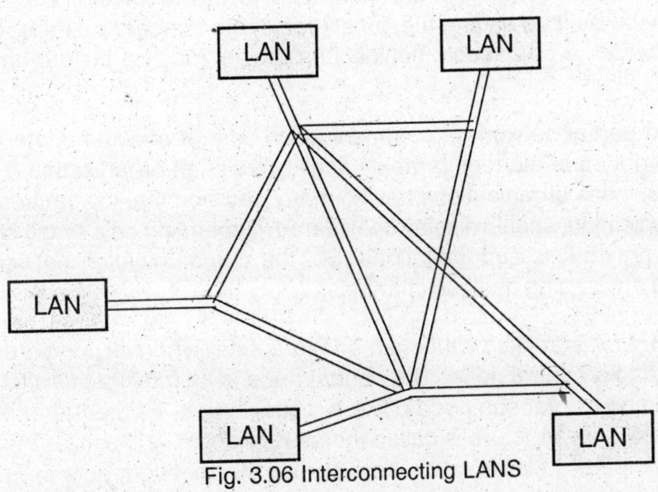

Fig. 3.06 Interconnecting LANS

Hub in Networking

Hub is one of the common components of the devices used in a network. It is called *the networking hub.* It is a centralised distribution point for all traffic on network. It acts like liason or centre for distribution. It means that it receives messages from the senders and stores once they are transmitted. The in-bound traffic arrives at the hub which receives and reproduces data to the computer connected to the same hub.

Network Topologies

Network topology consists of a lay-out or pattern of connection between the computers. In this type of structure, a single computer under the system acts as a server. It is also called as control computer whose responsibility operates as supervisor or act as a liason which directs and maintains the network In case of some other network structures, there will be no control computer or server. We now look into various types of network which seem possible to construct.

Any number of standard networks can be designed and developed to meet the requirements of the organisation. In case of LAN, there is the star or chain network structure which connects computers as per suitability. There may be several designs of LANs namely ring, bus, circle, mesh, tree etc or physical configuration. For instance, in case of a star LAN, it has a central controller and all network centres hook up to it. Similarly, in case of a bus LAN, a single cable is run and routed touching various centres on its route to provide a network linkage. In case of ring or circle LAN, each station having the equipment is hooked up together.

Types of Networks

We cannot suggest a particular line of communication network topology as universally suitable and applicable to all types of organisations.

The building up of a design depends upon the number of factors like size, nature of channel, number of persons and the complexity of an organisation's network. The objectives that are to be kept in mind in building a network is to achieve the purpose of communication i.e. prompt and accurate flow of information which is understandable to the receiver, listener or the reader. A simple network may be built up having the constituents, the sender and receiver. This is known as *circular communication*. A partial communication network may be built up that connects only two departments.

The simple and partial network of communication cannot accommodate all aspects of an organisation and may not meet the requirements of all types of an organisation. The requirements of modern complex business organisations having many decision making centres, interconnected by channels of communication, should also be considered. Depending on a single chain of command is fraught with many drawbacks and limitations. So, the communication network should reflect *multi-dimensional* and envisaging multiple channels.

1. *Star Network:* A star like picture is made to appear when all computers (nodes) in the network are connected to a central node. The central node is an intelligent switch which can only provide a data connection for various nodes, like a digital PABX. Exchange of information takes place via a central point. This structure is called the start of origin. It is similar to that of telephone central switch. The computer located at the centre, in a star network acts as a server, through which all communication must go through, any message must first be sent to the server which in turn retransmit the message to the destination. The problem in this star structure is that if the control computer fails the entire network suffers.

A star LAN has a central controller that provides interface by the network stations.

2. *Circle or Ring:* In the ring configuration, it forms a complete ring, wherein in nodes are connected in series. As a result, data flows from one node to the other until it is picked up by the appropriate target node. In order to control network access, a number of devices have been designed.

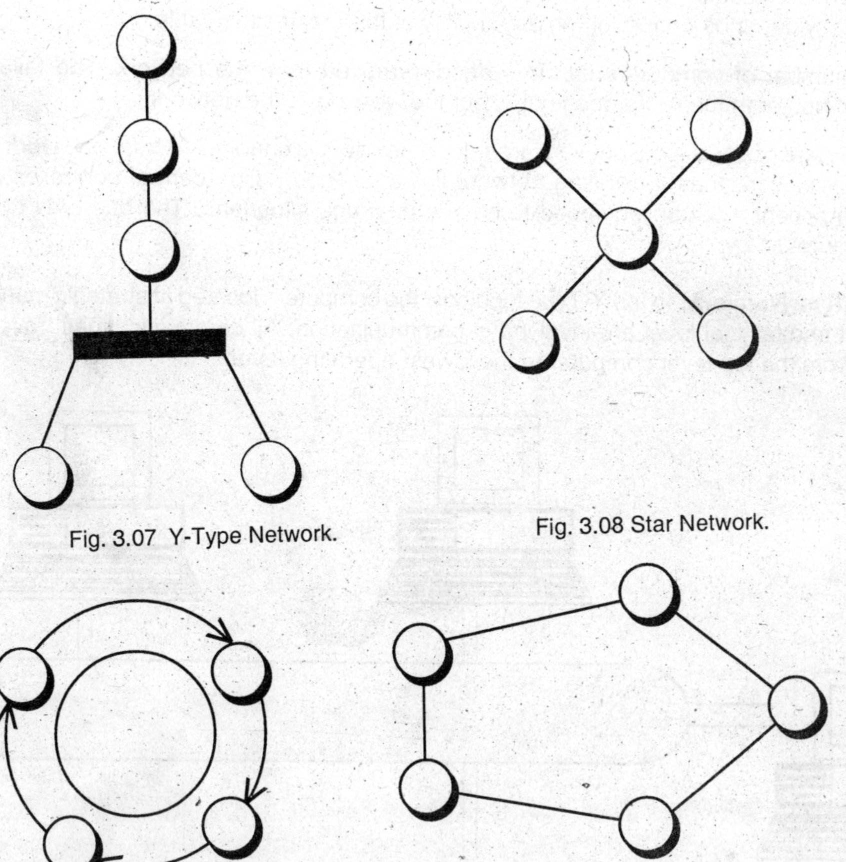

Fig. 3.07 Y-Type Network.

Fig. 3.08 Star Network.

Fig. 3.09 Circle Network.

Fig. 3.10 Loop Network.

In this network, each computer is hooked together to form a circle or ring configuration. Further, all workstations are linked to form a continuous circle. The data flows around the circle and the electrical signals pass around the ring from one centre to another.

In circle topology, the computers are arranged in such a way that all computers connected look like a ring. In this network, all communication can be sent by any computer to another around the ring. The messages go through round the ring. The cable takes the form to make a complete loop.

3. *Bus Network:* In the bus configuration, the technique of the node is not used. There is no central node to connect all the computers. Here, all the computers operating in a network share the same medium *i.e.* the cable. A number of devices have been designed to control the access of the network. There is a single cable to which all computers are connected. It is also called as the *broadcast* bus.

One computer broadcasts the message and all other individual computers in the system have to accept the message. We call this topology as bus network. The bus is the cable to which the computers are connected. All communications must go along the bus. The reliability and efficiency of bus topology depends on the length and quality of the connecting cable.

Any number of computers can be added, removed from the network. The failure of the individual computer in the route does not affect the working of the network.

In the case of a bus local network area, a single cable is channelled from one work station to another work station, thus facilitating network linkage. There is no central controller and each network component must be equipped to handle interface situations. The bus LAN appears as shown in Figure 3.11.

4. Y-Type Network: In the Y-Type topology, the computers located at strategic management, middle level and tactical level are involved in communication. All communications travel through downward from the top level computer to the lowest operating level.

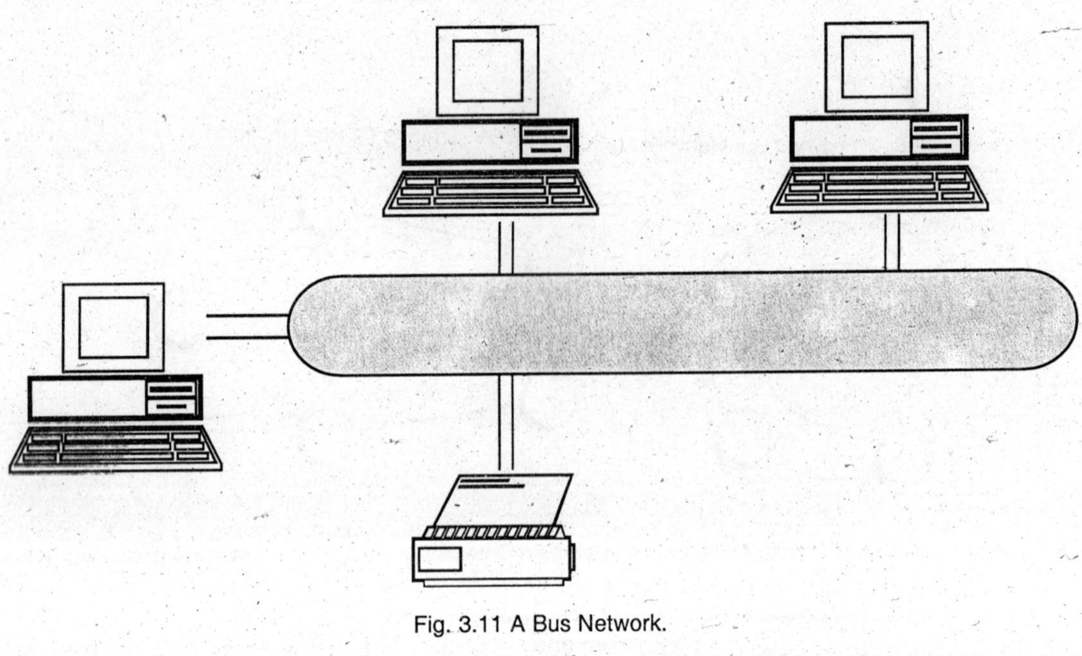

Fig. 3.11 A Bus Network.

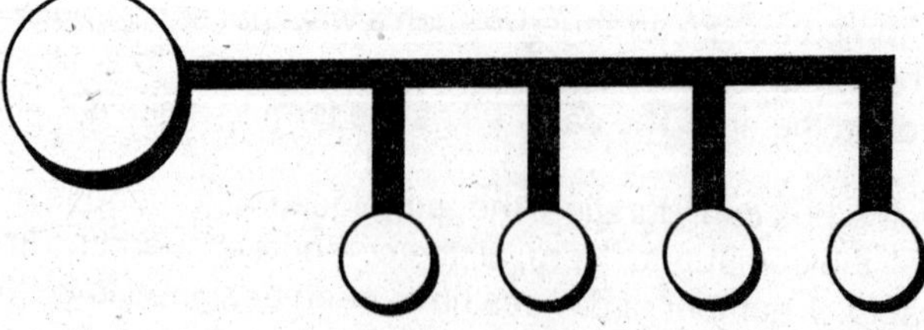

Fig. 3.12 Multi-drop Network.

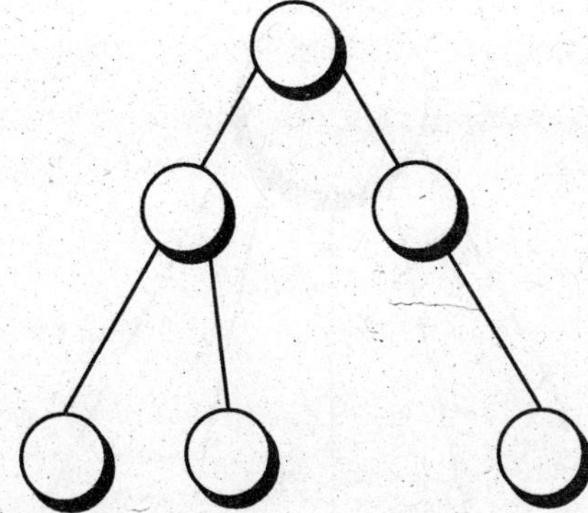

Fig. 3.13 Tree Network.

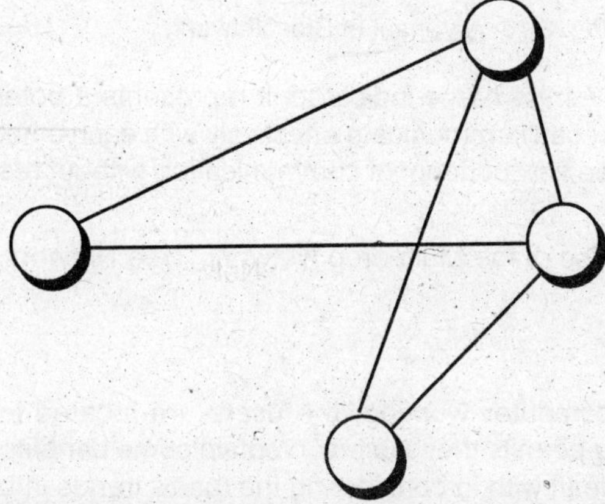

Fig. 3.14 Mesh Network.

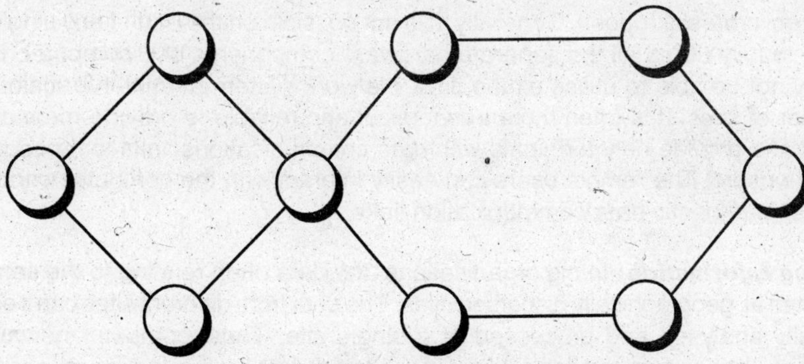

Fig. 3.15 Interconnected Rings.

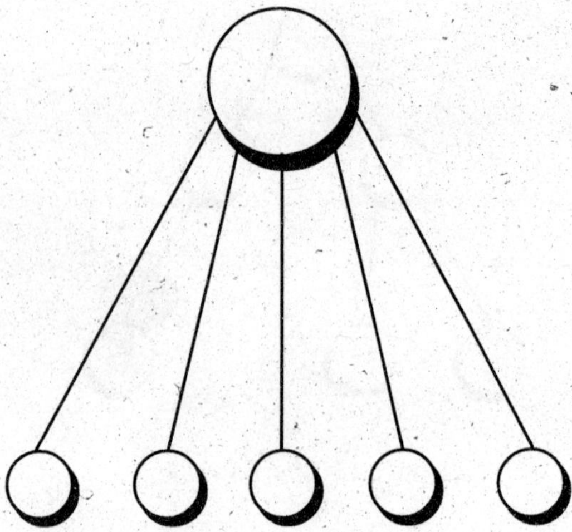

Fig. 3.16 A Variant of Star Network.

5. *Free Flow Network:* As the name indicated, it represents a potential communication structure, wherein every computer can communicate effectively with each other. The network figure shown is representative of the free flow concept of communication without restriction of the formal structure.

The other channels comprise of the Multi-drop Network, Tree Network, Mesh Network and Interconnected rings.

Advantages of LAN

In a network system of computer working, the users are located in their geographical distributed areas. The networking permits these users to obtain some benefits. The significance of computer networks will now be dealt with in considering the future trends in business details.

1. *Sharing of Resources:* Networks permit the sharing of physical resources. Computer physical resources that can be shared include software, discs, tapes, processors, memory, uninterrupted power supply, air conditioning, skilled operators, maintenance staff etc.

All these will add to the cost of installation besides large computers not only big in size but also costing several crores of rupees. Generally, it is not possible on the part of any single user who may not be able to fully utilise all the separate hardware components of a computer. Even if it is possible, he may not be able to utilise all the time. Network system permits full scale computing facilities a number of sites. It is often more economical and reliable to provide them at one or at most a few sites and provide only terminals with data communications links to its geographically distributed remote users. The remote users can easily interact with the computer with the help of these terminals and authentic data communication links.

2. *Sharing Information:* In big organisations, the data often relating to the same general subject is generated at geographically dispersed sites. The data from different sites can be connected and systematically analysed and processed at a single site. Thus, computer networks permit information sharing that makes available the consolidated data to the individual geographically distributed users at remote sites. The network technology permits vertical flow information i.e.

upward and downward. In addition, it is possible to design a computer network structure to permit hierarchical flow of data. With the help of the computer network, data can be transmitted to a larger computer as well as retrieve data from the larger computer through the network. Sitting at a terminal, the users can exchange and share information and queries and responses are conveyed through the network.

3. *Communication Links:* Terminals and computers are important components in the network to establish communication links by using existing communication channels for sending data between computers or between terminals. The channels of communication presently existing are telephone lines, microwave radio, optical fibre, cables and satellite links.

In communication, the most important piece of equipment is the modem which modifies electrical characteristics to suit these channels. Its function is modulation and demodulation. At another end channel, another modem changes the data received from the channel back into the original computer recognisable form.

Today, communication is supported by computer related support systems. LAN facilitates faster, wide and accurate communication which are indispensable in any decision making process. Managers spend quantity time in communication either orally or written form. The LAN concept of communication lets them expedite this communication among several levels and groups for exchanging data, sending messages and sharing information. LAN facilitates inhouses computer to computer communication reliably and speedily because of easy access to remote resources.

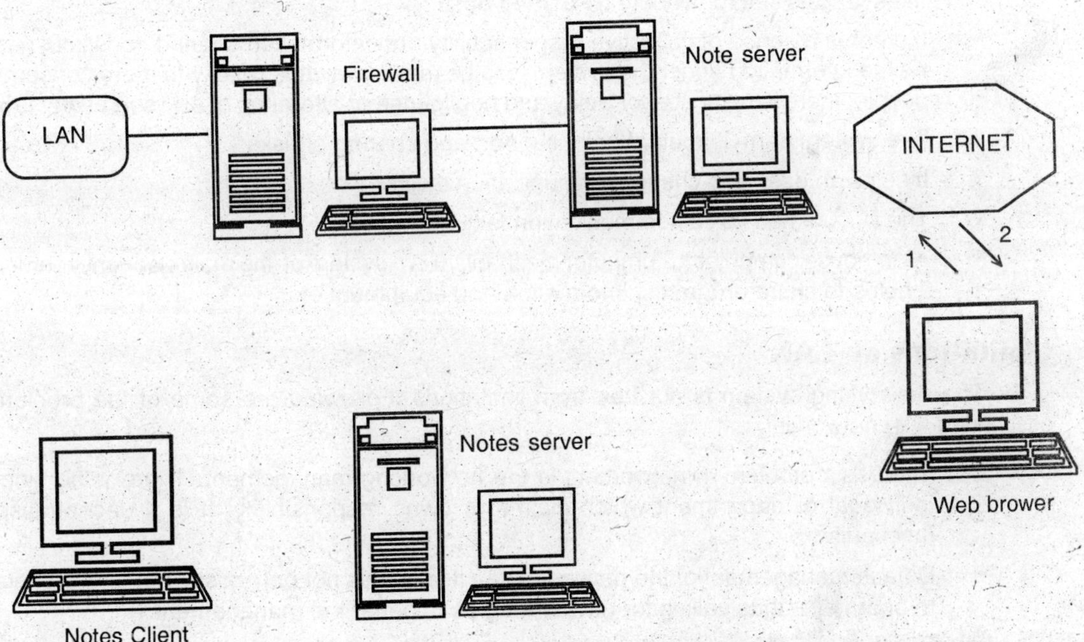

Fig. 3.17 Connecting LAN to the Internet.

4. *Time:* It is commonly seen that a lot of time is wasted in the preparation of final draft of any report or text document. Similarly, heavy amount of stationery is wasted in offices to prepare several drafts of documents before the final version is approved. Networking helps greatly to solve these two major problems. So, networking can be applied in the field of desk top publishing. All the computers within an office or an entire building are linked and texts and documents are passed around the office or building for review and improvement and subsequently seeing to it that the final version of the report/ document can be printed.

5. *Management Tools:* LAN is a management tool of getting the things done through people effectively and efficiently. In these days of changing needs of working conditions and organisations, the information technology oriented LAN lets the management to solve its basic problems. LAN acts as the monitoring and management control system which improves the performance of repetitive nature, relieving the worker from fatigue, boredom and introducing the elements of variety and novelty in routine work.

The other advantages continue below :

- There is no need to use large mainframe computers. It permits to employ a network of servers on desktop machines to do the same function.
- It operates at lower prices and higher flexibility.
- The networking system is of great help for services, businesses and small contracting business.
- The system connects the base computer via the modem which instantly enables to see the available slot for work to be carried out.
- It creates a sense of collective responsebility and information sharing consciousness. As the information under the system is to be made available readily to more concerned people, there is no scope for delay and negligence or alteration of any sort at any level.
- The system permits mutual help, support and sharing of risks.
- It helps an easy and cheap communication facility.
- The system has voice communication facility also.
- As in-house computer to computer mechanism is a system of the multi-user environment, it helps to share programs, information and equipment etc.

Limitations of LAN

The networking system is not free from limitations. Following are some of the problems associated with networking :

- The basic problem in networking is the networking management. There is no single individual or department which claims or owns responsibility. It is a decentralised mechanism.
- Default management of the network when it fails. It is not only costly but also complex to operate — thus calling for new strategies to better the management.
- Preservation of integrity of networking at all costs and levels is a difficult task unless automatic connections are provided.
- Configuration management problem which includes monitoring and controlling total networking from any point on the network.

- Any minor breakdown in the networking component may affect the operation of the whole networking. The day-to day maintenance of the network is a costly affair, and it is time consuming and requires expertise to manage it.
- Its working is complex, i.e. complex multi-vendor, multi-protocol, multimedia and so the technology requires global know-how.
- Design, procurement, project management and installation of cable and infrastructure will take a considerable amount of time. Small organizations therefore cannot afford to go for the installation of LAN or WAN.
- Problems like frequent technological changes, indigenous host suppliers can be usurped by the new cost competitive start-up, other modifications and alteration costs to the existing information technology cannot be ignored.
- There is a problem of password.
- Virus and software bugs problem may destroy the entire networking system.

Distributed Computing

In systems approach, there are two types of computing systems. They are Integrated Information System and Distributed Systems.

An integrated information system has several practical problems. The failure of the system may adversely affect the entire system.

In order to solve this problem, the concept of distributed system or distributed computing has emerged as an *alternative* to the integrated system which also has sub-systems.

The network computing is called as *distributed computing* as distinct from monolithic centralised mainframe computing. But this distinction is also largely disappearing as mainframe computers are being networked to PCs and mainframe computers acting as potential *servers.*

Network File Server

In case of LAN, the users store files on a file server which is a computer in the network and which is the central node. The file server can access data files. In a network, there are peripherals like printers, printer queues and modem etc. Among them, the file server in a LAN acts as a central hub to share the peripherals.

The purpose of a file server is to store files for application but the server does not involve in the processing of an application. The file server sends all or part of the data. When a file is saved, it copies the data file back to the file server across the network.

Limitations of the Network File Server

They read as follows :

- The drawback of this system does not permit simultaneous access to a single data set by multiple users. It means that it does not serve the data concurrently.
- Because of heavy traffic, the network can quickly become saturated.
- File server operates in files which are large database sets.
- The system prevents the user from sharing a file when another user is locked out.

Client/Server System (C/S)

The limitations and practical (operation) problems associated with the file server system led to the genesis of the client server system. It has the advantages of the network computing model along with the stored data access. Any local area network can be considered as client/server system.

Origin: The client/server computing system was first used in the late 1970s and started becoming popular and is being used regularly since the early 1980s.

Meaning: Client/server computing is a group of two or more computer systems connected via the network with associated software. The system is the main driving force of the growth of computing in economically potential areas, particularly in various businesses, banking and the Net. Both the server and the client have hardware and software components and packages. C/S computing is an architecture in which a system's, functionality and processing are divided between the client and a server.

Meaning and Nature of Server: The *server* is a computer and its software provides relevant services for other computers connected to it via the network. The server is called the *Back End.* The big computer that your modem dials to access the Net is the server or host on the internet which often has information available to those accessing the Internet. A server (back-end) gives stress on efficiently managing resources such as databases of information. Its main job is to manage resources optimally among various clients. The server manages the database among various clients.

For instance, in a banking application, a large computer is placed in a separate room as opposed to the personal computer on the desktop of the computer clerk, which is a client or the location is the server in which all the transactions and customer details are stored. The server with its software searches the information and sends it to the clients on a regular basis.

Meaning and Nature of Client: The Client is the computer with its software requesting for some services from the server. The client is called *Front End.* You are the client. People use *'Client'* software to access information available on servers.

Netscape is a web client giving access to information on a web server. The work-stations are clients who request services such as data, program files or printing from the server. A Client application (the front end) is the part of the system that users apply to interact with the data. The clients send requests and analyse the data that they received from the server.

For instance, in a banking application, the personal computer on the desk of the counter clerk is the client.

Whenever an enquiry is made, the client sends a request to the server giving particular details.

Benefits of Client / Server System: There are many benefits in the case of client/server model which solves all problems associated with the network/file server system. The following are some of the benefits of this system :

- The client and the server are the parts of the system generally run on separate computers. The server can store voluminous data and meet the requirements of the client's requests.
- The system is less expensive, with minimum disk storage and the memory is sufficient.

- Any number of users can be accommodated with productive, easy to use tools to enter and analyse the data.
- Client/server system satisfies the principles of flexibility. It is not rigid and allows all the inevitable types of hardware and software changes. This flexibility tends to take out that old server and plug in new servers without disturbing its functionality.
- Scalability feature is another benefit of this system. It permits scalability easily to accommodate changes in a work group. When many new workers are formed, it permits to plug into the network systems with the new client workstation.
- This system also focusses on the areas of system development. It means that each functional component can specialise to do something in the best possible way.
- Another benefit of this system is towards cost saving.
- It provides instant access to information for decision making, facilitate communication and reduce time efforts and cost for accomplishing the task.
- The system displays information on the users' requests, even though all data and information may be distributed in multi servers.
- The system can be integrated with other technologies like e-mail, document, imaging etc.
- It uses object-oriented technology in designing tools, enabling quicker development of applications.
- It permits integration of applications developed on different types of hardware and software, cutting down the software development project cost.
- The great problem is software maintenance particularly in the mainframe system.
- The functional departments of an organisation can be computerised and integrated. For instance, production, design, planning, finance and other departments can be integrated.
- With the internet technology being easily available, the order despatch to vendors, receipt of customers' orders, and tracking of shipments can be integrated with other functions like purchase, sales, shipping etc. The treasury function is to be integrade with the banking function and connected to the bankers.

Components of Client/Server

A client server system has four distinct components. Each focusses on a specific job. They are: database server, mail server, application server and network.

Based on the services rendered by the server, they are designated as the components mentioned above.

1. Database Server: A file or a database server stores all the data and information in an efficient way and provides the same to the client on request. The database server mainly deals on the following :

- To deal with a single database of information among many concurrent users.
- Controlling database access and other security requirements.
- Protecting database and
- Centrally enforcing global data.

2. Mail Server: A mail server receives, sends and stores the mail received for the clients connected to it. An internet service provider will have a mail server and a web browsing server including an internet user using the PC.

The e-mail software and web users are the software residing with the client and get connected to either of the servers based on the user's request. It is possible that on the same computer, both the server's software and hardware may reside with the same computer doing dual functions.

3. Client Application: A client application is called the Front End. It is a part of the network system that users apply to interact with the available data. Based on the requirements and design of the system, the business logic of the application may be shared between the front and back end. The client application's tasks are requesting and receiving information, validating data entry and performing application logic etc.

4. Network: Another component of the client server system is the network. The physical network may be twisted cable, ethernet cables or optical fibres. A large network widely dispersed may also consist of other components like hubs, routers and bridges etc.

The network and communication software are the vehicles that transmit data between the clients and the server in a system. Both the clients and the server run communication software effectively that allows them to talk across a network.

Network Software

The available network software are Microsoft NT, Novell Net ware and Unix.

1. Name Server: Name server contains databases of internet host addresses which translate word address into numeric equivalents.

2. Host: The individual machines at a particular location are generally called as hosts. The resource of a host machine is usually shared and can be utilised by any user on the Net.

Wide Area Networks (WANs)

Originally, the system of Wide Area Network (WAN) originated in the later part of 1960s mainly for research purposes. A number of autonomous computers located over a large remote geographical area is called the Wide Area Network. Opposed to LAN, WANs are used to transmit data over a long distance but not within a complex. They objectively connect a set of two or more computers on different and separate sites, separate cities or even located in other countries. The WAN system transmits data using separate devices like optical fibre media and satellite transmissions.

Accordingly, WAN uses packet switching methods or message switching methods. The special characteristic features of WAN are that different computers are located at different geographical areas and each have their own interconnections to the main network. The point of intersection of concentration is called the *gateway*. Thus, several computers are linked over a large distance in the WAN system. For instance, railway networking, airlines, intercity and intercontinental network are the categories of WAN.

Modem is one of the computer equipments which help to transfer data from one place to another and which are located at distance places. It allows sending information to a distant place by using personal portable computers with a modem. So, these can be transmitted from a distance field of business to the office computer via the telephone. For instance, it pertains to connecting office computers with that of salesmen who are away from the office. A networking system facilitates salesmen, dealers and others to have direct access to inventory files to know about the stock levels available. Recording is carried on instantly without delay.

Wide Area Network can be used to communicate, send and receive information within an office, between its branches, distributors, factory, salesmen etc. anywhere in an instant. It is a computer-based electronic network messaging system for corporate requirements and conditions. It has revolutionised the communication between offices, branches, warehouses, dealers and distributors etc. Businesses can receive reports in time or send instructions from where they can communicate to their branches, distributors or vendors located across the country. Thus, when a number of autonomous computers are located over large remote geographical areas, it is called WAN.

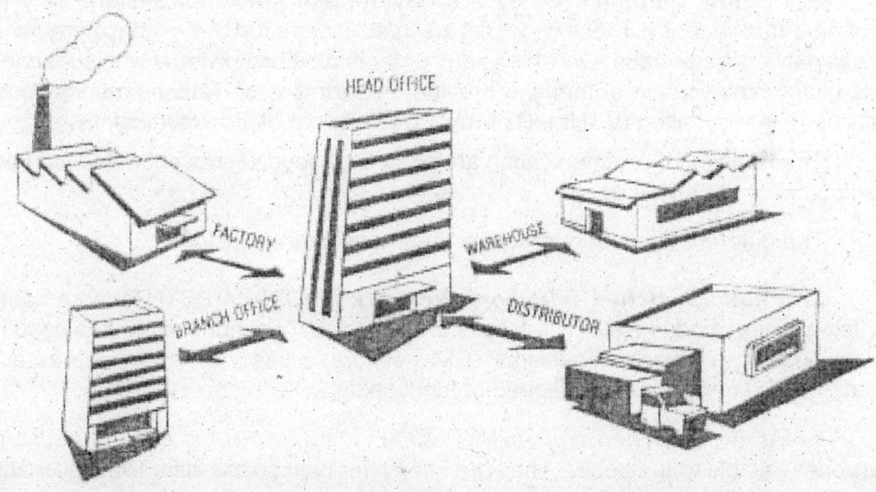

Fig. 3.18 Wide Area Network.

Objectives of WAN

They read as follows :

- To provide an effective communication between scattered sites.
- To share hardware and software by several users.
- To make accessible computer facilities available on sites to a larger community of users.
- To replace mail, cable and telex transmission and
- To enhance handling capacity.

The existing telephone networks are used to establish WAN to reach remote databases for the public bulletin board. Network services are leased from the vendor.

Types of Wide Area Network (WAN)

There are two types of wide area networks: private network and public network.

1. Private: A network designed and developed by one organisation is a private network wherein leased circuits (i.e. telephone lines) are to be used for installing WAN. Private WANs have a limited capacity to data and communication transmission. The first private net is ARPANET (Advanced Research Project Agency), an United States Network. Its creation was funded in 1969 as ARPANET and was designed to develop a geographically dispersed and reliable communication network for military use. The basic feature in case of all private WANs is to use private circuits to link the location which is to be served by the network. Another distinctive feature is that the user or the owner of the network has complete freedom to use the circuits in any manner they want. The owners of the network can utilise their circuits either to carry large quantities of data or for high speed transmission. They have every freedom to use any level of standard of technology available. But private networks generally have to notify telecommunication authorities by way of furnishing some particulars like location, circuits, modem, multiplexers and other ways of communication used.

2. Public Network: They are government networks designed by the government departments or agency. These networks are installed and run by the telecommunication authorities. These networks are made available to any organisation or individual who subscribe to this system. The telecommunication authorities are the Department of Telecommunications (DoT), Videsh Sanchar Nigam Limited (VSNL), Railways, Department of Communications etc.

The facilities of communication are shared by several subscriber individuals, organisations, institutions or departments.

The different types of public wide area network may include :

3. Public Switched Telephone Network (PSTN): A PSTN is more useful and designed for telephones, modems etc. It is mostly used for data communication. It is used in conjunction or as an adjunct to other mechanisms. This network is used for fax machines available at every location. It is known for its low speed of functioning.

4. Public Switched Network (PSDN): It is used in the case of public packet switched network available to the public. They are known for high speed also. Reliability and quality are the features of PSDN. It is designed in such a way so as to link the computer system and networks of one institution to many other institutions. It is commonly used for electronic mail services.

5. Value Added Services (VADs): In this service, there is the service provider who processes, stores and manipulates the data which is carried to the network for transmission. This service adds value to the data. The best example of VADs is electronic data interchange. This service permits trading partners to exchange trading and business documents like invoices, transportation and purchase orders. The VSNL is the provider of value added services in India.

In this, the owners of the Net and its users are put into separate categories. The users take network service on a rental basis by way of subscription. On the other hand, the owner designs and maintains this network. The subscribers link their equipment to the networks' facility offered by an external agency. It is a distinct mechanism of organised data communication network wherein the owner leases communication facilities and computers to manage communication link such as microwave station, communication satellite, trans-oceanic cables and other computer-supported communication systems. A network becomes value added on grounds as to what a computer adds to provide capability between the devices.

6. Integrated Services Digital Network (ISDN): This digital network is also a networking concept which uses digital transmission media. It integrates both circuits and the packet switching technique. The talephone networks have been utilising digital transmission facilities. Today, the trend is towards global application of the ISDN technology which offers fast digital connectivity. ISDN has the capability of providing for the integration of voice, video, data, fax and other advanced services.

This is a new service from Us-west that allows you to connect to computers at speeds of 56 or 64 kbps. To use ISDN, you must have it installed by US-West and have the ISDN device on each end of the connection. ISDN devices can bridge over two 'B Channel' for 12/128 kbps bandwidth.

Features and Advantages of ISDN

They read as follows :

- It is based on digital communication technology
- No voice interference
- High reliability
- Reduces retransmission
- Transmits data at the rate of 64 kbps per channel
- Data rates are higher
- Reduces waiting time for users because the latency of data transmission is smaller
- It carries both voice and data
- Offers flexibility to the users
- The operating cost is less hence it is cost-effective
- It works with two nodes namely Basic Rate Access (BRA) and Primary Rate Access (PRA).
- The speed of ISDN connection makes the graphics rich
- Permits to access websites and is usable
- Performance of PCs at home is improved
- The integration networks and services provide advantages for all those involved in the overall communication.
- Reduces cost in the offices as well as in the home environment.
- Two different networks are run to provide services such as telephones and data communication.
- ISDN accelerates the flow of information which not only increases the transmission speed but also multiplies it.
- Convenient features which increased its practical value are :
  - Call waiting
  - Diversion of calls
  - Automatic call-back
  - Logging of incoming calls
  - Calling number indication

- Do not disturb
- Conference calls
- Call charge indication and Transferred change calls and
- Packet Switched Network

Packet Switched Network: A packet is a block of data whose maximum length is fixed like a letter and the packet of information is sent from one place to another. A packet switched network is designed to meet the specific needs of subscribers requiring terminal-to-terminal, terminal-to-host and host-to-host communication. In the packet switched network, a sender's data is divided into blocks of data called the *packet.* Each packet includes an address along with headers and control information for the routing purposes. A packet switched network uses time flow and protocol network mangament throughout each data transmission sequence.

Packets are routed individually via the most efficient art from the point of origination to their destination where they are reassembled into their correct order. Packet assembler and disassembler (PAD) converts the data into packets then transmits the packets over the network to another PAD at its destination where it is converted back to its original form. In public packets network, packets travel over shared network facilities, eliminating the cost of a dedicated line between the sender and the receiver. The sender and the receiver just require an access line to the closest network access points.

Gateway Packet Switched Service (GPSS): Gateway Packet Switched Services is India's public Switched Packet Data Networks (PSPDN), and is the gateway to another international PSPDN. Gateway Packet Switched Network of VSNL connects Packet Switching Exchanges at Mumbai, New Delhi, Kolkata and other switches. The GPSS network is expressly provided for data transmission whereas PSTN is basically designed carrying speech.

WAN Devices/Hardware

Business information is the availability of raw material, inventory and process products. On the other hand, networking for e-commerce is the production line and distribution system. It is also a retail point of sale for the available information products.

The networks may be inter, intra, may function as local, regional international systems for e-commerce. Substantial data is required to be moved on at a distance greater than 3,000 feet. The advancement in sophisticated communication technology resulted in developing several new techniques for linking local area networks.

Paths are specified and the traffic has to necessarily pass through these paths. There are several devices which offer different degrees of discrimination and data capability. A network has several components like bridges. routers, hub, gateways, repeaters and switches etc.

A brief description of these components is as follows :

1. Router: A router is a complex and expensive device that is linked with personal computers. It is also like a bridge and a stand alone device on the LAN. The router has a module that is a part of the writing hub. A router is used to connect networks which are dissimilar. It provides connectivity between two LANs or WANs over a large geographical distance. It operates at the network layer three of the OSI model. Every router has to participate in a routing protocol to access the network topology. This helps the router to computer the best route from a sender to the receiver.

It is a device that can decide which of the several paths the network traffic will follow based on some optimality metric supreme and thus reduce traffic congestion on the LAN. Routers do the job of forwarding packets from one network to another based on network layer information.[1]

Functions and Features of the Router

The functions of the router are :

- To dig deeper into the envelope surrounding the data to find the destination for the data packet.
- To record the information contained in each packet or frame.
- It uses complex network addressing procedures to determine the appropriate network destinations.
- It discards the outer packet or frame and then repackages and retirements the data using these compressions.
- There are available sophisticated multi-protocol routers.
- It reads and examines the destination address contained in the Netware and IPX Protocol Router. It strips off the ethernet packet or token ring frame information and sends only the IPX packet and its encapsulated data.

2. Bridge: The bridge is a complex and expensive device that can be found within a personal computer. Bridge is a hand alone device on the LAN and as a module that is a part of the writing hub. It is a device used to connect two LANs operating under an identical LAN protocol over a wide area.

Functions and Features of Bridge

- To read the station address of each ethernet packet or of a token ring frame which is the outer most envelope around the data.
- To read and determine the destination of the message.
- To connect and pass packets between two network segments.
- A bridge does not look inside the packet or frame.
- To examine the address of each ethernet packet and to send across LAN to LAN circuits, only those packets addressed to nodes on the other sides.
- It is the object of the bridge to reduce the number of packets on the expensive long distance circuits.
- To pick up packets from one LAN and filter addresses which are meant for a destination on another LAN.
- Bridge passes the packets on the network.
- It operates at the data line layer two of OSI model.
- The amount of processing required is minimum.

---

1. *Computers Today, 16-31, August, 1999, pp. 80.*

3. Repeaters: It is a component of a network, a device which connects two segments of the networks cable. It retimes and regenerates the digital signals on the cable and sends them on their way again. In order to regenerate and propagate electrical signals, the repeater is used between two distinct network segments. This device is not popular in recent years.

4. Hub: In a network, the hub device is used to serve as the centre of a star topology network. A hub may be active or passive. It is active when it repeats signals sent through the network. It is passive when it does not repeat, but simply splits signals sent its rough this network.

5. Switch: A switch is used to reroute data to its destination, and is popularly found in switching networks. In switching networks, data is grouped and routed on the basis of pre-determined criteria.

6. Gateway: When two LANs are dissimilar, the component of gateway is used. Gateway operates on the application layer seven of the OSI model. Its main function is to convert data packets from one protocol format to another before forwarding it, as it connects two dissimilar networks.

It is a special purpose device that performs an application layer conversion of information from one protocol stack to another like TCP/IP.

Network Interface Card

The Network interface card is a board in a personal computer. At the manufacturing stage only, the card is installed before it is released into the market. Its function is to strategically network communication to and from that computer system.

X. 25

X.25 is a protocol for interfacing to a public packet switched network, but does not support the implementing of a network. As per the international Telegraph and Telephone Consultative Committee, one of its recommendations is that the most famous is X.25, which defines an interface into a particular data network, and also pertain to that of a packet switched network.

Intranet

Concept, Meaning and Nature: A micro internet is known as intranet. It is also referred to a system with restricted audience. Through the intranet system, a well managed and structured information flow is arranged to select individuals within the organisation. This is the family of internet services. The Intranet has access to internet but the internet has no access to the Intranet. The intranet has limited (private) accessibility. *Intra* means within and with reference to the computer network, it refers to private networking within an organisation.

Intranet simply means a network of computers which function within an organisation mainly to share data with each other. It uses the existing standardised WWW protocol.

In this system, there is the internal web server where substantial information can be stored. Anyone on the Intranet with a computer on network can view information documents located in the intranet server.

The browser software like Internet Explorer or Netscape can be used. For this system, Macintosh, Windows or Unix application can be used. Internal networks use TCP/IP protocol for data transmission. As a web server, it helps to share and dispense information within an organisation. The mechanism of intranet greatly helps the way in which information is shared, dispersed and broadcast over the network (LAN/WAN) within a company.

One of the essential ingredients in these days of fast growing competitive environment is an easy, fast, accurate and inexpensive distributions of internal information documents.

The intranet is an internal website used in an organisation to disseminate business related information and data to employees. In recent years, many business organisations have been searching for ways and means to improve employee communication. The application and usage of the intranet is a practical solution for distribution of materials more efficiently and thus reduce overhead costs. Documents, reports or a database are the sources in which all information generated is stored. The information is either generated on the LAN or WAN wide systems. With the increasing use of computing in organisations, more and more electronic documents are being generated-thus enabling easy and fast dispersal of information to potential net users.

Documents created in a LAN/WAN are linked with files or the source of information from various databanks and files within an organisation. More multi-tiered level sharing of documents on an inter and intra departmental level is possible to a large extent.

In the conventional method, several application methods are used, compared to using a specific document format.

Intranet facilitates solving all potential problems. In intranet, there is no problem pertaining to the multiple operating system, document's format, tiered level sharing and LAN/WAN.

A browser can be used as the front end which can tie everything from the back end to the front end. Inter and intra-departmental documents can be linked and shared seamlessly. There can be total control over documents, flow, sharing of data, creation, deletion, achieving and also resource centralisation.

Intranet Applications

The mechanism of intranet permits wide application. The following are the important intranet application areas :

- Broadcasting news
- Document management
- Inventory, purchase, orders, travel, library
- Linking internet sites
- E-mail for inter-office and intra-office communication
- Internal circulars called electronic circulation
- Bulletin boards
- Electronic chat
- Daily work assignments
- Executive information system
- Flow diagram and graphical contents
- Product and service literature on the intranet for quick access

- Shared database access
- Electronic meetings
- Collective writings
- In-house form requests
- Report filing and
- Sharing information by electronically generated documents, linking files or sources, information from various databanks placed elsewhere on the network.

Requirements

To design an intranet, it is essential to possess LAN and WAN, a web server up and running and clients using a browsing software to access Intranet.

Thus, intranets are internal TCP/IP based networks that allow information to be shared effectively within an organisation.

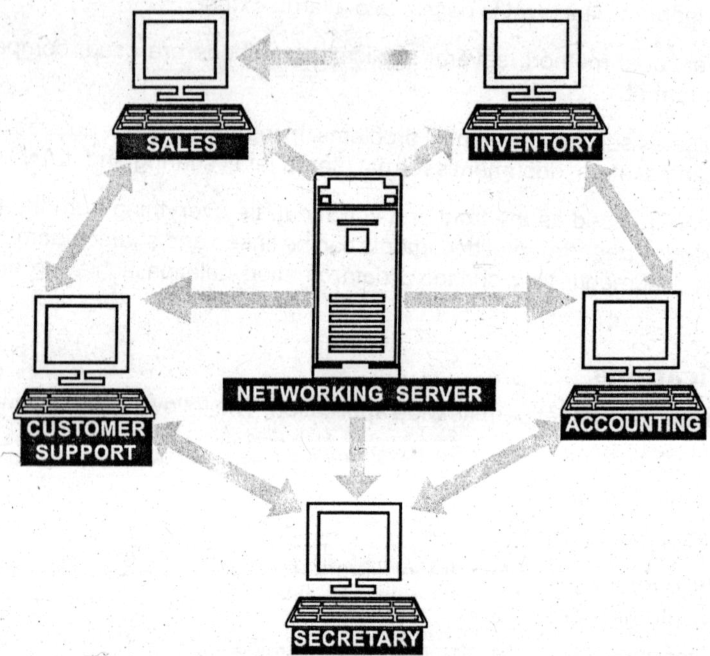

Fig. 3.19 An Office Network

Uses of Intranet

The system of intranet can be used as follows :

1. Communication: It facilitates to centralise corporate communication. Materials that become outdated on a periodical basis as on a monthly basis, are as follows: phone list, product/ service process, presentation contracts, proposals, requisition forms, marketing materials etc. can be placed on the intranet and will save manpower, wear and tear on covers and printers and they will be cheaper than a print shop.

2. Facilitating Employees: Intranet gives employees easy access to clients, products and relevant departmental information such as project reports and summaries, updates, catalogues and sales figures. Productivity increases as employees do not have to wait for co-workers to get back to them with job related information.

3. Interaction: Intranet fosters interaction with departments or offices which are normally isolated from each other and this is done through online newsletters and internal task forces.

4. Train Employee: Training a small group of employees on an intranet is far less expensive than sending them to a class or using CDROMs. Internet training allows companies to update/ modify information instant/aneously and the employees can schedule their training during the not so active business times.

The other uses related to Intranet are: inexpensive distribution, fast movement of data, no need to run to the file room to pick up a form, no need to put in a call to customer services, everyone on this network can access information and it ensures effective monitoring and strategic control of functions.

Features: They are as follows :

- Collects information at some central server or a distributed environment.
- Sharing resources in an efficient manner.
- Improves onward employee speed.
- Increases productivity.
- Congregates thoughts, ideas, comments, progress and discussions and
- Provides contacts which are easier and friendlier.

Groupware in Intranet

In intranet operations, groupware is used. Groupware means programs that help people work together collectively though they are located remotely from each other. Groupware services may include the sharing of calendar, collective writings, e-mail handling, shared database, electronic meetings with each person and be able to see and display information to others and other activities.

There are several resources solutions for intranets allowing easy use of the intranet and other applications etc. They are very useful towards a better understanding of this emerging technology.

Advantages of Intranet

As per the advantages, Intranet:

- Cuts corporate communication cost upto 70 percent.
- Increases productivity and efficiency levels.
- Meets one or more specific needs better.
- Addressing communication issues and
- Corporate intranet can provide information in a way that is :

- Immediate
- Cost effective and inexpensive
- Easy accessibly and usability
- Rich in format
- Versatile and
- Freedom of choice.

- Intranet security and safety protects information, SSL technology encrypts packets of information so that it is transferred securely.
- It is easy to use and there is no need to learn multiple software packages. The Internet Explorer is used to access all internal and external resources.
- It provides a way for people to easily retrieve the information they need.
- Intranet removes barriers to free flow of communication within the organisation and allowing groups to communicate and share knowledge.
- Intranet automates processing and eliminates the possibility of loss of paper and stationary.
- Intranet also provides the publishers who are spending a significant amount of time in producing different versions for the various client-platforms after preparing the content of news letter.
- Intranet ensures faster and more effective and increased productivity. It reduces paperwork to establish a paperless office.
- Intranet converts the conventional paper office into an electronic office by creating electronic documents for potential business communication.
- The intranet functions in such a way that it permits users on the intranet to access data from anywhere to anywhere on the network.
- It permits the user to create a personalised home page.
- Any member of an organisation has an opportunity to access the technology of intranet and to have access to information within the organisation irrespective of their hardware technology.
- All the facilities available on the web are also available on the intranet, browsing, hyperlinking and homepage.
- Computer makers are providing intranet products and services which will be easy to install.
- Conventional services take 2-3 weeks nearly to reach international customers when the documents are mailed. Intranet solves the problem by transferring the messages electronically.
- Web based intranet helps to reach the goal of simplifiction of information sharing.
- It saves valuable office time.
- This is by digitising all data and information.
- Keeps in touch with dealers, agents, brokers, customers etc.

Extranet

Meaning, Nature and Concept: The extranet is an extension of corporate intranet connecting internal networks of one company with the intranets of its customers, suppliers etc. The mechanism facilitates to create e-commerce application that links all aspect of a business relationship right from ordering to payment of the service.

Like intranet, extranet is also password protected, so that only approved people can get access to it. One way e-commerce is used with extranets for a large sales team that needs to order sales materials and brochures or products to be shipped while they are on the road.

All intranet is designed to facilitate internal communication, while extranets are created for communicating business related information to a particular vendor, distributor or customer. Therefore, extranets are generally more secure and password protected.

Several business organisations, particularly large corporations have been using extranets to improve customer services by making information and orders available within twenty four hours a day, seven days a week and 365 days a year.

Clients/customers in the extranet system can access real time information about project status, costs and development.

Dealers or vendors visiting the extranets can order products or service, check balances, review account information and history, look at pricing agreements and access database information.

Lucent Technologies and AT&T have commissioned World Internet Resources (WIR) to create an extranet. They have proved their metal in this project of communication.

As lines of communication are expanded, productivity improves between teams and departments. Project costs decrease while customer services increase leading to customer loyalty and satisfaction.

Definition of Extranet

Extranets are semi-private networks located outside the corporate firewalls which provide selected internal information to business partners such as clients, customers and suppliers as well as to remote employees. This expansive network supports activities such as sales and marketing, supply chain management, customer/product support, employee support, office equipment and ensuring supply procurement.*

Besides, it expands intranet technology by selectively making the information available to an organisation's business partners, customers and suppliers. This network is key to e-commerce as they combine the privacy and security of intranet with the global reach of the Internet. They are an ideal environment for implementing e-commerce business solutions, build potential business traffic on the Web far above what has been possible with various websites, search engines and banner advertising. So, extranet is the platform of choice for bulk business-to- business e-commerce extranet transactions.

---

* *Netscape, Feb. 15, 1999, p. 150.*

Extranet — A Business Tool

Extranet is an important business tool and has great advantage of the internet technology. The tool helps to achieve real cost savings and faster responses to changing business conditions. There are many reasons that makes extranet an important business tool. Consider the reasons mentioned below :

1. *IP-Based B2B:* Extranet is the future of IP-based business to business e-commerce. It is expected of this level of business transactions processing to increase several times. Its business is many times greater than the much publicised business to consumer transactions such as buying books and cars over the Net.

2. *Reducing Costs:* Extranet lowers cost by eliminating costly overheads and operation costs. In addition to eliminating the cost of proprietary EDI system, Extranet reduces resources that go into activities like order processing. So, many companies have achieved major costs and recorded costs savings by using Extranet.

3. *Saving Time:* This is a potential quality of the application of Extranet.

4. *Partner Relationship:* Extranet permits companies to establish stronger relationship with their various business partners by allowing them to share machines and related critical information with each other. A company's business is deeply intertwined with that of its business partner. So, by mutually forming beneficial relationships with their partners, the companies can increase their chances of success.

5. *Feedback:* Extranet provides instantaneous feedback on the existing market trends by monitoring of the information accessed on the site. It also provides the following benefits :

- Instantaneous feedback on product sales.
- Customer, supplier requirement.
- Giving companies the ability to keep their timings on the pulse of their business on a day-to-day basis and responses and communication with online clients and customers.
- Initiating quick and appropriate.

6. *Decision Making:* The launching of a successful extranet allows the companies to make effective and sound decisions quickly which they may not have had to make before. Thus, the extranet brings together organisations with divergent interests enabling them to experience a profound and profitable impact on how a company does business and how it appears to its customers and suppliers.

7. *Goals and Plans:* The extranet clearly predefines a company's goals and the means by which they will achieve them.

8. *Forecasting:* A well defined extranet network will enable companies to anticipate business problems. Creating a potential business practice requires dynamism and expertise. The mechanism of forecasting makes the companies to think about the issues, practicality those involving business solutions that will come up before they actually implement a system. Identifying these potential problems in advance enables the companies to develop solutions for future problems which inevitably arise.

Extranet Strategy

Maximum benefits can be derived from the extranet provided the strategy developed for this type of network must satisfy the following factors:

1. *Company Needs:* This defines the specific company needs, goals and problems that the extranet is going to address both in the short and long - term.

2. *Partner's Needs:* Determine business partners' needs and long-term strategies by consulting a large cross section of the partners.

3. *Business Unit and Functional Managers:* Get the business unit and functional managers to best understand the business issues, leading them to benefit most from the extranet system involved in strategy development process from the very beginning.

4. *Smaller Partners' Needs:* Extranet should work towards adopting business strategies to meet small business partners' needs.

5. *Trusted Partners:* Select a wide range of trusted business partners to participate in the pilot programme.

6. *Competitors' Strategies:* Analyse major competitors' strategies.*

Internet

Introduction: Focussing on the Internet here is a follow-up of the preliminary material after we understood LAN, WAN, Intranet and Extranet. This subject of Internet briefly and in non-technical terms, explains the internet concept in simple terms to the readers with little or no previous knowledge of computers. It also covers the nature of the subject, uses, application, operations etc. pertaining to the Net. The topic on Internet is included here with the primary object of giving the readers some idea about the principles and concepts of networking to help them succeed in using the Net for success as an entrepreneur, a manager or for other business purposes. While a good idea about computers is essential today, it would be more beneficial in learning the various areas of information technology with expertise and the related aspects of computers.

We frequently come across people talking about the Net in these days. Some business people, research institutions, educational institutions and a group of individuals know and use the internet to the maximum whereas some other people don't really know what it is. With the information technology opening up, people have moulded themselves in the computer culture in a big way, becoming potential IT professionals.

Internet — A Brief History: The Internet has its origin in military operations for defence purposes whereby virtue of its operations, the military personnel are scattered geographically in different distant places. To facilitate reliable, accurate and timely communication network, the Internet was designed for military use so that it is protected from disruption in case of destruction from a nuclear attack.

In 1959, the Pentagon's Advanced Research Project Agency (PARPA) created a network called the PARPA Net which permitted engineers, scientists and others working on military work all over America. In the early days, the initial object of the network was to share computers and information technology. It permitted the exchange of messages as per the system developed.

---

* *Dataquest, Feb. 15, 1999, p. 151.*

The PARPA Net subsequently was merged with another network called the Usenet News in 1979. This new organisation is a non-governmental parallel academic network.

Usenet news began to grow slowly and steadily and subsequently it became known as the Internet. The PARPA Net was relating to US organisations having US government associations.

In the global exchange of message, a new development in vogue today is the electronic mail (e-mail).

In the latter part of 1960s, the US government established five super computer centres. These centres acted as the main nodes of the Internet. To this network, all other networks of universities and research institutions were connected.

The designing of personal computers and their widespread use, because of its flexibility, market another important landmark relating to the Internet around 1980s. Till then, the mainframe computers with more speed, storage and memory, have dominated the technology field. Individual users, business organisations, educational institutions etc. went in a very big way to use micro-computers. The distinguishing feature of personal computers is that they do not have the capacity of sharing data and resources as they are stand alone machines. In order to solve the problem and to link computers together, the concept of LAN was designed which practically became more popular. Wide Area Network (WAN) was also designed which became widespread particularly with large companies.

Personal computers became more popular and widespread partly due to drastic reduction in the prices. Accordingly, online services like Telenet and Compuserve came into being. The concept of Bulletin Board Services (BBS) came into being, which greatly facilitated to connect individual computers, upto another computer in their vicinity for exchange and potential sharing of information. These are private networks which worked on different hardware and software platforms but could not talk to each other. TCP/IP, as an acronym stands for Transmission Control Protocol/Internet Protocol which are the procedures developed for interconnecting computers and exchanging the data.

Internet technology composed of TCP/IP, which gave birth to the Net helped interconnection of these networks, BBS communities and individual PCs of both home and office.

For exchanging information what is required is to connect any network or computer with the Net by using TCP/IP. Thus, the Internet became the network of all networks.

Yet another development in the history of Internet was recorded in 1990. In Geneva, physicists designed and developed a software for publishing, searching and accessing information on the Net. It was designed as a means to enable scientists to share documents with their colleagues. This is how the World Wide Web (WWW) became popular.

The development of the graphical browser called Mosaic facilitated to access information from the WWW. Thus, WWW has been growing enponentially, dominating the Internet. Thus, the Net came to the mainstream of life.

Internet — A Brief Indian History: Strangely, in India, the Internet is the product of educational and research undertakings. The expression "Internet in India" flashes many images upon the canvas of the mind. In India, the Internet has been for many years in the form of Educational

Research Network (ERNET), which was once available only to educational and research committees. In the early period, the Internet facility was not available on a large scale enabling people to get access to it. This is because of the policy laid down by the American Internet Manager, National Science Foundation (NSF), an agency of the American government at that time in the late 1980s. The US government set up five super computer centres which are primarily the nodes of the Internet to which the university and research labs networks were connected.

Internet in India was established in the late 1980s, which was a joint undertaking of the department of electronics of the Government of India and the United Nations Development Programme (UNDP), which used to extend technical assistance to developing nations. Many academic and research and development groups exchanged e-mails with each other using the ERNET. Thousands of scientists and technologists benefit with access to the ERNET facility, which is International in essence.

The Videsh Sanchar Nigam Limited (VSNL), a Government of India enterprise, is India's international telecom carrier, has also contributed its might giving to the expansion of internet technology in India. This backbone network in India is known as VSNL's Gateway Internet Access Network (GIAS). On August 15th, 1995, VSNL launched GIAS for the first time on a commercial basis in the country. It has also set up seven nodes at Mumbai, Delhi, Chennai, Kolkata, Bangalore, Pune, Ahmedabad including access nodes at Ernakulam, Cochin and Keonics. It has also launched intranet services at Lucknow, Hyderabad, Kanpur, Chandigarh and Dehradun.

A full range of internet services are now available. There are the remote internet access nodes which are connected to the main internet access node at Mumbai.

Present Position

In the early days the Internet facility was available to the government particularly for defence, research and development, laboratories, universities and computer science departments etc. In those days, getting connection to the Net itself was a difficult task for various known reasons. In the 1980s, the use of the Internet remained with the above mentioned authorities.

Now, the greatly publicised information super highway is accessible to anyone with time, interest and curiosity. The last fifteen years have witnessed an explosion of the internet activity. The use of the Internet is moving away from pure educational research to a network connecting millions of computers, many of which belong to companies using the Net for commercial purpose.

Concept and Meaning

Net is the short form of Internet, a new name given to the world wide network. The expression stands for inter-network. Computer is a network by itself. In simple words, the Internet is a conglomeration of a number of smaller networks and other smaller inter-connected machines distributed over the entire globe. Internet is a window to the global superhighway and to the cyberspace. So, it is a global system of connected independent groups of computers. It is the world's greatest democracy in terms of getting the information you as a net user require — which is available at your discretion.

These are the days of wonders and the potential of electronics. Among the modern wonders, the Net is one. It is the communication age, and Internet is a network of networks and a mother of all networks. It is a global network created by connecting these smaller networks with telephone lines.

The world network acts as a potential method of communication. Internet is a large repository of information available to the users. The Internet helps to get in touch with anybody around the world at the cost of a telephone call, proving to be economically viable.

It is an arrangement of a link between smaller networks and other individual computers all over the globe. Internet is the world's biggest software library, having opened doors to the vast amount of information available on the space information platform just by the click of a mouse.

Thousands of systems have been connected to the internet which have thousands of files, libraries and documents accessible to the public. Much of this consists of free or low cost shareware programs for virtually every make of computer. There are libraries of documents as well.

The Internet is a two-way communication method. Exploring internet potential brings the world on the screen of the users' computers. The basic principle of the Net is that the sender and the receiver are on the same line of the system.

To explain simply the internet is like the telephone system which is an instrument of global contact. There are many variant ways to connect to the Net. Similarly, there are different types of programs to run. Internet really is a way or path for various computers to communicate.

It is now the easiest thing through the internet to get computers talking to each other. We can communicate within the office, across the city or even the globe.

Most of the organisations having LANs are now interconnecting. They have crossed the threshold of LANS and enterprise wise networking, internet working or LAN to LAN connectivity is the trend of the hour.

The LAN can be inter-connected with the wide area networks. The routed technology is used to interact with other networks and VSATs (Very Small Aperture Terminal) to integrate remote locations.

The way to merge the world economy with the rest of the world has been paved, thus giving global body corporates potential opportunities to interact with manufacturers world over, to seek technologies and products world wide, Underdeveloped countries face stiff competition in terms of global recognition to multinationals equipped with advanced technologies and strategic marketing tools.

The success of a product in the market depends upon its quality and capacity to compete and sell in the world market. In a global marketing set up, there is a need to inform the potential global customer about the availability of a particular product with certain specifications, price, utility and other features.

The Internet connects computers and terminals often separately by way of boundaries to each other. Simply put, it is a global network and everybody has access to it with a PC connection. Thus, the Internet is accessible to all, but intranet is not freely available to all.

The main objective of the Internet is to facilitate the participating users to have mutual exchange of data-between the computers. To take advantage of these computers are a part of the Internet. The subject or data for mutual exchange may be numerical, alphabetical or a combination of both numerical and alphabetical pictures, movies, any text and anything that a computer is capable of accepting and storing. Graphic Users' Interface facilitates to see pictures also.

Internet — A Global Village

The world is a small place, a global village following the advancements in the information technology. It means that human potential technology has worked together, leading to globalisation. These words never used to be nor were more true than now. It means that with globalisation, one can sit in parlours or at home and join about millions of spectators watching the Olympics, the Asian Games and other international and national events taking place. The recent information technology revolution has transformed a communication conscious human society into an information-obsessed global village.

The distance between countries has been whisked away, thanks largely to IT. This revolution has been made possible by video recording and camera lenses that extended the range of our eyes. The new technology in human history permitted people from different parts of this planet to talk, see and communicate with one another electronically.

Earlier, the term global village was considered limited to the world of science fiction, but it is no longer a science fiction. Today, it has become a reality. Today, nothing is too far, too remote. This is why we say that we live in a global village. In a village, every one knows what is happening in their vicinity. Every one in the village has easy accessibility to information of the village. Similarly, information technology enables us to know what is happening around us and information is freely available with the benefit of easy accessibility to information related to various issues concerned with our lives.

Thus, there is tremendous interaction and inter-dependence which has bacome true of the whole world. Warious levels of improvement in communication and technological advancement have made this possible. The only thing is to ride this tigress of information technology and our skills lie in riding it to our advantage. There are a very wide range of possibilities available to us through this information technology. This technology may prove a faithful servant depending on how judiciously and to what purpose do we successfully master. Thus, there is a need greater than ever before to perceive the entire gamut of possible substantial relationships between information technology and business so that the formar is made subservent to our needs.

Internet — A Woven Global Village

Internet is the global information highway. The networks/computers operating in different environments are knitted to the Net by a common protocol suite and has evolved into one of technology's greatest damocracies, permitting the package of all kinds of information criss-crossing with full freedom among the Net users. Through this single channel, scholars, scientists, businessmen. librarians, journalists, artists and software developers are woven into a 'global village', information is vital in today's world. The problem of dealing with the accelerating glut of information is becoming acute and has eased to be within the ability of human beings, leaving them saturated. The human salurated interaction level, the urge to know the latest and in the fastest way has reached such new heights that its realisation through a global information highway of the likes of the Net was but imperative.

Information Highways

Communication highways are data transmission channels. The functions of these channels are to carry data from one place to another. The channels broadly categorised into three types are narrow band, voice band and broad band.

These bands indicate the rate at which data is transmitted. If the bandwidth of a channel is wider, it means it has more capacity to transmit data. For instance, telegraph lines are narrow band channels. They have the capacity to transmit about 5 to 30 characters per second (cps) voice.

The country has been eneavouring to build the global information highway. It is so essential for the sustenance of fast industrial knowledge and international economics.

Fig. 3.20 Global Village

Fig. 3.21 Global Village

Historically, telephone broadcasting and cable television are potential information transmitting media. Developments in technology namely micro-electronics, digital application, optical fibres, satellites, radio frequency range, micro and main frame computing has brought tremendous changes in information exchange. As such, long distance has become so cheap, quick and accurate.

Government of India approved in the year 1997, the creation of National Information highway at a cost of Rs. 700 crore, with plans to create the infrastructure for a national wide transmission of voice and data transmission. A national infrastructure is necessary by pooling in the transmission capacity existing in the country with three different departments, the Department of Telecommunications, Railways and the power sector. It takes place by intergrating available communication facilities of these departments as a network. The department of telecommunications has its own transmission facilities, The Ministry of Power and Railways has its own communication network. All these can be integrated to utilise the common facility and create national infrastructure, to constitute the potential national information highway. Initially, it was proposed to have a capacity of 8 megabytes per second with a facility to increase as and when demand requires.

Information Superhighways

In recent years, there has been sudden emphasis on international recognition about the information revolution. This revolution is popularly known as the information superhighways. But it needs a well coordinated and comprehensive information infrastructure which will cover the use of computers, telecommunications and office systems technologies. This information infrastructure facilitates collection, processing, storage packaging and dissemination of information which may be in the form of voice, data, text and image. Vast amount of information is available on database world wide which must be explored.

Superhighways connect large cities and countries and from these large cities, they come to smaller freeways and pathways to link together small towns whose residents travel or move on slowly with narrow residential ways. The super highway is the high speed net. Information super highways involve the availability of information on-line at all levels- schools, homes, offices and so on. We often hear about superhighways in computer telecommunications in recent years.

Superhighways are very much a part of the communications. Americans call it National Information Infrastructure. In India, the National Informatics Centre (NIC) dedicated national information highways to the nation in the year 1994.

Information superhighways is an advanced version of the already existing information highway. It is a satellite-computer optical fibre communication system which facilitates the transfer of massive data along with audio, video and graphic information at high speed.

Information Superhighways (ISH) have been commissioned by the National Information Centre (NIC) which provides free exchange of information among software and databases, educational institutions and hospitals etc. A large number of networks already operating in India such as Educational and Research Network (ERNET) of the Department of Electronics and the Remote Area Bunisess Message Network (RABMN) of the Department of Telecommunications are part of the ISH which is super-imposed on the giant National Informatics Centre Network (NICNET), India's largest satellite-based computer communication network. NICNET already has about 700 satellite earth stations in 500 cities and towns around the globe.

Applications of ISH

With a large database, ISH enables organizations, public or private and individuals to have access to substantial specific information in various dimensions :

- Video conferencing by the ISH would enable business organizations or others to conference simultaneously from different cities.
- The database of ISH containing around 15,000 journals including 1,000 full text journals would enable users to have access to all these journals, by cutting costs of subscriptions considerably.
- ISH has an impact on the media too. The user can select from the newspapers only those news items which would be of interest to them.
- Books fed into the computer database could be read on the computer monitor, with pages being turned over with the click of a button.
- ISH offers latest services such as transmission of laser videos over the computer network from which users can select the movies of their choice from thousands of titles stored in the computer databases.

Number of Networks that Constitute the Internet

It is to be understood that the Internet does not necessarily mean collection and connection of a large number of networks. Sometimes, a single computer can form part of the Net. In this, a single computer is connected to a network or service provider which is mainly linked to the Net. Thus, transmitting information or data from one network to another network is done. So LANs, WANs as well as the large commercial online application is also not of the Net character but through gateways, they can be connected to the Net.

So, as regarding the number of computers or networks that make up the Internet, there is no fixed number to constiute the Net system. There is no limit to the number, for this may be in thousands or millions. Globally, lakhs of cmoputers and networks form a major part of the Net.

So, any number of computers can be connected to the Net. The system is so fast, convenient and flexible, making it the only method best suitable to connect universites, educational institutions, labs and research institutes around the world. The academic users can use the Net with different software packages to participate in subject related discussions over the network. It facilitates to create documents and software libraries on the Net making them accessible to all the net users. What is required to connect any network or the net computer up with the internet is the ability to use TCP/IP for exchanging this information.

Size of Internet

How many people are using the Internet is an important aspect to know. According to some studies, ending January 2000, there were about 250 million users. The following is the break :

Canada & USA	131.1	million
Europe	64.23	million
Asia Pacific	42.6	million
South America	7.10	million
Africa	2.36	million
Middle East	1.29	million

The figures indicate that the number of net users is growing at a staggering rate. The number of web pages on the Internet recently swept past the one billion mark. They are growing in number over the years.

For example, one billion hours amounts to 1,14,155 years and one billion minutes make 1,902 years. If you got in your car and drove 100 kms per hour, it would take you 1,141 years to drive one billion kms. Even one billion seconds is beyond thirteen years' worth of time.*

Who Owns and Manages the Internet

The world is getting networked in a big way. Today, there are millions of internet users the world over to whom it has become a means of cross border transfer of information, it facilitates direct contact between the individuals, groups and institutions from different countries. Voluminous information available on the Internet becomes available instantaneously, which can be accessible to millions of individuals.

It may be mentioned that the Net is not owned by any single individual or organisation. The management and control of the Internet is completely decentralised and it is entirely managed by individual and organisational volunteers. Every user pays for his part. Each network meets the expenditure for the installation and operating costs as well as those connecting up with the other networks. The Internet is a cooperative environment and as a social as well as technical in essence-catering to all segments of the society. It is the responsibility of the users to ensure the trust and loyalty of the community.

Glorious Dreams — Realms of Reality

The Internet has brought a revolutionary change in computing and communication. It works towards strategies to interact with everyone, thus satisfying the world's growing inclination towards global communication — who are eager to seek information at all levels.

---

* *Computers Today, 16-31 March, 2000, pp. 72-73.*

It is supported by satellites that will gird the planet at low altitude like a rotating system of chain mail, transmitting signals from any one point on the planet to any other with speed and capacity of fibre optics cable.

Internet provides a range of facilities and information to computer users. Access to the Net has opened up a whole world of information to the subscribers by using the latest stored program control (SPC) as well a satellite and fibre oplics technology to provide global connectivity to these subscribers. This has greatly moved towards facilitating international trade, commerce and industry which needs reliable, fast, accurate and heavy load carrying communication links. The telecommunications network is universal in application and India is connected with communication links to the rest of the world to meet the requirements both in terms of quality, quantity and variety of information.

Global communication systems are providing a multitude of services-voice, data, accessibility and a variety of communication media- copper, fibre, microwave and satellite links. The technological advances in miniaturisation, signal processing, compression, fibre and satellites are shrinking the distinction between different types of services. These communication services viz., voice, fax, date, e-mail, video conferencing, television, radio etc. ensure instant access to information, people and machines throughout the globe. The informatics revolution brought in by the technological advances in the field of satellites, cables, switching, computer, devices, etc. is influencing radically the way the economic activities are being carried throughout the globe, making it virtually one gigantic market place a global village.

The development in sophisticated communication technologies giving overseas communication services has shrunk the world, thus making the world one big family. Nearly 150 countries can be contracted from India, by using satellite and sophisticated gateways exchange and the concept of global village has now become a reality. Distances between countries have been bridged and people have been brought closer to each other. Across the globe, corporations, individuals, business houses etc. have been reaping the benefits of the Internet in a big way.

The Internet has moved towards eliminating the barriers to free and fast communication and allowing groups within the companies and groups outside to communicate and share knowledge. The internet technology is applied to the network of components i.e. making navigating, tracing and making information retrieval far simpler than ever before.

It offers many advantages, most notably is of the use and communication to any hardware platform that supports the web browser. The internet users can download data from the websites.

Information is available on the Net on any topics of study and the data traffic has been increasing considerably in the recent years. Higher the capacity of the Net, more is the speed with which data can be accessed by net users. New technologies have enabled the network towards enabling access to the global village and offered the world opportunity for distributed computing possible. The technologies include :

- Network File System (NFS) and
- Network Information Service (NIS)

The Net is all set to revolutionise the information. The internet technology is based upon accepted standards which is an unanimously accepted norm and widely used. The internet is based on the following three main standards :

- TCP/IP — (Transmission Control Protocol/ Internet Protocol) for connectivity.
- HTTP — (Hypertext Transfer Protocol) for interfacing with data.
- SMTP — (Simple Mail Transfer Protocol) for electronic mail.

Information Available on the Net

Information on various subjects are available on the internet which can be accessed by any one. For instance, the following are the themes, a few to mention, available on the internet as broadly classified :

- Agriculture (international food and nutrition database, agricultural weather statistics, market news, drought information, newsletters.)
- Archaeology (thousands of databases of archaeological investments.)
- Bulletin Boards System (huge amounts of scientific, technical, non- technical information, environmental protection and hundreds of files on a wide range of subject areas.)
- Business and finance (business, finance, research databases.)
- Computers-literature (weekly news bulletins on topics like workstations, super computers, interviews, news etc.)
- Education (covers colleges, universities relating to information on scholarships, ranks, fellowships, research, faculty development etc.)
- Environment (information relating to environment data in text, graphics and table form.)
- Games (game server permits interesting online games including bucks, moria, tetris sokoban and other adventure games.
- Geography (access to countries, cities, regions and to access their information like population, latitude, longitude etc.)
- Health (health information including AIDS, its statistics, risks, treatment, reasearch news etc.)
- History (databases of American and European historical topics.)
- Internet and resources (information about people, organisations and resources on the Net and related online services and resources.)
- Language (choose from online Webster's Dictionary and spelling references, pronounciation, definitions etc.)
- Libraries (include databases like library, catalogues, current articles, information databases, other libarary systems, library and system news.)
- News (articles from USA today.)
- Physics (nuclear physics, statistical measurements, radiation levels and other information for the US.)
- Space (NASA Space link history, current events, projects and plans at NASA.)
- Sports and Athletics
- Technology (information technology articles.)
- Travel and
- Weather

What to Do on the Internet ?

Users of the internet can do anything as per their areas of interest which are available on the Net. However, the following are some of the important things which can be done through the Internet :

- Online news services
- Daily news can be read
- Listen to music
- Playing sounds
- Electronic fund transfer
- Cybershow room
- Cyber payments
- Consumer durable services
- Credit collections
- Credit ratings
- Distance education
- Cultural information
- Educational research
- Foreign exchange
- Travel and tourism
- Medical health
- Publications and journals
- Libraries
- Legal services
- NRI services
- Photography
- Advertisements
- Stock market
- Student related higher education information
- Yellow pages
- Histories
- Court judgements
- Consultancy
- Banking
- Shopping
- Commodity pricing information

- Electronic bulletin boards
- Reading, asking questions, answering questions, participation in discussions and other news groups
- Teaching and marketing and
- Payments etc.

Features of Internet

They read as follows :

- Computers have the capability to communicate with each other. If connectivity is given, information can be exchanged between computers.
- The communication function between computers facilitates access to information residing in one computer from another computer.
- A group of computers in a net system are connected with the help of wires, cables or the wireless.
- The interconnected computers can communicate with each other with the help of software.
- It is the software which constitutes the network.
- The device of the modem is to be used on both the sides connected to a telephone line which facilitates that the two networks can communicate with each other by using the modem.
- A network may be a simple network of two computers, an office network of more than two computers, network of networks, larger network and networks around the world.
- Information can also be obtained through commercial network packages like bulletin board packages etc.

User Groups of Internet

The internet is used widely as a valuable information source on several different subjects which are available to the public. Presently, the user group of internet services are :

- Corporations
- Commercial organisations
- Universities
- Government institutions
- Research institutions
- Commercial users
- Individuals
- Entertainment users
- Homes for pleasure and
- Medical groups etc.

The Internet comprises of the world wide network of computers, and it is increasingly being commercialised. Its importance and uses have been greatly recognised by a wide cross section of public and the use of internet is moving away from pure academic and research communities to networks connecting millions of computers, many of which belong to companies and other organisations using the internet for commercial purposes. On the other hand, the service providers on the Net are also undergoing a sea change from contributions by government funded agenices to private oprators as well as major telecommunications carriers, These commercial operators have interconnected their network to form Commercial Internet Exchange (CIX).

Thus, information on the internet and oportunities to use it are rapidly growing and the last 15 years have witnessed an explosion of internet activities.

The internet is changing the way people communicate world over. This new technological innovation is gaining popularity faster than any other communication media today with the fast expanding universe of the internet, every one can have access to information on the internet. It can be used both for communicating with others, fun, business, games, movies etc. The experiences of the Net users reveal that internet-based resources and businesses are identifying new ways for promoting and selling their products or services on the Net, thereby mustering new customers, increasing their turnover and ensuring increased profits.

In the early days, the internet was made available only to the government, academic and research institutes. But today, it is used extensively and the number of users connecting to it from home continues to grow dramatically. The primary uses of internet are shifted from research to commercial application, moving to customers and business application has been increasing by lakh of users annually.

Gateway

It is a generic term used as a name for computers that forward and route data between two and more networks. Gate is a short form of gateway. Technically, it means a computer that transmits files or e-mail from one network, which is a window of a country to another window of another country. With the help of interface machines, the networks are connected when more than one data network is connected, this called the gateway.

The network of a building, premises or office is a gateway to the Net. For instance, sending an e-mail by one office network to another office network or by one country's net to another country's net is a case of sending messages online. Gateway is a computer or the program running on the internet which transfers files or e-mail messages or commands from one network to another (C. Crumlish).

India's Gateway to the Internet

The Videsh Sanchar Nigam Limited (VSNL) is the sole overseas communication organisation in India and India's only international communications carrier. It has opened a window or gateway to Global Information Services (GIAS). Thus, India has one backbone network that operates at a very high speed and carries the bulk of the online traffic. All other smaller networks are connected to this backbone.

VSNL has contributed substantially to the expansion of the GIAS network in India. It has been providing access services to the Internet on all India basis. It has its main internet access node at Mumbai, connecting other internodes in other countries. In view of the ever growing internet access needs, the system uses satellite media, submarine cable etc. to cater to the potential Net users.

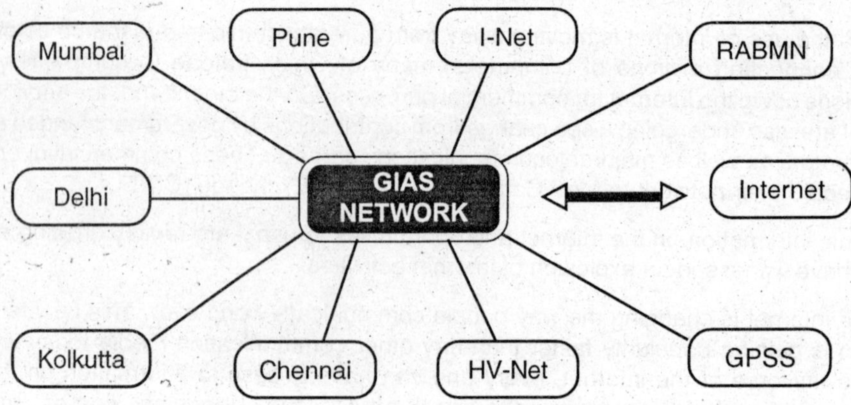

Fig. 3.22 Videsh Sanchar Nigam's Gateway Internet Access Services

Working of the World Wide Net

Small local or regional networks are connected to the World Wide Net (WWN) which is a complex web of various networks. It is like a modern road network of transcontinental super highways connecting large cities. This follows the coming of smaller freeways and pathways to link together small towns, whose residents travel on slower and narrower residential ways. The net super highway is high-speed internet. A computer is connected to this super highway that uses a particular system of transferring data at high speed.

In the US, the major internet 'backbone' can really move data at rates of 45 million bits per second. Smaller computers of particular geographical regions are connected to the internet which transmits data. Individual computers or smaller networks constitute a source of feeding data to these region. In the system, there is no one central computer running the internet. The resources of the internet are to be found among thousands of individual computers.

Upload/ Download

This refers to transferring files via, 'ftp' Uploading is moving a file from your computer to a remote host on the Net. Downloading is moving a file from the Internet to your computer. It is a 'to and fro' system.

Importance of Internet

The most remarkable facet of the emerging digital economy is electronic commerce. E-commerce is radically changing not only the way businesses serve and communicate with their customers, but also the way they manage their relations with both suppliers and partners. Both the new internet based companies and traditional producers and services are transforming their business processes into e-commerce processes. In an effort to lower the costs, improved customer service and increased productivity, the value of e-commerce transactions world wide is growing expontentially. Many developed countries and some developing countries consider the Net as a unique opportunity leap-frogging whole stages of industrial development.

The Net, apart from enabling potential e-commerce, is also contributing to the rapid internationalisation of the services sector. It makes it possible to unbundle the production and consumption of information-intensive service activities. These activities e.g., computing, accounting, role of personnel, marketing and distribution play a fundamental role not only in service industries but also in manufacturing and primary industries.

More and more people are gaining access to the Net and more and more of them are shopping on-line, because it provides a level of convenience to merchants and customers. The Net is fast becoming the method of choice for transacting businesses globally. In the days to come, all business persons will conduct an ever increasing number of business transactions online. There are several internet access application solutions available in various forms — this is being used by net users in a big way.

They provide cost effective and easy functioning, thus allowing upto the minute flow of information. The network of computers around the world is growing substantially. There are many sources and providers of information on the Net, and almost as many ways to access them are available to the Net users.

The net users are increasing and net business booming, with millions getting to it world wide. The marvellous internet technology is offering ample opportunites and interacting with others from any where to any where at any time. It is a sort of mixing of anonymity and adventure, which most businesses exploit to develop their business. There are no barriers to online entry. Merchants, customers and others can easily access to the Net with initial investments.

Networking is a fortunate business segment that has assumed the role of potential infrastructure industry. Internet and the growth of the world wide web have accelarated the growth of e-commerce and created opportunities. Internet is the medium for e-commerce and the single biggest agent of business. It is changing the way we pay, create, communicate and invest in smooth business transactions. Not only does it open up whole a host of new business opportunities, it also allows and enables traditional business to :

- Streamline their business operations.
- Reach newer markets.
- Reduce costs.
- Improve business cycle time.
- Improve customer service levels.
- Increase efficiency and
- Build potential ties with business partners scattered worldwide.

Businessmen have viewed the internet to be an important business application tool of the furure. People are moving to take advantages of opportunities created by the internet at a fast pace. Internet-based orders reaching out to the customers is a valuable business tool.

The internet revolution has established itself in India. With the advent of suitable infrastructure and favourable online business policy, there is likely to be an exponential growth in Net applications for e-commerce. The last one year has seen a sharp increase in the number of internet users and an improvement in the overall quality and prices of online services offered. Easy access to the Net is also triggering a boom in computer sales and websites for the global extension of marketing. Major companies have either set up or are in the process of setting up their websites for global recognition.

Shopping and Shopsite over the Internet

The popular area of selling and buying goods in the international niche market has expanded to online shopping websites. There are reasonable sites for rare, classically conventional and modern goods. The more comprehensive the e-commerce solutions, the more sophesticated online shopping services can occur. There are more opportunities to the people to spend money on internet shopping which is a convenient method of buying desired products.

The Internet has completely revolutionised the way we shop. The buyers need not rush home after a frantic spree around the stores and supermarkets shopping for day to day products. Buying and selling transactions online take place in a quite different manner. In conventional shopping, people go to the stores and supermarkets. We are nearer to the online virtual supermarket, final vision screen, where we make a selection by clicking on the products desired to buy, witness a shopping basket graphics file up with graphics indicating your purchases and finally find credit card details to pay and settle for the online purchase. Credit card is an important pre-requisite for online shopping.

A shopsite with reference to e-commerce is an online store creation system. The site allows merchants to bill the user on the basis of the catalogue of products to sell on the Net. It also deals with tools for site creation and management, sales and purchase statistics secure encrypted transactions and online order fulfilment.

Cyberstore - front on Internet

Cyberstore-front Inc. offers storefront creation, order processing, business administration and management tools with unlimited lasting capability and the most comfortable shopping, It handles all aspects-designing websites from logo creations to credit card merchant account, so that the business can accept real time credit transactions. It has great capability, functioning 24 hours a day and seven days a week.

Internet for Small Businesses

E-commerce solutions are available for both small and medium sized businesses. There are developers of integrated e-commerce applications for both these categories of business.

E-commerce builders is one such solution, which brings e-commerce to small businesses with potential online resources and articles about e-commerce marketing, promotion of websites, with software programming and designing tools for these small businesses ensure their global recognition.

The EC- builder is the first product to bring the power of e-commerce into the hands of small business users. This is known as simplicity — a simple point with the click software application.

Software EC-builder Pro 4.5 is an enhanced credit card transaction processing gateways. With the EC-builder and EC-software one can:

- Easily create an e-commerce website for small business.
- Automatically promote small businesses to search engines.
- Customise online store with any image or video.
- Add media files and banners to the website.
- Host online business with any internet service provider.

- Accept credit cards and complete e-commerce transaction and
- Accept multiple product orders with a built-in shopping card.

Feature of EC-builder

EC-builder helps to get small businesses online enabling sale transaction in hour. Multiactive Software Inc is the leading world wide development and market of innovative sales, customer management and internet commerce solutions.

Internet commerce solutions form Multi Active Software (MOS) Inc. include EC-builder, Maximiser Enterprise, Maximiser, tracker and sharkware.

Maximiser Enterprise 5.0 is the leading sales and customer management solutions for small to medium sized businesses world wide. The products are used by organisations and individuals within the financial services, telecommunications, insurance technology and manufacturing companies.

With the availability of IT enabled e-commerce solutions, its acceptability is growing rapidly among small, medium and home based business and people poised to capitalise upon this retail market. Many solutions providers are offering e-commerce capable web sites, online promotion and work on strategies to upgrade facilities, thus allowing potential customer relationships, build customer base and ensure long-term customer commitment to their business. There are many products which brought the power of e-commerce into the hands of small retail business users. The simplicity and sophistication and affordable price software are both far beyond expensive site creation tools.

Thus, the application of the world wide web and Net for e-commerce is no longer a luxury and confined to large businesses, they are not for priviliged businesses, government and home users but all have access to it. Even small businesses can have their own website and do potential global business. It has produced a revolutionary new way for small businesses to communicate and interact with customers and new potential customers. This will be possible by assuring customers online security and providing services at the earliest.

Personalising the Net

Until now, the Net has been a vast repository of freely available information. One of the greatest joys of surfing is the ability to go off on a bizarre tangent, with new sites just a click away. However, the era of personalisation is fast approaching and the ***Web is at crossroads in its evolution.***

Will it finally fulfil Marshall McLuhan's prophecy that lighting communication will create a global village where any important news and information spreads through the community like wildfire or will people withdraw into themselves, focussing more and more on their own narrow interests?

Howard Rheingold, author of *The Virtual Community,* believes in sociability. "There is a hunger for community that grows in the breasts of people, especially as more and more informal public spaces disappear from our lives," he says. Stanford University's Norman Nie takes the opposite view, believing that "the more time people spend using the Net, the more they lose contact with their social environment".

Will the internet bring us together in virtual communities or will it tear us apart as we filter our view of the world so effectively and personally that we lose the shared experience that is at the heart of any real community? This leaves those who hope to provide the Net with its news coverage in a quandary whether to concentrate on the community or on the special interests? Walter Bender, principal investigator of Massachusetts Institute of Technology's News in the Future Consortium, believes personalisation is the key. "Modern telecommunications are leading inevitably to the smallest news product imaginable: the personal newspaper, or Daily Me," he explains.

This would have content culled from all over the Web, personalised just for you. It could take into account your diary and include travel directions, and follow your football teams's progress — perhaps the only way we 're going to see a sports section not dominated by Premiership clubs.

What makes the question of personalisation versus community so fraught is that the Internet is ideally suited to either approach. Chat rooms and increasingly advanced messaging and conference services let people contact each other whatever their geographical location, and huge portals such as Yahoo! and MSN can provide news as one aspect of very general community service.

On the other hand, esoteric groups with little funding or experience can tailor sites to their own specific interest — think of the frightening number of Star Trek sites on the Web. The increased accuracy of search engines lets surfers home in on what they want quickly, leaving everything else by the wayside. Content providers are trapped between the Scylla of people wanting to know something about every thing and the Charybdis of people wanting to know everything about something.

One thing everyone agrees has to be avoided is simply transferring content wholesale from the old media - websites differ from print as much as print differs from broadcast. Its a ludicrously obvious point, but reading from a screen is not nearly as enjoyable as reading from a page. *Wired,* the technology culture magazine, once received a guilt-stricken e-mail from a reader who had ploughed through an entire issue online and wanted to pay for it. The publisher replied : "If you can read that much from a screen, you deserve to have it free." New media barons have to focus on what differentiates the Internet from old media, and so far, few seem to exploit its strength and understand its weaknesses.

For instance, the simplicity of publishing material on websites means they can be constantly updated. The magical clickability of hypertext means readers can follow their own path through the material, delving into areas more deeply than would be possible using offline publication. Similarly, the online reader can easily browse vast archives for specific information.

David Card, senior analyst at Jupiter Communications, believes there is a market for content online. "At the moment, we're seeing errors in scope. Too many sites have eyes bigger than their markets," he explains.

David Shenk, the author of two books on information overload, believes personalised news is inevitable, but thinks it is "very dangerous". He fears that people not exposed to general news will become blinkered.

E- transaction: Handle with Care

Electronic commerce like any other business involves the exchange of some form of money for soft or hard goods and services. But for many, payment processing on the Internet is a major problem. The whole process seems unnecessarily complicated and can be a nightmare to set up. In an interview with Indiatimes.com, Jayanta Chatterjee, chief knowledge officer, Venture Infotek Global, explains how online payment processing works and points out some of the pitfalls that businesses should try to avoid.

Excerpts from the interview :

How prepared are we to use electronic payment systems for e-commerce?

Implementation of electronic payment systems for e-commerce is in its infancy and still evolving. The technical, economic and legal components of electronic payment systems are yet to be comprehended to the desirable extent.

As a result, there are a number of competing proposals and implementations of electronic payment systems. One thing is clear to everyone involved in electronic payments. Electronic payments ultimately are far cheaper than mailing out paper invoices and then later processing received payments. It is convenient for customers and it saves the company a lot of money. Estimates indicate that the cost of billing one person varies between ₹ 50 and ₹ 70. Sending bills and receiving payments over the Internet promises to drop the billing paying cost to an average of ₹ 5 per bill. The total savings is huge when you multiply the unit cost times the number of customers that could use electronic payment.

What are the most preferred ways of payment for an e-commerce transactions?

There are many basic ways to pay for an e-commerce transaction ranging from cash on delivery (e.g. VPP), wire transfers (Inter-bank, Intra-bank-Net Banking), payments cards such as credit and debit cards, stored value card and Cyber Currency.

But the most preferred means of e-payment has been payment cards (credit and charge cards), which online shoppers use for a majority of their Internet purchase. Payment cards provide built-in security for merchants because they provide greater assurance that they will be paid through payment card issuing companies than through the sometimes slow direct invoicing process.

The elaborate series of actions associated with using a payment card are often transparent to the consumer. Several groups and individuals are involved: the merchant, the merchant's bank, the customer, the customer's bank and the payment card company that issued the customer's payment card. All of these entities must work together in order for customers' charges to be credited to the merchant's accounts (and vice versa when a customer receives a payment card credit for returned goods).

How different is the use of payment cards on the Internet ?

Most people are familiar with the use of payment cards. When you purchase one or more items, the clerk runs your card through the online payment card terminal and your card account is charged immediately. The process is slightly different on the Internet, though the purchase and charge process follow the same rules.

Laws prohibit merchants from accepting payment cards credits to their account until the products are shipped. That is, an Internet stores cannot charge your payment card until the day that they pack and ship your merchandise to you.

Payment card transactions follow these general steps once the merchant receives a consumer's payment card information, which is sent via a Secure Socket Layer-protected Web page.

- The merchant must authenticate the payment card to ensure it is both valid and not stolen.
- The merchant can check with the consumer's payment card issuer to ensure that funds are available and put a hold on the funds needed to satisfy the current charge.

- Often a few days, following the consumer's request for purchase, settlement occurs which means that funds travel through the banking system into the merchant's account after the purchase has been shipped.

When customers arrive at a stores electronic check-out counter, merchants want to offer them payment options that are safe, convenient and widely accepted. The key is to figure out which choices work the best for your company and for your customers. You will have to make some choice and choose the best one or two solutions for your situation and budget.

But payments in e-commerce represents some challenges and several risks.

What are these challenges and risks involved in e-commerce transactions ?

The cyber world is different. The identity of both buyers and sellers is a challenge. On many occasions, the consumer is not genuine and may be using some one else's card, which was lost or stolen. There are also times when you may be dealing with a fraud merchant, who may deliver sub-standard goods to you. And above all, there is considerable risk of leakage and tampering with credit card information flow on the Internet.

How can e-transactions be insured from such problem?

Electronic payment technologies and services providers will have to develop a secure online payment gateway uniquely designed for regional ground realities taking care of infrastructure bottlenecks yet creating a fairly secure payment system.

As such, Internet business will typically require a separate account and the cost is likely to be higher because the risk is greater. In a retail store, the merchant sees the card and the customer and can compare signature, obtain ID or other means of verifying authenticity. There is greater risk of fraud when the card is not physically presented such as telephone or Internet orders. Therefore these transactions typically carry a higher processing fee, which is another challenge for those working on e-payment technologies.

E-payments: A new way of life

As the Internet continues to transform commerce as we know it, the method of payment is one component which is critical to successfully conducting business across a network. An intense battle is on between the conventional and electronic modes of payments for value-exchange on the Internet. While it is unlikely that cash payments will die out because of their robustness in the face of technical difficulties, a few ungainly documentary methods may quickly disappear,because some electronic payments systems that address the same appear to be much more effective, says Piyush Khaitan, founder of Venture Infotek Global Ltd. He further focusses on the electronic payments system and questions related to it,

What does an electronic payments system mean?

E-payments system is a mechanism wherein payments take place electronically without actual exchange of cash or cheque. Banks are the backbone of the payments systems as they act as a guarantor to the seller and recover money from the buyer. Some of the popular e-payment products are :

- Card-based products-credit card, debit card and stored value card.
- Electronic Clearing Services (ECS).
- Web banking, Internet commerce and other related products.

Why do we need e-payment systems?

The total personal consumption expenditure in India is $ 225 billion (₹ 10,00,000 crore) out of which only $ 2.5 billion (₹ 12,000 crore) happens electronically. Compare this with the US economy in which out of $ 6 trillion personnel consumption expenditure, $ 2 trillion happens just using credit / debit cards. Thus we rely for practically all our transaction needs on cash. This increases the amount of currency in the economy. This high amount of cash in circulation has its own disadvantages :

- The cost of printing and maintaining the currency is a very expensive affair, especially in low denomination notes.
- A high demand for currency results in shortage of currency.
- The high incidence of cash transactions has an undesirable effect of tracking these transactions very difficult and leading to loss of revenue in the form of taxes like sales tax etc.

All these factors points to the immediate need for developing a strong e-payments system.

What are the key drivers for e-payments ?

Growth of e-payments systems in India will depend on certain key factors such as :

1. ***Regulatory:*** The government is taking a serious note of this issue. The Saraf Committee, set up by the Reserve Bank of India (RBI) in 1994, has identified and suggested a road map to address the technology issues related to e-payments. As a follow up to the various recommendations, we now have legislation in place to recognise and deal with electronic transactions. Likewise, guidelines have been announced for the formation of a consumer credit bureau, issuance of debit cards and stored value cards and also technical standards for the same are now in place.

2. ***Competition:*** With the advent of the new non-PSU banks like HDFC Bank, ICICI Bank, UTI Bank etc, MNC banks are forced to innovate and compete vigorously by offering enhanced value propositions to consumers. We have seen a suite of new payment products unfold. Also, PSU banks and now even the smaller ones are in the market with a variety of offerings. All this means more and more e-payment products and systems.

3. ***Consumer Preference:*** Increased middle income affluence, opening of the economy, awareness and sophistication in urban and semi-urban households due to the reach of cable television have all contributed to the Indian consumer demanding and using e-payment systems that provide convenience, security and status.

4. ***Infrastructure and Technology:*** The telecommunications infrastructure in most metros and mini-metros is now world class. Also, bandwidth and international gateways are easily available at affordable cost. Trends in mobile commerce online transaction processing and knowledge management demonstrate that e-payments will grow at a very fast pace.

What do you think should be done to increase the number of electronic transactions in India?

The government has already announced guidelines and defined a clear-cut regulatory framework, whereby it has become easy for banks to introduce e-payment products. What is perhaps missing is a definitive road map, which agreed to targets and a tracking and feedback system.

The second need is to bring down the cost of the transaction. For example, each point of sale terminal costs about ₹ 25,000, ATM machine ₹ 8,00,000, magnetic stripe card about ₹ 10-25 and smart card about ₹ 100

These costs are abnormally high by international standards because of the very high customs and other duties. If all such duties are abolished, we will see an immediate affordability of such technology and consequent reduction in the use of cash.

I remember a ₹ 5 note actually costs more than 5 rupees to produce and had a life of only 30-35 days. A payment card, on the other hand, typically lasts 2-3 years. This will encourage the use of cards and result in more transactions.

The third thing is that utility companies should come forward to accept e-payment instruments as an official payment tool and should provide consumers the convenience to go for such payments.

Job Hunting on the Web

When Ajit Joglekar's job as systems analyst in an Andheri based unit became victim of a downsizing operation, he decided to go to the web for professional help. Discarding the traditional route of job consultants and placement services, he began scouting india's leading job sites — the likes of jobstreet.com, naukri.com — jobsahead.com — posting his resume on these online job joints.

Three days following his cyber roamings, he had signed the dotted line with a leading Mumbai-based software house, at a salary atleast 40 per cent higher than his earlier assignment. Roughly translated, that meant a 13 per cent jump for each day he was ironically 'out of work'.

A search on WWW.google.com led Mr. Joglekar to some of these jobs, following which he was besieged with phone calls from organisations looking for someone "just like him." The fact of the matter is when it comes to jobs and careers now, self help, using the Net as a tool is in.

Potential job aspirants say this sure beats chasing after headhunters and agencies that may or may not open the right doors. I feel that both can co-exist. However, looking for a job online allows applicants to take control of their job search. With just a few mouse clicks, they can post their biodatas, pick and choose the companies they prefer to work with and even monitor the safe passage of their curriculum vitaes into the relevant hands.

There are of course the odd instances when people putting out their resumes in the hope of attracting some big fish have found themselves instead hooked and cooked when they received responses from their own companies' HR departments for posts that sounded suspiciously like their own.

Oops ! The occasional embarrassment aside, job seekers are finding the Web a virtual storehouse of bigger opportunities and broader career horizons. There's also the all-important perk of by-passing files of snail mail crowding the desks of hiring managers.

Today, most leading companies (both Indian and global) post job listings on their own sites. A regular tapping of these could lead you into a unexpected pastures and a juicy job, well before some other contenders opting for the good old Mumbai postal department path.

In most job searches, speed and access to information are key. On the Web, one can reach thousands of companies by simply leading the cursor up the right cyber alley. You can also access the job listings that appear in hundreds of newspapers. Typically, classified advertisements run only on Wednesdays or Sundays and appear a few days after being submitted to a newspaper. The same advertisement, however, will get online within 24 hours of submission and even stay there until the post is filled. Therefore, if you're looking for a job and you're in a hurry, the Web might be your best bet. If you're willing to go to a different city to work — that is happily move home lock, stock and barrel — from your existing base, you stand an even better chance of getting picked up. The Web's global reach will provide you with access to jobs in places you only read of in exotic travel brochures.

Therefore, if you want to be a keeper of a game park in Kenya, you know what to do if you're very worried about confidentiality, the good news is a number of sites today after ways in which privacy is guaranteed. Meanwhile, there are a few tips you can follow to ensure your web search for jobs does not lead you to a dead end.

TIP 1 : *Gearing to move on* : If you're fine about relocating, you will probably find the world an open field. Infact, the more open you are to change, the more positive your chances of hitting upon a job that satisfies your wander lust.

TIP 2 : *Narrow your search* : A bit of spadework always helps. Do your homework on companies and fix your sites only on the ones you really want to work with.

TIP 3 : *While creating resumers,* keep hiring managers in mind. Your resume should be short, crisp descriptions of who you are and what you do best are perfect for the on-line world. Infact, make sure you highlight your skill sets. These will probably show up if an HR chief somewhere does a keyword search. Also, make sure your resume is in tune with the profile of the company you are applying for. Talk the 'language' of the company, you might find yourself getting heard !

TIP 4 : *Choose your website carefully*, discriminate, act snobbish. Just remember, only the best site is suitable for you, Settle for the leading names in the business and only post your resume when you're absolutely sure the site is credible and effective.

Is the Emphasis on IT Justified ?

Yes, IT can Change Lives and Our Country: The economy of a country is no longer measured by the strength of traditional industries but by its technological advancement. Information Technology should be looked upon not as an end by itself but as a means for achieving overall development.

The IT sector is perhaps the last opportunity in regaining competitive advantage for the country, to develop rapidly, to improve the standards of living of our people and to grow out of poverty.

Unlike traditional industries, the IT sector is people intensive and creates vast employment opportunities. This implies a very low capital output ratio and an opportunity for all of us grow quickly. Presently, it is estimated that over 300,000 software professionals are working in the country. According to the NASSCOM report, India will be able to export software, worth over $ 50 billion by the year 2008. The domestic market is likely to expand to $37 billion at the same time. This growth is expected to create an additional 22 lakh jobs in India.

Some feel that this kind of growth in IT will benefit only the elite. I do not subscribe to this view. I think IT will primarily be responsible for eradicating poverty as well strengthening democracy. I believe that IT will be useful as a tool for every poor citizen to demand and secure his right to information. The Government of Karnataka has already taken several initiatives primarily to take the administration to the doorsteps of the common man.

We have plans to set up 7,500 Mahithi Centres (IT kiosks) all over Karnataka. Presently, the state has land records of 60 lakh farmers in the computers. We plan to make this information available on the Net. The same Mahiti Centres will be able to provide many other value added services like e-mail, internet information, birth and death certification, panchayat taxes, information on government schemes etc. These kisosks will also provide the details of different government schemes and the amount spent in each and every village.

IT can make land registration simple and easy. People go to sub registrar offices for registering sale deeds, mortage deeds etc. as well as for an encumbrance certificate. This process is extremely cumbersome. To simplify the procedures for citizens, my government has already initiated computerisation of the department. So far, over 100,000 documents have been registered in a computerised environment. This will give relief to Bangalore citizens. Later, the project will be extended to the entire state.

The Government is using IT to protect the state's natural environment . The forest department has already implemented computerised systems to track poaching and other forest offences, improve wildlife management system as well as manage rare species under the Western Ghats programme.

The new technology can be used to effectively eradicate poverty and empower women. The latest technology in eradicating poverty is via selfhelp groups for women. These women groups are encouraged to save money. The government steps in with revolving fund as well as bank credit. This method is found to be the most effective in delivering rural credit as well as eradicating poverty.

IT can use e-governance as a tool and deliver a government that is more proactive and responsive to its citizens. It'll play a vital role in coordinating with the government departments as well as undertake a few critical projects that are likely to be used in more than one department.

Since most decisions in our system of democracy are taken at the village and district levels, IT provides an exchange database at a single point made available to all decision makers. You can also analyse the data in an intelligent manner and provide a sophisticated decision support system for the use of all decision makers. These are but a few aspects where IT can change our lives. There are of course many more ways.

The Masses get no Benefit from It

Laloo Yadav, Rashtriya Janta Dal Leader said that the impression that I am against Information Technology (IT) is completely wrong. When I said, 'Yeh IT, YT Kya Hota Hai, what I meant was that It is not all that important. But some BJP leaders, wanting a bit of fun at my cost, made it appear that I had mistaken IT for income tax, It was deliberate and mischievous".

Let me set the record straight — I'am not anti-IT. I do realise that IT has relevance in some fields and does provide job avenues. But IT cannot be the main thrust area of a nation like ours. For a country like India and a state like Bihar, the priority has to be agriculture and rural and economic development.

The use of IT is confined to the hi-fi log. The masses have no access to it and get no benefit from it. Agar yeh such nahi hai to Chandrababu Naidu ke highly successful IT pradesh mein kisan atmahatya kyon kar rahe hain? Bijli ke rates kyon high hain? (Why are farmers forced to commit suicide in Andhra Pradesh? Why is the power tariff being hiked?)

To those who harp on IT, my question is — Can IT plough the fields and provide electricity to farmers? Besides, how do you expect people to make use of IT in places where there is no power most of the time? It might be a priority with the urban elite but for the common man, the priority is still drinking water, health education and power. Without these, Internet and e-mail make no sense.

Indeed, if IT is as important as it is made out to be, why are they having to resort to manual counting of votes in the US? Where are all their super computers? What good are they? The American presidential election has exposed the tall claims of blind IT devotees.

It is obvious that IT cannot provide solutions to our problems. Take Bihar, for instance. Farmers here have produced more than 80 metric tonnes of paddy this year. But they are not able to sell it in the market because they are getting less than Rs. 200 a tonne, which is lower than the cost of cultivation. The Union government is not able to purchase their produce at the minimum support price. Why? Because it has made a commitment to the World Trade Organisation (WTO) to purchase a certain amount of agricultural produce from the world market. So our own stuff is rotting unsold. What will be the result? Farmers will stop cultivating their fields and our agriculture will suffer. Does IT have as solution to this problem? It needs common sense, not IT wizardry, to realise the implications of this ruinous policy.

People should know that India is being treated as a huge market. Our shops are being flooded with multinational goods — butter, milk, tomato sauce, you name it. Imagine, even salt might be imported from foreign countries! And all this being done with the help of the IT-backed electronic media. In the process, our dairies and indigenous industry are being harmed. Do you need IT to tell you these simple things?

That's why I do not attach much importance to IT. It can never be our sole thrust area. Too much reliance on IT is an alien apporoach. It does not cater to 90 per cent of our population. A more indigenous approach is needed to solve our problems.

Online Market Place

In recent years, there has been a drastic shift in the buying patterns of consumers, which is leading in the direction of simplicity. Buying at the online market place is very easy, simple, fast and secure. Business partners who know the potential features of online market place are turning Net to the to buy goods or services. Products are ordered online and payments are made online. Customers are attracted to merchants' websites considering them to be cost-effective online transactions. Shopping is convenient in an online market place, as it is free of hassles, no pressure with instant approval-subsequently increasing online purchases.

Buyers the world over are appreciating the convenience of shopping online. The online market place and online shopping features have gone from science fiction to reality within a very short period. The Net is the force behind its revolution. It is a virtual store online. Online storefronts and sites are usually supported by a database that allows for easy updating and searchability. The sites have the capability to process online orders using credit cards. Online market places are opened for business without any restriction, from anywhere to anywhere at any time, 365 days year with round the clock services.

Shopping online is an online market place which has taken over the internet world by storm. It has enabled businesses to reach a vast audience which earlier was inaccessible. Now, technology has allowed all businesses large and small, to powerfully present electronic storefronts and shopping online. Both the online marketplace and shopping transactions are rapidly becoming common sites on the Net.

Virtual Private Networks (VPNs)

The VPN is a network that uses a public network service as its wider area network backbone. These are more popular now not only in India but worldwide. In India too, the use of VPNs is gaining popularity. It is a sort of public network for private use, assuring maximum online security and speed. But the fact is that the VPNs market in India is still in its infant stage, but because of the favourable information technology policy, the telecommunication policy moved forward towards liberalisation and its accessibility.

This network mostly provides what is being called Internet Protocol Security (IPSEC), an emerging standard among the security protocol. Typically, the VPN software is run so that communication to and from a remote terminal like a hand-held notebook computer is securely provided to the user's office base. The recent release of Windows 2000 means that for the first time, such a security protocol comes built in with the operating software and need be separately implemented.

There are three types of VPNs :

Intranet: Intranet is also called as site to site or LAN to LAN. It extends secure private networks across the Net or other public network services.

Extranet: The Extranet VPNs are an extension of the Intranet with the addition of firewalls to protect the internal networks. They are ideal for e-commerce. They allow secure connections with business partners, suppliers and customers.

Remote Access VPNs: They are called as Dial VPNs. They allow individual dial-up users to connect it to a central site across the Net or other public network services in a secure way.

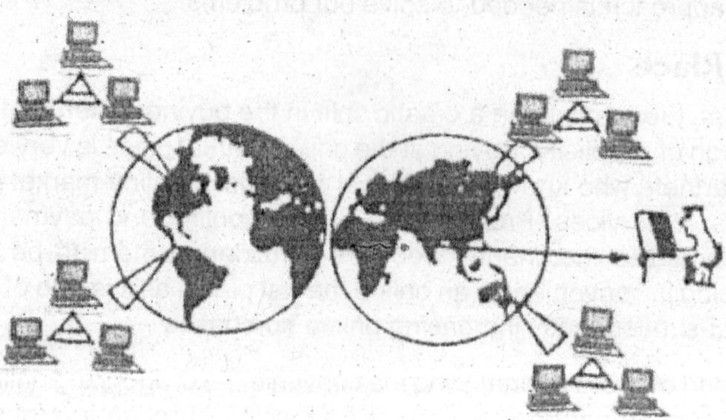

Fig. 3.23 A Global Network

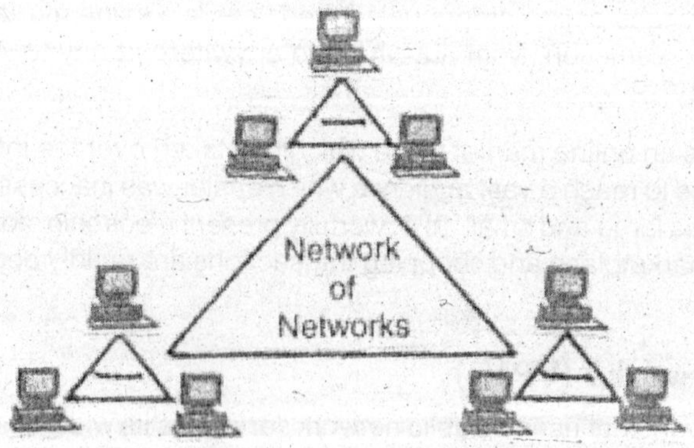

Fig. 3.24 Network within a Network

Protection to VPNs

They are as follows :

- The most promising is the Internet Protocol Security (IPS), an open Internet Engineering Task Force (IETF) which chooses standards that provide secure communication transparency.
- Point to Point Tunnelling protocol (PPTP) developed by Microsoft.
- Layer 2 Forwarding (L2F) developed by CISCO for remote access also.

Uses

- They help companies by reducing the overall operational cost of WAN through reduced telecom cost.
- It replaces dial up connection to remote users and leased line or frame relay connection to remote sites with local connections to an internet service provider.
- VPNs permit to increase the span of the corporate network and boost the efficiency of the organisation.
- Permits employees who are on move or travelling employees to access the network from any place and respond to messages faster and answer queries quickly.
- Offers e-mail facilities, internet access and control database services to users in remote offices.
- VPN uses the Net as the transport backbone to establish secure links with business partners. They extend communication to both regional and isolated offices.
- They significantly decrease the cost of communication for an increasingly mobile work force with potential sales by businesses.
- Product development can be accelerated. Strategic partnerships can be strengthened in a potential way.
- Eliminates the use of expensive lease lines or frame relay circuits. It is a secure way to access corporate network resources over the Net or other public or private networks.
- They include a number of security features including encryption, authentication and tunnelling. It replaces traditional dial up connections to provide access to remote users and telecommunications.
- Helps to connect LANs in different sites instead of using the public switched telephone network or dedicated leased lines. They can be used to give customers, clients and consultants access to potential corporate resources.
- VPNs cut long distance telephone charges because a user typically dials a local call to an ISP. They provide flexibility and cost savings as corporations extend their network to include remote employees and business partners.
- They save telecommunications cost by using the Net to carry traffic (rather than paying long distance phone charges) .
- They minimise operational costs by outsourcing the management of remote access equipment to a service provider.

Problems

They are :

- Many users worry about security whether the data over these networks are safe or not. Customer security needs to be maintained at all costs.
- Lines may be clogged up resulting in delay, lack of sophisticated bandwidth causes problems of prioritising the usage.
- Poor infrastructure is another problem.
- Failure of networks and the Net itself can play havoc to online business.

Cyberspace

The term 'cyberspace' which was often used in science fictions, has become a common use. It is used in prefix for many terms like cybercash, cybertrade, cyberpayments, cyberlaundering, cybercrimes etc. The expression was used in 1985 by William Gibson, an American author, in his science fiction book titled 'Neuromancer'. The book popularised the term 'cyberspace'.

It continues to be used in today's business language. It denotes information superhighways or 'infobahan'. It means a combination of computer, communication, telecommunications and the entertainment industries.

It stands for the shared imaginary and potential reality of various networks. The term is used synonymously for internet, and it includes talk, computing payments, shopping and other activities via computers and working through the computer network.

Cyberspace links are global in essence and the combination of five industrial segments like computers, communication, tele comprises of communication, electronics and entertainment which are required by consumers.

It is a new terminology in common use, indicating things happening in society leading to advances in technology in the areas of telematics and micro-informatics.

The virtual world is created when people exchange or organise information electronically, To communicate via cyberspace, an individual can send and receive e-mail, post views to a new group or set up a personal home page.

The Open Buying on the Internet (OBI) Consortium

In the year 1996, a round table was formed composing of buying and selling organisations. The object of this forum was to create an open vendor neutral scalable and secure inter-operable standard for business to business electronic commerce. This finally led to the formation of the consortium.

It is a non-profit organisation, dedicated to developing an open standard for business to business internet commerce. It is being managed by Commerce Net as it is an independent collaborative firm. Buying and selling organisations, technology providers,financial institutions and other interested parties on an annual fee basis are eligible to become members of the consortium.

The object of the OBI specification is to facilitate the rapid implementation of internet-based economic solutions by utilising inter-operable standard based internet purchasing systems. The characteristics of this system are universal high speed access, inexpensive paperless information and transaction and platform independent software services.

Thus, this will benefit buying orgainsations, supplier organisations and technology and service providers including marketing and trading hubs.

Objectives

The objectives of the OBI are to provide :

- An open vendor and platform neutral architecture for internet purchasing to allow companies to fit these solutions into their information technology infrastructure.
- Consumer choice, to allow the creation of buying and selling partnership for high volumes, and low dollar commodity goods.
- Inter-operability among purchasing systems to conduct business to business electronic purchasing, independent of technology providers.
- Healthy competition to allow buying organisations to select suppliers and technology providers based on their own criteria and not on the basis of proprietary technology.
- Standard solutions meeting the common means of organisations to conduct business to business electronic commerce.
- Public documents (requirement, architecture, specifications and guidelines) to allow all interested parties to implement OBI- based solutions.

National Informatics Centre Net

National Informatics Centre Net (NICNET) is a premier organisation in the field of information technology in India. It provides state-of-the-art solutions to information management and decision support requirements of the government and the corporate sector. The Centre set up a satellite-based nation wide computer communication network with over 750 nodes connecting the national capital, the state capitals and district headquarters to one and another. NICNET is a very viable gateway to the Net at the national level.

NICNET maintains its leading edge with the incorporation of a powerful Ku-band based national info-highway as an overlay network on the existing structure. It is connected with over 200 international networks in 160 countries through Gateway Packet Switched Service (GPSS) and has dedicated internet access through direct high speed link to SPRINTNET, USA, with more than 700 micro-earth station nodes in all state capitals, district headquarters and selected commercial centres. NICNET has the widest reach among online users in the country.

NICNET, in its present configuration, connects all central government departments, state government, secretariats, district administration headquarters and some public sector organisations in a single intergrated network. In parallel with setting up of its massive infrastructure, NIC has developed a large number of informatics services for almost all sectors of the government such as economy, industry etc. Any of these services make extensive use of NICNET, resulting in timely, efficient and reliable flow of information at different levels in the government hierarchy.

There is also court information system on NICNET. Access to NICNET for the national and internet e-mail will be provided from any of the nearest satellite earth stations of NIC spread over 500 cities and towns in the country. Connectivity will be provided on dial basis. The high cost of data circuits over STD or intercity dial up is not required.

Access to NICNET for other Net services will be provided from any of the major state capitals and important commercial towns.

NICNET—Internet Services

Its internet services include :

- Global electronic mail
- Views and News — usenet
- Remote login (telenet)
- File Transfer Protocol (FTP)
- Information servers-navigators
- Interactive access
- Remote database access
- Emergency message communication facility
- International mail facility
- Electronic data interchange
- International remote access and
- Internet access.

NICNET— National Info Highways

NIC was constituted in March 1975 and entrusted with the responsibility of bringing about a revolution in the work ethos. NIC's satellite-based computer communication network, NICNET went into operation in 1988. The reach of NICNET users went beyond the Indian borders as the network connected them to other international netowrks to provide access to all information on a global level.

Info Highway Services

The Info Highways provide a wide range of modalities of connectivity to its customers, who can access the network through the low speed VAST network or through PSTN of the Department of Telecommunications (DoT) or through internet working. As each of the remote stations as well as at the hub, facilitates connectivity and is created for providing WAN transit networks in the world, Info Highway services bring to users a host of services including :

- Inter-personal communication
- Emergency message communication
- Access to more than 200 networks in 160 countries
- File transfer
- Electronic data interchange
- Integrated nation wide banking service
- 400 e-mail services
- Multimedia communication
- Tele-conferencing
- Full text and bibliographic retrieval
- Hytelnet, WAIS services

- VLDS access services
- Distributed GIS
- Large scale data broadcast services
- NICNET Info Highway also offers special value added services like EDI, image transmission, multimedia transmission, teleconferencing and directory services.

Info Highway Features

They read as follows :

- The network supports high communication at variable data rates beginning up to 2.2 mbps through KU-band SC PC data pipes, at each of the remote sites. Modular design enables the upper limit to be pushed by multiples of 2.2 mbps to cope with the growing demand of these services.
- NICNET info Highway implemented as an IP-backbone network to facilitate creation of intranets and easy internet connectivity.
- The Network Control Centre (NCC) has a seven metre antenna. This antenna has automatic tracking facility and has all its major modules duplicated for high reliability and availabilty.
- The NCC has a Star Network Management System (SNMS) to monitor the network.
- The network has the capacity to increase the speed at selected nodes upto 2.2 mbps without any major investments.
- Each remote station uses a 1.8 /2.4 metre antenna equipped tracking facility to work with inclined or bit satellites.
- To overcome rain attenuation in the KU-band, the master station is designed with the automatic uplink power control.
- Remote stations have the necessary interfaces to support both synchrnous and asynchromous circuits.
- Remote stations can be configured locally or from the Master Earth Station (MES). These remote stations will provide both operational as well as monitoring information to the network control centre.
- The highway incorporates a cost-effective data broadcast facility which uses the same RF portion of the MES but has separate sets of digital equipment. The data broadcast network will initially support 32 data magazines. This can be extended subsequently to support data magazines in the multiple of 32.
- Multiple gateways of 266 kbps each set up at Bangalore, Mumbai, Kolkata, Chennai and Delhi (to be upgraded to 2 mbps at Delhi).

How to Connect to the Net

Any person who is desirous to get connected to the Internet, necessarily has to obtain an account from VSNL. The interested Net users can participate through the VSNL by paying a prescribed amount to the latter.

There are two different rates to get connected depending upon the status like students, professionals, individuals, commercial orgainsations etc. There are two options of dial up account available to use the gateway internet access services. They are terminal dial-up or leased services and TCP/IP dial-up service.

The procedure involved in getting either the terminal account or a TCP/IP account is similar. To get this account, the following two steps are involved :

- To get a modem form the computer suitable for use on telephone ines.
- To contact the VSNL to obtain the application form and fulfil formalities to initial the Internet connection.

After a careful scrutiny of application, if it is found satisfactory in all respects, the subscriber will be given a login name and password. The subscriber is subsquently ready to log on to the VSNL terminal account to go on to the Internet.

How to Get on to the Internet

Getting on to the Internet is a very easy procedure. One is required to fulfil the following criteria to get on to the Internet :

- To have a compatible personal computer
- To use internet software, to possess a modem
- To get online via service provider i.e. VSNL in India, which will give the e-mail address after opening an account
- To get the personal computer hooked onto the internet
- To get an internet account from the internet access provider
- To connect the telephone lines to the modem and the computer
- To load the window operating system
- To connect to the internet using dial-up networking of windows
- To launch a web browser i.e. the microsoft internet explorer or netscape navigator.

TCP/IP

The acronym TCP/IP stands for Transmission Control Protocol Internet Protocol. It relates to the internet account and deals with procedures developed for interconnecting net computers and communicating data. Internet is called network, because of the use of TC/IP. Actually, TCP/IP has given birth to the Internet. The TCP/IP account facilitates to connect any network or computer with the internet. Today, it is possible to initiate interconnection of all types of networks, private BBS communities and individual PCs in both home and offices. Internet works because they follow a simple procedure of the TCP/IP account.

An individual computer or networking computers have to use protocol in order to achieve the object of messaging across a network. It is the practice under the internet management to follow a set of rules laid down which is known as the *protocol*. It defines and sets certain standard rules which all computers want to link with each other to confirm to these pre-determined standard set of rules codified in the networking protocol. Different computers maybe running on different types of operating systems. Though they are running on different operating systems, the protocol enables them to communicate effectively. Thus, TCP/IP helps the user to transfer data from one computer to another computer.

The TCP/IP account is must for an internet connection-without it, one cannot approach the Net. When once the user connects to the Net, it means he is making connection to any other computer on the internet.

VSNL, as the second level of access, provides a direct TCP/IP account. The subscriber can use transmission control protocol / internet protocol software to connect on a dial-up or leased basis to the GIAS system and access online services available on the Net. In this mode of access, the users will be required to use software for e-mail, file transfer, remote login, mosaic, WWW etc.

Computers talk to one another via the Internet. This communication is possible through a common mutually agreed set of forms and procedures, which is the *protocol* used for potential information exchange. The technique is designed to ensure upto date transmission of data between the two computers. IP stands for Internet Protocol which receives the data from TCP and trasmits to its destination. As such, any kind of information can be sent over the Net.

It is a feature of the Net computer that every computer linked to the Net has a unique Internet Protocol (IP) address which distinguishes it from other computers on the Net. The address is four sets of digits separated by dots. The INTERNIC, i.e. the Internet Network Information Centre is the one which gives IP address to those getting connected to the Net.

Some Internet Concepts

I-Net: India's domestic Public Switched Packet Data Network (PSPDN), I-Net is provided by the Department of Telecommunications (DoT). I-Net, in its first phase of operations, has nodes at eight locations. I-Net is inter-connected to Gateway Packet Switched Service (GPSS).

I-Net is a domestic switched network which is connected to the GPSS, and subscribers of these networks would also have an access easily to cities of India and they would also be able to avail advantages of I-Net in addition to subscribing to GIAS.

NUI: The acronym NUI stands for Network Users Identification. Subsciber's access to Gateway Packet Switched Service (GPSS) is permitted through a confidential user access code called Network User Identification. The subscriber can use same NUI from Mumbai, New Delhi and Kolkata for accessing GPSS using local dial-up numbers.

RABM: This acronym for Remote Area Business Message Network (RABM) is a data network of the Department of Telecommunications, exclusively developed for communications from remote locations of India. It is inter-connected to Gateway Packet Switched Service in Mumbai.

Easynet: The Videsh Sanchar Nigam has an agreement for database access through EASYNET—the knowledge Gateway system of M/S Telebase Philadelphia, USA. This provides an easy access to over 850 databases around the world. EASYNET system can also be accessed through the gateway packet switched service if the user obtains a password from VSNL by paying prescribed annual password fee.

Free-Net: This is a community bulletin board system which provides free access to local residents. There are many free nets, which extends to all, initiating full internet access.The National Public Telecommunications network support freenet based in Cleveland, Ohio.

HV-Net: It is a high speed VSAT Network of the Department of Telecommunications and it is interconnected with the Gateway Packet Switched Service (GPSS).

Ether Net: It is a local area network technology. The technology has created an ethereal universe and user to become an internaut.

Point-to-Point Protocol (PPP): The PPP software allows a Macintosh or PC to act an internet host. You can use Mac or PC applications to read news, send/receive e-mail, transfer file etc. The only hardware requirements are the modem and telephone line. CS DC uses PPP instead of SLIP because it is a newer and more robust protocol. It is also faster when properly configured. The Serial Line Internet protocol (SLIP) is similar to PPP in functionality. It is older and not as flexible as the PPP.

Netiquette: These are seen as a few unwritten rules of conduct on the internet. A set of guidelines on legitimate behaviour on the Net has been implemented. It covers net using abuse or libel over the Net users.

Kilobytes Per Second (Kbps): It is a standard for measuring data transmission speed. Another standard is cps-characters per second, which is generally $^1/_8$ the kpbs rating. A 56 kbps connection transmits 56,000 bits per second. A page of text is about 2,000 bytes or 16,000 bits.

V. 32 Bytes: This is a modem protocol that allows modems to communicate online speeds of upto 14,400 bps (bytes per second), and upto 57,600 bps when the data is compressible. Realistic data transfer rates average at about 1,500 characters (bytes) per second using the Zmodem or PPP.

Internet Service provider (ISP): The Internet Service Provider has made internet access available to the private person. Commercial services charges people either a flat fee or an hourly rate, and they inculude America Online, Compuserve, Netcom and Prodigy. There are more and more local providers emerging in large cities as well. Internet access service is provided by designated service providers. In most parts of the world, this access is provided by the service providers for a fixed charge.

In India, the sole provider is the Videsh Sanchar Nigam Limited (VSNL), the Government of India's designed external service provider. It has two types of services. For ₹ 15,000 a year plus registration charges, it provides 500 hours for one year — whichever is exhausted earlier via the TCP/IP protocol. It means the subscriber can receive text, picture, sound clips, movie clips — whatever is available on the worldwide net.

Another method is that VSNL provides a shell account or text only without graphics or sound service for ₹ 5000. The bona fide students get this service at concessional rates. The VSNL holds monopoly in association with the telephone department as the Internet Service Provider.

Those who opt for the text only service need not invest in a standard browser like Netscape Navigator or Internet Explorer. VSNL provides a menu where users can directly access websites through their URLs or one of the half a dozen internationally known search engines such as Yahoo, Infoseek or Lycos.

The modem is the most popular internet access device which connects a computer to a telephone line, which in turn connects to the modem at the host computer. This is known as a dial-up account because the computer takes route through a process similar to dialing a phone number to gain access to the concerned person.

Access to internet is connected or provided by an Internet Access Provider (IAP). The provider may be a small local operator or one of the large commercial online services. In India, VSNL is the only internet access provider, with its scheme — the Gateway Internet Access Services (GIAS) which enables subscribers to log onto databases, send e-mails, read news, download files, remotely running programs on distant hosts and a range of other applications.

The VSNL has the following options for enabling gateway internet access services :

Shell Account: By using the dial-up access linked to the GIAS Host, the primary level of access for internet users is using this service set up by the VSNL at each of the nodes. By connecting to the host computer, the users would be able to use all internet services. In this node, the users would be using a simple terminal emulation from their PCs and will not require any special software on their machine. The limitation of this access node is that access is primarily limited to text based services.

TCP/IP Account: VSNL as the second level of access, provides a direct TCP/IP Account. The subscriber can use the TCP/IP software to connect with a dial up or leased basis to the GIAS system and access online all services on the Net. In this node of access, the users will be required to use software for e-mail, file transfer, remote login, mosaic, world wide web etc.

Packet Switched Network Access: This third level of access provides access via packet switched network i.e. I-Net, Remote Area Business Message Network (RABMN), Gateway Packet Switched Services (GPSS) and HV-Net. Subscribers of these netoworks would be able to avail full range of internet services using the Shell Account and TCP/IP Account.

Internet Agents

The expression 'Agents on the Net' is commonly used in search engines. Agents are programs that intensively search the Net to give specific results to the Net users. Agents can also be customised and scheduled according to a user's need.

So, agents simply mean programs that will enable users to do bidding automatically. Agents are run over the Net on an individual computer everyday. Agents can find the following for the net users :

- The latest news
- Download it to the computer
- Monitor internet traffic
- Report on its total usage
- Find the best deal on the CD one wants to buy
- Perform important web maintenance task and
- Perform jobs cooperatively.

On the Internet, agents are called 'spiders', 'robots' (simply bots) and knowbots. The popular search tools such as Lycos, Infoseek and Altavista use spiders.

The user first has to select the needed task and the agents automatically go off and perform the required tasks. A variety of several languages can be used to write agents' programs.

Working of Agents

1. *Gathering News:* A simple internet agent is one who gathers news from a variety of sources while you are not using your computer or while you are using the computer for another task. Newsagents can work in several ways. In the simplest example, you fill out a form saying what kind of news you are interested in and at what schedule do you want your news delivered. Based on that information, at present intervals, the news agent enters news sites on the Net and downloads news stories to your computer where you can read them as HTML pages.

2. *Best Bargains:* Shopping agents will let you search through the Internet for the best bargains. On the Web, you fill out a form detailing the product you want to buy. When you send the form, the shopping agent launches programs that search through a variety of shopping sites and databases on the Net. The agent looks into the databases of those sites and finds the best prices. It then sends back to you the links to the sites so that you can visit the sites with the best prices and order the products from there.

3. *Web Maintenance:* Web robots or web maintenance spiders can perform important chores related to web maintenance. On websites, particularly large ones, very often HTML pages include links that become outdated. In other words, the objects being linked to have been taken off the Net. Whenever a user clicks on the link, an error message is sent. A web maintenance spider can look at every link on every HTML page on a website and trace each link to see if the linked object still exists. It then generates a report of dead links. Based on that report, the system administrator can rewrite the HTML code, getting rid of the non-existing links.

4. *Extra Load:* When robots and spiders do their work on a remote internet site from where they were launched, they tend to put an extra load on the sites' system resources, for example, by swamping the server with too may requests in too short a time. Because of this, some system administrators are interested in ways of excluding robots in certain circumstances by not allowing robots into certain web directories. A variety of ways have been devised to limit robot access including creating a file called Robots. txt. that describes the areas of limits to the robots, which the robots would automatically adhere to and not visit the sites.*

Some Network Security Measures

Presently, internet security measures are not adequately available. Many people believe that it is not an application technology. In addition to the above, appropriate measures may be adopted:

- This will retain customer loyalty to a great extent.
- Physical access to the servers may be controlled.
- Total security is almost impossible, so strategies must be worked out to enable people to detect breaches of security.
- To create an awareness and develop a culture among the members of the groups.
- It is also necessary to identity levels of protection for various aspects of information transmission.
- It is more safe to use a separate password to run servers.

* *Computers Today, 1-15, April, 2000, pp. 76-77.*

- In tune with the advancement and the emergence sophisticated technology, the outdated hardware and software programs and communication devices must be replaced from time to time.
- To adopt network auditing facilities.
- Use of fibre optic cables are more desirable as they cannot be easily trapped. In case of twisted pair cables and coaxial cables, they should be concealed to prevent easy access to information.
- Use of encryption coding in business messages and data communication ensures security.
- Even passwords can be encrypted. It is also desirable to avoid passwords embodied in communication access scripts.
- See through devices will also help to a great extent.

  (*for details, see the chapter on e-commerce security*)

Advantages of Internet

The use of the Net has grown among people considering the advantages of being online and accessing sites on individual discretion. To mention, it is of publishing and propagating information, the ability to provide continuously upto-date information, freedom from the time zone and other constraints etc. Following are the advantages of being on the Net:

1. *For Operations*

- It is cost effective
- A great equaliser
- By establishing relationships with merchants and customers to exchange products and services
- Business can gain contracts with strategic online planning
- Flexibility
- Automation of operations
- Saves time
- Unlimited transactions not limited by their human factors and
- The entire process is automated.

2. *For Pleasure*

The Internet can be used at home :

- To exchange electronic mail instantly with college friends or family members.
- To participate in group discussions on topics that interest you, through the public newsgroup or bulletin boards.
- To find educational tools. Universities around the world, book stores, libraries and school systems are sharing online information, enabling students to register online for registering in these universities. Here, qualification matters to a large extent.

- To entertain — it is fun and easy to spend an hour surfing from one topic to another and one site to another.
- To shop-commercial electronic storefronts are growing in number. You can now order flowers, music and computer equipment over the Net.
- To read about interesting sports and leisure events and choice topics.

3. *For Business*

From the business point of view, the Net can be invaluable. It can be used to :

- Get technical support for products being used by consumers who are new net users.
- Distribute software.
- Provide technical support, bug fixes and product information to the customer.
- Publish information such as technical or marketing literature to the net users.
- Communication or collaboration on various projects.
- Market and sell products online and
- Boost your business while away from the office with a global online recognition at the click of a button.

4. *Others*

They are as following :

- It facilitates the ways to share information.
- Send, retrieve and receive e-mails needed.
- The user can send mail to others on the Net.
- Just typing the correct e-mail address facilitates online communication fast.
- Internet can be explored as a form of pleasure, entertainment or fun or for personal communication — its main application being access to information in a big way.
- ISD is cheaper in terms of charges.
- It is no matter for the internet as to what kind of computer to use.
- Daily millions of messages are sent by individuals, corporations, organisations and government etc.
- It enables the people all over the planet to communicate within seconds.
- Internet acts as a international computer which is connected through a network at the user end.
- The widespread deployment and universal acceptance of internet technologies have created an opportunity for new class of low cost clients who focus on accessing internet based information services. The client primarily runs the internet application such as browsers and e-mail.

Internet-Uses, Services and Applications

The subscribers of the Net can obtain benefits from the existing potentials of the Internet device. It is a global information super highway to the cyberspace and can be used both for pleasure, business generation and commercial purposes. The user of the Net can log onto the databank, send e-mails, read news, download files and remotely run programs on a distant host. The range of other applications or uses to which internet connection can be put to is continuously getting enhanced with the availability of hypertext information, world wide web, video and audio files.

The growth of the Net i.e. the window to global information superhighway has revolutionised the way global network is related for international access to global information.

There are several services or uses available for which the Net can be put to. The wide variety of uses of internet available is expanding slowly. It is recognised today that it is a single global unparalleled technique for most of the problems. It is a superpower along the highway which offers solutions to all sorts of global problems.

One cannot explore the vast potential of the Net and the resources offered by the computer, unless some electronic tools are used.

The important uses or applications of internet are as follows :

- E-mail
- Usenet
- Telnet
- File transfer protocol
- Archie
- Gopher
- Veronica
- Mosaic
- WAIS and
- Real Time Chatting

E-mail

The basic use to which the Internet put is e-mail or electronic mail which abolishes the distance between the countries, friends, business associates etc. The essence of networking, i.e. the e-mail, permits to send messages quickly and easily. They travel almost instantly over the network to location around the world. E-mail is the most widely used Internet service. Messages given by e-mail may include text, graphics, voice and video.

The internet is the most suitable global medium for sending e-mail. Corporations, individuals, educational institutions and research institutions are using the internet for transmitting data through electronic mail. Electronic transmission is greatly facilitated by the internet wherein the user types the message and it travels instantly over the network to the receiver. It permits to send messages to a specific person or group. Network information allows the user to send messages on an electronic bulletin board for all to access it.

UseNet, News Groups, News

The concept of UseNet pertains mainly to the Net. The members of UseNet operate with an understanding of the other members of UseNet to share and exchange news between the user groups. It is a way to share information and discussions organised into thousand topics (from celebrity matters and fan clubs to academic discourses). Similar to list servers, this forum is very public, open to anyone on the Net.

News groups are composed of articles posted by readers and contributors on particular topics. A post is called an article which is nothing but messages to a news group. There is a separate program known as news reader which is operated to read UseNet news. It facilitates to establish a link with the news group or the subscriber to the news group, read articles or post articles on the news group. Thus, the UseNet is a public forum.

UseNet is a quite distinct and different system of global communication network, and it is not exactly similar to the Net. The news group is the basic block of UseNet, composing of a collection of messages with related themes. On the other hand, the network groups are referred to as conferences, forums, bulletin boards or special interest groups. It is news internet, which is one of the useful internet applications. There are thousands of these news groups available online in different languages.

It is also called as Net-News. It is one of the important segments of the Net. As a popular online application, NetNews (NN) is a system of interactive communication composing of various topics. There are several thousand groups ranging from recreational to scientific matters. The quantity of information we receive is approximately equal to a 500 page book per minute. The quality of information varies from excellent to not so good information.

The UseNet is a distributed bulletin board system strategically spread over to hosts throughout the entire world. There are discussion groups on almost any topic which can access in an instant by typing 'NN'. The entire news feed uses upto 500 megabytes per week.

A group of people using the Net is called the user group. Under this service, the users can communicate with a group of people at the same time by sending messages to all the people in the group. This is called news group e-mail. One can leave information on the electronic bulletin board where the user can invite responses.

There are seven major categories of news group. They are :

- Computer science and related topics.
- Group concerned with news network and news software.
- Group discussing recreational activities, hobbies and art.
- Group discussing scientific research applications.
- Group that addresses social issues.
- Talk groups or a forum for debate on controversial topics and
- Miscellaneous activity that does not fit in any of the above categories.

A part of the internet computer space is devoted to news groups, electronic notice boards, bulletin board service (BBS) and other areas of special interest. It is a program which presents these discussions, enabling users to ask questions, circulate opinions and get help etc.

How UseNet Works

Global Bulletin Boards: UseNet is a global bulletin board and discussion area. It collects messages pertaining to different topics into newsgroups which are freewheeling discussion areas in which anyone can participate. Newsgroups can be found on many host computers. There are thousand newsgroups that cover just about every topic you have ever imagined and many you probably have not thought of and would like to enter into a discussion.

Posting: To participate, people send and read messages that are posted on the newsgroup. There are two kinds of newsgroups: moderated newsgroups and unmoderated newsgroups.

In a moderated newsgroup, a human moderator receives and reads all the messages for the newsgroups. The moderator then decides which messages should be posted. The messages to be posted are subsequently put on a newsgroup server and other messages are discarded. In unmoderated newsgroups, all the messages are directly put on the server. Newsgroups and all their messages are stored on a UseNet server. They are organised by broad categories and then broken down into specific topics for target discussions by Net users.

Duplication of Messages: UseNet servers communicate with one another so that all messages posted on one server are duplicated on other servers. While there are many UseNet servers, not all servers carry all newsgroups. Each site decides which newsgroups to carry to ensure quality topics and discussions.

Pictures, Multimedia: Pictures and multimedia files and even executable programs can be posted in newsgroups for other people to see and use. However, because of the technology used in newsgroups, these files must be specially encoded to be posted. To view, play or use files, you will have to first transfer them to your own computer and then decode them with a special software package. A common encoding scheme used on newsgroups is called *unencode*. There are versions of this encoding and decoding program that works on the PC, Macintosh and Unix Computers. Mime is another encoding scheme.

Reading and Responding: Newsgroups reader software lets you read messages and respond to newsgroups. The software gives you ways to manage your newsgroups besides enabling you to subscribe to these newsgroups, which means that new messages will automatically be delivered to you when you check the server. You will also be able to cancel your subscription.*

TelNet

Yet another important segment of the Net is TelNet, which enables the Net user to log on from one computer to another computer via the Internet. Thus, it refers to both the protocol and the terminal emulator that allows Net users to log onto other Unix hosts. TelNet permits to access other computers via the internet by using TelNet. As a protocol, it allows the users to be on one computer system and do work on another host computer which may be located very near or it may be a distance communication. Thus, TelNet allows the user to log onto a remote system. It is an internet program that gives the user power of the internet to connect to database library, catalogue and other information resources around the world. There are several sites dealing with different areas of interest around the world, which can be searched on the Net. They are agriculture, bulletin board systems, business and finance, computers, education, environment, games, geography, geology, and the government.

Cyberspace has its libraries, in which TelNet is one of the keys to these libraries. TelNet application strategically permits users to log on to another system to avail and access the services available on the host systems. The user can use the TelNet by grouping data into voluminous database across the Internet network.

---

* *Computers Today, 16-30, April, 2000, pp. 80-81.*

File Transfer Protocol (FTP)

This is the most important service available on the Internet. It is a protocol for transferring files on the Net. A Unix system that has files will enable the user to access the FTP program by logging onto those hosts, using a username of *'anonymous'* and your address as a password. On Unix system, the program that does this is named 'FTP'. Zip files. (used on PCs) require binary mode transfers, and the user will just type 'bin' at the ftp prompt once he is connected. It is a client server protocol which permits the user on one computer system to transfer files to and from another computer system. The user knows the addresses of the host computer at the remote site.

FTP is a method or tool as the name suggests, to copy files from the remote host to the main host and vice versa. It is the best method of transferring files from one computer to another computer over the telephone lines.

Anything available on the Internet can be obtained by way of copying the data/documents available on the Net. There are libraries of documents. As such, one can also get a copy of the recent US Supreme Court judgement from the Net, besides obtaining FTP copies of historical documents. The users can get songs, lyrics, poems, credit collection, credit rating, distance education, fashion design, shopping, journals, photography, virtual gallery, yellow pages etc. from the Net.

Archie

This is a program that allows the user to search for information stored on anonymous and large FTP sites on the Net. TelNet can be used to access Archie servers. It can be accessed by e-mail. It is in other words called as the search program.

This program helps to look through several anonymous file transfer protocol sites. It indicates the location of all these files required by anyone. There would be many anonymous file transfer protocol sites. It is the function of the internet application of the Archie server to collect services, and as such, each of these services is responsible for keeping track of file locations in these anonymous FTP sites.

Archie servers have the capability to communicate with each other and gather and combine their information into a huge global database. There is also a facility of periodical updating database. A file can be searched and located in the database just by giving a keywork to search for. So the Archie server tells us where the files are located. The Archie catalogue subscription maintains a list of about l,200 internet file transfer protocol archive sites of approximately 2.5 million files containing 200 gegabytes of information. The current catalogue requires about 400 megabytes of disk storage.

Gopher

Gopher is part of the Internet. It has the capability to *'Go For'* textual information from a huge public database. Simply put, it is a potential file finder one can see on the computer screen the rest of files presented by Gopher.

This is a menu-based information retrieval system that allows the user to locate and retrieve information on the Internet. There are a list of government gopher services available in/pub/govt. text.

This use of the Net would permit the user to hop around the Net looking for information in various informaion libraries or servers, without having to struggle hard to know where the materials are specially located. We often hear net users talking about *gopher space* In the Internet, there are several hundreds of inter/connected libraries called *gopher libraries.* So, all gopher libraries make up Gopher space.

The distinctive feature of gopher is that it practically goes around and collects the potential information required by the user and displays it on the computer screen. This is the fundamental difference between Archie and Gopher. The inter/connected menus of Gopher allow the user to burrow deeper and deeper into the database until he gets the information needed for which he is looking for. The gopher service of the internet was developed at the University of Minnesota.

It searches information from a large database. It is a file tracer or finder which displays on the computer screen lists of files and drab text documents. It is a menu-based program that enables the user to look for information without the knowledge where the material is specially located.

So, gopher space is another word used to describe the entire gopher network spanning the Net.

Veronica

Veronica, an acronym popularly known, stands for Very Easy, Rodent Oriented Network Index to Computer Archives. This technique of internet application helps to find neat files in the gopher space more quickly. It is a search tool that would permit the user to quickly scan the gopher space for a particular file or essential directories. As precursors to search engines, these *'client programs'* will search the Internet in various ways and return either lists of sites or actual data to the Net users.

Veronica is a program that can be accessed through gopher. It requires the user to enter a keyboard. It searches quickly through a database of over 5, 500 servers and over 10 million gopher items of files and directories.

Veronica is both fun and amazing because it not only finds files but also gets all these files and directores. It is a big database of information that is available through gopher space. This program helps to track all the gopher menus that can be accessed by the user.

Mosaic

It is popular graphical interface for accessing the world wide web gopher and other services. Version 2 is still being tested and is buggy but has more options. Performance under PPP has much improved and proves satisfactory to those preferring desirable image downloading.

Mosaic brings the way we use the internet into the new era. Its feature is that it is an easy way to reach audio. video-text and graphics.

WAIS

The acronym WAIS Stands for Wide Area Information System. Its task is to search or scan internet libraries as soon as the user types in the word or specific topic. WAIS, as a result, returns a master index providing links to all the sites relating to the user's request. There are WAIS programs designed to work independently of the Web with the help of special gateways software, and the user can reach these programs. It is a distributed database protocol for sophisticated searches over the Net.

Real Time Chatting

This is a program available to users across the Net to talk to each other in real time. Internet Relay Chat (IRC) supports a channel metaphor; where each channel is on a unique topic and can have a number of simultaneous users. IRC tends to be full of immature people flaming each other. *Flaming* is the posting of offensive remarks to newsgroups. What happens when someone does something controversial or stupid in mail, news or IRS ? It is a nasty or unpleasant response to a message that someone has sent out. If you get flamed by a stranger, do not take it personally. It is best to stop any further communication in this online chat programme.

Chatting interactively in real time is also one of the most widely used services on the Net. It permits the user to exchange messages or voice in real time on the Net, but the user has to use a suitable kind of software. There are several factors which influence the quality of exchange of voice like application, the capacity of the computer and the compression method adopted etc.

Limitations of Internet

Though there are potential uses of the Internet, shortcomings also follow with this global technological link. The following are some of the important problems associated with the Net :

1. *Ethics:* As the internet is growing fast, so is a host of ethical concerns about its application ethics and norms. Researchers, scholars and the early users of the Net would like to protect the internet from censorship. But law enforcing agencies particularly in those countries where the Net is widely used and has intermingled in the threads of the social fabric are considering means to curb impersonators, pirates and other improper users. At present, censorship is mainly intended to protect children against gaining access to indecent data on the Net.

2. *Pay-Service:* In the beginning, everything that was available on the Net was free. It was intended to provide help to researchers around the world. But as the popularity of the Net grew over the years and is growing, a number of pay-service networks are appearing.

3. *Copyright:* Problems of copyright and security have already surfaced.

4. *Disinfestation:* The existence of the Internet as a democratic information infrastructure. seems threatened by the notorious web-based terrorists who attempt to spread disinformation and the software giants who are trying to define webonomics are working towards preventing the detrimental rates of cyber crime.

5. *No Owner:* Some people think that the Net may eventually end up in being a medium of ideological propaganda. But at the moment, such concerns do not seem to be well founded because unlike other technologies of the past, the Net is a diversifying rather than a centralising force. It is not owned by anyone.

A Network Computer (NC) is a stateless system designed for accessing network information and services. It is the network server on which all software, data and configuration information rests. A network computer runs specialised software known as network computer operating system which is special to its server vendor. There exists no option, and the hard drive exists for the enhancement or local storage of private documents.

6. *Traffic Jam:* The rising popularity of the Net is creating traffic jams and at certain times of the day, the networks are so crowded that it is practically impossible to connect with certain servers and go online.

7. *Lack of Autonomy:* Though there are advantages, the NC model is not without its limitations. The end users lose their autonomy to run their own software, create and keep their own data and to configure their own systems.

8. *Crimes:* Internet theft and cyber crimes are on the increase. Today, there is no safe strategy for the information put on the Internet. It is a public network. The mechanism of internet must ensure unwanted access to this information and ensures security to customer to customers. A number of cyber crimes came to light in recent years which have been identified and investigations were also conducted throughout the world. They are mostly taking place in companies, banks, private organisations, government departments and public sector organisations.

There are two types of cyber crimes. They are :

- Data related crimes and
- System related crimes

Data related crimes include tampering with the data , unorganised locking of data, entering into various databases etc. System related crimes include tampering with programs, change in program logic, trozan horse program, trap doors and super japping etc.

9. Cyberlaundering: Cyberlaundering is yet another new internet crime. It provides facility for the transactional transfer of financial value through the Net. It facilitates an unprecedented anonymity and security for users involved in financial transactions. Consumer articles are taking online. There is no technological breakthrough that can bring cyber based transactions within the perview of law. Laws of most of the countries do not cover cyberlaundering as it has not been anticipated as a futuristic online exercise. The technology makes it difficult to unravel the names of the persons involved in cyberlaundering because it traverses countries and their laws. A transaction passes through and the problem is which country has the right to impose tax has the right to take action against the violators of the law.

10. Security and Privacy: Online communication requires that the security and privacy of information given by customers be ensured and these are the two most important issues today.

The fact is that privacy and security are generally used synonymously and interchangeably. But both are different problems. They are used in the same breath because of technical reasons, but these two problems need separate solutions.

The security factor involves inclusion into the private network connected to the Net. The privacy factor is concerned with the information that goes out over the internet itself. Snooping into the contents of a message is the most important privacy problem. The users need protection.

11. Language: Internet use is associated with English language and with urbanisation in a multi-cultural and multi-lingual global world, the benefits of internet technology are available only to few people. Language is the biggest problem to computer literacy. The social impact of computerised english language should not be ignored. In a multi-cultural and multi-lingual country, using the computer for vulnerable business is Insignificant. Alternative languages are to be worked out to meet the requirements of the different countries and regions within the country. Thus, the majority of the Indian population has no access to the Net.

❑❑❑

E-commerce Websites

Web-Meaning and Concept

The Internet Technology has woven the world into a web and hence it is called the World Wide Web (www). The Web is a part of the Internet for all practical purposes.

In recent years, the concept of Internet has emerged as an interface, a window opening into the world of information- a way of getting to where an individual plans to go.

A web is a magnificent and elegant communication structure. The world wide web is an area or part within the internet. It is like a big library. Websites are like books and web pages are particular pages in the book. Pages may contain news, images, movies, sounds, 3D worlds, animation etc. Web pages can be accepted anywhere and everywhere in the world. When a computer is connected to the Web, the user has equal access to global information in terms of his area of interest. The Web helps to look at a document on the Internet in an instant. The essence of the system is, that these documents as well as links between them constitute a web of information.

The phenomenon of World Wide Web has made the network easier to use, operate and navigate. Web is a group of internet users who developed and designed it as a general purpose architecture for substantial information retrieval. It is composed of different files, libraries and directories distributed throughout the internet and connected with the client server architecture. The World Wide Web displays pictures, text, sound and even interactive programmes. It has the capability to attract people who seek information in their areas of interest.

Website — The Concept

The 'Web' is a term related to the web pages associated with a particular organisation and they may pertain to one subject or an array of issues pertaining to our daily lives. A Website is a combination of the home page and on-line collections of documents that spans many internet servers—they are all connected by 'hypertext' and contains tools that enable searching of sites by the users.

This topic will help you to understand how e-commerce on internet works and how service providers help you to build your own e-commerce websites. In this new business medium, it is necessary to get your business on-line, maintain it and work out strategies to attract customers to your website. Marketing and promoting business on-line is quite distinct from traditional offline. The new member of an e-commerce enterprise needs marketing and promotion to stand out from millions of other sites. The era of personalisation is approaching fast and authorities on information technology believe that personalised news will inevitably happen, though it will have some drawbacks. It is said that lightning communication will create a global village, where information will spread like wild fire and the possibility is that people will withdraw into their cubicles with emphasis on their narrow interests.

A lot of companies have been developing web venues from a design perspective, slick colours and flashy graphics that look nice and attractive. The web designers also represent product industry etc. In addition to producing greater functional sites, some web design companies have created venues designed to meet corporate objectives, drive new and existing customers to these sites and generate substantial returns on investments.

The website is a business tool of an organisation or individual used to generate revenues, streamline operations and improve communication with the customers. The objectives of developing an effective website are as follows :

- High quality service;
- Cost effective website;
- Marketing solutions for companies of all sizes;
- Exceptional customer services;
- Reduce operating expenses and
- Returns on investment.

Web technology is a universal access tool to acknowledge information and opinions, allowing each individual the power to choose and personalize what they want to see.

Today, there are tens of millions of pages on the web, and tens of thousands more are added daily. In this overwhelming flood of information, the possibility exists for a website to be last amongst competition. So, specialised organisations should address business and internet e-commerce sites solutions. If a user wants to build and deploy a website, it is to be remembered that it is a business, just like any other store, a website is a business, not an advertisement.

Many have failed to understand one basic principle-when other people enter your website, they have entered your place of business. This means that they have entered your website for using the services as per their choice and needs.

Website-Meaning and Nature

A website is a door through which the customer can enter the virtual company. Interactive websites can be developed by using the latest technologies like Java script, CGI, Shockwave, DHTML etc. A website design should be visually appealing as well as professional looking.

Many companies are advertising their website locations and their e-mail addresses on their stationery, on TV, radio, advertising in newspaper, magazines, bill boards and the public transport network. The web addresses are an open door to information enquiries and orders for services. A presence on the Web promotes image of the product, assures quality services to customers and encourage new customers to visit these sites. Information is printed on the catalogue, price sheet, brochures, newsletters, advertisements, forms, handouts, vendor data etc.

Getting on the web means getting a company's address on the information super highways, giving prestige and promoting image and leaving an impression on the customers.

It is a link together of more than one web page and you have a recipe for your eyes, hence the term 'wibsite'. The term 'website'* has special significance in browsing the Internet.

The world wide web has sites pertaining to various areas of interest. There are retail sites, portal sites, hardware, manufacturers, record company sites, artist sites etc.

---

* *Robert Ainslai.*

Site designers design and develop page and product lay out templates to meet their needs by making large product database easily available and efficient. Anyone can build a website in a business like any other store.

Once a website is created, the next step is to navigate the world of online marketing and promotion, to bring potential customers to the site and help them there once they find these sites. They are customer oriented, giving them all the information and services that they need. Publicizing the website is an important task on the part of the company. Business built up as per the traditional supply chain find benefits in dealing with suppliers over the site.

There are many service providers to design a site and handle e-commerce transactions, there are useful tools to create attractive, compact graphics including sound, animation, video and analyse visitor statistics.

Frequently Asked Questions

To get started an effective e-commerce transaction, it is imperative to do some groundwork to get established on the web, which is a potential venue for business. With some materials and principles in mind, one can proceed to commence e-commerce online. There are so many frequently asked questions (FAQS) by the business, and they have been addressed below.

Addressing some Frequently Asked Question (FAQS) on E-commerce Website

1. Web Cost: Every business planning to go on the Net will put a question as to what is the cost of the Web facility. The answer to this question is very simple. It truly depends on the type of service available online. Spending upon e-commerce service software and support on computer hardware are major components. Similarly, high-end solutions and internet services will cost more than the basic online brochure.

2. Starting a Website: Remember, an e-commerce website is an extension of business, making it imperative to develop business plans. Gathering information on the target market to figure out exactly what role the website has to play in business and subsequently decide proportional and appropriate internet services that will meet specific needs are to be given priority. Besides, it should work towards preparing and obtaining a feasibility report, study market plan details based on the business strategy and establish short-term and long-term services for online business.

Fig. 4.01 Spider on a Web

3. *Finding Website:* Among several FAQS, how will people find a merchant's website is the most frequently asked question. There are various ways to promote a site. The basic question is from where does traffic come from? The answer is unequivocally clear. Search engines and online directions portal giants such as Yahoo, Infoseek, Excite, Hot Bot, Altavista will help people find the website, so promoting a site on the locations is vital.

4. *Updating Site:* Updating the site includes the provision of latest information and changes, keeping the site current is crucial for online business. There are several options for mailing sites to update and revise websites. They range from installing administration software to online processor-based administration.

Revising and updating a website is a potential concern for business. Keeping the site current and updated is vital to its success in the eyes of customers. Providing with practical options for keeping the site current is the standard element of the development and expansion of online business.

5. *Procuring Orders:* How to receive orders from users is an imperative question regarding any business proposal. Though there are several methods of getting orders, the popular and standard method of receiving online order is by e-mail. Alternatively, there is a possibility to have e-mail, or fax in ordered forms as well as digital forms on the site are automatically faxed to the concerned business. As such, it eliminates the need for a computer in business locations and can be somewhat simpler to maintain than e-mail ordering systems.

6. *E-mail Account and Domain Name:* The user can have an e-mail account that reflects the domain name. The mechanism permits to establish as many e-mail accounts as required to the user. In addition, it is possible to install a feature of forwarding all messages from multiple accounts to one-e-mail address.

7. *Features of Website:* Website design is very contemporary, requiring the services of graphic artists and web developers. A web page may generally include a logo, photos, artwork, background and the text. It is complete in all respects with appeal and functionality for easy navigation.

A website design should contain the following features : colours, header, logo, photos, title, subtitles, keyword and description, placement with search services, descriptive content and copy, navigational links to other content areas, links to e-mail, graphics and images, sized for quick loading of pages, hit counters, meta-tags list website in the search engine and list website in directories.

Furthers :

- Different companies may have different website faces.
- Contents website also considerably vary from company to company.
- Check facts by going around the website presently available that intrigue us.
- Look around competitors' sites.
- Keep site distinguished from competitors' site.
- Site can be simple and complex depending upon the potential, types and online experiences of the business.

Types of Web Sites

It is practically not desirable to have a uniform face of websites for all companies. Different companies may have different faces of these websites. The contents of their websites also differ widely. The size, competitor's site, experience, budget, design skills and other factors influence in the selection of e-commerce sites. Generally, the e-commerce websites can broadly be classified as follows :

- Simple web page
- Multiple web page
- Shopping basket and
- High end e-commerce sites.

A brief description of these sites is given below :

1. *Simple web page:* A simple web page may deal with basic things, for instance say 'hello'. A single page website is simple and is a desirable one for the e-commerce website. It is very simple to design. The page may contain basic features of the product or service and the company such as :

- Corporate logo
- Address
- Phone, fax,e-mail, number and addresses
- A link to e-mail address
- Contact page etc. and
- A brief product description

A simple web page has certain drawbacks. They are:

- It does not provide full information to the visitors.
- There may be a number of enquries and doubts to be answered through e-mail.
- Product or service specifics are not available.
- Visitors may not show interest in the site contents and contact.
- It is difficult for people to order and enquire about the services.
- It may not probably attract more business.
- A simple website cannot withstand the competitor's website.

2. *Multiple page website:* Because of some practical drawbacks and limitations in case of the simple web page, this led to the designing of the multi-page website. In this, a site may have several pages, and each page may deal with one aspect. For instance, each page may contain the information on each of the following;

- Corporate profile
- Corporate machine and philosophy
- Contact address (e-mail and website)
- Product
- Services

- Solutions
- Software technology
- Reseller arrangements
- Case studies
- Success stories
- Affiliates and associates
- News
- Free train and rates
- Catalogue online form etc.

A multi-page website permits to this type of website with graphics, a profile of the business and catalogue of products and services. As online forms are available, the visitors can easily contact as well as make early inquiries or place orders for the services desired by them.

3. *Shopping Basket:* An e-commerce site to be effective and sound must be flexible, dynamic and a complex high end site. It is because of the fact, that as the business grows both in size and the number of customers, more variant services may be required to be rendered from the e-commerce site. For instance, a typical customer from a particular country may need a full-fledged online store to browse, select and check out many items easily and quickly without the need to contact many people personally.

All these requirements resulting in designing a website is known as 'shopping basket website'. The features and advantages of the basket website are :

- Look at different items
- Add items to the basket
- Make modifications to total order before submitting credit card information
- Responding to customers' suggestion
- Site is easier to operate
- More useful to customers
- Tied it in more effectively with accounting user registration and inventors' systems
- A full-fledged shopping basket online stores space, time, efforts and skills.

4. *High-end-E-commerce Site:* In the high end e-commerce site, the online store is connected to other information systems, orders are taken automatically and processed automatically. So, the business will become more efficient with the help of database. Under this, it is possible to confirm the identity of the customers and customize pages. It also satisfies the needs and requirements of the individual visitors to this site. Besides, it also provides discount for different types of customers. The special feature of this site is that it integrates online purchasing with accounting, inventory, manufacturing and shipping.

Thus, the e-commerce website can be basic, multiple page, small or large, complex or powerful depending on various factors. The mechanism permits to change at any time according to needs, but a site cannot be changed just for the sake of change. It is not a fashion. Any change calls for new strategies which means incurring more costs.

How To Design A Good Website-Products and Services

Hyper Text Mark-Up Language (HTML)

The tools include :

- User interface engineering
- World Wide Web consortium
- Yale Webs style guide.
- HTML100
- Bare Bones Guide to HTML
- Web references
- Web master only
- Web receiver and
- Marketing the web with a faster face.

All these services help design a good website. They are the potential resources for web developers. The User Interface Engineering conducts all sorts of interface research and helps web designers to develop websites. The world wide consortium is an international standard body, defining official specifications for HTML and other web-related languages like XML and scripting languages etc. Web reference gives a lot of technical information and serves as a potential resource for those accessing different websites.

On the other hand, the web master only gives the sources for information and tools help designers to develop dynamic and exciting websites.

Web Colour

This includes Browser safe colour—which is of potential use for labouring on the web. It contains a 216 colours palette. The Two 4 colour page has great colour potential with colours in both RGB values and ashex values. It is an online colour composing engine. The phoenix is used for e-mail with features like browser safe and other colours. In the Netscape's Colour Cube, suggestions to convert RGB images to Netscape colour model are given. It is non default for the Web.

Graphics and Clip Art: The following are the graphics and clip art products and solutions:

- Paint shop pro
- Adobe Image Ready and Image Styles
- Macro media fireworks
- View pro
- Microsoft photo draw
- Zoom web clips
- E-mages
- Tudog clip art
- Web graphics resources

- Mining co-logo design
- Graphics by silver
- The Stock zone

Animation: This includes :

- Animation factory
- Animation zone
- Animation online and
- Amazing animated banner maker.

Essential Requirements in Designing a Good Website

This topic outlines the basic steps of setting up a potential and profitable website without technicalities. The road to successful e-commerce is riddled with various pitfalls. Armed with proper knowledge, one can avoid mistakes that may be experienced by many online merchants who may go out of business even before they really got started.

In this topic, several commonly found, stumbling blocks to e-commerce have been identified and considering them, it may lead to offer easy solutions to ensure the survival of online stores.

How to design a good website, what are the essentials to build a good site is being concentrated here.

1. ***Legal Aspects:*** The web designer must consider copyright issues anytime when copying images on the web or scanning photographs and images available elsewhere. In case of clip art files, the problem has reportedly taken a serious dimension. But generally, many images are copyrighted and scanning and manipulating of company logos requires skills on the part of the web designer.

2. ***File Size:*** As far as possible, it is always prudential to keep the file size small. Visitors at websites in these days will not have to wait too long to look at pages. Besides, larger images load slower. In fact, the good principle that needs to be followed by the web designers is that they should limit the size of all the texts and images on a web page between 25k - 30k in total. Buttons should be limited to not more than 5k. Larger illustrations and photos should be within 25k - 30k. Some designers reduce a graphic's file size by making it black and white. The graphic file size can be reduced by making the image dimensions smaller by using transparencies and turning off interlacing.

3. ***Add Graphics:*** Visitors are less attracted when only the text is included. They may leave the site in most writings and many may not even like the site since they might not be interested to look, read and hear to understand the contents of the website. In most cases, sites are unprofessional because of misspelled words, typos and incorrect grammar implies that they are not professional business persons.

Text alone will not make the website attractive. In the early days, the internet was a text place. It is the graphics which has made the world wide web popular. It is also easy to pack as much information into a page of words as into one picture or image. A picture is worth a thousand words. But creating graphics for the web is not an easy endeavour. It is a skilful art. There are solutions such as Graphics Interchange Format (GIF) which is mostly used for logos, cartoons and illustrations and joint photographic experts group for photographs and detailed art work files. There are graphic programs such as Paint Shop Pro, Adobe Photoshop, Corel, Photo-Paint etc., which permits to select file types when graphics are saved.

4. *Consistent Design:* A website and graphics fit the professionally designed site lay-out. It should be always keeping to the same pattern or style and unchanging. A preview or post view helps to fit into the design. Resizing older designs and creating new graphics is desirable to fit the spaces in the site desired. There are many solutions that will make it easy to fit business person's information into a consistent design. The solutions also allow to select from a dozen site designs.

When a business person titles a site, he includes not just the name of his business but some keywords which many people are likely to search for. Some important words or phrases of site text are called keywords which many people are likely to search for. Some important words or phrases of site text are called keywords. Selection of a title along with several keywords form part of and parcel of the web design. Keywords do not appear on the screen in the website. They are important. The search engine will find these words. The search engines visitors use Altavista, HotBot, Infoseek, Lycos, Webcrawler, Excite etc.

The search engines have the capability to make note of the keywords and help searchers to find them. Keywords are included as META tags because they do not appear on the screen. But they are hidden inside the code that makes up the site. The visitor can view, read or take printouts about this hidden descriptive information from the homepage which he visits.

5. *Title of the Web Page:* There should be well thought out titles for the website which should be finally selected. It also should contain a short description and several keywords about it. Generally, the title should be made to appear in the title bar at the top of the web browser windows. The title is very important. The search engines pay attention to the title of the site alone. It is to be remembered that a website's title should indicate pretty well what the site is about. When titling a site, it is not just the name of the business that is imperative but it should contain some words which people like to search. The wise selection of the website title is a key factor in ensuring potential business and using a phrase to describe a business name in the title will help web users to distinguish one site from the other.

6. *Personalization:* The Personalization feature is essential to the existing external website or internet. The feature must allow website visitors to select which lines of news, product and/or service topics they wanted to see each time they browsed the web page.

7. *Repeating Visit:* A website containing information must generate frequent repeated visits to the site. The customers or clients are presented with only those news items, announcement and special offer links which they consider important. It may have an impact of generating frequent repeated visits to the site.

8. *Compelling Message:* The website must be designed in such a way to deliver a compelling message to buy and appreciate the attractive and effective text and graphics crafted by experts like web designers with over active imagination and understanding.

9. *Evaluation:* Another imperative is to accurately evaluate and increase the use of the appropriate search engine, establish banners and links to bring qualified visitors to the site. Besides, it requires the harvesting or purchasing of leads to increase customers' base and generate additional sales cut and the cost evaluated periodically from individuals and organisations. The object of evaluation is meant for the sole purpose of raising standards of the web to a new and sophisticated level and the design must attract national and international clientele. The site should be easy to navigate and simple to purchase items, adding new features such as auctions and coupons have added advantage. These features allow to constantly update the site. There must be capability to combine offline promotions with the website.

10. *Competitors:* There are many popular and familiar sites on the world wide web. If you plan your own website, then it gets imperative for you to check out strategies to compete and gain superiority over the existing sites. There is no other potential alternative. You have to possibly make the website more effective, technically efficient and visually appealing. You alone cannot do it. There are critics for your site. Follow the standards for website development. The contents of the site, design, technological and navigational aspects that a site possesses is equally important.

Thus, it involves special skills and resources to design and establish successful presence of a website in cyberspace. Keeping a website upto date in both content and technology is vital to reaching and maintaining the potential technology friendly audience. A continuous use of a variety of measurement tools to ensure long term success has been deemed necessary time and again.

A web design philosophy is simple that its design be based on the perspective of the customer, which inevitably decides profitability.

11. *Working Hours:* The website is to be kept open for operation 24 hours a day, 7 days a week and 365 days a year.

12. *Simplicity:* It should have the capability to process orders of customer's safety, simply and easily. All that is needed is to check e-mail from home and ship the product to the customer ordering for the services. It is that simple.

13. *Anyone can Operate:* There should not be any need that every user be a cyber geek to build an online superstore.

14. *Marketing Website:* Without technical experts, it is not possible to market the Internet website. The websites will never achieve effectiveness unless customers can find it.

15. *Cross Links:* Maintaining as many lines from similar or related websites to the main website is good for building traffic to the site. The cross-link facilitates sites to automatically take advantage of added traffic.

16. *Tracking Visitor's Selecting Topics:* An effective system should have the capability to track visitors and to identify which visitor has selected which topic and when. The users should spot marketing trends and the most and least popular topic selection made by the visitors. It is essential for successful e-commerce trends.

17. *Dynamic Site:* Any company creating a website must satisfy a condition that the site must be dynamic and responsive in order to meet the information needs of the customers.

18. *Dedication:* The site needs to be dedicated exclusively to e-commerce marketing and selling products online.

19. Security: Security is to be available to the website easily, rapidly and at lower cost than more expensive. The other two important aspects are increasing the bottomline of e-commerce and allow the growth of business.

20. Site Promotion: Promotion of site online is the key to successful e-commerce. Everyday thousands of new websites are appearing on the Internet. So, a site is to be strategically promoted, otherwise any site will be invisible. It is more appropriate here to know the basics of site promotion in the context of e-commerce.

A sound principle of website promotion is that it is better to put into specialised areas relating to the field of business rather than keeping the word to everyone on the net, stratifying the Net. It is not possible to reach everyone. For instance, cable at the satellite television channels have divided the television viewing audience. So, the advertiser cannot reach the potential audience but now these channels are fast changing, attracting audience of diversity.

There are several methods of promoting business sites. But the selection of an appropriate and effective one would work towards promoting a particular business.

The best way to go about promoting a site depending upon the product, service, coverage, type of site, competition, newness etc. is by working out strategies to hire services of professionally reputed firms having a good track record and good reference. However, a site is to be marketed in a variety of ways. Newer and newer ways of online and offline methods are emerging frequently. But it is essential to keep an eye on them. This will promote potential business.

Methods of Promoting Site

There are two prominent methods to promote sites. They are: Online promotion and Offline promotion.

1. Online Promotion: The following are some online promotion tools :

Search Engine : When a site is built, its promotion takes place in the form of submitting the Universal Resource Locator (URL) of the website to the major internet search engine. There are a number of search engines like Yahoo and Altavista. But Yahoo is the direct and best known search tool. It is a directory of websites. Following the instruction given in Yahoo submission URL, the site's information is sent. There are smaller and larger search engines and directories as well as specialised engines that meet the target audience. There are many other ways to get people to the site.

2. Announcement: There is the Yahoo Announcement site list, with the help of it, one can opt for the preferred site. Zinerack and E-Zine list sites are useful for the listing of electronic magazines. Besides, there are several internet-e-mail mailing lists such as PAML as well as Yahoo's newsletter list where it is possible to even place an advertisement.

3. Web Advertising: Internet advertising is another dimension of e-commerce. Web advertising is still in the infant stage and is not well recognized particularly in India where it is still developing. Online advertising like graphics is an expensive one. As such, small businesses cannot afford to go for web advertising. The target audience group exposed to web online advertising is not significant. It is much lower than for the similarly priced radio or television advertising. Therefore, only large companies with a larger market audience and budget can afford web advertising.

4. *Usenet and Mailing ist:* Usenet still shows a sign of a widespread canvas and a good place to promote business. The term *Usenet* is also called as news groups. Online Usenet news group is accessible with the news group-reading features and is a good place to promote business. Another advantage is that news groups and the mailing lists are free, so they are cost effective. But while selecting Usenet, one must be careful because all groups may not accept commercial postings. They have their own written and unwritten rules not favourable for business promotion.

5. *Cross Linking:* *Link* is another fundamental unit of hypertext. A link is information embedded that connects it in some way to another mode. Cross-linking is one of the site promotion tools. It is the cheapest way to promote business. It is a technique wherein one has to use a search engine or directory to find some other good sites relating to the field of business, then cross link with them and this provides a link to them from one site and they link back. The company can contact the other sites and make necessary arrangements for crossing of sites. It is always desirable not to have too many cross links, otherwise the visitors may lose interest and prefer to jump another site which is more interesting and not boring. A single link is reasonably good.

6. *Hiring:* Another best way to go about business promotion is hiring someone. In this, e-commerce solutions providers arrange to submit the site to dozens or hundreds of search engines for a nominal fee. In hiring a particular method of site promotion, it is always effective to target specific search engines. It is good to hire someone with reputation, someone who is professional and genuinely knowledgeable with a successful track record.

7. *Spam:* What is Spam ? The unsolicited commercial-mail and Usenet hostings are known online as Spam. Generally, people get annoyed a lot in the case of junk faxes and postal mails. Besides, Spam is free, and hence people use it, causing a real problem on the Internet. Therefore, those who have been online for long time are experienced to receive dozens and even hundreds of Spam e-mail every month. It tends to result in inconvenience with so many unrelated spam messages. It leads to problem of servers being a victim to crash due to hung amount of free spam e-mail being overloaded. The only remedial measure is to make Spam illegal and imposing fine.

8. *Offline Promotions:* There are still many people particularly in India who are outside online. Such a group of people are still the majority of potential customers. E-Commerce site is only a part of the entity and is not separate from business. It is the part and parcel of business marketing plans. It includes both URL and e-mail address and offline. The internet information can be made available everywhere, phone number and addresses are there. Bill boards and business cards also can be used to contain URL. Therefore, a balance is to be maintained between the offline and online marketing of sites.

Searching the Web

A web is searched for information services by visitors, online services usually provide access to the World Wide Web. A web has a number of pages, from which information is obtained. There are various models for searching the web:

- Searching by directory
- Searching by topic
- Searching by key word and
- Searching with search engine.

Each www is a unique name to go round called Universal Resource Locator (URL). With URL, the user can log on to a website or web page. Manoeuvering around a web page is possible by using the keys. Navigation is a process of moving within the hypertext web to establish hypertext links on a page.

To obtain information on a particular subject of interest on the Net the Web is used. The Internet is the large repository or space platform of information placed by users. As such, the size of the Internet is very large - so searching for information and mobility on the Net is complicated. As separate software packages are designed and developed for searching the web for information, the software package is called *search engine.* There are many search engines, which are available for use to find information:

- Altavista
- Web Crawler
- Yahoo
- Lycos
- Infoseek and
- All Web

Software Tools

The products and services for successful e-commerce must help to design sites and handle e-commerce transactions. There are several tools which help create attractive, dynamic, compact graphics, exciting, containing sound, animation, art etc. The following are the graphics and multimedia tools to enhance sites:

1. ***Paint Shop Pro:*** Web designers mostly use this tool for designing graphics.

2. ***Macro Media Flash and Shock Wave:*** The tool is used to create a small, efficient and attractive vector animation in the site.

3. ***Real Server and Real Tools:*** Real audio and real video are the widely used tools for streamlining content on the Web. Its services include creation and serving multimedia content.

4. ***Macro Media Firewalls:*** This is a software of web graphics.

5. ***View Pro:*** It is a program of Windows 95, 98, NT image processing to handle image formats on the Microsoft windows environment.

6. ***Microsoft Photo Draw:*** It is a photo editing program.

7. ***Snag-It:*** It is a program designed to create animation and movies on the site. Other features include multimedia, screen and video capture.

8. ***Quick Time Pro:*** It is designed by Apple, which allows viewing and helps create compact movies with sound tracks.

9. ***Abode Image ready and Image styles.***

Issues in Web Site Strategy

Every business must strategically create and play a website to be effective. Otherwise, it will find itself lost in the business bandwagon in future, with business strategies changing in a big way.

- Are you using all the available web design technology to maximize you web design development objective?
- Will your budget allow you to meet your objectives of website design?
- Have you properly identified your target audience?
- How can you ensure that you can be found on top of the search engine?
- How can you get audience attention?
- Are you trying to syndicate your site?
- What are the most cost effective ways of producing a site?
- Are your future objectives realistic?

Do you have all the answers to these questions? If so, you may have to compare your answers with your competitors.

Ways of using Web Sites

- Some business people use the website for selling physical items which might be shipped, and picked up by customers. For instance, cars, books, plants, computers etc.
- To sell information in one form or another by using the downloadable software, digital photographs, articles by subscription and more.
- To sell services, writing and editing, accounting, psychic advice etc.
- Combination of two or more of the above.

The sites of any business may fit into any one of the above categories of a website.

World Wide Web Consortium: It is an international standard body that defines official specifications for HTML and other web related languages such as XML and scripting languages.

Yale Web Style Guide: It is a potential well researched and comprehensive guide to design websites with strategic planning.

Web Reference: It provides technical information and web resources most useful both for beginners and experts.

Web Master only: It is a premier source of information and has tools to help develop dynamic and exciting websites. It also helps in maintaining lists and online resources.

Benefits of Website

- Specially designed site is addressed to needs whether it is small office, home office, mid sized business-they are just curious about products or services to reach a global audience.

- People learn about solutions available to enable them to manage information technology.
- Gives users a global visibility, helps and makes convergence to e-commerce in future business more transparent.

Site Services

It includes the following :

1. Hosting: It includes the presentation of the site using existing internet services or host them on the high bandwidth server.

2. Design: This service covers preparing attractive, appealing, contemporary web graphics including animation, three-dimensional design, page background, logo creation, digital video etc.

3. Programming: As one of the site services, it helps in the creation of sites. It includes programming by using the web developer tools such as PERL scripting language. It is possible to automate the creation of sites. It means large data can be converted into the web format.

4. Support: Technical support is always available on the Internet from the beginning for web users.

5. Presentation: In addition to design, the capability to create text on pages that presents business professionally is equally important. The activities may include writers and proofreaders having skills in technical and public relations writing.

6. Features: They include custom designs of all major site enhancements on the web like Java scripting, real audio, sound services, custom forms, animation, database presentation and secure online transactions.

Browser/Web Browser

Web client software is that which allows you to view or '*browse*' the World Wide Web. Netscape and mosaic are both *'web clients'* that let you browse information on the Internet organised on the website.

A browser is an internet computer program which reads documents from the client and displays it on the computer screen. It has the capability to display internet files by mixing graphics, pictures, tables, text, sound and animation (multimedia). It glances through a file, reading bits and pieces in a casual way. It reads desultorily, it means jumping from one thing to another, without rational or logical connection, rambling, hasty, loose.

A browsing program helps to display information on the World Wide Web. It is a client program or application program. The Internet server provides information while the browser is used to search through information provided by a specific type of server. In the Internet operation, the user can view and navigate efficiently and quickly through information.

Netscape navigator and the Microsoft Internet Explorer are the popular browsers, which offer graphical interface to the World Wide Web.

Browser works on Internet software, which is unique in essence, which permits the user to witness or browse the Web. One can access the web through the browser. A browser can read documents, fetch documents and access files by FTP, read usenet news group,Telnet into remote sites and even travel around gopher space. In short, everything about Internet discussed above can be done by using a web browser. Web is able to accomplish all this. The URL lists the exact location of any Internet Resource.

There are many web browsers available to access on the Internet. They are Netscape, Internet Explorer, Opera, Smart Browse, Netquest, Netcaptor, Net positive and Neoplanet.

Among them, Microsoft's Internet Explorer is the most popular, running around nearly 60 percent. Netscape stands in second place.

These browsers have their own modest download sizes.

Web Browser and Internet Clients

The following are the popular web browsers and Internet clients useful in the web world :

1. *Opera:* It is small, using fewer systems software and is a commercial browser. It is from Norway.

2. *Netscape Communication:* It brings the web to the world, including e-mail calendering and more.

3. *Lynx:* It is used to read text only. It is very small and very fast.

4. *Microsoft Internet Explorer:* It is a browser best integrated with windows including enhanced navigation tools such as Explorer Bar.

5. *Cute FIT:* A web browser programe written in a very systematic manner widely used for commercial File Transfer Protocol (FTP). It can be used to move files to or from ISP or the web server.

6. *Neotrace:* It is used to see graphically on the Internet, where packets make their way through the wires. The process of e-mail movements from the sender to people around the world and the problems connected to the site can be observed.

7. *WSFTP:* It is designed for Windows 95, 98 and a functional FTP client.

8. *Web TV viewer:* It permits to see as to which site looks to the growing number of people using the television to surf the web.

E-commerce Hosting Services

The essential tools needed to enable a website for e-commerce may include :

- Registration of domain name
- Using Secure Socket Layer encryption and access to a secure server certificate.
- Electronic commerce software for building and managing a web-based store.
- Real-time credit card payment systems service,
- Internet access dial-up.
- E-mail account,
- Technical support right from the beginning

- Additional credit card payment systems option from Cybercash
- Employ Private Secure Socket Layer (PSSL) certificate instead of using the shared certificates,
- Presentation and
- Internet connection and a web browser to keep the products in the web-store upto date.

E-commerce hosting services such as Yahoo store (http://store.Yahoo.com/vw) and E-commerce online (http://www.icatcorp.com/products) can help one develop an e-commerce website. The hosting service provider will then run your e-commerce system on its own web server.

Using a web browser such as Netscape Navigator or Internet Explorer, you can connect to an e-commerce hosting service and develop an e-commerce site in a few minutes simply by answering a few questions. Yahoo store charges a minimum of $ 100 per month for the use of its site-building tools and for hosting the site which you as a person built, depending on the number of items your company is selling. ICat commerce online charges $ 50 per month for similar services. Although Yahoo Store and I cat Commerce Online are two of the best known hosting services, AT&T, IBM, NCI and GTE also provide hosting services for large complex companies. Many hosting services for large companies base monthly charges on the number of transactions those companies conduct. For example, AT & T charges $ 395 for the basic services that include the first 500 transactions.

Internet Browsers

The following is the list of browsers and their download size for Window 95/98 NT platforms.

Browser	Download size
Netscape	4.08;15.1 MB
Internet Explorer	5.01;17MB
Opera	3.61;1.3 MB
Smart Browse	3.9 MB
Net Quest	3.2 MB
Net Captor	5.04;770K
Net Positive (for Beos)	
Platform R4 for Intel)	1.2 MB
Neoplanet	5.0; 3.5 MB

Website Service Providers

World Internet Resources (WIR): Electronic commerce development creates e-commerce. venues for WIRs produce e-commerce sites.

WIR helps merchants to maintain a successful e-commerce presence while integrating web-based transactions with existing sales and distribution channels. WIR uses the AT&T secure buy services to ensure all credit card transactions are safe. It has created the following e-commerce sites :

- *Scents for Less :* Discounted home brand men's and women's fragrance and cosmetics.
- *Smartwiz :* Children's educational and family software.
- *Swintec :* One of America's leading business equipment company.
- *Capelbos gift basket :* It is New York metropolitan area's premier retailer of fresh fruit and gourmet gift baskets.

WIR thus helps develop and build secure extranet systems geared to improving relations with client, customers, vendors, distributors and manufacturers.

The products and services of WIR are as follows: World Internet Resources (WIR) is an interactive business communication firm specializing in website development and online marketing solutions for corporations of diverse industries and sizes. WIR was founded in 1995 to creates undertake and redesign print brochures and other corporate literature and thereby unifying communication efforts. Online presence pertains to including cyber costs and multimedia for the web allowing to broadcast company meetings, lectures, training etc.

As a world internet, resources produce e-commerce sites and they offer the following related services :

Fig. 4.02 Search on a Web

Database Integration

The service of database integration is intended to provide an interface from a website into business related data. It enhances work flow and customer service by providing visitors to access the website to real time customer information, account information, sales history, shipment tracking etc. In addition, it will integrate the website with existing sales and inventory databases.

WIR has an inhouse database department specializing in the following:

Java (IDK 1.1)	CGI	X Windows systems
JDBC	ORACLE	Visual Basic
Visual J + +	Sybase	VB & Script
C	Informix	Visual Inter dev
C + +	DB2	Visual C + + 5.0 6.0
MSSQL	Windows NT server	JavaScript
4.x 6 x 7.0	Perl	ASP 2.0
ADO 2.0	ODBC	OLEDB
Developer Studio	Power Builder	SQL windows
x view CORBA	RDBMS integration	–

Client: Its client include AT&T, Tiffany & Co., Lawn Dector, Daiichi Pharmaceuticals, Exogen, Fujipoly, Gleicher Manufacturing, Milestone, Scientific, MAAC Conference, National Institutional Tournament, National Trust for Historic presentation and Team Hormony Foundations.

Development: WIR is interested in creating a new website and improving design functionality and interactivity to existing online venue. Development includes facilities from internet or extranet creation to e-commerce application and database integration.

Its comprehensive development process involves:

Discovery: This involves bringing into the forefront business objectives and creating a long term online business strategy.

Identity: Examining the unique attributes about the company/product to determine the most effective way to represent them online.

Creation: Establishing a great looking site design, structure and compelling content that will appeal to customers and keep them returning on a regular basis.

Education: It includes information about the company and industry while enhancing knowledge about doing business on the Web.

Marketing: Some of the services of marketing include the following :

- Website coding for higher search engine directory listing.
- Search engine registration.
- Reciprocal links with sites related to product, customer or industry.
- Banner ad, creation, placement and search engine keyword buys.
- Targeted e-mail campaign with a direct link back to site.
- Offline advertising, marketing promotion like radio, cable, TV etc.
- Online research analysis and recommendations of effective online marketing and offline e-marketing strategies to reach target audience.

Frontera Design: Frontera designers specialise in simple and elegant to cutting edge websites and e-commerce sites using Java Script, Customer CGI, Scripts and dynamic HTML. Frontera design provides professional complete graphics and designs for website development, motion graphics, multimedia, print and training.

Its activities are as follows :

Website Development: It includes: Site planning, Design development, Forms, CGI, Java script, Shockware/flash dynamic HTML, Database integration, E-commerce, Video, Audio, GIF, Animator, Animated banners.

Multimedia: Digital video, Quick time UR, Authoring, Interface design.

Motion Graphics: Design, Production, 2D/3D animation

Print: Brochures, Advertising, Business systems

Training: This pertains to : Education and instructional media development.

Web-Elegant Structure

It is an internet service that provides hypertext access to information on the Internet. You may access Gopher, WAIS and other services from a WWW browser. Web is an elegant structure of information despository and communication. It is a part of the internet which displays pictures, text, sounds and many interactive programs in a magazine page like manner.

Web is able to catch anything and give access to Information on the internet. It is a reservoir of voluminous bits of data. It is a new terminology in information technology. As a matter of fact, the existing dictionaries have to be rewritten to take account of the IT terminology. With the browsing program, a Web can be displayed. It offers wider scope for communication and exchange of information globally on a wider canvas.

Web-Origin

The World Wide Web (WWW) address first started appearing on billboards in 1995. The online life is dominated by the Web only. In the early days, WWW was mainly used :

- As a publicity vehicle.
- To put brochures online.
- To provide information to customers, and
- To general hype-use of publicity and advertising to make people aware of a product.

Thus, the web is a face and WWW is an engine of the Internet, which is seeing explosive growth since 1994.

The origin of the Web can be traced to begin in the early 1990s as an effort in creating hyperlinks between pages of text at the CERN physics research facility in Europe. Another development was that the web browser software became capable of displaying graphics too.

Thus, the Web has become a glamourous face of the Internet and is available and accessible early to use graphical images, point and click for navigating through lakh pages of information. Promoting a website is the way to make the presence of a business known globally.

The web site helps by acting as :

- Advertisement
- Brochure
- Catalogue
- Storefront
- Order desk and
- Service centre

The Internet Service Provider (ISP) account gives :

- An e-mail address
- Space to put a website and
- Helps to register a domain name

There are website creation softwares to create and launch websites without learning any HTML. For instance, EC Builder is a popular website creation software.

Factors for Growth of Web

Here various factors responsible for growth of the Web are being concentrated upon. Following are some of the key factors :

- International recognition of Internet and its potential.
- Extensive global use, both for business and non-business activities.
- Encouraging and favourable information technology policy of various countries.
- Availability of security, privacy, authenticity of technologies like encryption, SSL, SET etc.
- The proliferation of PCs, LAN, WAN, Intranet, Extranet, Modem etc.
- Availability of open standards such as TCP/IP, HTTP and HTML
- Cross platform support.
- Multimedia support and ease of use.
- Complementing the system infrastructure.
- Web application development from Intranet to outside of an enterprise through Internet.
- Evolution of e-commerce i.e. online shopping and availability of sophisticated solutions.
- The number of internet users has been growing at a staggering rate. In January 2000, the number of internet users worked out to be about 250 million. More and more people and companies are taking advantage of Internet and shopping online. Nearly a third of the Internet 250 million users are accessing the World Wide Web.
- The emerging information superhighways facilitated global access to companies and business.
- One stop IT providers and developers have been providing the most caring services, meeting professional and technical needs, extending excellent support on common issues associated with internet connectivity.

- The facility and effective working of the reseller program or partner program. Reseller program is an excellent choice for every professional who provides IT without investing on high end equipment and technical support stage.
- Availability of web solutions and services including web hosting on different platforms, co-location, web design development, promotion, hosting promotion and customised programming and
- Cost-effective, user-friendly, global visibility and convergence to e-commerce being made more transparent.

Web Page

A web page is like a specific page in the book or magazine which we take from a library. A web page may be news, images, sounds, text, animation etc.

A business can be established on the Internet by providing the web page with pictures, text, graphics, forms, audio, video and animation. Pages are produced in a structured form to suit the web medium that reflects the company's unique identity and is a distinctive web marketing program. It integrates internet marketing into the overall marketing plan.

The number of web pages have been growing at a stagerring rate in recent years. The number of web pages on the Internet swept past the one billion mark. This clearly reads the success story of the Internet. Today, we are talking about the number of web pages, about one of them for every man, woman and child in India. It is a stagerring amount of information that has been fast growing.

Every page contributes to the business potential for many companies as witnessed in the recent years. A page contains interactive illustrated affairs displaying headings, graphics, background, patterns, colour pictures and containing imaginary cross referenced pages along with the tedious text diligently formulated. It means web pages are all too often a triumph of style over contents shown on the Net.

It is like a magazine page. Preparation of a web page requires special and diverse blend of telents and experience to build up a web-based extension of business.

In these days, anyone can create a web page. As a matter of fact, many people feel that the creation of web pages can be created easily and develop as an professional online service. We can see a lot of good and bad web pages on the Internet. A good website design requires an experienced professional design team.

According to some estimates, every month, 1,50,000 users are added and more than 20,000 pages are added everyday. So, it is essential to be present on the web or get out of business, as it is the order of the day—the early birds reap benefits quickly is a known fact.

Home Page

A status page of a site is called the home page. The shop window into which the user enters, first is called the home page, from where all other sections or pages can be accessed. If the website is bigger, the smaller the URL of the home page. The bigger the site, the more it is to have more pages.

A World Wide Web consists of millions of web pages. A homepage is a starting point or organisational centre for the collection of online documents or the World Wide Web. If you are a businessman or organisation, the customer's first glimpse of your services on the Internet can be crucial to giving them information about you, in the way you want it presented. It may include text, graphics, sounds, movies and links to other pages with related topics.

Types of Web Design

Web pages can be designed in the following ways :

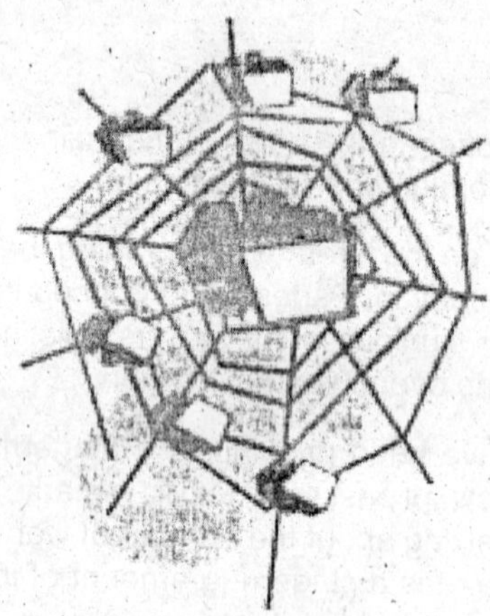

Fig. 4.03 An Electronic (Computer) Web

- Simple static web page
- Interactive web page
- Dynamic colourful website and
- Combination in between them.

A dynamic website enhances the traffic and prompt return visits of the customers. The web design service providing firms offer:

- Graphical icons in the making
- CGI programming
- Database programming
- Cold fusion mark-up language
- Copywriting and
- Lay-out.

Blending the code and text in perfect harmony offers an eye catching website. Services are being offered with various hosting and designing options, all balanced with the latest technology.

Links and Hot Links

Every web page contains text, graphics, pictures etc. and there is some link between the pages as to the text, picture etc. Any part of the text which is underlined on a page is called as *hot link*. When clicked on an underlined word or words, part of the text will bring a new page on the screen. The text on a new page may have further links of its own either to other pages in the same site, or outside to those of other individuals or organisations.

Web Facilities

A web facilitates to see pictures, hear sounds or watch movies. When the program talks, the Internet talks, navigates transaction with the computer at the other end and brings pictures, text, program etc. as desired onto the computer screen. The Web permits to display pictures as a part of the text or in the middle of the text. This facility has made the web so attractively accessible, fascinating, interesting and now most popular to the people and is widely used today.

Both internet and web have media, as that is the basic medium in text. The other media includes sounds, movie clips, animations and interactive programs. The viewer program is used to view or play a particular type of file.

C-Web

It is a short form, stands for Centre for World Wide Web service over NICNET (National Informatics Centre Net). The C-Web is the first web server in the country to navigate through the Internet for the exchange of multimedia documents between computer users internationally. The WWW Gateway to Internet provides a powerful browsing and searching facility for a seamless world wide digital web of information. NICNET has now weaved the entire country into one single communication entity for reaching out to the world at large. The establishment of the most advanced WWW server in the world through BASIS web server at C-Web adds a new dimension to Internet services over NICNET.

Operating Systems

- Linux
- SGI Irix
- Soloris and Sunos
- Microsoft Windows NT Server and
- Many other flavours of Unix.

Programming/Mark-Up Languages/Protocols and APIs

- Java Servelets
- Java Server Pages (JSP)
- Java/Java Script
- Java 2 Enterprise Edition Development
- CGI
- Perl
- C/C++
- XML
- Enterprise Java Beans (EJB)
- HTML
- TCP/IP
- Firewalls and Networking Security
- Cryptography/PGP.

Databases

- Oracle 8
- MySQL/msql
- Microsoft Access
- Microsoft SQL Server 7.

Servers /Applications

- Allaire's JRUN
- Orion Application Server
- Netscape Enterprise Server
- Apache
- Stronghold
- NCSA Web Server.

Multimedia

- Macromedia Direction
- Macromedia Flash
- Adobe Photoshop
- Real Audio Producer
- MP3 Production
- Digital Multi-Track Recording.

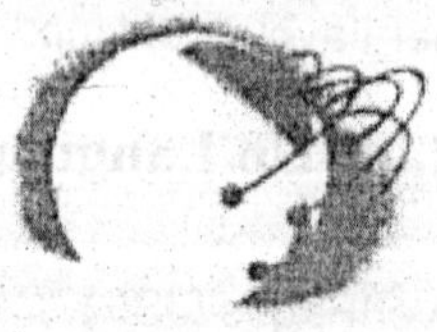

Fig. 4.04 Internet-A Global Transparency

Advantages of WebSite

- Quick access to the web market worldwide
- Attracts new customers for their products and services
- Integrates into business to increase revenues and expands customer base
- Provide a value added service to the customers
- Ability to update and manage the site seven days a week and twenty four hours a day

- Strengthens relationship with current customers
- Cooperative promotion with e-commerce solutions providers
- Establishes long-term customer commitment to business
- To deliver marketing message to a worldwide audience of millions of clients/consumers
- Helps to create a new channel for sales
- Takes position for the future and stay ahead of the competition.
- Possible to create a profit centre by selling advertising space to third parties.
- Website is a unique and new opportunity for business of any size
- Helps to increase sales as well as the growing revenue beyond that way which was once impossible by using the traditional method of commerce
- The online shopping tool, B2B, B2C, C2C, B2E transactions, which allow to Top into the global market place.
- Showing to information superhighways
- This gives an opportunity for business to focus on core business activities.

Top 15 Websites

The top 15 websites are:

- Amazon.com
- Barnes and Noble.com
- Microsoft
- NextCard
- CDNow
- First USA
- 1-800 Flowers
- eBay
- Enews
- Network Solutions
- Lowestfare
- Onsale
- Visa
- SunMicrosystems and
- General Motors.[1]

The top three web advertising categories include :

- Computer Related goods
- Books and
- Credit Cards.

1. *Computer Today, 16-30 September, p.35,99*

Web Server Types

There are two types of operations of the web server:

- To establish one's own web server with the help of hardware vendors. It is a costly system and
- To use another person's server by paying a rent. A web server is also called a website.

The use of the web requires a complex infrastructure of :

- Servers
- Browser software
- Knowledgeable web designer
- Site designer and
- Programmer to work.

Site Connection Methods

There are two methods to connect a site to the internet. They are:

- Uploading to Internet service provider's web server by using internet standard File Transfer Protocol (FTP) and
- By saving the website onto a directory on one's own or provider's webserver. Both methods serve the purpose.

Programs to Create A Web Page

Web page can be created by designers using the following programs:

- HTML
- Java
- Dynamic HTML and
- Java Script and other Advanced Programs.

Customised programs are written for the following features with different rates :

- Banner rotation
- Guest book
- Vistalog
- Database connectivity
- Auto respond
- Bilingual programming
- Search engine
- Counters and
- Forms.

Options for Building a Website

There are three options for building a website. They are :

- Buying a web page design program
- Learning to code in Hypertext Markup Language (HTML) to create pages.
- Paying someone to make pages and
- Ec Builder Wizard gives options of dozens of different site designs and colour schemes.

Cost of Web Creation

- Site Creation
- Periodical fee
- Cost of creation of finished HTML files
- Updating cost
- Evaluation
- Site hosting
- Site development and
- Site promotion.

Some E-commerce Websites

There are some well-known websites : www.eBay.com, www.amazon. com, www.rediff.com, www.satyamonline.com, www.cnn.com, www.psinet. com, www.Yahoo.com, www.bidorbuy.com.etc. There are sites and sites which can be visited – so start surfing and enjoying the sites of your choice and needs.

Fig. 4.05 Around the World Through Internet

Some Popular websites

1. E-Bay (www.ebay.com): Established in 1995, E-Bay is the world's largest auction site that is available round the clock. It has more than 3.8 million registered users and more than eight million unique visitors. Currently, there are more than two million items in more than 1500 categories listed for sale. Items traded include antiques, books, movies, coins, stamps, collections, computers, dolls, figures, gems and jewellery, photo electrics, potteries and glass, sports goods and toys.[1]

This site is specially designed for online sales. It has developed an auction format on the Web that has attracted some lakhs of registered users. The company runs a novel business that is growing at a phenomenal rate. When it comes to business, e-Bay cashes on all the strategies that prove beneficial to the developers of the site and satisfy the customers with e-commerce.

2. Yahoo (www.yahoo.com): David Filo and Jerry Yang set up this company in 1994 to generate revenues from online advertising. In March 1999, Yahoo's global network traffic grew at an average of 235 million page views per day, up from an average of 167 million page views per day in December 1998. For the fiscal 1998, net revenues stood at $ 203 million, nearly a three-fold increase over the net revenues of $ 70.5 million in the 1997 fiscal.[2]

3. Amazon.com (www.amazon.com: Seattle-based Amazon.com is the world's first and largest online bookstore. It was founded in 1995. The company has grown from being an online bookseller to an internet shopping hub, offering music, videos, auctions, toys and consumer electronics. Now it is working out strategies to emerge as an online shopping super store allowing anyone, from major manufacturers to creative housewives, to sell merchandise through its website. Commencing on September 30,1999, more than 5 lakh new items including vacation packages and maternity clothes are available through its new Z-shop programs. In view of its expanded offerings, the company's customer base has grown enormously. It has also generated vast revenues with its online marketing programs.[3]

Today, Amazon.com has 4.5 million active customers, many of whom experienced e-commerce for the first time through the site. The site's market grasp is firm and its technology impressive with sophisticated personalisation, account management and customer service features. Book selling and buying will never be the same.[4]

4. Internet Entertainment Group: The entertainment company provides most useful incentives for using its e-commerce site. Of all the marketing strategies that we would never have thought of, let alone believed, would work-giving away pornographic pictures while users get stock quotes in one of them. That is Sexquotes, a website owned by the notorious Internet Entertainment Group, which does just that, showing just how wrong we can be. Please, no jokes about keeping abreast of the market place.[5]

---

1 *A. K. Mohanty, Information Technology, Jan. 2000, p. 48.*
2 *Ibid*
3 *A.K. Mohanty, Information Technology, Jan. 2000, p. 48.*
4 *Mark Gibbs, Information Systems, Computer World, April 1-15, 2000, p. 78*
5 *Ibid. p. 79.*

5. Doubleclick (www.doubleclick.com): The fact that e-commerce best targets international customers remains undisputed. This site sells online advertising space worldwide. It has internationalised its website, which supports 13 languages and has served so far billions of advertisements across many potential sites. Its earnings include revenue from international operations also. Its speciality is to customise for the local markets and this localisation is crucial to getting revenues front international business.

6. Federal Express (www.fedex.com): The doyen of the shipping industry is the Federal Express, which has a firm grasp of the benefits of e-commerce. It is a company which provided customers with customsed package tracking and shipping software.

7. American Headhunter (www.americanheadhunter.com): This is a unique site. The most unusual wares are sold via the e-commerce sites. Strange products are available on the Internet.

8. K-Tel (www.ktel.com): It markets and distributes consumer products through retail stores and by direct response marketing. K-Tel products include albums, compact discs, casettes, housewares, automotive accessories and other products and devices.

Some Indian Websites

1. Electronics for you (www.electronicforu.com): This site strives with a complete section, to educate the Indian businessman of how he can use the internet to further his business and gain substantial revenues.

2. Asia.Internet.Com: This site offers and focusses on Asia pertaining to areas that include news and resources on e-commerce and information technology in India. The internet news section provides a number of articles on the Indian markets. The site includes an exhaustive list of global ISPs.

3. Economic Times online (www.economic times.com): The interactive edition of this Indian business newspaper provides substantive sub-continent-focussed technology and potential business coverage, major company and sector profiles, quarterly reports, currency calculators and market data. An archive of recent stories is housed within the site for easy searching.

4. Silicon India: The interactive version of the Silicon India magazine includes up-to-date and well designed sections on Indian technology and business news, links to Silicon India magazine, features authentic articles and search engine capabilities.

5. Times of India Interactive (www.times of India.com): The Times of India group has created a complete Indian portal with web directory, India Times news features, links to other news and classified services and listings of computer and internet related sites.

6. Eth.net: Eth.net, an information and news service, provides a compendium of recent interviews with top Indian and international business leaders and experts on technology, e-commerce and the growing trends of the internet in India.India is yet to establish itself in the information technology bandwagon.

7. Rediff on the Net (Rediff.com): The first e-commerce site in India, and one of the most trafficked portals for both Indians and non-resident Indians, Rediffmail.com provides a wealth of India-related business news, a search engine, e-commerce and web solution services.

8. India Info (www.Indianinfo.com): This site includes news on all subjects portaining to India with search engines and e-commerce. India info.com contains an index of Indian portals-various topic and region-specific sites and largely serves the non-resident Indian community.

9. E-commerce Magazines and News: E-commerce Times Business 2.0 , Red Herring wired news, Tech Web, CNET in Asia, Commerce Net.*

Working of Web Track

These aspects will lead to a better understanding of the working of a web track :

- Accrue's software does not rely on analysing web logs to figure out how a website is being used. Instead, a *'sniffer'* sits on the Internet and analyses the traffic to the site. This sniffer is a computer that runs software that examines all the TCP/IP packets coming in and out of the websites. This leads the sniffer to know the personality of the visitors.
- To track traffic through a website, the sniffer must first identify who is coming to the site. Accrue can do this in a number of ways. If the site uses cookies, the software uses the cookie as a way to identify someone. Accrue can also use the Open Profiling Standard (OPS) information stored on a person's web browser. OPS enables people to determine the kind of information about them that can be made public. If no cookies or OPS information are present, the software uses the person's IP address.
- The sniffer examines packets as they come into and go out of the site. It notes any time an action is taken such as when someone requests a web page, and whenever that action is completed, such as when the final packets from the page are delivered-it tracks who is making the requests, where they are coming from, where they are going and similar information. This information is contained in the TCP/IP packets. The sniffers discard all the intermediate packets transmitted during each action, as only the beginning and ending packets are needed. All the intermediate packets are discarded by the sniffer because they lack useful information.
- Information is sent from the sniffer to a database, where all the information is stored.
- Many kinds of reports can be created out of the database, such as the average amount of time people spend on a site, the average number of pages they read per visit, the most popular pages on a site, sites people have just visited, sites they are going to visit and similar information pertaining to customers who visit the sites.*

Information Technology, Feb. 2000, p. 19.
Computer Today, 1-15 March, 2000, p.105.

Fig. 4.06 Information Tracking

Web Design Strategy

In the knowledge economy, the Internet surely cannot be just for downloading information. It is got to be about developing and creating new concepts. In the context of e-commerce, the future lies in evolving web designs, with a multi-designer using multi-skills. Weaving designs around the web is a basic step in successful buying and selling through the Internet. What is needed is to work in cognisance with a common platform of designers to exchange ideas and experiences on the subject of design strategy for potential use of the Internet.

To design a strategy for the e-commerce site over the Net is not a traditional strategy. The basic issue is that each concern has to explore opportunities in relation to its requirements and facilities offered by the Net and use the technology suitably.

The weaving designs around the Web require the activity of new generation people with internet knowledge in using it. The Net is a reality today. What is required is to find out, how to access it and what to do with it for trading? The traditional personal computer is to be replaced by new interaction and the cutting-edge technology following the paradigm shift in the area of information technology. It has created value changes and underlined the importance of going to the Internet. There is a need for a new vision to define what are the benefits of online global business and for proper education and making business ready to share the potential market without which global business is not possible. You need to move in today's business bandwagon in gaining substantial revenues.

The process of online business is low cost, easy to use and gives wider access to businesses being launched on the Net.

A strategy involves **continuous** efforts by firms to redefine craft and find better ways to accomplish objectives. In designing a website, experts must have a finger on the pulse of the cutting-edge technology, in creating elegant and attractive designs of websites. It demands to keep up-to-date with the ongoing changes in the industry, changes in technology or issues which are area specific. It is always desirable to engage professionals to act as consultants or advisors as well as designers and HTML programming for building successful websites- that is in terms of content and the format of the sites. The new technologies enable to create and launch effective sites that offer unequated value for the clients in terms of information about the products for which there is demand.

Web development means custom-internet solutions. The designer must assess the goals of the business firm and target the audience of each organisation to create an effective online presence. Using smart design and rich functionality, the designers must create dynamic and data-driven web sites that effectively communicate messages and enhance the image of the company and ultimately help increase traffic to the site. Publicity and advertising on the Net is a potential source leading to recognition.

The design must attract national and international clientele, with most current and innovative technology possible. The sites should be fully interactive and animated using the latest micromedia flash and the flash generator technology. The tour of the state-of-the-art web experience is enjoyable and results in repeated visits to the site preferred.

Creation of an effective website is not an easy task. It requires coding and computer skills much more than required in the case of HTML. Besides, it demands advanced graphic design skills and strategic marketing expertise, to attract international clientele for long-term economic growth. Promotion of the company's products and services to the market-whether regional, national or global, is the ultimate motive behind creating a website.

A website must suggest answers to questions put forth by online shoppers:

Why to shop here ?

How to order ?

How to contact ?

What is its portfolio ?

What is affiliation ?

What is the reseller program ?

What are its benefits ?

WWW e-commerce services should focus on business to business and business to consumer communication. The inhouse web designers may have a rare mix of engineers, programming, writing, layout, design skills specialised in internal net and www applications, HTML programming, interior architecture, animation experts, graphics, fine arts and design etc., together produce attractive and appealing sites.

Completing, editing or modifying any portions of the completed website also requires professional skills.

Sometimes, site hosting concerns may reserve the right to reject hosting of websites containing objectional materials or contents or quality standards, because there are forbidden sites, evil deaths and rape. So, websites featuring forbidden sites like bestiality, rape, pee, poop sex, fisting and pregnony are objectionable to sight. It must be ease of use demanded by merchants world wide.

Low cost, easy to use and payment processing solutions for web business are most important factors for the success of e-commerce. An affiliate program that is integrating into using tools enables to recruit other websites to send traffic customers to our site, rewarding them with a small commission or store credits is winning strategy. It is a great way to promote traffic and sales online.

The developer must deliver quality software to enable and facilitate the e-commerce needs of companies and customers of a wide array of sizes.

Domain Name and Search Engine

Earlier Conventional Methods: Domain name system on the internet is a very recent method. Before the advent of the domain name, the communication process through the Internet was a very complex one. For instance sending an e-mail over the Internet was complex and the difficulties associated with this system were among others, as follows :

- To know destination numerical address of the machines.
- To know the path that the message should take.
- To specify most or all the machines between the sender and recipient and
- A changed location changes the e-mail addresses of the recipients.

What is Domain Name: In order to solve the complex problems associated with the process of communication, an improved and sophisticated system has been devised. Each computer which is linked to the Net has a unique address which is called the *domain name.*

The domain name is the key in identifying business on the internet/web. Every identity of the user on the Internet is established by this key. A domain name may have two or three parts depending upon the word.

A domain name, also called internet domain name, is a part, a place or an apartment in a complex, a town or even a country. Basically, a domain with reference to an internet is accessible to humans in terms of reading and writing. With the help of the domain name, the computers easily and strategically communicate with one another. It takes place in the form of a complex series of numbers which the computers use to communicate with one another.

What are the Functions of Domain name

- It permits the user to type or bookmark an intelligible word or phrase. This helps to access a website, access e-mail address, access file transfer protocol (FTP) site and access other internet accessible machines.
- The Internet Protocol address or IP address is important in internet operations. Under the domain name system, the IP address can change and many can do while maintaining the human style address.

The Internet Service Provider (ISP) usually helps to register a domain name and also link domain to space on the server. A domain name is the internet title for business. Today, most domains end with .com, registered with an organisation called Inter Nic in Washington DC.

Today, there are many domain registration organisations and the so called internet savvy have established online stores and many are trying to get domain ending stores and other terms. The business people will have to contact InterNic by paying an annual prescribed fee to get

.com, .org, or .net and other such domains. A business located outside the US or its own country may have a central registrar for its domains.

For instance, .ca for Canada, .uk for Britain and .au for Australia. They may be preferred to have a domain specific to their country. It is always useful to have an appropriate domain name, but strictly speaking, it is not that imperative. Generally, the web address should be short and precise relating to the name of the company. It is preferable to have an e-mail address at the same location, so that they are easier to find and easily accessible.

Domain names have certain characteristics-they are to remember that they correspond to a series of numbers called internet protocol numbers which serve the routing address on the Internet. They are generally used as a convenient way of information retrieval and reaching the area of choice on the internet.

The Internet Domain Name System (DNS) consists of a directory, organised hierarchically with all domain names. When a domain name is registered, it will be associated with the computer on the Internet designate when the period of registration is in effect.

Domain names end with .com, org, and .net and they can be registered through companies known as *registrars.* An alphabetical listing of these companies appear in the registrar directory.

Types of Domains

The merchants doing business online are required to understand several levels of domains which are in use on the internet. Following are the various types of domains:

1. Top Level Domains: Top level domains contain all the 'endings' for websites like e-mail addresses, file transfer protocol and other internet accessible machines. It is the responsibility of every country in the world for administering top level domains under their respective control. They include, for instance, .com-commercial businesses, .Net-network (internet-related) organisations, .org-non-profit organisations, .edu-educational institutions in the United States, .gov.-United States government agencies, .mil-US military and .US-other sites in the United States (rare).

Originally, these domains were restricted to the owners within the United States of America. But today .com, .net, and .org domains are now available for use by servers anywhere in the world. But they are mainly administered in the United States.

A new set of seven North American top level domains have been approved, which are as follows :

- .firms-businesses or firms,
- .store-businesses offering goods for purchases,
- .web-entities emphasizing activities related to the web,
- .art-entities emphasizing cultural and enertainment activities,
- .rec-entities emphasizing recreation/entertainment activities,
- .info-providing information sevices and
- .nom-for those wishing individual or personal nomenclature.

Still there are other domains which have to be sub-domains of the country to which they belong. For instance, they include: .ca-domains in Canada, .uk-domains in the United Kingdom,

.au-Australia, .ru-Russia, .at-Austria, .fi-Finland, fr.-france, .de-Germany, .il-Israel, .it-Italy, .jp-Japan, .kr-Korea, no-Norway, .es-Spain, se-Sweden, .tw-Taiwan and .ch-Switzerland.

Top level domains, however, do not correspond directly with a particular machine, but they refer to a type of domain or to a region.

2. *Multiple Domains:* When a company wants more than one domain, it can do so. Such domains are called *multiple* domains. Depending on the nature of business, products, services etc., a company may want to consider more than one domain. If the business of a company depends on the recognition of the name of the company and name of the products or services, it may have more than one domain. For example, multi-active has a domain for its original product Maximizer (Maxmizer.com). Later,the company added a domain (Multi active.com). It followed by domains for other products (maximizer enterprise.com and eC Builder.com). The URL is generally typed to find a site.

3. *Larger Domain:* India is a larger domain in 'IN'. Hosts and local networks are grouped together to form a domain, where domains are later grouped into one or more larger domains.

4. *Sub-Domains:* Sub-domains may relate to organisations such as NASA and Compu Serve. In this category, involvement of national or provincial domain name authorities is not mandatory. Once a domain is owned, it is possible to set up as many sub-domains as required. It means it permits an organisation to go any or many levels deep, further down the domain chain. The mid-level domains and sub-domains are accessible under the domain umbrella. The system, the network administrator of the ISP can set up sub-domains by setting the company's domain name server (DNS) computer. It is the function of the DNS computer to tell those linked to the Internet globally where that mid level domain is, and which sub-domains are under it exactly.

5. *Repid Domain:* This is a new domain reservation service created to accommodate and serve clients who need domain names registered without an active website in place. Rapid Domain has many advantages like reducing the hassles and reserving the domain names.

6. *Which Domain to Use:* It is one of the frequently asked questions (FAQs). The business firm must think twice and select an appropriate domain or domains. A suitable and best domain is one that must closely matches the name of the business.

The domain normally ends in'.Com.' The suffix to a domain is'.Com.' The prefix to a domain is 'www'.

In case of major web browsers like Internet Explorer and Netscape, when you just type a word (name), the browser normally appends "www" to the front and ".com" to the back automatically. For instance:

If you just type "Altavista", the browser automatically appends. "www" to the front of "altavista" and ".com" to the back. It may appear like this: http://www.altavista.com.

Owning the first .com address is not always feasible. There are lakhs and lakhs of organisations on the Internet. Business firms need to work out strategies for potential accessibility by the clients.

Another variant approach is that if a company does not possess a domain, it is best to search for reasonable.com variations relating to the company name, business type and so on. If there is no possibility of registering at .com, select an appropriate alternative in .net, .org, or at local geographical top-level domains such as .co, .uk, .ca and so on.

Domain Numerical Addresses

Domain names avoid the number confusion and allow sequences that look like human language to be assigned to blocks of numeric addresses. Hence, instead of typing '207'.46.130.149' you can simply type in name 'www.microsoft.com' into the web browser. Domain names developed in 1080s now have become so common and no one uses the original numeric IP addresses directly. The top level domains such as '.com' or sub-divided into second level domain *i.e.* network were in turn split into the third level domain i.e., host computers and so on.

There are about 250 top level domain names out of which the '.com' is the most sought after. At the end of March 2000, there were 157, 19, 462-domain names, out of which 94,82,427 were .com addresses.

Precautions in using Domain, site etc.

- Protect the authenticity of your online identity by registering web addresses in all of the top-level domains (.com, .net and .org) — it is simple, yet many people tend to ignore this. Take the recent case of the multiple NASA sites: while nasa. org is the official site, nasa.com and nasa.net were registered and pointed at as porn sites.
- Be wary of registrars who ask to 'point' the domain name at their own site. Instead of letting registrars make www. your new-name.com as an alternative address for their own site while they are holding the name for you, it is better to display a standard 'site under construction' notice. This saves any confusion regarding the ownership of the site.
- Beware of sites that offer reservation services for a limited time only, typically 90 days. The registrar should offer unlimited 'reservation' and DNS services for domain names purchased at its site.
- Check out the freebies or additional services such as e-mail forwarding, website forwarding, under construction page or sample page. It is better to know beforehand what you are paying for.
- Have a list of possible names ready when you visit the registration site. Make use of 'tools' such as 123 domain me .com that offers a service whereby you can specify keywords you would appreciate in a domain name : Within a short time, it will send you a list of all the permutations of these keywords that have not yet been registered with InterNic. Similarly, www. unclaimed domain .com provides a free listing of unused and unregistered names and www. thesaurus. com offers some unusual domain names.
- While registering names, think of close matches, common names and synonyms. Consider this: a porn site Intel-Inside .com is using the chip grants' name to attract customers to its site. Similarly, then Microsoft filed suit against two Texans who registered microsoft windows .com and microsoft office .com and similar domain names, alleging an infringement of its trademarks and misleading the public.
- Finally, don't forget to renew your account, or else you will have to pay a heavy price. Britain's foremost cancer care charity dealt a massive below because of an administrative goof-up by the domain registrars NSI. The Marie Curie Charity, which helps thousands of people cope with cancer lost the domain www.mariecurie.com to the hardcore cafe porn site after NSI failed to inform the charity that its renewal was due.*

---

* *Computers Today, 1-15 April, 2000, p.68.*

Registered Domains

The total number of registered domains world wide stood at 1,44,37,101 as on 31st January, 2000. The number of dotcoms was 88,11,662. The following is the list of the number of domain sites country-wise.*

Country	Code	Number
Germany	.de	9,53,398
United Kingdom	.uk	7,64,230
Argentina	.ar	1,52,182
Australia	.au	1,22,061
Netherlands	.nl	1,21,242
Switzerland	.ch	1,08,450
Italy	.it	99,950
Denmark	.dk	93,181
Japan	.jp	65,017
Brazil	.br	59,628

The following are regarded as the most popular website names ending July 1999.

Country	Code	Number
.com	1,87,73,027	Commercial
.net	1,24,32,542	Network
.edu	51,41,774	Educational
.JP	20,72,529	Japan
.uk	15,99,497	United Kingdom
.mil	15,61,756	US military
.us	15,55,882	United States
.de	14,26,928	Germany
.ca	12,94,447	Canada
.au	9.07.637	Australia
.org	8,21,933	Organisations
.gov	6,83,363	US Government

Steps in Domain Name Selection

Initlally the search for domain name availability remains when searching for a domain, then remember the following points :

- Use or name something easy to remember,
- Do not use more characters, generally not more than 26 characters,
- Use any letter, number and hyphen,
- Punctuations are not allowed,
- Try to have.com domain,

* *Computers Today, 16-31, March, 2000, p. 73.*

- Try product/slogan names which are in use as an acronym,
- Prefer also .net,.org,etc. Registration to the following domains are also possible-.cc,.nu,.to and .tm,
- For other countries, add country extension such as.net.in:.org.pk (they stand for India and Pakistan),
- Is the name easy to remember and use?
- How does it look on the business cards?
- Impression,
- Does it create an impact? and
- Less length is desirable.

Universal Resource Locator (URL)

The acronym URL stands for Universal Resource Location/Locator and it is related to the internet web page. The URL is to be typed into the browser enabling accessibility to a web page from any network computer. It is an internet address. Every resource on the internet has its own location identifier, enabling the user to identify the source of any information on the internet.

There are two parts in URL. They are :

Access method or protocol used by the server and

Computer's domain name

To benefit from the vast information on the internet, the user will need an internet address. Every resource on the internet has its own location identifier. The URL is an internet address which lets the user identify the source of any information on the Internet. If the URL of a web page is known, one can key it in to access it immediately from any interconnected computer in the world. Every web page has its unique name with the help of which the user can directly enter into the page. So, the identification of the page or site is termed as UTL.

The URL is an address you use to reach a specific place or thing on the internet, from a document to a sound. Akin to your address, it is the combination of letters or numbers people need to reach a page on the Net. For example, our URL is: "http://www.albion.edu/admin/comp/newit/computin.htm." You can access various URL web pages which are advertised in newspapers, billboards, banners etc.

When a company rents space on a server for its sites, they are given such an address. To do business online over the internet, it has become a practice or norm that larger enterprises register as top level domains. There are many top level domains like http://www.sony.com, http://www.times of india.com,http://www.sony.com etc.

So, Sony as a company name or an abbreviation can also be used. However, the name comes directly after www. Sony and is followed by.Com. .Com is the country code and.com is a North American commercial site.

The control of the top level domain differs from country to country.

Cybersquatters: The world wide web is gaining wide popularity and many businesses are going to have a place there. As a result, an unfortunate state of affairs is the emergence of 'cybersquatters'. Because of the problem of getting a domain, an unscrupulous practice of cybersquatters has emerged. For registering a domain, a prescribed fee is payable say US $ 70 approxirnately for two years. Cybersquatters are the people who pay the prescribed fee to register dozens of domains, actually not relating to their own business activities. They do so in the hope that someone may want the domain and buy by paying a high price for it. They are like ticket scampers. Such practices need to be prevented particularly some of the more extreme cases of cybersquatters - is to establish that the domain should match the well-established trademarks and the trademark should belong to the trademark holders only.

The unauthorised use of brand names in web address is called cybersquatting. Most organisations as a precautionary measure of for multiple registration and also register under '.co.in' domain to curb cybersquatting of their registered name or trademark.

Cybersquatters have made hay while the sun shone. Even otherwise, the sale of domain names was a big business. For instance, business.com was sold for a whopping US 7.5 million and it was Year 2000.com for US10 million. But now it is tough going for cybersquatters. The Internet Corporation for Assigned Names and Numbers (ICANN) hit back on October 24,1999 with a brand new policy for settlement of domain name disputes. The Uniform Resolution Policy and its rules go well beyond the mandate for curbing cybersquatting.

Indian Domain Name

Domain name registration under Indias' country code '.in' is not a free service. Registration can be made against the payment of a token fee as is the norm prevailing abroad. This norm of charging fee came into force with effect from 1st March 2000.

Earlier, Indian companies and organisations were allotted free '.in' domain names by the National Centre for Software Technologies (NCST). The domain.co.in 'was available for registered commercial organisations and '.gov.in' for government organisations. Now even those entities who have already got a free domain name and active websites, will have to cough up the fees.

There are nearly 2000 domain names ending with the country code '.in' registered with NCST, of which 1,300 have been registered by commercial organisations —0 they are .com.in and .org.in.

Domain activities involve domain registration, domain parking and domain forwarding. Hosting packages for domain names are available for hosting various sites and URL addresses.

The NCST is the body authorised to register names ending in India with a specific country code. The list of organisations registered under the country code read like a who is who. Most organisations have a precautionary measure and they opt for multiple registration and also register under the '.com.in' domain to curb cybersquatting of their registered names or trademark.

Internet Corp For Assigned Names and Numbers (ICANN)

The Internet Corp for Assigned Names and Numbers (ICANN) is the internet's top governing body. It is a non-profit organisation responsible for maintaining the infrastructure for internet addresses. A committee of ICANN recommended to the board of directors that a policy governing the creation of new categories of domain names called 'Generic Top Level Domain Names' be created in an effort to categorise websites in a better way and make them easier to find. It helps expand the market and makes navigation through the web easier.

Registering Domain Name

Every domain name and FTP basics have to be registered. The following steps work towards getting the domain name registered :

1. *To Have Space:* It is necessary to procure a web space. The space may be a directory, a folder oa web server computer, which is accessed by file transfer protocol. It is necessary to have an internet service provider, to set up some web server space. Web pages are put here and the need to be able to map this space to www is important. For example, www.marketbuilder.com.

2. *Finding Address:* Intertnet domain registration service requires addresses. So it is necessary to find out domain name server addresses from the Internet Service Provider. The internet protocol addresses are in the form of numbers. For example, Multi-active software has DNS servers at dns. mult-active.com (204.239.26.1) and dns2. multiactive.com (204.239.26.10). The ISP gives IP numbers and names to the domains being registered.

3. *Selecting Domain:* The next step is to search for a domain. The desired domain may not sometimes be available. For example, if you want a .com domain address, it may not be available. But there are several back-up options and addresses such as .net, .org, .edu., and .gov.etc. Network solutions INC., Net Names, Register.Com and Uninet are the search and registration services available worldwide. When a choice for a domain name is entered in an online form, to pick up the appropriate .com, .net, .org ending domain, theNetworks solutions website tells whether it is available for registration or not.

4. *Registering Domain:* Next step is to registering an available domain. At this stage, the user is actually buying the domain. Normally for registration, a fixed registration fee is to be payable, which may vary, depending upon the domain type the user is registering and the country which is administering. But in case of .com, .net, and .org, the standard price is US $ 70 for the first two years.

5. *Map:* Next is the getting of the ISP to map the new domain using DNS computers. After ascertaining that DNS mapping is done, it is best to upload the site to the web server space.

Advantages of Top Level Domains

The following are the major advantages of top level domains:

- It confers a status and increases the prestige of the business. Today, most organisations consider it as status to have this top level domain.
- Having a top level domain in company name ensures a protection to the name and no other entity can register with the same name. This feature has substantial commercial advantage. The Internet Corporation for Assigned Names and Numbers (ICANN), a private sector and non-profit corporation, adopted a policy for the introduction of new top level domains tecently.
- Top level domain facilitates change provider at any time and one can simply move his address to another machine. There is fixed or tied arrangement to its provider.
- It is easier to remember. The internet top level domains (TLDS) enable users to locate websites in their chosen fields of interest and there is advantage in relation to e-mail address.

Search Engines and Directories

The search engines and directories have different criteria for searching the result of a search. Each search engine and directory has its own criteria for searching. For example, a web page specifically written to come up at the top of altavista will not be favourable in Apollo.

The directories and search engines are becoming more sophisticated , following that the different search criteria may constanlly be changing. Therefore, it is desirable to create a website that individually addresses and deals with the unique properties of each directory and search engine.

This issue can also be solved by creating multiple copies of the initial web page. Each copy is framed so as to include several keywords, phrases and then these multiple pages are registered with the ideal search service. The advantage of structuring multiple copies are: the site is shown more than once, receives the visibility, increases the probability for a political client to view products or services, aggressive and successful marketing strategy and increases traffic visiting the site.

A periodic and regular inspection and maintenance of the website in the directories and search engines is crucial, because listings sometimes get dropped from them. A periodic inspection and updating of listings in directories and search engines ensure their accuracy, currency and availability are imperative to assure potential interest business. Thus, periodic inspection helps to maintain position and the visibility of websites amongst the many websites listed.

Some special and exclusive pages may be targeted for scientific industries by promoting these pages through all major search engines and directories. A direct method of gaining visibility to a specific website is to be visible with a '*Banner*' and each banner is linked to a website, clicking on the banner directed to the site.

Search Engines	Directories
Altavista	Apollo
Excite	GTE super pages
Hot Bot	Galaxy
Infoseek	Info space
Lycos	Magellan
Northern Lights	New Riders Yellow pages
GOTO	What is new Tool
What-u-seek	Yahoo
Anzwer	The Mining Company
	Looksmart.

There are about 1,500 search engines and directories on the Internet.

When a website is built to be submitted, the URL of websitesare linked to the major internet search engines with title and industry description and keywords. There are hundreds of search engines and directories and among them, there are both small and large search engines and directories. Generally, the smaller search engines and directories are of not much use. Similarly, there are some specialised search engines which can be selected to reach the target audience. For instance, if a merchant sells engineering supplies, he can submit the site's information to a search engine or directory designed for engineering and other technical or engineering personnel. The Internet user can search by any one of the appropriate search engines or directories to register potential business.

It is subsequently imperative to accurately evaluate and increase the use of appropriate search engines to benefit the internet user and the firms that are accessible on the Net. It is a very useful tool, usually organised on a web page, that allows you to search the Internet, enter your terms, and depending on the search engine, and you will receive from 100 to 1000 'hits' or subject matches. Click on a match, and you will immediately, enabling easy and quick accessibility to information on the web page- a 'link'to attract potential internet users.

The keywords do not appear on screen but they can be used by internet search users. Search engines are automated tools programmed to crawl or spider across the web. The popular search engines are Altavista, HotBot, Infoseek, Lycos, Web Crawler, Excite etc. They find the words users are searching. The best known internet search site is the internet directory. Search engines are an important source to visitors to specific sites. However, the search engines alone are not the only way to go to the websites.

Top Search Engines

Search engine placement solution is also equally important. This solution service will greatly help web pages in ensuring the application of standard ways in the search engines. This is very important. A substantial number of world wide web users use Big 8 engines to search and find what they are looking for on the Internet. The Big 8 are as follows: Yahoo, Infoseek, Lycos, Excite, Altavista, Web Crawler, HotBot, MSN and Snap. The last two search engines have been included recently.

There are several reasons why people prefer to have a site position at these locations. One important reason is that when these resources are used to conduct a specific search, the average user may not view more in the first ten pages of results. If the site is not found in the first ten pages of the search result, it is better to forget the site being found by using a search engine.

People prefer pages to the top of the list for the key words or key word phrases. Service providers help to get site superior positions on these resource pages. This results in increase in traffic to the specific site, because the site is at the top of the few of the list.

Yahoo

To search a page, Yahoo! is generally used. Many internet users use this search engine because it is one of the oldest and the best known search tool. It is a directory of web sites. Since it is not an automated search engine, it does not index all the texts on every site possible. But sites are put into categories based on information of those sites which the administrators send to them. Thus, the user can visit the search engine yahoo ! and submit the site's information to it manually.

There is a separate guide known as Yahoo! submission URL that contains instructions for doing so. However, Yahoo is a good place to see for attractive and strategic methods to promote a site. Yahoo's Directory list contains a good source of information about all directories and to them also one can submit it. There are hundreds of search engines and yahoo! has links to most of them. This information we can get from the search engine list category.

Who Provides Registration Services

The following are the services available for searching and registration of services:

- *InterNIC* : In the US, InterNIC is the clearing house for the domain name registration.
- *Network Solutions INC* : In the US, earlier it was the only domain name registrar, but today also it is widely used.
- *Register.Com* : This service extends domain name registration service relating to some international domains.
- *NotNames* : As a registration service of UK, its service has the potential to search all domains worldwide.
- *UniNett* : A detailed listing from Norway of registration authorities around the world.

The user can search for available from these service providers. Some of the Indian companies that offer registration services are Delhinet, Indic Links, Innovative creations, Planet India, Web India Internet services, Webworks, Cyberweb Global service and India web promotors, Dot com services and Satyam Infoway Ltd.

Java Language

Java is an object oriented language developed by the Sun Microsystems incorporated in USA. It is one of the best suited solutions to e-commerce. Microsoft has also come up with its own solutions known as Microsoft Transactional Server (MTSMSMQ). Java has the capability to work on any platform that has Java Virtual Machine (JVM). Java platform is important to the internet and java technology forms the basis for the strategic revolution of software development.

Java translates the byte code into the native language and relates accordingly to the machine-it works the same way as the speaker, who in his hand, translates a foreign language into his mother tongue and then records the same accordingly. Java provides the knowledge of e-commerce. Unlike other programs which have their own niche or specific function, a java program can perform a wide variety of functions like providing audio-visual back-up, animation etc. It provides an excellent interface on the Net. What oxygen is to human beings, Java is to the internet as the worldwide web lives, works and even sleeps by the language.

Java is one of the important programming tools related with the web technology today. The other tools are Active and Java Script.The Sun Microsystems has developed Java computer language, which enables applications to be run to the concerned firm from the internet. It is on similar lines like word processing, graphics and spreadsheet programs which are run on the PC.Also, it is similar to the C++ computer programming language.

Java is an object-oriented language which means programs which can be created by using the pre-existing components. In this, there is no need of writing the entire program.

Java runs the inside browser, provided there is a Java enabled browser like NetScape.

Java Script

Java script is also an object oriented language. It means the script works by manipulating objects. It is a scripting language which is easiest to learn and not complex. Java Script helps the users to write scripts even without substantial programming experience. Java Script is an interpreted language. It is more useful to the web designers to facilitate functionality and interactiviity in relation to the web pages. Certain things which cannot be obtained with HTML can be obtained with Java Script.

It is a strategic interpreted language because its commands are executed by the browser. With the help of the Java Script commands, it is possible to create a web page. It is applied for by internet users following a wide variety of sophisticated, interactive features.

Java Knowledge helps in the following ways :

- To build and develop portable java-based web applets and applications,
- To use packages to create Java Code,
- To use Java graphics, library to build GUI,
- Create network and client/server application in Java,
- Portability of the language is the distinctive feature of the Java,
- It performs a wide variety of functions like audio-visual, animation etc,
- It is an object oriented language that can run on any platform,
- It permits easy downloading from the internet.
- There is a provision for security and programs based on Java cannot be backed into,
- It has a feature of scalability. It means any number of users can use it from any part of the world,
- Java is most useful to those in the field of commerce. It is fast catching up in recent years. The Java is one of the potential solutions related to e-commerce.

Hypertext

Hypertext is also called the *generalized footnote.* In a web page, words are abnormally, excessively or hyperactively underlined. When the underlined words are clicked, it takes the user to other web pages.

The word *hypertext* was originally coined in the year 1965. But earlier in the year 1945, a paper predicting the use of hypertext was published.

Operationally, hypertext means non-linear or non-sequential text. It means the text contains no single order or method that determines the sequence in which the text is to be read. In other words, the text is organised and written in such a way that the reader has to necessarily and easily jump around from one topic to another topic.

Organizing a text in a hypertext manner is found in a conventional paper document. But today, the hypertext is best brought to life on a computer. For example:

Newpaper : The front page of a newspaper is the best example of a text, out of which the newspaper page is hypertext. Topics in a newspaper are arranged in such a way where the reader can easily jump from topic to topic or from theme to theme if he wants more details on any one topic specifically.

Novel : Similarly, a paperback novel is yet another best example of text, out of which the novel page is the hypertext. In the case of a novel, on the flip side, it does not encourage to skip around. The writer of a novel assumes that he will be reading in a fixed sequence, reading one page right after another.

So in the hypertext, words are made into buttons that have the capability to cross reference in a program. It can be used to link graphics, animation and other texts. The best example of hypertext is the help system of windows wherein the user can select individual hot words on the screen which are then linked to the additional pages and layers of text.

The system of hypertext is more useful when presenting an reference in voluminous textual information. The hypertext authoring programs provide graphical links for animation, sound, video as well as text.

Hypertext Document

There is a simple data format known as Hypertext Markup Language (HTML). One of the features of the world wide web documents is its hypertext structure which is created by HTML. HTML permits the user to easily link words or pictures in one document to other documents and the resulting document is called *hypertext document.* The hypertext documents are transferable from one platform to another. Thus, the world wide web provides a way to interconnect computers running different operating systems.

Operationally, the web means a huge collection of interconnected hypertext documents. But what exactly is hypertext? This is a frequently asked question, and it is the same thing as the file. Broadly speaking, hypertext is a text with links, and with the help of links, the user can select hypertext documents as per his requirements. The help menu of the program indicates a hypertext help document and links available for accessing potential information.

The web facilitates the subscriber to jump or hyperlink from one web page to other pages on the web. Does this sound too good to be true? Well, it is. Thanks to the facility called 'Hypertext'. The world wide web is based on hypertext, making it possible for you as a user to go roaming around the web, bounding from document to document, and using nothing but links in those documents.

Because *gopher menus* are linked together, a whole world of information is available to the user with just a few key strokes. Imagine if we were able to take these links one step further-instead of linking menus, we could link '*documents*' together. You could read one document and find keywords in that document that really interests you, touch that keyword and automatically be taken to a new document somewhere else in the world and this new document could even have links to other documents around the world and so on.

It operates by joining words from a page of data on one computer towards words on the pages of another computer. It may be words or anything. The processing of words by one computer and another computer is called hypertext *transfer protocol.* The world wide web is formed when all the participant computers of the Net appreciate this strategy.

Applications of Hypertext

The applications of hypertext cover the following:

Computer applications

- Online documentation,
- User assistance and
- Software engineering.

Business applications

- Directories
- Reference books
- Legal research and legal documents
- Trade shows
- Product catalogues and
- Advertising.

Educational applications

- Foreign language

Entertainment and Leisure application

They include news, newspapers and magazines.

Basic Elements of Hypertext

The following are the aspects of basic elements of the hypertext:

1. Links: Links are an important unit of hypertext. It connects nodes. Links are provided at their departure point, which helps the user to activate in order to follow the link. As the links are anchored at the departure point, activating the anchor man is to follow the link to its destination node. A link may be a standard link which connects two nodes. There are some hypertext systems which are known as superlinks which connect a large number of nodes. A plain link is just connection between nodes.

2. Nodes: A node is a point on the steam, line or point at which a curve crosses itself. A node with reference to hypertext means a collection of data organised around the specific topic. The data is related or linked to another body of information. Hypertext is a network of nodes. There may be many nodes in the network and each node is linked to some other node. There are many hypertext systems and accordingly, different terms are used for nodes. For example: In hypercard, a card is a node, in hyperpad, the node is a pad. A node is a screen full of data.

3. Buttons: A button is a knob pressed to operate a key on the keyboard or it is a button on the mouse used to operate. A button is a visual cue in a node that alters for the user that the link exists. It means a button is a visual representation of a link in a node. A mouse button or a suitable function key of the keyboard can be used subsequently, causing the system to activate a link to display a different node.

4. Annotations: A note or comment added to a text is called *annotation*. It is annotated by the author in the margin, by adding notes to a text, book, manuscript or magazine, giving explanation or comment in this regard. One of the basic elements of hypertext is annotation which is a special link method. It maintains a potential link to small and additional amount of information. When a reader comes across an annotation in the primary material, he refers annotated material and returns after completing with the annotation. Annotations are quite similar to foot-notes and citations in the traditional text. In hypertext, annotations are less intrusive because they are not shown. This is a plus point in this case.

5. Editors: Hypertext is more popular because it uses the basic element of editors. The conventional meaning of the word editor implies a person who edits a book, a newspaper or magazine by adding, deleting, improving, making corrections and substituting words without disturbing the essence of the matter. An editor with reference to hypertext pertains to one who enables the user to create a node and link it into the network. In the hypertext system, an editor is a part of the network.

6. Browsers: A browser is an internet computer program which reads documents and displays files by mixing graphics, pictures, text, sound and animation. The browsing program helps to display the Web. Similarly, the hypertext browser is also a program or sub-program which displays a diagram of a network of nodes. There are two types of nodes in the hierarchical browser. They are parent nodes (located at higher level) and child nodes are linked to each parent node.

7. Trails: A record of the nodes is called a *trail.* A trail is accessed by the user while viewing the hpertext network. The element of trails in a hypertext system is a useful device for refining hypertext networks. When the user spots a problem while searching for information, he can refine the network.

Built-in Programming Languages

It is another basic element of hypertext. Inbuilt programming languages greatly help users to a great extent to customize the system to meet one's specific requirements. To facilitate this, many hypertext systems have built-in-programming languages. Knowledge pro is an instance of a program that has a built-in programming language. Similarly, the hypercard on Macintosh is a language called hypertalk. The IBM linkway also has script language like the hyperpad.

HyperText Mark Up Language (HTML)

This pertains to using or containing more words and they are verbose lay-out instructions< > marks. The language is used to create web pages and to connect web pages to other pages. The acronym also stands for horribly tangled messy language.

The computer code creates and displays documents on the world wide web. Web browsers interpret the underlying HTML code to show the user the text, image and sound when he accesses the site.

Static sites are made up of a series of interlinked HTML files. These files contain links to graphics and text with the additional use of Java, animation, sound and forms etc.

E-commerce Process and Payment Solutions

Introduction

How can business firms and individuals go for internet business unless solutions and software technologies are available for facilitating their operations? There are many software operations and solutions with their respective global initiatives to deliver e-services and solutions for merchants and customers globally. It includes financial services encompassing e-business, e-information and e-commerce solutions for business to business and business to consumers to modify critical application services.

E-business solutions are not just creation and set up of online web stores. E-commerce solutions mean quick solutions to boost business and automation requires electronic technical solutions. In this, there are two options.

They are :

- Conventional shopping cart program and
- Customer business solutions.

E-commerce over the internet involves all routine transactions but in different ways. Consequently, every financial transaction in one way or the other has to depend on some electronic form or process to boost business

Business today requires cost-effective solutions to meet the new way of business to facilitate its operations. This involves using public networks, private leased lines, local area network (LAN), wide area network (WAN), payment process, authorization, authentication, security, privacy of sensitive personal financial information, software and hardware consultation etc. For banks and other financial institutions, e-commerce can translate solutions into internet banking credit card processing, back end/front end, integration, visa e-payment, transactional banking facilities for their corporate clients, electronic data interchange and dial-up PC banking solutions.

There are several firms-top tiered, middle-tiered and bottom tiered, providing solutions to commercial organizations that are looking at expanding their current front office and back office operations to the e-commerce arena.

Merchant solutions are potential terms of doing business over the Internet. Without merchant solutions and other related solutions, merchants cannot accept credit cards, so merchant account and credit card processing is usually coupled with a little technique.

Merchant solutions providing firms offer IDs to anyone who is interested in establishing his presence on the web and wanting to conduct business. Single window solutions also have been designed and made available for conducting business on the internet quickly, easily and securely.

Solutions

E-commerce solutions technology helps to run businesses more successfully by suggesting strategies to build, integrate and operate various information systems. They also provide custom solutions that leverage internet technology to improve business processes. Professional service providers provide creative solutions to business problems, giving business a competitive edge through the innovative integration of internet technology into the existing business systems.

Solutions are available for all. They are :

- Business to business (B2B)
- Business to customers (B2C) and
- Business to employees (B2E)

They are related to e-commerce.

A wide range of internet software products are made available, having been revised, refined over the years and then customizing them according to requirements. With expertise in e-commerce, intranet, extranet, security and privacy, professionals help to plan, architect and implement reliable and secure internet solutions to fit specific business needs.

Systems integration business solutions across all computing environments are tailor-made for specific business needs. The devices span the life cycle of a solution through solution development, installation, role-out and end-user training. These are available solutions, integrated and easy to use electronic commerce system for the suppliers and buyers of products and services. It is easy today to create and operate individualized web stores and streamline both the whole buying and purchase requisition process and payment process.

Sell side applications and buy side applications are also available. Sell side applications include facilities like flexible presentation, dynamic merchandising, wide customer access, order management etc. while the second category of application facilities include self service ordering, automated approval, shopping list, reporting etc.

Gold Rush — Need for Solutions

The Internet is the gold mine in the new millennium. It is a *profit valuation* for business to generate profits through the Net. There is wealth in it as with any gold rush, people and companies want to dig into and exploit the Internet to gain fortunes. Millions of people are getting connected Internet worldwide, making it the world wide web. The more people get connected, the greater the opportunities for the Internet miners who subsequently benefit from global fame and ride the boat of fortune.

These are the days of the wireless world. But the internet miners need tools to get at the consumer's gold. It is here where businesses need creative e-commerce and e-business applications, solutions, products and services to exploit the internet mine more fully. The real solutions should be on the application side. The solutions needed should be that the platform should be standardized with common language, browsers and industry protocols, Expectations are there, that is the expanding net application space to pull in revenues, offering in this space one-to-one application systems for online marketing, e-commerce and potential sales.

So, every company must have e-commerce solutions to gain substantial fortunes. E-commerce is completely a new paradigm which is all too convenient and available at affordable prices. The most successful e-commerce model depends upon solutions, to acquire and keep customers through huge choice and relevant information, E-commerce is successful with effective solutions, products and services for various businesses. It is increasingly becoming clear that only a cyber structure is not enough to support substantial growth. That kind of growth needs specific solutions and world class global solutions.

The profit-strapped, net struck cyber entrepreneurs should have vision and money to invest in sôlutions , products and services. Due to low entry barriers, cyber competition is perhaps more fierce, calling for different level of improvements in the existing infrastructure, in better contents and solutions, faster delivery; payment, settlement and on-line support.

The solutions supplied must be quick, efficient and effective to meet organizational challenges whether its goal is an electronic journal e-commerce site for online products and services sale, corporate communication, domain name parking and e-mail account.

Internet Access Solutions

Information on the Internet is available with the click of the mouse. What is needed is access to the wealth of information. In today's business, access to information is essential. Business needs solutions developers, providers who realize the need of internet access and provide reliable services to the business. For this, we need strategically innovative and technology proven concepts.

A variety of access solutions are available for a range of business sizes which will cover all individual and organizational needs. Generally, the range of services and access solutions depend on particular needs. Solutions are available from simple dial-up access services to tiered (T3) access services. They are internet access packages to match potential business needs.

The advancement in sophisticated technologies in recent years resulted in a major breakthrough in data transmission. These take you to places on the internet within seconds.

Effective Solutions

Empowering an e-commerce online is to increase its capability and potential to do transactions at minimal expense. E-commerce services are designed to achieve it through competitive and effective solutions. As such, these solutions must ensure :

- To reduce transaction faces
- To sell to 100% of customers by accepting credit cards electronically
- To track sales in real time.
- To have cross selling and up-selling of products.
- Remote management of storefront and products.
- To have easy management of storefront and products.
- To have fully protected and secure transaction capabilities and
- To increase customer base worldwide.

Professional Experts to Design Solutions

Building solutions related to e-commerce requires world class professional experts in computer graphics and design to combine art, technology and design, specialized internet systems, multimedia designs, website design, digital video applications, computer animation systems, computer- based architectural modelling, logo, business system, design and 3D modelling.

The website design and development requires a team consisting of computers, graphic designers, business and legal professionals etc. who work to make sure worldwide web (internet) exposure matches an organization's portfolio of commerce, advertising and marketing goals.

Building websites is easy and complex. To be successful, it must satisfy the following requisites:

- Be cost effective,
- Be traffic intensive,
- Generate revenues and
- Adjust to the landscape of the Internet.

Areas of Solutions

Businesses which implement solutions to conduct online business will stay competitive in this evolving market place. There are several solution providers for e-commerce which provide turnkey solutions for selling products or services over the Net. Problems of any scalability and complexity are addressed and solved with contemporary technology. Solutions are available ranging from simple shopping carts to server clusters accessing a corporate databases. It may be thousands of miles away over a secure connection offering real time product stock and pricing information as well as order insertion to keep in touch with the past and the contemporary technology. The client involvement is also minimum in an effort to make the development and implementation process as transparent as possible.

The solutions are required on several areas. Some of them are as follows: web design, development, getting started, turnkey solutions, machine critical development, multimedia, counselling, reseller, promotion, software, merchant solutions, internet resources, domain registration, merchant processing for online acceptance of credit card payment, establishing presence on a cyber mail, corporate e-commerce solutions using EDI and industry proven e-commerce solutions software, security, shopping cart system, online web store, real time online credit processing, web-based graphics and design, intensive site planning and e-mail marketing system.

Solutions Provider

Solutions provider companies offer powerful, affordable, large and small and secure solutions to help increase sales. They assist revenue growth over and beyond the target which was once impossible traditionally. E-commerce solutions are based on e-commerce technology. The new devices allow businesses to enter into the global online market place as well as to expand business horizons. The number of companies that are taking advantage of the Net to change and create new businesses are increasing phenomenally because of the availability of both affordable and secure solutions.

Companies offer a comprehensive source of e-commerce solutions that cover all needs of clients to sell online and benefit customers. The sophisticated e-commerce software will build web stores from the ground up, building product catalogue, shopping cart, electronic payment processing, real time credit card transactions and merchant accounts.

The internet service providers have been providing internet connectivity service, solutions for corporations and individual users. The solutions provide wider potential on the world wide web.

The service providers also provide a wide range of service including potentially efficient connections for business networks, website development and hosting, co- location facilities, internet application development and other strategic business solutions. Many tools are designed to provide businesses the potential to boost profits by selling products on the Net via the virtual store front. A business can quickly set up an online store front presence with little technical expertise. Solutions enable the businessmen strategically to use electronic shopping carts, handle real time credit card processing, web design development, hosting, promotion and reporting etc.

In the process of making business more successful, the adoption of carefully thought out designed solutions, products, services and alliance strategies are essential.

Numerous IT firms have emerged as potential market players among providers of e-commerce solutions to business and media organizations get their retail advertisers online, making it a potential business trend.

Solutions must cover an impressive array of easy to use features that make e-commerce easy. The ultimate e-commerce software solutions must produce and maintain a complete online store, an inventory of products and services available for display and ordering over the internet complete with thumbnail images. Ultimately, the providers of e-commerce solutions should find perfect strategies to cater to the internet and intranet business needs. The desire to do business online has never been greater. Yet a simple internet presence is no longer enough. What is needed is to exclusively create innovative effective solutions for the internet that is one shop online shopping solutions.

Fancy Technologies

There are several new and fancy technologies that make the web an exciting and dynamic place to do business. Many of these technologies provide a practical and convenient interface which are appreciated by online clients. Providing appropriate solutions based on business needs is equally important as applying these solutions in ways that are practical and dynamic. There are specialisation organisations which help to answer difficult e-commerce questions. The interactive advantage of e-commerce solutions are that the merchants quickly increase their visibility in the market, generate substantial revenues, establish potential market presence, with unlimited exposure of their products to an international client base, expand product availability, increase customer convenience in advertisements and test promotions of products.

Thus, e-commerce solutions save customer's time and money, allowing them to shop where and when they want, compare different brands and prices and initiate purchases at their own discretion both at home and office.

In addition to this, e-commerce solutions can significantly reduce cost of opportunities. The technologies should be exploited by users accessing different websites. Custom solutions will be tailored to suit the needs of customers and will not squash the available internet technologies in a feeble attempt to make them look impressive. E-commerce is definitely more difficult than simply selling and running a standard website or online store and it can go from simple to extremely complex issues, demanding suitable technological, non technical and legal solutions. They are concerned with online catalogues, the shopping cart system, interactive and multi functional database, website design, e-sales sites, internet marketing, merchant accounts, payments, digital signatures, authentication, security privacy and credit cards are some of the issues relating to e-commerce which need to be addressed.

Everyone recognizes that e-commerce is the next big opportunity for buyers, financial institutions and customer. But doing business on the Net means finding a suitable servers, and cost effective and reliable way to collect payment and process transactions. It is the solutions that facilitate the need of customers with a server-based transaction process system that enables various businesses to authorize, process and manage credit cards and electronic cheque transactions in real time. Online environment is necessary from any computer with an internet connection and a web server.

The solutions must address the fact that merchants simply send the information needed to process transactions over secure and encrypted internet connections, a sophisticated transaction process system, with reliable payment authorization solutions. Online business must get more advantages from reliable commerce servers, powerful databases and fast secure leased line connections to financial institutions right from the web browser. The need for an authorauthorization solution should be given to the customers for successful e-commerce.

Online Commerce Solution

To get products online with fully enabled commerce, solutions may include:

- Acceptance of credit card.
- Acceptance of first virtual.
- Secure, encrypted ordering form.
- Digital storefront.
- Low start-up and monthly cost.
- Marketing products or services to global consumers.
- Corporate intranet.
- Internet solutions and professional services.
- Hosting services.
- Easy to use, enabling one to maintain an online store complete with a shopping basket and secure server support.
- The developer should build a custom store, tailored to the exact needs with a complete administrative control with the browser-based administration.
- For a retailer who wants to expand into internet sales with a reliable easy to use web-store application, it is essential to develop designs to benefit them accordingly. The developer must offer a wide array of tools to help build an online store front and increase the bottom line by developing the custom web store.

Solutions for Successful E-commerce

For the success of e-commerce, solutions to the following areas are:

- Encrypted password/ message
- Digital certificate
- Public key infrastructure (PKI)
- Certificate authority

- Cryptography
- Electronic money
- Credit cards
- Authentication
- Digital signature
- Merchant account and payment
- Unbreakable algorithm and
- A new crypto-code having larger key length and larger block size than DES.

Other Solutions Read as Follows

- Credit card software
- Processing
- Shopping cart software
- Database development/applications
- Real time credit card transactions
- Website design
- Internet web marketing
- Hosting services
- User training
- E-commerce solutions
- Telecommuting
- Hardware and
- Communications.

Essentials of Good Solutions

Building effective e-commerce solutions is not complex but to be effective and successful, it must address the following issues:

- Quick response.
- Efficient working.
- Effective solutions.
- Most cost-effective, fastest, easiest.
- Traffic intensive.
- Generate revenues.
- Low cost transactions.
- Adjust to the landscape of internet mechanisms.
- Continuous technical service and update.
- Suitable to large businesses and small corporations.

- Government, non-profit, civil groups, business of sizes, individuals and families helping to manage financial affairs and solve problems and plans for the future.
- Meeting the needs and requirements of clients and merchants in an electronic environment.
- Specialised in business to business liaison, business to consumer and consumer sales and marketing.
- Develop and result-oriented sales and marketing programs to increase bottomline results.
- E-commerce solutions to help businesses to deal with potential business issues.
- Providing merchants with a turnkey product and ongoing site maintenance at affordable prices with classified banners and website constructions.
- Creating simple solutions that retailers want to adopt.
- There must be customized e-commerce solutions.
- The whole process of setting up an online store must be easy regardless of the size of business.
- The simplicity and sophistication of software, inexpensive site creation for small and medium based business is necessary.
- The solutions for business should increase revenues and expand customer base.
- Solutions should always be available being specialised in all aspects of internet commerce for companies of all sizes, assisting in designing, hosting, promotion and subsequently implementing the online internet store.
- Customer ordering system or providing customer interactive programming for the web site should not be ignored.
- The shopping cart system must place internet store online at the customer's finger tips in a matter of hours.
- The solutions must be designed to meet the needs of customers, merchants and developers of websites who need more advanced features, easy to use technology by professionals yet be affordable to them.
- Business solution developers should secure and support growing needs, designing the network and maintaining with expertise the online business.
- A wide range of high quality solutions and services are required including internet services such as web hosting, intranet, hardware solutions, software and consultations for business needs that is expected of the one-stop IT provider.
- Solutions must automate payment processing from credit card authorization to fund capture and settlement by making website payment operational 24 hours a day.
- Selecting the world's best internet commerce software solutions must be a *revolutionary solution* E-commerce solutions for small and medium-sized business should be prioritised as they can develop innovative e-commerce and customer management software companies evolving e-business solutions and the e-commerce web system.
- It should be easy to implement and maintenance free, and use leading security measures to ensure that the customers' confidential information is also protected. The ease in use is demanded by online merchants.

Web development for e-commerce solutions is a critical aspect. The developer must provide:

- Internet commerce system
- Shopping cart system
- Internet access and
- Product payment.

Internet commerce consists of the above mentioned areas. One of the areas of internet commerce management is the online product management system which involves the administration to strategically and efficiently add or update a database of items and categories through various web browsers.

Advantages of E-commerce Solutions

E-commerce solutions are trusted by thousands of online business people on the global canvas who access the Internet in a big way. The well trained and experienced staff of the services have been extending support to various aspects of e-commerce operations.

Payment solutions are available for the virtual storefront by setting up security to accept credit and cheques on the world wide web. Thus, there are a blend of total solutions presently available to the business community.

Service providers developed advanced solutions for business needs required for internet transactions as well as customized solutions. They have applied the best of the new technologies in an innovative way as required in e-commerce. The businesses can use emerging solutions of internet software technologies to create online stores. Without the latest technologies, administrative and legal solutions, it is not possible to create online stores comfortably, attractively and conveniently for the shoppers to securely transport and protect sensitive personal financial information.

The following are some of the benefits of effective e-commerce solutions:

- Support internet based electronic business process.
- Provide the strongest security framework to facilitate all secure commercial transactions.
- Availability of training and educational facilities.
- The selling technologies help to implement shopping cart and complete e-commerce solutions to help lead businesses into the new millennium.
- Shopping carts, a secure server, merchant account credit card processing, online payment and processing solutions are beneficial categories of effective solutions.
- Solutions are available for both small and large businesses.
- Timely availability of solutions and their cost effectiveness are additional features.
- Availability of services such as hosting, administration, design and maintenance of websites, improving sites, registering domain name, installation set-up, configuration confirmation, customization, free sale, post sales, storefront etc.
- Some companies are providing a free trial use of solutions.
- They provide the easiest, most secure and the least expensive method for selling products and services online.

- One can build one's own online store quickly and securely initiate business transactions.
- There are solution providers offering consultation development, management and trained services which extend support through any internet project development.

Technology Standards for E-commerce

There are technology standards for e-commerce including various aspects governing internet commerce which employs several standards. Several of these are as follows :

1. *Electronic Data Interchange (EDI):* This is a common document structure designed for permitting businesses to transit information over private networks. Today, EDI plays a critical role is setting the stage for a major presence in corporate websites as well.

2. *Open Buying on the Internet (OBI):* The internet purchasing round table has created the OBI service released by OBI consortium.

3. *Open Trading Protocol (OTP):* This is related to online payment activities. OTP is intended to standardize the various payment services. It was created as a compelling stand and to the OBI by a group of companies including AT & T, Cyber cash, Hitachi, IBM, Oracle, Sun MicroSystems etc.

4. *Open Profiling Standards (OPS):* It is a microsoft and firefly backed standard permitting users to create a personal profile of preferences and interests they want to this share with the merchant . The objective of this standard is to help consumers protect their privacy without banning online collections of marketing information.

5. *Secure Locket Layer (SLL):* It is a secure protocol designed to create a secure mechanism servertry to using a public encryption.

Secure Electronic Transaction (SET): It is also one of the secure devices pertaining to suitable encodes and the credit card numbers stored on the merchant server. This standard is created by Visa and Master Card. There's wide support for SET in the banking industry.

Trust: It is a partnership of companies which aims to build and ensure their trust. They should not violate the privacy of consumers.

E-services/solutions

They include:

- Network consultation
- Internet access
- Web solutions
- Co-location
- Client/server applications for internet and intranet back office and small office services.
- Exchange server solutions
- Turnkey solutions
- Systems and network integrator
- Internet working services

- Design maintenance
- Support networks in LAN, WAN environment like UNIX, NT, Novell etc.
- SQL, ASP, JAVA, C++, Visual Basic, PERL
- Web Hosting
- Website design and development
- Intranet, extranet, internet service
- Reseller programs
- Shopping cart/sales cart
- Securing, privacy (encryption, SSL, SET etc.)
- Credit card online
- Payment methods, digital signature, authorization
- Graphic and design services
- Database and Online catalogue
- Logo development services
- Copywriting services
- Sales and marketing consultation on and off the internet
- Advertising service on the web and other media and
- Domain name.
- Developers performing all sorts of interface research will help both programmers and web designers to make their products work better for the Net users.

E-Business Solutions Matrix

The fact that e-business encompasses so many activities can make it difficult for organizations to identify their potential to tap the electronic opportunity to nitiate business by way of substantial investments. A simple tool that can help is the e-business solutions matrix developed by Unisys Corp. According to Unisys sources, by organising various aspects of electronic business into distinct and understandable elements, companies can approach e-business with a clear strategy that results in a clear pay-off.

The matrix divides e-business into three categories for substantial gains:

- Attract
- Interact and
- Transact

The Strategy to Attract: The focus here is on marketing and gaining potentially new customers. It starts with simple and static websites but can include activities such as online advertising, *Web casts* and online recruiting. It can even include embedded channels within various product offerings. For example, a site that sells airline tickets will appreciate allowing a credit card company to offer a special introductory deal to customers who buy tickets for a special destination.

The Strategy to Interact: The e- business pace picks up in the interact category. Here, companies are interacting with customers, adapting offers in real time and providing authentic one to one marketing. For example, an auto maker may provide the customer self-service, a retailer may adjust pricing on-the-fly or a bank may recongnise that a valued customer has overdrawn an account and automatically transfer appropriate funds. This can also involve information turning internal expertise into saleable information or making government records available to the citizens online.

The Transact Strategy: The most challenging potentially beneficial e-business opportunities are found in this strategy. It is clear the way e-business provider meets the load, whether it involves selling products online, conducting business-to-business or taking advantages of online procurement. Such activities involve the integration of all systems and departments of individual business firms and potentially the systems and departments of the firm's partners and suppliers.

ATTRACT		INTERACT	TRANSACT
Operational Efficiency	Brochure of website	Knowledge portals	E - procurement
	Employee Communications	Interactive channel support	E-business (EDI)
	Interactive recruiting	Customer self-service	Dynamic supply chain
			Industry exchanges / trading networks
Revenue Growth	Advertising banners	Games and entertainment	Web merchants
	Sponsorships	Dynamic benchmarking	Web as a new channel
	Webcasts	Information repurposing	Product portals
	Online direct marketing	Interactive learning	
		Adaptive/ 1-to-1 marketing	
New Markets	Navigation Portals	Adaptive knowledge development	Problem portals
	Channels within Products	New infomediaries products	Dynamic logistic
		Customised product design	interlocking communities / market places

Source : Information Systems, Computer World, Feb. 1-15, 2000, pp. 59-60

Shopping Cart

A shopping cart is a part and parcel of online catalogue that keeps tracks of the item which have been decided by the buyer to buy. The concept of shopping cart is very important in case of online shopping. E-commerce service providers arrange for shopping carts to be used by net users to keep track of products and integrate a wide variety of different payment methods into the web site. Shopping carts are required when a large list of product/services are offered for sales.

It is a shopping cart in which the customer selectively adds certain quantity of products to a list. It is nothing but a list to which the customers add each of the items they want to purchase, The cart is to be added and then checked out. The shopping cart device in e- commerce permits the customer to selectively add a certain quantity of products to a list or shopping cart.

There are many methods of payment for purchase. But at the time of the check out, the payment method is selected and the transaction is completed. Shopping cart provides a way of selecting items and adding them to a shopping list for purchase.

A good shopping cart will allow the customer to enter an order at the website for any product by the following procedure:

- Select
- Quantity
- Size
- Colour
- Obtain payment information such as credit card or cheque numbers.
- Compute shipping charges and
- Sales tax.

If the credit is used with real time system like authorize net, it means that credit is already authorized and the system only needs to fulfil the order.

Shopping cast allows the customers the familiar and comfortable sense of shopping with this device which is a shopping convenience to shop over the Net. For this, a shopping cart program is used. It facilitates the customer to:

- Add
- Remove
- Change and
- Alter items without difficulty.

The quantity of items anytime and the check-out button is always there when customers are ready to complete their purchases. Other features of a shopping cart include:

- Multiple shopping option
- Number of items
- Order weight
- Order value and
- Automatic credit card verification.

The current feature of the e-system is advanced shopping cart capabilities. Product selection can be stored in personalized shopping carts to which users can add, edit and remove products both during the course of a single visit and across multiple visits to the sites of choice.

Features of Shopping Cart

1. *Inclusion of Items:* Detailed information is submitted to the shopping cart when the customer shops at a merchant's website. Information such as product, item, quantity, product description, shipping value, weight and price per item etc. are accessible.

2. *Viewing Information:* The customer can view information about the items added to the shopping cart. The other features of the shopping cart is helping the customers substantially by giving the Zip code for shipping and tax calculations. There is a facility of modification to the items in the cart.

3. *Totals:* The customers view the sub- total page and proceed to the total page. Total page presents a final sum to the customer. The sub-total page, shipping and tax details are summarized. The customer can get detailed information with the final order.

4. *Real Time Transaction Processing:* Shopping on the Net provides an opportunity of real time online transaction processing. There are several payment methods for buying. Based on the type of payment method selected, it gives an opportunity to the customer to process the order and return real time confirmation to the user.

5. *E-Mail:* The information about the order is received by the merchant and the buyer.

6. *Transaction Report:* All transactions take place on real time, enabling the merchant to receive all orders and transactions.

7. *Shopping Cart Services:* The shopping cart services on the Web may include the following services:

- To provide easy to use powerful, low cost solutions for conducting secure electronic commerce.
- Set up quickly and easily online stores without having to learn new programming skills.
- Provide secure socket layer security, protecting both shoppers and merchants when their personal, confidential and financial information is in transit over the Net.
- Set up a shopping cart account and start selling products or services online.
- Provide a cost- effective merchant account solutions either solely or with partnership and
- Provide an effective product management system which enables the administrators to easily update or add a database of items and categories through a web browser. Software enables the administrator to handle large product bases easily and efficiently.

Some Shopping Cart Systems

1. *Shop Plus:* Shopping cart systems help to build a store or mall on the internet. Within the website, the store can be customized. It permits to use frames, or no frames, single product pages, options within products, price changes, unlimited product bases and global shipping charges and unlimited tax options.

2. *Shop Site:* It is a flagship shopping cart solution. It is a high-end flexible online store development system that provides merchants with the ability to build and maintain a catalogue of a wide range of products and services. This system provides tools for site creation, management, sales and traffic statistics, secured encrypted transactions, online credit fulfilment, credit card processing, real time and order delivery.

There are two versions of shop site. They are shop site manager and shop site pro.

3. *Comcity:* Comcity provides shopping service to keep track of product lists and integrate a wide variety of different methods of payments into the website. It extends support for sales cart, a commercial released from the Internet shopping cart.

Shopping Cart Software

Is it necessary to have shopping cart software? Generally, no such software is necessary when only a single item is offered. When a merchant is selling more than a few products, it is needed to have some kind of shopping cart software on the website. This type of software is more useful from the customer's point of view. This software permits visitors to browse the pages of a choice site and select items leisurely before placing an order for the selected items. Today, in the market, there are available many shopping cart software packages for this operation.

On the other hand, the shopping cart is generally not required when only a few items are offered to sell. But when a large list of products are offered, the shopping cart is essential to help the customers keep the online transaction straight and add items regularly. This provides potential turnkey e-commerce solutions. There is no need for the merchant to purchase any products off the shelf or from the third party shopping cart software.

Merchant Account — Meaning and Nature

What is merchant account? Why is it important and who needs it? A merchant account is needed to accept credit cards. It gives the business the ability to use the credit card as payment for the products or services being ordered online. A merchant account is a contractual relationship between the customer and the merchant and a processing bank or any independent organization. A merchant account is not a bank account. So, there is no need to deposit or withdraw from the bank and does not carry any balance. The usual banking rules and procedures do not apply to a merchant account. It is a potential *online liaison* between this merchant and the customer. The processing bank or an independent organisation may necessarily insist on opening a bank account called the *merchant account* with their banks.

The merchant account is essential for online business in e-commerce. A merchant account is simply a service that will take credit card orders. It is a totally secure process wherein the funds are directly deposited in the merchant's bank account.

The account gives an opportunity to the customer to do online business with an extremely popular payment method i.e. *credit card processing.*

Merchant account is a special account supplied by banks, financial institutions or independent organisations which allow the concept of payment by credit cards. Without the merchant account, it is not possible to accept payment by credit card.

Is it necessary to have a merchant account to sell on the Net? The answer is that it is not necessary, only when a merchant wants to accept a credit card, the merchant account is to be set up. There is no need to have a merchant account like a bank account. If there is no merchant account, then it becomes imperative to have one for potential online business.

It is the merchant account service providers who authorize the credit cards transfer from the customer and deposit the funds for their purchases right into the business account. Merchant accounts are available from some banks and other independent providers. For instance,

Card Service International, a leading transaction service provider, offers small to mid-sized business merchants a variety of services like credit cards electronic cheque, internet transaction services etc.

There are many other alternative methods of payment like cash on delivery and cheque payment, which do not require a merchant account. But it is necessary in case of accepting credits in the context of the potential internet business. Banks, financial institutions and other independent merchant accounts service providers offer potential services to get a merchant account started.

Many banks may not offer the service of availability of the merchant's accounts.

To set up a merchant account is not a complex process, but with the risks associated with security, many banks are not coming forward to issue these accounts. Here, Cards Service International comes into the picture.

The merchant account can be used to accept credit card payment in online stores. It is also safe to process credit cards over the Net. The Secure Socket Layer (SSL) offers an encrypted connection, and the merchant can receive information about fraud screening if any, on each online on each transaction.

Types of Merchant Accounts

There are two types of merchant accounts for accepting credit cards.

1. *Card Present Accounts (CPA):* Under this method, both the customer and the merchant must physically be present at the same location at the time of transaction. The credit card is swiped through a card reader or at the point of the sale terminal. Subsequently, the Shoppers sign the authorization slip for the sale receipt.

2. *Mail Order/ Telephone Order (MOTO):* This method is quite opposite to the above method. In this method, there is no need for the merchant and shoppers to be present at the same location physically. The card is not swiped through a card reader and no signature is obtained. In case of mail order, business or catalogue method, the MOTO method of payment is used. As such, all internet transactions are considered as MOTO transactions and only require a MOTO merchant account.

3. *Total Merchant Service (TMS):* Total Merchant Services include a wide spectrum of activities. The basic question is how to get a business started, accepting the credit card. There are a few basic steps that constitute total merchant services:

- Selection of bank rate which may very according to the type of business and

Selection of payment acceptance solutions. They include :

- Internet processing
- Credit card processing software and
- Point of sale terminal equipment and third step is security.

4. *Merchant Identity (ID):* Merchant Identity (ID) is essential to do business on the Web. It is the basis for accepting the credit card. Merchant ID relates to machines which are programmed with this ID. It gives approval for the sale against the credit card. Merchant IDs are issued only for use on the Net.

Mail Order/Telephone Order (MOTO) facilities are also available. MOTO transactions are those transactions in which there is no imprint of the credit card nor does the merchant have the autograph of the cardholder. In this the, chances of fraud are more.

E-commerce solutions providing firms offer Merchant IDS to parties interested in establishing their presence on the Web and who want to conduct business on a wired global canvas.

Digital Receipt for Online Shoppers

A Receipt is a written statement evidencing that money, goods and other things which have been received. It indicates that the amount for the goods have been paid with the signature and with a rubber stamp saying *paid* or *received.* In a conventional commerce paper, receipts are issued acknowledging a business transaction. A digital receipt is an internet version of the traditional paper receipt. The receipt can be delivered via e-mail or a website database. It facilitates delivering receipts over the Net. It is an innovative device that will bring proof of purchase to the PC. Customers and online shoppers are increasingly relying on their computers to manage information and access to internet with one another. It is a new technology which is an open solution created by leaders in the industry. This new electronic facility will allow customers to easily track and manage their purchases and utilies the Net to communicate with retailers to perform basic post purchase transactions.

The Association for Retail Technology Standards (ARTS) of the national retail federation and shop. org, a consortium of the leading online retailers, have formally accepted a proposed standard for delivering receipts for business over the Net.

The digital receipt is the product of an alliance formed and led by the NCR Corporation and that includes Hewlett Packard's Verifone Division, America Online intuit Microsoft, Office depot, Valicent Inc (formerly known as receipt.com), RCS and VISA.

Cash Register-3 of Cybercash also issued a digital receipt in the form of proof of purchase (POP) to verity that a customer has paid for the services.

Digital Certificate or Authentication Certificate

A specially constituted certification authority issues a certificate in the e-commerce payment process. This is called digital certificate or an authentication certificate. The company receiving such a certificate can then put the certificate upon its site.

Certificates convey the name of the subscriber and other identification information such as an e-mail address, the public key of the subscriber, the validity period for the certificate, the name of the certificate authority that issued the certificate and the certificate serial number.

More and more internet companies are stressing on the use of digital certificates by their customers to protect the security of the consumers and their own transactions. For online merchants, digital certificates act as a passport to access the Net and are becoming a critical tool for boosting consumer confidence in the security of their website and in online commerce in general.

Digital authentication technology is contributing to the growth of e-commerce by working on strategies to establish between the participants of online transactions. This technology includes digital certificates which are issued by certificate authorities.

Digital certificates provide benefits that allow online stores and consumers to utilise the Net to the maximum such as authenticating the identity of participants on both ends of an online commercial transaction and authorizing credit card payments. Digital certificates also improve security concerns in non-commercial transactions by authorising access to key information without passwords, providing non-repudiation, i.e. legally binding the proof of messages sent over the Net and verifying the integrity of information exchanged online.

Payment System

The payment mechanism which constitutes the core of e-commerce process has become an important business strategy. It is simply because the payment mechanism has the potential to change the very essence of commercial transactions, business and industry models throughout the world. Payment processing systems play a critical role in e-business and any company considering launching its business must have chalked out plans well in advance. It is strategic business needs.

There are a number of payment options available. They are broadly classified as offline payment option and online payment option.

1. *Offline Payment Options:* These options mostly relate to the conventional payment methods. Under this method, an individual may use :

- A phone
- Drop a cheque into the postal headbox
- Earn and use discounts
- Bills
- Drafts
- Cheques
- Moneyorder
- Credit cards and
- Cash on delivery.

Electronic payment via the web is coming out of its infancy stage and many customers prefer using more traditional payment methods such as cheques or cash on delivery

2. *Online Payment Options:* Doing business online is an innovative strategy and the payback or payment through the e-shop is one of the most critical and challenging issues for any such business. How to make payments for online buying is a frequently asked question.

Electronic payment via the web is catching up gradually. Even today, many customers prefer using the traditional payment methods such as cash on delivery.

3. *Payment Process Software :* The Payment Process Software is used to facilitate payback for purchase. This software is usually sold as a service rather than as a product. It means there is no need on our part to install it on the web server and run it yourself. It is just sufficient to pass the credit card data to the software company's server and they take it from there. Most companies allow to buy the software and lease it for a monthly fee.

There are hundreds of companies making payment processing software. The best known and popular payment processing packages are Authorize Net, Cybercash, IC Verify and PC Authorize.

The merchant must be totally confident about his selling process. Utmost care needs to be taken since this is very crucial to the shopping experience of the user. The act of passing one's payment details to an unknown person may make the user hesitant to acknowledge the selling process and the payment process. The entire process also needs to be safe from both the merchant's and customer's perspective. To do this, a number of systems could be used to make the ordering page secure.

One of the popular systems today is SSL, which is supported by most of the browsers. This system encrypts the credit card data being transmitted so that it is very difficult for another person to decipher. It also certifies that the message is arriving from an authentic point (browser). This is done by using a digital certificate.

1. *Cambist Merchant:* Cambist Merchant Solutions allow merchants to accept secure credit card payments on the internet. From Cambist Inc, this payment system requires no additional hardware or software and is seamlessly connected to the merchant's existing website. Real-time payment authorization makes it possible for the customer's funds to be automatically deposited into the merchant's bank.

2. *Verifone:* Verifone makes it easy for users to make payments without re-entering credit card data. Its *wallet* software offers a user friendly graphical interface that lets users point and click at the potential site to make payments. A receipt manager files the purchase receipts and exports receipt information into personal finance programs such as Quicken. This is especially useful for keeping track of the expense and for maintaining the proof of purchase.

3. *Verfone:* Is one of the few organisations with all facets of product life cycle. Its portfolio comprises of internet payment software. E-payment server software and e-mobile payment software products enable end-to-end e-payment transaction processing that bridges the gap in physical, wireless and the Internet applications on a global platform.

4. *Cyber Cash:* Cyber Cash Inc has introduced the first payment processing system services, using its own secure Agile Wallet technology. Called the InstaBuy payment processing system, it enables webstore operators to offer their customers a secure and convenient way of making payment for online purchase. Customers use InstaBuy for both added security and convenience. Merchants use the services to streamline the payment process and increase consumer confidence and loyalty to their e-commerce sites.

5. *E-Cash:* This is a software based payment system that allows users to send electronic payments from any PC to any other PC or work station, using any computer network including the Internet. Called e-cash, it is introduced by Digcash Inc and requires merchants to open a bank account with a bank that issues e-cash.

6. *Pay-Base:* The pay-base suite of products from bottom line technologies provides enterprise wide payment software and internet enabling payment information solutions to business and financial institutions worldwide. From e-commerce to checking and curbing, the pay-base mechanism is geared towards improving processes.*

---

* *Dataquest, Feb 19,1999, p.149.*

Payment Services

E-commerce over the Internet is complete and successful only when there are effective online-payment services. Today, there are many real time online payment systems service providers. Providers are incorporated companies which approve this kind of payment. They are mentioned below :

- Authorize.Net[IM]
- (Authorize. Net (US)
- Future Cash
- (Future Cash (France)
- Banesto
- (Banesto (Spain)
- Cambist
- (Cambist (US)
- Card Service International (US)
- Credit card network (US)
- Data transfer Associates (US)
- I-Bill (US)
- I-Check (US)
- Merchant Online (US)
- Net Bank (UK)

Payment Methods

In e-commerce business, there have emerged a number of buzzwords or catch phrases. What are buzzwords for e-commerce payment process? E-money, e-cash, virtual money, electronic cash, electronic cheque, electronic wallets, cyber money and micro-payment are the various new phrases which are jargon related to payment methods on internet business.

In modern commerce, things are moving and changing at such a break neck speed that the technology gets outdated for those of us bewildered and besotted by the technological maelstorm that has overtaken the traditional systems of communication, the form of internet and its growing use in commerce.

E-cash and virtual money revolution unravels the mysteries of money and non-money. We are in the plastic money era wherein e-money, smart card, e-cash electronic wallets and cyber money are related to global business trends today. It is this enigma that grips modern day commerce. These buzzwords have become the currency of the Net. The most fascinating aspect of e-money is that it travels through cyber space. It is global money with the smart card facility. The links in the money circle are getting bigger, numerous and more complex in essence. The spendable value leverage over reserve and money base is growing. With money creation bypassing national and international boundaries, monetary policies have been constantly reshaped and new legislations are coming up along with security, privacy authentication and the encryption technology.

However, the following are some of the presently available information technology based payment methods.

1. *Digital or Electronic Cash:* Buying products or services over the internet finally results the payment for It. Digital cash means electronic cash or e-cash which allows the person to pay for goods or services. It is a process of transmitting data and information from one machine to another. E-cash issued by a bank as specified sum represents real money. The special feature of e-cash is that it is anonymous and reusable. This is the main difference between e-cash and credit card transactions done over the Internet.

To facilitate e-commerce, e-cash is designed as a new concept to make cash payments using computers connecting over various global networks. The e-cash is stored in the hard disc of the customer's computer in the form of an electronic wallet. The customer can spend e-cash for the purchase of items from any shop. Electronic cash can be used for paying or receiving payments between the customer and merchant, persons or for other important money transactions.

There is a separate software, which is used on the customer's own computer and the customer can withdraw e-cash from his own account in a bank. There are a number of secure e-cash solutions which provide security, privacy and the authentication of online transactions.

After finalising the selection of items through shopping cart and placing orders, the customer sends a request to the customer's bank server for sending cash from his account. The bank in turn verifies authenticity, balance and other details and sends back a secure e-cash packet. The packet is stored in the electronic wallet of the customer's hard disc. The e-cash reaches the chosen destination site over the Net.

To use digital cash, both the customer and the merchant need to have an account with a bank that issues it. The bank provides customers with the *'Purse'* software for managing and transferring their digital cash. Customers convert funds from their regular accounts into digital cash and then transfer it to the purse software, which stores it in their hard drives in encoded form until it is spent.

2. *E-Money :* Electronic money, e-money or digital cash is an electronic surrogate for coins and bank notes (example : cash cards or cash issued online for use over the Net) which is stored in an electronic device such as a chip card on computer memory and which is generally intended for making relatively small payments. The EU is making progress towards the implementation of a directive covering issues of e-money. The aim is to have a technology neutral legal framework that harmonises in the supervision of electronic money institutions and protects consumers.

With merchant accounts and payment process in vogue today, there are electronic money institutions and credit institutions (banks).

The credit institutions (entities) accept deposits and cheques which are subject to the Banking Regulations Act and directions of the Reserve Bank of India.

The structure of electronic money institutions is quite new and distinct. Similarly, the treatment is also different. So, electronic money institutions and conventional institutions are two different entities which would not be identical.

Electronic money institutions are subject to fewer controls and are restricted to in the case of e-business transactions.

3. *Digital Money:* It is a form of electronic or internet media. This is a grab-bag term for the various electronic payment schemes on the Net. Yahoo lists 21 companies offering a form of digital money.

4. *Electronic Cheque:* It is mainly used for paying utilities and phone bills. Currently, this is being tested by cybercash electronic cheque such as pay now and take money from the users' cheque accounts to pay utility and phone bills. This is in vogue today.

In virtually all aspects, an electronic cheque has the same features as a paper cheque. Indeed, in its simplest form, some systems merely require the customer to fill out a form in the web store. This data is then transferred to the merchant where it is converted into a paper cheque using blank cheque forms in a standard office printer. A further level of security can be obtained by utilizing the third party inputs for additional services such as verification.

5. *Electronic Wallet (E-Wallet):* It is, payment method under which the credit card numbers in an encrypted form are stored in the hard drive. Relating to the purchasing of goods at the website, the electronic wallet support is done by just clicking a pay button to initiate credit card payment by the e-wallet.

This is a payment scheme, such as cyber cash internet wallet that stores your credit card numbers on your hard drive in an encrypted form. You can then make purchases at websites that support the particular electronic wallet. When you go to a participating online store, you click a pay button to initiate credit card payment via a secure transaction enabled by the electronic wallet company's server. The major browser vendors have struck deals to include electronic wallet technology to increase the sales of their products.

The term electronic wallet is used in electronic payment which store credit cards and cash. In the e-commerce online world, the digital wallet is installed by being plugged into the web browser. In addition to storing cash, it stores the mastercard number and shipping information. The use of a password is necessary to enable the user to access the contents. Its basic function is to implement the encryption which permits secure electronic transaction (SET).

Electronic wallets are based on SET to hold electronic credit card and they have been developed by browser manufacturers such as Netscape and the Microsoft Internet Explorer. It may be noted that for the acceptance of transactions from electronic wallets, merchants need to incorporate SET into their servers.

The e-cash is stored in the hard disc of the customer's personal computer in an electronic wallet. The customer can spend from it for purchase of items from any shop accepting e-cash. The bank server sends a secure e-cash packet which is stored in the electronic wallet of the customer's hard disc. The exact e-cash required for the total value of purchase is paid from the electronic wallet in the customer's computer. The customer can make payment using a credit card number by e-cash through an automated clearing house (ACH). The merchant gets the payment immediately in debit-based transactions from the customer's bank in the merchant's bank account through the ACH, through a bank transfer. In credit transactions, however, the merchants get paid through a normal credit card processing cycle.

It is one of the improved methods in payment technology. E-wallet is not a new payment mechanism but more of a way to store details in a common area, to be specific, a virtual wallet. This will enable the buyer to make a payment by flicking open his wallet rather than having to fill in fields in online forms. A number of companies have competing versions of the e-wallet, from Microsoft's passport to the Java wallet.

Other ways of increasing credit card security have come from Cybercash and Verifone, both provide consumer with a helper application called a *'wallet'*. In the process of setting up the wallet, the consumer provides his/her credit card information and receives an encrypted code that refers to credit card in return. When making a purchase at a participating web store, the wallet passes the code to the merchant. The merchant then hands over that code, along with purchase price, to the wallet issuer who verifies the transaction with the credit card company and transfers the funds to the merchant along with an authorization to *ship* the product.

The e-wallet software from Idealab, an internet business development company based in Pasadena, California, commits itself to making online shopping as easy as pulling out a credit card. Presently, one has to fill in the fields manually, a cumbersome task which is said to have resulted in abandoning online shopping carts (or lists of items at web stores that the visitors have selected for purchase) frequently.

When the e-wallet software is added to the bottom of a windows desktop, a single click will propel shoppers through e-commerce check-out lines by automatically filling in the name, credit card, shipping and other information needed to complete a transaction. Shoppers simply drag icons of their credit cards over an e-commerce page and enter a PIN number, so that other users cannot shop with the same wallet.

6. Micro-payment: The major advantages of digital cash are the relatively low transaction costs and the fact that it can be divided into smaller denominations that are used in the real world. This makes it suitable for use in low value transactions such as paying for a stock quote or news article. These small denomination tokens are known as micro-cash and transactions with them are called micro-transactions or *micro-payments.*

Transactions amount between 25 cents and $10, typically made in order to download or access graphics, games and information—they are known as micro-payments Pay-as-you-go micro-payments were supposed to revolutionize the world of e-commerce. One early scheme, for example, let visitors to ESPN, Sports Zone use their cybercash/cybercoin accounts to buy a $1 day pass to the site's premium content without having a spring for a full month's subscription. But many potential customers have been unwilling to play along with the micro-payments.

As a payment scheme, it is more in practice in the US. Under these, transactions in smaller amounts are typically made in order to download or access graphics, games and animations, and in other words, it is called as micro-payments.

Disintermediation : Internet business eliminates the conventional middleman system. It means that e-commerce eliminates traditional retail intermediaries such as retail stores and mail order houses etc.

Electronic Cheques

Automated Clearing House (ACH)

The ACH service is a payment service that allows both online and traditional merchants to accept and process e-cheque payments. It may be either from the website front or through the quick commerce virtual terminal.

ACH service makes it easy for online business to add an e-cheque payment option to their websites. Customers who wish to pay for a purchase with an e-cheque can simply select the e-cheque option and enter the requested bank account information. ACH service encrypts data using SSL30 encryption technology and transmits it to the secure server for posting the transactions which are automatically settled each day. Then the system debits the customer's account via the automated clearing house and transfer funds to the merchant's account. If the account numbers are entered incorrectly or the account has insufficient funds, then the ACH checking service system intimates the merchants.

Traditionally, merchants without commerce -enabled websites can also use the ACH service to handle periodic billings. Businesses such as health, clubs, tanning saloons, subscription services and health practitioners are typical examples of business that need the ability to periodically deduct funds from their customer's checking accounts.

The ACH is the electronic network which transfers and clears funds between banking institutions on behalf of merchants and their customers. Each transaction takes nearly 48 hours to clear the ACH service which should not be used by merchants who sell soft or digital goods that are normally downloaded immediately upon completion of the sales of goods ordered by net users.

Cyber Cash

Cyber Cash Inc. is an organisation, a world leader in e-commerce technologies and services for the benefit of merchants and customers. It has introduced a service known as cash register payment service. It made e-commerce simpler for many online merchants. Cyber cash enables commerce across the entire e-market spectrum from electronic retailing environments to the Internet.

Cyber cash provides a full line of software products and services allowing marketing, billing, financial institutions and consumers to conduct secure transactions and other e-commerce functions. It uses a broad array of popular payment forms. The cyber cash payment solutions support credit, debit purchase cards, cash, cheques, smart cards and alternative payment types. The leading brands of cyber cash include Instabuy, Agile wallet, ICEUERIFY, PLUERIFY, Cash Register, Net-verify, Pay now, Web Authorize and PC Authorize.

Cybercash, cyber cash logo and agile wallet are trademarks, service marks, registered trademarks or registered service marks of Cyber Cash Inc.

Cyber Cash is a pioneer in credit undertaking and the leading provider of internet payment technologies and services. It greatly helps merchants to accept secure payments on the Net with more ease, flexibility, reliability and is cost effective.

Secure Payment Options of Cyber Cash

1. ***Secure Payment Card:*** They include Visa, Master card, American Express, Novus, Discover, Diners Club. JCB, Cartie Blanche. etc. are the cards available from which consumers can select any one for the safe purchase of products and services online.

2. ***Cyber Coins:*** It is used for small cash payments for instantaneous electronic delivery of information products and services to the customers.

3. ***Pay now Electronic Cheque :*** The feature of this option is that it enables consumers to pay their bills directly through the web server.

GM Card easy Pay Wallet

GM Card easy-pay wallet was introduced in the year 1999, in partnership with General Motors, Cyber Cash and HouseHold international. The services are offered to card holders of the provider. The wallet will make it more convenient for the member cardholder to make secure purchases on the internet and will allow greater use of the card online. It is an internet-based service, which enhances customer loyalty. It is an important development in the strategic application of the electronic wallet which has come to stay. The wallet will store a shopper's name, credit card information, shipping details and other relevant facts. The stored details can be called upon to make an online purchase quickly and easily.

Concentric Network Corporation

Concentric Network Corporation (CNC) is one of the leading companies in providing e-commerce solutions. The cybercash's industry leading cash register payment service is featured in CNC's e-commerce retail packages. Cybercash has a strong partnership with CNC, which is a popular service provider offering small and medium sized merchants and tools needed to succeed in e-commerce. Cybercash and CNC are working together to make e-commerce simpler and easier for many online merchants. Its feature is integration of Cybercash's credit card processing technology into e-commerce services. Otherwise, previously merchants had to piece together their own internet e-commerce processing solutions by establishing separate relationship with the internet payment processors.

Internet Payment Features

The internet payment features include :

1. *Real Time Payment:* This facility enables the merchant to complete online transactions immediately. Shoppers receive confirmation that their purchases were approved in real time. The merchant gets the payment for the sale of goods or services by transfer to their bank in real time.

2. *Scalability:* The e-business has come to stay, continues and is growing at a faster rate. The system must have the capability to manage and support the growth of their transactional volumes. It requires additional payment features. The Internet Payment Service (IPS) has to manage scalability. The merchant's growth of revenue depends upon the ability of payment services to ensure that much scale with increased transactions.

3. *Additional Payment Features:* Installation, upgradation and additional payment are also needed. The level of integration and maintenance is an important factor. Cybercash's cash register 3 service is renewed, which is an integrated one. Cybercash takes the responsibility of managing and maintaining the software.

4. *Multiple Payment Methods:* The common forms of payment methods include cash and electronic cheques but credit cards are the primary choice of payment in e-commerce. Most of the merchants are giving multiple options of multiple payment methods to extend their business.

Internet Payment Services (IPS)

Taking credit card payments online. every merchant on the internet needs to have an IPS and merchant credit card account. A complete and successful e-commerce is not full unless the merchant's website must be able to access and process secure online payments. Cybercash is an instant of IPS, which enables the merchant to accept online payments from their customers and securely process the payment service.

The IPS is needed to the merchant that provides security to deal with credit card authentication, confidentiality in transaction, server use integrity and server use integrity and server virus protection. The IPS includes SSL and protecting security with encryption of the customer payment information.

The financial institutions of the merchant provide him with a bank account that enables him to accept, process and deposit payment from their customers. These issues are very important to facilitate e-commerce.

The main reasons for IPS requirement are :

- Merchant needs guarantee to get money for the goods or services sold.
- Customers need confidence and be comfortable shopping from the website.
- Merchant needs security to deal with credit cards authentication, confidentiality in transaction and server host integrity.

Payment Gateways

A payment gateway ensures securing credit card payments to be made over the Internet.

Communication between the user and the website host is encrypted using the Secure Socket Layer (SSL) mechanism, built into the standard internet browser. This ensures that even if someone were able to monitor the traffic between the user and the website server, they would not be able to read it.

Encryption should be used on all pages on the website that handles the card details. The website owners do not then need to keep records of their customers' card details. These are handled by the payment gateway provider. The data transferred to them is protected by a service of firewalls.

The payment gateway provides to deal directly with the relevant bank and then informs the website hosts whether the transaction has been successful.

Videsh Sanchar Nigam and E-commerce Gateway

Videsh Sanchar Nigam Limited (VSNL) has developed the potential to explore the possibility to sell services and products online and accept payments. This scheme allows merchant servers to link up to the main server, thus enabling them to conduct substantial e-commerce. The facility is available www.e.com.vsnl.net.in.

Presently, the VSNL has been using the Net for e-commerce for its own international transactions, presenting its bills to international carriers such as British Telecom. More recently, customers' applications were being received online, with the groundwork done for receiving of payments online and order confirmation online.

Its value added and leased line service were full buyer-2000 compliant. In the case of international voice services, it had achieved compliance for 36,000 circuits as against the current operational level of 19,000 circuits.

Credit Card

Back Ground: In recent years, there has been a remarkable shift in the purchase pattern of consumers which requires a direction of simplicity. The Internet has driven consumers to buy goods and services because it has become easy to do so. Products are seen online, ordered online with payment made online, shipped quickly and delivered right to the buyer's door. Consumers are preferring to be driven to this service by the merchants who advertise their websites and this leads to avoiding overhead expenses.

As such, credit cards are the currency of the Internet. People using the Internet for their purchases make payment via the credit cards.

For these and various other reasons, the acceptance of credit cards is crucial for success in the booming e-commerce market.

The Internet has become a global marketplace with a wide variety of goods and services available from any computer around the world. Banks and financial institutions, seeking ways to improve services and make financial transactions more convenient for customer, are encouraging and undertaking the usage of credit cards in a big way.

Large corporations are being challenged to find more effective ways of conducting business at a faster rate, lower cost, fewer people, high level quality, confidence and credibility.

Many companies are implementing credit card purchasing as a part of the re-engineering efforts to facilitate the purpose of and payment for goods and service.

The most popular credit cards are Master card, Visa, American Express, Discover card, Diners Club and Federal Reserve ACH.

The following steps may be involved in accepting credit cards :

- Total merchant services
- A bank rate for business
- Payment acceptance solution
- Internet processing
- Credit card processing software
- Point of sale terminals and
- Complete secure payment application.

Cash, accepting cheques and money orders are popular methods of payment for commercial transactions. In e-commerce credit card, the merchant account is kept with the financial institutions. Credit cards are accepted online. The buyers will enter their credit card information in the order form and the information is forwarded by e-mail as an encrypted, compressed and encoded attachment, which is quite difficult to intercept and decode. In online payment, the credit card benefits both the merchant and the customers.

Credit cards are the most popular way for paying for goods and services on the Net. The more card types you accept, the better your sales will be.

Payment solutions when available, enables the website to accept credit card payment in real time. Significant savings are also realised by eliminating inhouse manual processing.

The Internet Payment Service (IPS) such as Cyber cash enables the merchant to accept online payment from customers and security process payment transactions from a merchant's web storefront through the existing system of financial institutions and credit card processors. Payment information is encrypted through a direct link to secure commerce servers from the web. Technology permits to e-mail a payment confirmation when the transaction is approved and subsequently send the customer an e-mail receipt. Accepting credit cards greatly helps to make purchases online with instant approval.

The credit card market is strategically moving towards development. There were only 5 lakh credit cards in 1994 but in 1999, the number touched 33 lakh and per card usage went up to ₹ 27,000 per annum from ₹ 12,000. The average number of cards per person went up to 1.4, leading many to believe that the acceptance of credit cards as a way of life is a beneficial business strategy.

The opportunities for growth in the Indian credit cards industry are unlimited. The credit card concept is picking up across different cross sections of the country. But still, the Indian card market is in its infant stage and untapped and hence offers wide potential.

The consumer is more exposed and better travelled and this trend in itself has caused a sea change in his spending capacity.

Non-traditional areas where the usage of cards is on the increase, certain segments have shown the most dramatic growth in India like gas stations, supermarkets and other outlets catering to daily necessities. There is a shift away from spending on travel and entertainment also. A market research professional feels that impulse buying and unplanned purchase is becoming more common. This tends to lead to an increasing use of cards for smaller ticket items. Penetration to these is the key to the growing credit card industry.

Encouraging customers to thrive on credit is the trend of co-branded cards. Internationally, issuers like department stores and petrol pumps offer customers loyalty benefits for using their own brand cards. As in this case, it can help a cardholder with travelling and entertainment, provide an additional financial cushion, assist in productive assets creation and gets moving only in emergency, saves time on payment of utility bills, permits purchases across the globe and this is a means of identification for further retail loans/personal benefits and providing insurance.

Smart Card (Electronic Credit Card)

The smart card is a plastic card, the size of a credit card, with an embedded micro processor and memory, used for storing information related to banking identification, medical data etc. When inserted into a card reader, it transfers data to and from a central computer. It can be programmed to bring about self destruction if repeated attempts are made by unauthorized personnel to use it.

Smart card is like a credit card of a bank relating to the bank transaction and it is the most convenient device to draw cash from Automatic Teller Machine (ATM), but also to check weapons in and out of the armoury and for personnel tracking and identification purposes. The present technology also permits users to turn their uses into ATMs to make electronic payment or have more money downloaded from their bank account. The ATM card system has been launched by many banks, enabling the users to draw cash from their unmanned terminals.

Smart card permits users to access a variety of services at specially positioned card reader stations. A plastic card will help to buy stationery, books, groceries, operate bank accounts, make long distance phone calls, payments and get access to the Internet.

The US-based Fischer International Systems called *smarty*, could be inserted into the 3.5 inch floppy drive of any PC, converting it into a smart card reader. So in future, the users could operate their cards at home and turn their PCs into the automatic teller machine to make electronic payments or to draw money from their bank accounts.

A smart card is a multi-functional micro-processor and memory on a computer chip is embedded in a plastic- it is literally a *computer in a card.* This specimen card has the inner workings and the computer enables users to see the card.

Popularly called a smart card, the card in the computer comparatively has less computing power than a PC. In advanced countries like France and the US, smart cards are produced and are in wide use. They have a simple processor and a small memory. Days will come when smart cards will soon be replacing credit cards. They only read memory into which data can be placed. In each card, there is a central processing unit. In other words, it is a mini computer. There is always an interaction between the smart card computer and other external devices which read the card and enter the data on to it.

The features are:

- The amount of sales or purchase is stored in the card's memory,
- A credit is given to the retailer's account and
- A deduction is given from the cardholder's credit balance.

When a transaction takes place, say a purchase, the information as to the amount of purchase, the name and address of the store and the data is stored in the memory. It requires a device known as *the card reading machine.* The machine is also connected to a home computer, a television set or a printer which displays a full record of all purchases made with the card.

Types of Credit Card

1. Credit Card: The credit card was originally pioneered in the early 1959s. A credit card is a plastic card with the particulars of the cardholder's name and address embossed for easy transfer by contact printing. This contains no memory. A single plastic card will help the cardholder to buy stationery books, groceries, operate bank accounts, reserve tickets, make long distance phone calls etc.

2. Magnetic Strip: It is a credit card with a black magnetic strip. This is more popular and widely used in the UK. It has about 250 bytes of space for storing characters.

Conventionality, this black strip consists of 3 tracks-a 79 byte track used for travel applications, a 40 byte track for banking applications and a 107 byte track for personal identification number (PIN) and other applications. This card can be read, that is, its information can be downloaded by card readers but it cannot be written into traffic and it is one way only. It has small, amounts of memory but no computer on board.

3. IC Memory Card: This card has the capability to store about one megabytes of data. The best example is the photo CD card, storing a number of pictures and other special function cards to store data for easy transportability.

A smart card is quite distinct and not similar to the cards mentioned above. A card to be called as a *smart card,* must be able to think for itself- this is it possible through a computer and atleast a small microprocessor. The smart card device has been around in India for over a decade with a different name called the *slim calculator.* It is called as *super smart* because in addition to onboard memory and the onboard processor chip, it has a keypad.

An electronic system has been used even for credit for card service. For instance, Bank of Baroda has introduced in some of its branches, the electronic data delivery system for dealing with the credit card business. According to this new system, the electronic instrument can act as liaison or transaction between a shopping centre and the bank's central office. It is expected to allow the bank's cardholder to use the card in shopping centres for any amount on the basis of instant approval which it receives from the central office within a few seconds.

Smart Card — An Internet Currency

In the Net business, the smart card functions as a separate currency. Credit cards are the currency of Internet. Almost all online purchases are paid via these cards, which provide a secure, fast and easy-to-use method of payment for both merchants and customers. There is much value of credit card acceptance in the online market place. Acceptance of credit cards is crucial for tapping the potential internet commerce market.

They have the feature of instant approval and business time is saved. Credit card usage on the internet means finding a secure, cost-effective and a reliable way to collect payment and process transactions. There are service providers with a secure-based transaction processing system, which is necessary to enable various businesses to authenticate, process and manage credit cards and electronic cheques transacted in real time.

The merchant has to simply send the processor necessary information needed to process customer's transaction over a secure, encrypted internet connection. The rest of the work is handled by service providers that is processed by means of sophisticated computer supported transaction processing systems. The merchant has the advantage of fast, reliable commerce servers, a powerful database and fast secure leased lines connecting to major financial institutions.

Authorize Net is one of the popular service providers which provides the following:

- Authorized.Net virtual terminal
- Authorized. Net web link and
- Echeck. Net.

The transfer of information can be done by using a terminal like retail stores and use processing software such as POS charge or PC. Authorize that can be installed on desk top and then transmit the transaction to the processing centre, or on online real time credit card processing gateways like Authoize. Net or Total Merchant Manager.

Another method is the process by telephone system that allows to transmit the transaction over a telephone key pad.

Capturing customer's credit card information can be obtained by other methods-Verbal, Mail, fax, online shopping card, order form and swiping the card in person.

Strategis to process a credit card and ensure that the money is sent to the merchant is an interesting area of study in e-commerce. An order can be taken over on the Net, phone, fax, walk-in-strategy, offsite and trade show.

CompuBank-Real Time Banking Online

Compubank is the first US financial institution to protect online banking customers with insurance protection against possible unauthorized transactions in their online accounts. The aim of privacy of personal information about the customers is of paramount importance. The customers of Compubank are able to access their accounts, conduct bill payments, account transfers and retrieve cheque images or statements. The customer can access his bank account from home, his office or anywhere in the world. It has developed as a successful global banking phenomenon.

Compubank has global presence due to the high level of convenience in terms of cancelled cheques, monthly statements, current balance, overdraft protection, cheque re-order, funds transfers and direct transfers given by it.

The bank is one of the leading institutions in the internet banking services. Its state-of-the-art banking systems allows for real time cash management.

Compubank's bill payment process permits to make payments to a business, corporation, individuals, or a charity via the PC or telephone.

The internet banking agreement provides for the terms and conditions governing the basic internet banking services and bill payment services offered by Compubank. Internet banking services cover all banking services like funds transfer, bill payment services, wire transfers etc.

Services

Compubank has charted out a list of services to benefit its customers They are :

- The customers can use their visa cheque card for purchases as well as for cash withdrawals. The card can be used for purchase at grocery stores, hotels and other merchants and ask for cash back.
- The customers can use their ATM cards at Over Cirrus, Money Maker and Pulse ATM terminals across the United States and abroad.
- The banks' free bill payment allows to make payments to a business, corporation, individuals or a charity via the PC or telephone and the bank accepts all the direct deposits for customers.
- Its funds transfers services cover transfers initiated by customers between their accounts with the bank.
- It allows customers free and direct transfer of funds into their Compubank accounts from accounts at other financial institutions .
- Wire transfer from their accounts facility is also available.
- Cheque reorders.
- Overdraft protection and
- Downloading personal financial software.

Card Service International—Payment Solutions

Card service International is an independent transaction service provider. The company has the credit of having serviced some lakh merchants and processing billions of dollars in the bank card volume. It services extend from small to mid-sized business merchants. Its activities include a variety of services including credit card, electronic cheques and internet transaction services. Some banks have relationships with card service International. It works with the kinds of businesses that most banks consider risky. Highspeed Technologies has exceptional merchant account program offers available to its clients through the card service.

Card services, SSL Application Programming Interface (API) offers e-commerce website builders and provides an encrypted connection to Secure Payment Engine. It helps those merchants who want to get online account fast with a limited start-up budget.

All Card service International merchants receive the following benefits by using the Link Point, Secure Payment Gateway Technology. The following are the three unique and user friendly payment solutions available to serve the e-commerce needs of any merchant.

1. ***Virtual Link Point:*** Virtual Link Point allows merchants to manually enter details of credit card transactions on a PC through a secure connection to the Net. Virtual Link Point is the internet equivalent of a point of sale (Pos) Terminal or PC - based transaction software without hardware or maintenance expenses. Sales, returns, authorization and real-time reports are all provided by Virtual Link Point.

2. ***Link Point HTML:*** Link Point HTML is a simple yet sophisticated product and requires a little hands - on work by the merchants to use it. It wraps around the merchant's existing website, allowing online shoppers to select and order products and securely pay for them with a credit card. All the same services provided by Virtual Link Point are available with this product.

3. ***Link Point API:*** Link Point API is the most sophisticated level of service, enabling software companies, commerce service providers (CSPs), Internet service provider (ISP) or cyber-wise merchants to add Secure Socket Layer (SSL) payment capabilities to their products, services or custom store fronts. Additional features such as fax and shipping calculations and electronic soft good download (ESD) i.e., software, pictures and texts are included.

Advantage of Credit Cards and Payment Over the internet

There are many reasons to accept secure credit card and cheque payment over the Internet. The following are the top 20 reasons to support this mechanism.

1. ***A Universal Medium:*** At present, credit cards provide customers the only universal medium of exchange that can be transmitted electronically. Although, in many countries, credit cards are not as widely used as in the US and Europe, they are still the most globally accepted medium of exchange for various business transactions.

2. ***Currency Exchange:*** Credit cards automatically handle currency exchange for international sales. A customer, for instance from the US, may buy a product in Indian rupees on a website by presenting his credit card but the credit card company will charge in US dollars from the customer and pay store owners in rupees after subtracting a modest exchange fee.

3. ***Improved Cash Flow:*** Under the conventional method of management, the merchants have to wait for 60 or more days for payment. Under the credit card method, processing system and internet funds for purchasing card transactions are sent electronically through the banking system into the business checking account within two to three days.

4. ***Reduce Expenses:*** There is no need to process and mail invoices, manage and collect the expenses.

Total merchant services offer a range of processing options including electronic terminal processing, PC-batch processing and mail order telephone order batch processing.

5. Credibility: The prestige and goodwill of the business may go up using the credit card method. Many people are displaying cards and logos on ads on web pages and they gain credibility with their online customers. Safety and Security is ensured to the customers to buy from the merchants over the internet through credit cards. Today, not only established business persons accept credit cards, but it has become common among small businesses.

6. Working Capital: Accepting credit cards and payment over the Net will increase the amount of effective working capital. Money can be actually realised in just 40-48 hours. As a matter of fact, the merchant is not extending credit to their customers or waiting for cheques to be cleared. Another advantage with this is that merchants use the customers' money to purchase products from their suppliers before shipping them out to the customers.

7. Profitability: Many merchants nowadays are accepting credit cards for many reasons. One of them is that they increase profits. Selling on the Internet is offering service to the public on a global canvas. It means that there will be more customers and there will be more sales. Increased sales means more profit. Some research studies indicate that accepting credit cards recorded more sales than those who do not accept credit cards. A business person not accepting credit card means losing potential customers. So, accepting credit cards will increase the bottomline. If there is no credit card, the business person potentially misses out on e-businesses. By this, firms do not turn out valuable customers away simply because the business does not take credit cards.

8. Customer Convenience: Encuring customer convenience is of utmost importance. A card is carried along with a purse and it is easy for the user to pull out a credit card from the wallet or a purse. In recent years, many people recognized the convenience and the importance of the smart card. Many prospects became suspects of paper cheque dealings, The customers get many freebies offering by banks like free air mails, extended product warranties, free long distance, cash balance, rebate towards using specific cards, gifts and other bonus.

Payment over the internet and accepting secure credit cards make it easy for people to buy products/services online. The convenience of shopping any time, from home or office is the major reason for the consumers to buy products online.

9. Impulse Buying: The merchants can sell products or services by asking customers their credit card number over the phone. There are a number of problems in dealing with a traditional medium of paper cheque. Just by contacting on phone, prospective customers can be converted to a long-time customer by accepting credit cards.

Another reason why to accept secure credit card and cheque payment over the internet is that it makes it easy for customers to buy products online when impulse strikes.

10. Win Competition: In the context of the internet business growing at a faster rate, a merchant who does not accept credit cards will definitely lose potential customers and subsequently there will be decline in sales.

The computer who appreciates credit card acceptability will be benefitted by selling more and attract more customers. There are many customers who buy through credit cards. A merchant who does not advertise the acceptance of credit cards for his online businesses will lose substantial business. So, in the new method of business, merchants can withstand competitors and get sales increased by the acceptance of credit cards.

Online customers will choose the internet merchant who accepts secure payment towards the service products they order.

11. Security: Credit cards provide a secure, fast and easy- to-use method of payment for both the merchant and the customers. It provides and protects sensitive payment information with encryption technology.

12. Avoids Time Delay: The time delay associated with the traditional payment method is a major deterrent for ensuring smooth purchases, which is eliminated in the case of credit card acceptance. The time it take to process an order with a cheque payment receiving such from the buyer, depositing it in a bank, waiting time for clearance etc. will add to the time it takes to deliver the product to the customer.

13. Instant Approval: Another merit of using credit card is that it permits customers to make purchases online with instant approval by providing them a high level security.

14. Increased Sales: The past transaction history for the last few years indicates that payment over the Internet turns a website from an electronic brochure into a money making virtual storefront.

15. Make Money with Covenience: With the commerce enabled website, one can sell on the fast track every day of the week automatically without hiring a clerk or manager to run the stores.

16. Instant Gratification: Online shoppers want to buy for instant gratification. If they cannot order for products, services online, they must keep looking for a site where they can.

17. Level Playing Field: On the Internet, no one knows you are a small business. Small business firms operate on par with big business firms on the Net. It is a global business canvas for firms to do online business.

18. Increases Market Size: The commerce enabled website gives access to credit card users on national and international business levels.

19. Customer Loyalty: The findings of some research studies indicate that online buyers tend to return to sites where they have bought access to products and services on these sites.

20. Enhanced Advertising : Accepting credit cards online increases the credibility of business firms.

Credit Card Fraud

The whole concept of the credit fraud is a bigger risk to merchants than customers.Everybody is concerned with working out strategies to protect the consumer using the credit card for online purchases. It is actually the merchant who is actually at risk and stands to lose to a large extent. The merchant bears all liability in transactions where the credit card is not physically used or the card holder's signature is not obtained on the sales receipt.

The internet merchants have to take the same precautions as in mail or phone orders. Generally, they are at risk of getting fraudulent orders. Asking for the e-mail address of the online customer is the best precaution. The impact of fraud online stores can be detrimental to the merchants.

Processing of Credit Card: Following are the guidelines to implement the processing:

- A form is needed on the site which the customers can use to place orders.
- The seller needs to have a credit card merchant account. An e-commerce merchant account with a bank is necessary to process an e-commerce transaction.
- A payment processing software which will serve as a link between the site and the bank is imperative.
- With the help of HTML and the CGI script, it is essential to work out strategies to create a form.
- The CGI script performs the function of passing the credit card information to the payment processing software, which in turn sends the information to the bank.
- Different banks may insist on different requirements for approaching merchants.
- The application processing procedure may also vary from bank to bank.
- The processing may take some time which may vary between four to six weeks.
- Some banks work out strategies to collect application fee.

Credit Card Processing Equipment

Processing equipment is needed to process credit cards. Customers prefer to present their cards for swiping as banks consider swiped transactions. *Swiped transactions are those that actually have the credit card present and it is run through a magnetic card reader or terminal.*

The credit card family group of equipments have various devices. The industry standard equipments are Verifone Jr. XI's, Tranz 330s, Tranz 380s, Tranz 420s, and Tranz 460s.

Credit card terminals plug into any standard phone line along with the power outlet. The terminals can be connected to the back of the modem of fax machines.

Tranz 330 handles home- based processing needs, which are swiped and keyed in transactions.

The card reader is a magnetic card reader which connects in line with the key board and permits to swipe the customer's credit card on the PC.

Steps in Credit Card Service

They are:

[i] Customer visits the merchant's website.

[ii] Customer makes the selection of products services and

[iii] Customer purchases from shopping cart. This means that the -

- entire website front-end processing is on IPS's service.
- data is linked with the secure socket layer private key.

[iv] Data is sent to the gateway.

[v] Data is unloaded with the private key.

[vi] Merchant fulfils order.

[vii] Data is verified and settled.

[viii] Money is sent to the bank.

Kinds of Transactions

The bank usually considers transactions of two kinds. They are:

Swiped Transaction: It is transaction in which the credit card is presented and run through a magnetic card reader or terminal. The banks have a better discount rate for doing swiped transactions.

Keyed-in Transaction: It is a transaction considered when the product or service is sold by the interactive order form page which needs to go with the website. 21st century resources commercial domain accounts make this very easy with a program called Form Mail installed on the domain.

Processing of Financial Transactions (E-commerce Process)

The settlement of financial transactions of e-commerce over the Net is not simple nor does it take place on a conventional basis. The working of financial transactions in the electronic way of doing business involves various contemporary technologies and processes, which are upgraded over the years. However, the following are the various steps involved in these transactions.

1. *Browsing:* There is an electronic catalogue on the website and the user has to browse through it and decide on the lists of products he wants to buy.

2. *Order Form:* After the selection of items to buy through the electronic catalogue, the user has to fill an order form, giving particulars of the products, their price along with other details like tax, shipping fees etc.

A customer enters an order on a merchant's website wherein all relevant transaction information is encrypted and transmitted to the Quick Commerce Secure Server, which is linked via a detailed leased line to the credit card processing network.

3. *Electronic Payment:* The online shopper has to select the process of payment for the products he has bought. Generally, in the case of e-commerce over the Net, customers prefer to go for e-payment. At this Juncture, there are two important aspects to be understood, i.e. the correct credit card number and the type of credit card to be used.

In electronic payment, the shopper need not send his procces credit card number, and it is enough to indicate the type of credit card intended to use. The shopper only sends preliminary information for instance, his electronic signature. With the help of this signature, the merchant verifies that the signature is that of the particular shopper, who wants to buy and order products or services online is authentic.

4. *Receiving Order Form:* The order form detailing the items that the shopper wants to buy are filled out along with other particulars and the merchant receives the order form.

5. *Identification and Tracking:* The transaction information is sent via leased lines to credit card network, where the validity of the card is checked and the availability of tunds on that accounts is verified. An authorisation code is returned via leased lines to the secure server, and the authorisation is encrypted by the Quick Commerce Secure Server and transmitted in encrypted form to the merchant's web server, which subsequently triggers meeting the order of the customers.

The techique of the transaction identifier of the software helps to identify and track the transaction. This ensures safety of business and works towards averting any risks which result due to online fraud.

An e-mail reciept is sent to the customer. The customer also receives from the merchant the identifier and the electronic certificates. Two certificates are necessary to complete the process of getting a bank card. They are :

- One certificate identifies the merchant and
- Another certificate identifies a specific electronic payment gateway.

6. Verification: With the help of electronic certificates received by the shopper from the merchant, the customer creates the following two documents : Order information (0I) and Payment Instruction (PI).

The software of the customer encrypts these messages and includes the customer's electronic signature in them. The OI and PI are then forwarded to the merchants. In turn, the customer's OI is decrypted by the software, The electronic signature of the customer is used to verify that the order is an authentic one. The verification is then sent to the customer to the effect that the order has been made. This tends to avoid risks in business and ensures customer loyalty.

7. Credit Card Information: The shopper has necessarily to send his credit card and bank information to the electronic payment service. This brings forth the authenticity of the shopper who appreciates online buying.

8. Encryption: As soon as a shopper makes a purchase, the payment information is sent to the merchant along with the order form. The information is scrambled by using the first key. It is called encrypted information. A unique second key is used to remove loopholes, if any in the information. The encryption key encodes personal financial information which is decoded by the electronic payment service with the help of the second key.

9. Payment Gateway: In the working of financial transactions, there is a specific payment gateway. It is an electronic gateway to the banking system where online payments are processed. The electronic certificate issued by the merchant identifies the specific payment gateway. Without the electronic certificate, it is not possible to complete the transaction of the credit card by any means.

10. OI and PI: The customer receives electronic certificates which are used to create both order Information (OI) and Payment Instructions (PI). The messages in them are encrypted including the electronic signature. These two documents are in turn forwarded to the merchants. The merchant decrypts OI, uses the electronic signature to verify the genuineness of the order from the customer. The customer in turn receives from the merchant verification to the effect that the order has been made.

11. Authorisation Request: In the working of financial transactions on the Net, the merchant creates an authorisation request for the payment. It includes the merchant 's digital signature, the transaction identifier and payment instructions. All these in encrypted form make requests to the payment gateway.

12. Capture Request: Soon after the completion of transaction, the merchant requests the payment from the bank. Capture request is created by the merchant which contains details like amount, digital signature and other information relvant to his website.

13. Bank Card Payment System: The payment gateway verifies with the help of the merchant's digital signature that the message is from the merchants. The payment gateway sends an authorisation request to the issuer of credits to the customer. It sends a request for payment to the bank. In the financial transactions settlement, the credit card payment system is used for business online.

14. Customer Interface Online Stock/Credit Verification: A customer can log on to a website, enter a customer code and password and automatically be linked to a specific price matrix, live from the back office database. As items are added to a shopping cast, the stock system can be checked for availability and sales allocation made in real time. A customer's credit availability *i.e.* the non cash transaction can be verified and allocated in real time.

The customer's shopping profile can be stored for a fast shopping interface and maintained for future Customer Relationship Marketing (CRM). As the shopping cart is accepted, the items are transferred from a temporary file stored on the back office system to a confirmed sales order. The customer is sent an e-mail message, confirming the order with a tracking number.

15. Dispatch/Distribution: The order can be scheduled by the back office system for delivery based on the user's criteria.

Picking slips are generated by system for the main warehouse. A single order can be split over and distributed, depending on the physical outlay of the warehouse. As a buy has been completed, picking the goods follows, which are sent for scanning and order consolidation. The system will then track when an order is complete and issue packing instructions. The goods are scanned as a complete order, packed and shipped. A shipping certification may be sent via e-mail to the customer.

16. After Sales: This is a fully integrated after sales module which may be allocated to a cash centre. It includes :

- Call logging
- Product/customer recognition
- Customer history and
- Reorder/replacement of customer goods.

EDI Traditional Stardard

The EDI system has its own interface with standard mapping. This allows the user to share information with other internet systems including :

- Placing electronic order with suppliers.
- Receiving electronic order from customers.
- Interfacing to courier/ logistic companies and
- Interfacing with banking institutions.

Traditional Messages

The traditional EDI has a very large role in business to business integration. It is a complementing new technology for web-based solutions.

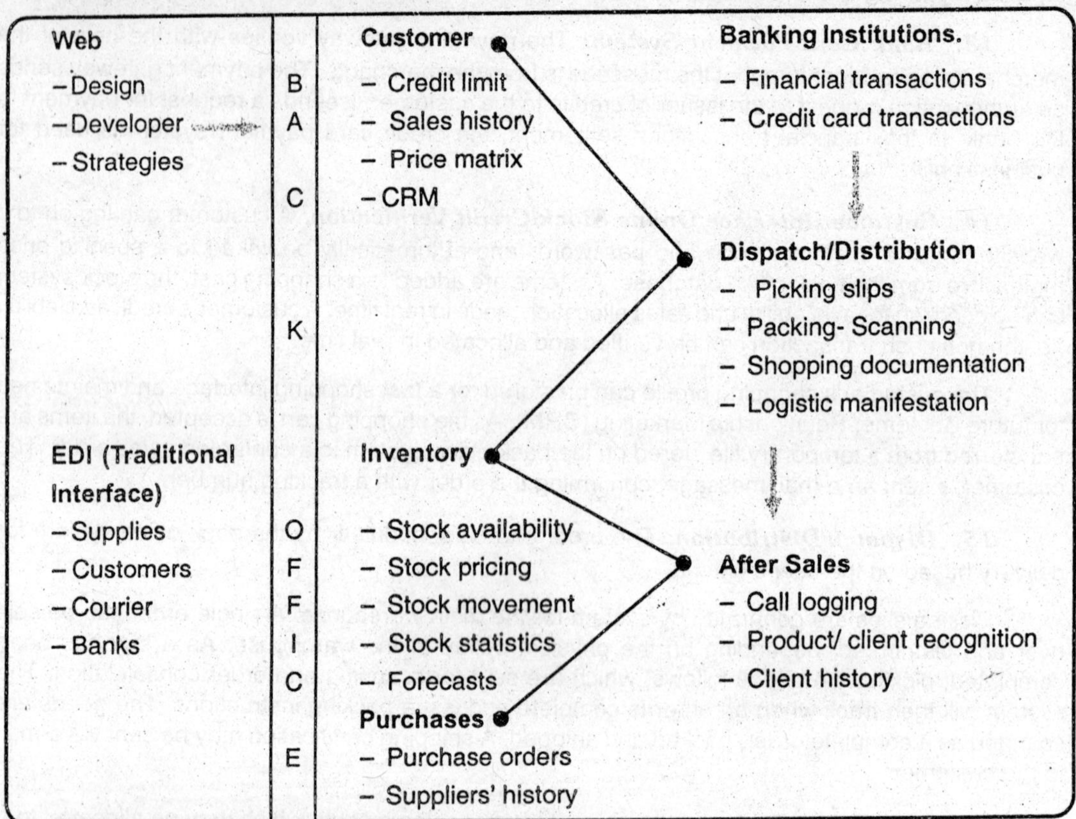

E-Commerce Solutions

Net Sales Inc.

The software of net-sales is one of the oldest and most trusted providers of full services, out sourced e-commerce solutions for online retail digital distribution and business to business processes.

Its capabilities include:

- e-commerce site, design and hosting.
- legacy system integration.
- catalogue systems, contents and management.
- complete transaction processing and back-end operations.
- risk management
- customer service.
- digital and physical fulfilment of management.
- marketing support and
- reporting and data mixing.

By outsourcing to net sales, businesses can focus on their core competencies while the software manages the complexities of their e-commerce applications.

Net-sales provides e-commerce solutions for online sales of downloadable fonts and related digital process.

The Net-sale's full service, customized outsourced e-commerce solutions ensure full fledged strategies to enable online retail, digital distribution and business to business success.

PSI - Net

PSI Net was founded in the year 1989. It is one of the largest and most experienced providers of IP-based commucation services for various business processes. It offers a complete range of internet solutions that helps cut costs, processes substantial productivity stratetgies to expand into the new market and improve the way of online business. It is the premier provider of internet solutions and services for online global business.

As a powerful competitive force, it helps customers leverage. It is the world's first commercial internet service provider (ISP) which operates as one of the largest and most advanced internet access networks, and its solutions extend to various businesses, government and educational institutions.

Products and Services

Access

- Offers complete range of reliable high quality access service.
- Provides a wide variety of internet access solutions for today's business.
- Extends solutions from the entry level on demand access to high speed leased link service and private IP networks.
- Provides remote employee access to the Net, wherever their work takes them to more than 150 countries world wide and
- Manages networking services.

Security

- Network requires protection from unauthorized access to the server, database and other information assets.
- It offers a wide range of managed internet security services that provides protection for online business. They include protection for Router Waller, PSI - Net Secure Enterprise and LIOF Security System.
- A range of managed internet security service like packet filtering and firewalls that offer strongest possible protection for business are equally imperative.

Application: There are many useful reasons why many business firms connect themselves to the Net. One of the best reasons to connect business to the Internet is to make use of applications that reduce cost, boost productivity and give a strategic application edge. The reliable high quality applications include voice, e-mail, internet faxing, video and audio casting over the Internet.

Hosting: In recent years, more and more businesses are setting up their websites to market their products and services. Besides, they are also using Internet facilities to store and distribute corporate information of all kinds.PSI - Net offers facilities like PSI web, Dedicated NT, Co-location, PSI - Net Multimedia and Web slant. These contribute towards substantial online business.

E-commerce: With the growing application of the Internet, more and more business firms and consumers are discovering the convenience of the Net as a sales and marketing medium, allowing sales 24 hours a day everyday. It requires real time electronic transactions and electronic shopping carts that can manage mulitple purchase,multi currency payments and contemporary security measures to protect consumers. PSI-E- commerce Solutions include the following:

- Provision of global networking for business.
- State of the industry frame relay network.
- Its specific designing for business grade internet traffic
- PSI-Web communication
- PSI-Web world pay and
- E-commerce express.

Its other services include :

- Corporate internet access and private IP networks
- Strategically managed internet security
- Web and database hosting services
- Electronic commerce solutions
- Voice, fax, live, audio, video, and other applications.
- Extending full time service to small and medium-size businesses including government aqencies, educational institutions and information service companies
- Providing the most advanced fast packet internet access network e-commerce solutions
- E-commerce solutions that enable the business to sell over the Net
- Hosting services on the website including other important business data
- Applications that allow the Net to make business more productive and
- Security measures to protect information data of the customers.

PSI-Net allows to sell products/services around the world 24 hours a day everyday. PSI-Web world pay and e-commerce express solutions can include real time transactions. electronic shopping carts to manage multiple purchase, currency transactions and security measures to protect merchants and customers. Its products and services include access, security, applications and hosting pertaining to online business.

Net Source's E-commerce Solutions

It is a specialised e-commerce solutions provider for online business needs and it can custom program e-commerce solutions for statrting a website.

Some of its solutions for e-commerce include :

Main Frame Intergration: This synchronises a company's onsite catalogue database with the websites database.

Shopping Cart System: Provides customers to shop for mulitple items that will be stored in a single shopping cart until they are ready to order.

Credit Card Valuation and Charging: One can vaildate a customer's credit card and charge them online, thus reducing workload considerably.

Secured Transactions: In order to protect the privacy of customers, this strategy offers them secured transactions. On this server, the user can purchase his own secure certificate for the online transactions.

Password Protection: Net source program is a security system that allows only those people who wish to have access into the site. Its services include :

- hosting services.
- e-commerce marketing
- techonology
- design, services, clients and multi-media.

Buying and selling of goods and services across the internet is the trend today. An e-commerce site can be as simple as a catalogue page with a phone number or it can range all the way to a real time credit card processing site, where customers can purchase goods and services by downloading and receiving them on the spot. E-commerce merchants can range their small businesses with a few items for sale all the way to a potentially large retailer.

AuthorizeNet Solution

Its solutions include the following products :

Authorize Net Virtual Terminal: The product allows merchants who have access to the Net to manually enter transactions without the need for an internet storefront. It is a perfect solution for traditional businesses looking for a faster and easier way to authorize and manage online credit card transactions.

Authorize. Net Web Link: The existing internet storefront can be linked by the supplied HTML or by a proprietary shopping cart/store builder programme. It brings fast, reliable and secure transaction process capability to the storefront on the Web.

Echeck Net: It makes it easy for web- based and traditional businesses to accept electronic cheque payments.

Reseller List: This includes the list of resellers.

Online Payment Methods: After the completion of the shopping cart, it is imperative to total the amount on the cart and then check out the payment strategy. During the check-out stage, the payment is selected and the transaction completed. There are many ways to accept online payments on a website. They are :

Credit Card: It is the simplest method to note the credit card number and process it. A web page is to be built to take advantage of this method of payment.

Cyber Cash (Authorize.Net): Cyber cash is a cashless method of securing payment. The service providers give description through the website for details of this service. For this, they charge a certain amount including set up fee, and with or without monthly fee associated with cybercash. The party can also choose to accept payments automatically using cybercash. The other systems of online payments are Authorize Net.and manually processed credit cards.

Sillcomm Internet and E-commerce Solutions

Sillcomm Corporation founded in 1998, is a privately held company, headquarted in Dayton Ohio. It developed internet business solutions for diverse range of clients. It has specialised in providing graphics, photography, web designing, client servicing, server programming and marketing. It has developed the most enriched, attractive and user friendly sites.

Sevices: Its e-commerce service solutions include:

- solving problems,
- web designing,
- web programming,
- web hosting,
- graphics,
- photography and
- marketing.

Products: A client server page (ASP) has the benefit over traffic HTML documents of being data generated by HTML code at the run time.

It means that HTML is produced only where the ASP page is loaded so that it can be tailored to specific circumstances. It is currently working on various aspects of ASP application, that will perform general functions for different industries. These applications will be ODBL complient data compliant that perform functions such as online application scheduling, real-time data acquisition, shipping cart management and office automation.

Virtual Focus: Virtual Focus Inc. has been established for providing internet commerce systems and the home of the virtual cart shopping cart system and virtual catalogue product management system. It has specialized in all aspects of internet commerce for companies of all sizes. It assists in designing and implementing an online internet store, customer services and ordering system or providing customer interaction. Its popular virtual cart shopping cart system lets the user to place goods on the internet store online and at the customer's finger tips in a matter of hours. It is easy to install and maintain the virtual cart and virtual catalogue systems.

Lakota Group Business Solutions: Lakota group is specialised in web-based programming and making solutions that provide businesses with an effective online presence. It guides business through the process of setting up shop on the web. It has been offering four areas of service to the clients. They are :

- Cilent discussion
- Articles/essay databases
- Payment centre
- UPS resources.

Lakota Group Inc. is an e-commerce development firm. Its phillosophy and approach to e-commerce is based on the idea that each participant in e-commerce must maintain an ongoing education by continuously applying new knowledge and technology to generate more revenues from online business. Its portfolio includes serving a number of local state level, national and international clients. A wider range of online services makes for great online services.

It has been offering services such as newsletters, account access, user registration, special coupons and area information etc. Its solutions help to provide a wide front door for business.

E-commerce Development

This includes :

- web graphics design
- website design and lay-out
- database managment solutions
- e-commerce and shopping cart software integration
- real audio and video.
- interactive application (chat, classified, auctions, search program etc.)
- mailing list management,
- site traffic statistics software,
- proprietory administrative facility that gives control over contents,
- cansultation
- market research and feasibility study.

WebSite Hosting

Lakota provides e-commerce solutions for website hosting covering the following:

- unlimited server space at great rate.
- reliable servers with back bone internet connection.
- daily back-up copies of all files.
- front page 98 extensions.
- Online server interface.
- CGI-bin access.
- e-mail accounts
- secure server access and
- proprietary scripts to enhance website business.

Website Promotion

Lakota's website promotion solutions include the following :

- classified search engine promotion.
- banner advertising on major portal sites.
- link exchange services and
- consultation.

Custom Programming

Its custom programming solutions include the following :

- HTML, DHTML, CSS and XML
- Java script and UBS
- PERL, ORACLE,Cold fusion and java and
- Visual basic, C++ and FoxPro.

Jellett- Blotek- E-commerce Shopping Mall

MTT Solutions: The corporation is dealing with maintaining accuracy considerably, security and privacy of customers and employee personal information. It is concerned with identifying the purposes for which personal information is collected at or before the time information is collected. Unlike local mail, the number of stores is not limited by physical space.

Selling up with MTT's electronic commerce service can improve online stores traffic. Its e-commerce solutions offer merchants services through the use of wizard, the ability to quickly create a potential online store front. Merchants can create a personalized look and feel for their stores, using graphically rich, industry relevant templates.

Shopper Services: Many internet solutions require customers to type on their credit card details every time they want to buy something. This gives more opportunities to tamper with the information of the customer. The solution is that these details should be kept securely by a strategic e-commerce infrastructure in a database located behind the firewall, with no direct access to the Net. It is so secured that the information should be transmitted to the bank only when a purchase is made, and travelling to the bank over secure and private non-internet connections. This addresses and eliminates the possible potentials for anyone to capture and rescue all credit card information.

In addition, a multi-layer security model also ensures protection of the consumers. It includes security technologies as the internet part of the system ensures several mechanisms and features protecting the personal and financial information.

Benefits of Single Secure E-commerce

The benefits can be read as follows :

- Order 24 hours a day, 7 days per week
- Shopping simplicity and conveniences set up of the shopper account to simplicity future purchase.
- Shipping and taxes are calculated automatically
- Credit card payments are available in real time
- Funds are transferred when the goods are shipped
- Receive shipment notifications available via the e-mail
- Use shipping cart functionally
- Use any browser to shop
- Guaranteed transactional security using the latest world leading encryption technology and
- User name and password protected account for shipping accessibility and convenience.

Merchant Services: Getting online with commerce enabled website e-commerce service provides many benefits for business and customers. This service provides the following benefits to both merchants and business :

- Reach new markets and customers with worldwide distribution protentialities
- Provides any time, anywhere access
- Add value to the selling process
- Lower cost of doing business
- One-to-one marketing
- Gather customer related information
- Market uniquely as per the customer profile
- Product testing and
- Merchandise cross-sell and up-sell

MTT's E-commerce Package

This includes :

- Back end integration
- Import uitility for databases
- Remote publishing capability
- Online help
- Mulitimedia product capability
- Featured products
- Web-based client
- Fulfil digital goods
- Subscription based service
- Shopping carts.
- Custom template design and
- Store-front templates.

Level 1: This is a fully functional browser based e-commerce application that allows merchants the ability to set up and manage all aspects of their online business, equipped with an internet access connection.

Level 1 Key Functionality

This includes :

- Browser based creation and maintenance.
- Support of unlimited products in catalogue.
- Payment gateway integration for real time payment authorization and settlement.
- Detailed statistical data provided in real time.
- Large selection of store templates from which to choose.

- Sales promotion and management.
- Advanced sales analysis and reporting back office manager's tool.
- Automatic tax and shipping calculations.
- No additional software required.
- Up selling and cross selling.
- Shopping cart and check-out.

Level 2 Key Product Functionality

- Support unlimited products in the catalogue.
- Wizard and online help
- Import/export facilities.
- Store support animated graphics, both sound and video.
- Ability to specify product attributes such as colour and size.
- Numerous templates for a wide choice.
- Offline store creation with the ability to publish remotely.
- Automatic order and payment process.
- Dynamic store that supports database searches by category item or key words.
- Shopping cart and check out.
- Payment gateway integration for real time payment, authorization and settlement.
- Detailed statistical data provided in real time.
- Sales promotion and management.
- Strategic up selling and cross selling and
- Pricing.

Virtual PIN: This is for consumers who are not keen to transmit their credit card numbers across the Net. The PIN service provides an additional level of security. First Virtual issues a virtual PIN to the customer, once they have been provided their credit card number over a voice telephone. Customers can then use their virtual PIN in lieu of a credit card number. For each purchase, first virutal sends the user an e-mail message asking them to confirm the proposed transaction. Once first virtual receives back the confirmation, the credit transaction is processed and an e-mail is sent to the merchants authorizing them to ship the ordered goods.

Privacy Bank: It is on similar lines as the e-wallet but with slight different ideas. This payment method has Privacy Bank.com which operates by storing customer information having agreed to supply the products and later using it to automatically fill out forms on web pages that these users visit. The catch is that e-commerce sites need to accept the privacy bank service in order for it to work effectively.

The users have to sign up with privacy bank.com and enter personal information to whatever extent they design. They can enter minimum amount of information such as their name, address or they can provide credit card numbers and other personal information—they have to be assured of security by those managing these sites.

ATM/Debit Cards: These cards are used widely in Europe and are increasing in importance in the U.S. with card data reporting a 42 per cent annual growth rate last year as opposed to 15 percent for credit cards. The major advantage for the merchants is that they carry significantly lower transaction costs than the checks.

Real Time Payment Process: E-commerce over the net requires real time payment processing. Through the internet, the business parties can make use of real time payment systems. It means that the customer's payment will be approved by a service provider before receiving the order and then transferred into his account.

Real time payment processing means to process the customer's payment information right from one's own website. This offers customers greater security in purchasing from the site. The customer's transaction goes straight from the website to the card processing network and back again. It is convenient of having processing tasks done automatically. *Payment processing is the ability to accept credit cards over the Internet.* The functionality of software provides with the capability of processing the credit transactions in real time, just as they would at a point of sale terminal. A real time web page confirmation is given to the buyer and also e-mail order confirmation to both the merchant and the buyer. Transactions are processed online in real time.

Purchasing Cards

Purchasing cards are credit cards which corporations issue to their employees for buying products and services at the selected sets of businesses. Purchasing card transaction volumes, in the United States totalled 20 billion in 1997 and they are widely tipped to become the standard for business -to -business purchases on the Net.

E-charge

The e-charge system allows customers to change web purchases to their normal telephone bills. It is currently only available to merchants in the US and Canada, although an expansion into Europe is planned this year. It is in the pipeline.

Virtual Sales Slip (VSS)

The expression VSS refers to electronic transactions on e-commerce over the Internet. It displays detailed information on any transaction which is generated by the merchant's online store and downloaded to the digital wallet. The VSS contains particulars on typical items such as:

- Conformation of order
- Shipping details
- Tax, if any and
- Total amount of sales etc.

Online Catalogue Shopping

Web pages called catalogue shopping, displays sales items by merchants.

Cyber Cafe

The features of cyber cafe include :

- Internet browsing
- E-mail
- Internet training and
- Many other features.

With this facility, the people are able to send and receive e-mail with the click of the mouse.

E-commerce Exchange

For successful e-commerce, the provider of electronic commerce and credit card processing services are necessary. For this purpose, e-commerce exchange has been established as one of the leading providers of electronic commerce and credit card processing services. Many e-commerce solution providers have formed a powerful strategic alliance with e-commerce exchange as potential partners. The partners use e-commerce exchange (internet based e-commerce software) to strengthen their services by providing customers with pre-approved and turnkey electronic commerce solutions.

Tips on Electronic Commerce Exchange (ECX)

They include :

- Fast set-up
- Quick approval.
- Easy installation
- Simple website order integration
- No credit turndowns and
- Low start-up investments.

E-commerce Merchant Accounts Merchant Credit Cards

Quick Commerce: Quick commerce is a powerful internet based software tool that is a real time authorizing terminal and a complete secure transaction processing system. It facilitates e-commerce merchant accounts, merchant credit card and merchant business credit. Merchants can use virtual terminal and weblink to settle credit card transactions without the need for a separate software. Credit card transactions are authorized immediately upon submitting e-cheques which are also supported by quick commerce systems.

E-commerce requires a system specializing in merchant access and quick commerce transaction selections for traditional and non-traditional markets.

Quick commerce accepts all forms of non-cash payments like Master Card, American Express, Diners Club, Electronic cheque and coast to coast network of merchant accounts are also served.

This rapid growth has fuelled to improve quick and easy set up of merchant accounts for traditionally hard to place businesses such as home-based business or new merchants-business owners with credit problems, high risk business and others which are considered non-conventional by banks and other card processors.

E-commerce needs a powerful combination of a turnaround advantage and an inexpensive way to implement secure online credit card processing. Quick commerce is that which can have a new merchant accepting both credit card and e-cheque payment. Electronic commerce payment solutions need to succeed in the ever changing global market place and this is possible by working out strategies compatible to online business.

Features of Quick Commerce

Virtual Terminal: Quick Commerce Virtual Terminal enables the business with a quick commerce account to authorize, process and manage credit card transactions from any computer with an internet connection and a net browser. Virtual Terminal replaces the standard authorization terminal or software and provides the best solution for merchants who manually enter credit card transactions for mail or phone order sales.

Virtual Terminal is an ideal solution for businesses of all sizes because it removes the complexity and expenses normally associated with authorizing and processing credit card transaction expenses and it is much faster than the standard dial-up authorizing system.

Business with quick commerce simply accepts access to the quick commerce virtual terminal through the website, using any industry standard web browser. After logging onto the system using a unique ID and password, merchants can access the complete range of quick commerce service. This includes authorization for purchases, credit and returns including status and activity reports.

To authorize credit card transactions, the merchant simply completes an electronic form that provides the quick commerce system with the information it needs to complete the transaction. Thus, the information is encrypted using forty or 128 bit Secure Socket Layer (SSL), 3.0 technology and is then sent to the quick commerce host server. This server then sends the data through the authorization network to the appropriate card issuer's bank over a secure and proprietary connection. When the process is complete which takes about five seconds, the merchant subsequently receives an authorization number and the quick commerce server stores the transaction. Transactions are atuomatically settled and funded within two to three days.

Merchants can also check the status of transactions and automatically bill customers for recurring charges are run on a variety of reports.

It is the world's leading internet based payment authorization and transaction processing solution which authorizes, captures and manages credit card transactions.

Web Link: Quick commerce web 0link allows internet-based business to authorize process and manage credit card transactions without worrying about the complicated software, hardware and expertise normally associated with the processing of payment over the web.

When online customers are ready to purchase products or services from a merchant's website, the weblink either captures the necessary information link name, credit number etc. from the site's own secure transaction page or displaces a standard web link transaction page posted on a quick commerce server for the customer to fill out.

This information is encrypted using 40 or 128 bit secure socket layer technology and is sent to a quick commerce transaction server. The server then sends the data through the authorization network to the appropriate card issuer's bank over a secure proprietary connection. When the authorization process is complete, the customer either receives an approval or decline response.

Features and Benefits of Quick Commerce

The benefits read as follows :

- Quick commerce enables to take secure credit cards and electronic cheque payment 24 hours a day, 7 days a week real time without even needing to speak to customers.
- It can increase internet sales as much as 1500 per cent.
- Credit card customers buy 2.5 times more merchandise.
- Credit card customers buy products or services as and when they desire.
- Payment plans make larger purchases easier.
- By accepting credit cards, they often legitimize business to customers.
- No credit turn-downs regardless of previous credit history.
- Equipment is 100 per cent financed. No large out of pocket initial investment.
- Fast turnaround funds are transferred into the account within 48 hours.
- Emergency equipment replacement including fault equipment are replaced within 24 hours.
- Access and process transactions anywhere around the globe where you have internet access.
- Automatically accepts, authorizes and processes credit card orders directly from the website.
- User friendly easy to use programme.
- Solutions for automated processing of internet merchants.
- Handles recurring monthly payments from credit cards.
- Secure socket layer security is best on online dealings today.
- Reporting capabilities accessible via the Net.
- More sales on the Net through acceptance of credit cards worldwide.
- Authorized transactions within five seconds and e-mail customers' order to merchant for fulfilment.
- Encourages impulse buying online.
- Converts website from e-brochures to virtual storefront.
- Merchants can sell online service and offer immediate product downloads that is information software.
- Merchant's secure payment orders page can be set up to have the same look and feel as the rest of their site.

E-Online Banking

Introduction

Banks as we all know are for the safety and security of our economic assets. A web customer can shop on any website, but payment will be through e-banking.

The battlefield of business has changed and e-commerce is the potential war front industry of the millennium-whatever is predicted on the e-commerce boom, that are likely to tap up revenues. Many banks outside the country are in the front curve in developing a customer friendly online presence. Many underlying changes are fast emerging and personal finance is being heralded in by the Internet.

Online banking and internet banking services have established themselves in the US and other countries. In recent years, in India also, a few banks have been offering net banking facilities. Many other banks are working out strategies related to e-banking services.

The opening of global (online) business doors and getting information with the click of the mouse only highlights the potential demand and for internet connectivity.

E-banking is one of the e-commerce facilitating segments. The application of information technology in the banking sector is an excellent opportunity for the industry. But the technology should not be seen as a mere aid to speed up processing and crumple costs but as an additional avenue for delivering services to online clients. This was why the growing popularity of the ATM did not result in the absence of bank branches, instead ATMs moved to off-site locations and strengthened the position of banks giving the facility in the retail market.

Today, In view of global business, the individual is not the icing. E-commerce needs a financial backbone which is foolproof and conducive to online customers. It is in respect of e-commerce, whether in the form of business to business, business to customers and customers to customers - all need this financial backbone. This will demand from banks to build up greater trust in their teachnological capabilities, brand image, move from supply driven to the demand driven paradigm. In advanced countries, the click of the mouse has taken the centre stage and banks are edging their way towards cyberspace with innovature services taken to retain these customers.

The Concept and Meaning

Online banking, e-banking, electronic banking, net banking or banking over the internet are the buzzwords of business today-they are commonly used in the banking industry. It is the information technology which has revolutionized the way of the banking both at the local, national and international level. It is a cutting edge technology, a new business paradigm.

Internet banking services mean that any enquiry or transaction should be processed online without any reference to the branch (anywhere banking) at any time.

Online banking, a little known concept so far, has soon taken centre stage. So, it is imperative for us to understand that online banking is all about doing banking transactions over the Net.

E-banking is a concept which will enable anyone to conduct business with a bank from the comforts of the home or office. The need hitherto is to personally visit the bank to conduct one's business and with e-banking on the Net, the working hours of the bank is done away with. Instead, all one will have to do is to tap a few keys, go to the bank's site, identify himself and get on with his business at any time convenient to him.

It is called as banking on the Net, which has been in practice for more than a decade now, and gained popularly since 1994 because it has used a friendly way of online business and is cost effective. The leap forward in this service happened when the banks started offering online banking service to its customers.

The Electronic Delivery Channel Includes

- ATM
- Telephone
- PC
- Intenet banking and
- Online banking.

Online banking is the latest service available to the customers. Electronic bill payment is one of the key services offered by banks. Today, banks are running an online front. There are many reasons for this movr :

- The net is the future for all potential businesses and
- Value added services are must in the increasingly competitive banking world.

Need for Computerization

In recent years, banking and non-banking financial institutions have been experiencing several changes due to liberalisation and financial sector reforms. The advancement in sophisticated information and communication technology is supporting power for the fast computerization of the banking operations. The online initiation of the banking sector is a new paradigm revolution from paper-based to online transactions. Thus, the Indian banking sector is moving towards computerisation and is entirely dependent on computers. A large amount of accounting and financial transactions are now handled very efficiently and quickly with the help of computers.

On account of globalisation, privatisation, deregulation, inter-linking of money, liberalisation of the capital market, foreign investment, taxation reforms and various other factors are responsible for bringing about a sea change in the last one and a half decade.

These economic reforms to some extent have been facilitated by technological improvements in communication, computerization and automation of the banking services. The emergence of e-mail, Internet and e-commerce have resulted in substantial business, global operations as well as extensive use of credit cards, smart cards and diversification of banking operations — these underline the need for the use of sophisticated electronic technology by way of computerization. On the other hand, customers need easy to use service and time saving operations, tele-banking, online banking etc. It is the information technology enabled computers which are designed to meet new challenges.

Accordingly, thousands of bank branches are computerized, where the computers are centrally located. Banks are actually the first in the technological race to adopt computers ever since they emerged. Not only the central office but branches also are equipped with terminals. The networking mechanism facilitating online accounting enables them to interrogate the central computing system for information exchange and monitoring of business developments. This greatly helps to timely ascertain the current balances, deposits, overdrafts, interest charges in tune with computerization and pre-printed long stationery is designed to print out customer statements and other reports.

Today, more new operations in the financial institutions are done on computers. Operations by computers improve the service and efficiency and reduce transaction costs. Information technology is enabling the availability of traditional banking functions by electronic means. There are many factors helping to accelerate this trend and a paradigm shift such as devising micro computers, widespread use of personal computers and the decreasing cost of computers etc proves beneficial to the banks going online.

Automatic Teller Machine (ATM)

The automatic teller machine is commonly used in bank financial transactions. It is an unattended or unmanned device usually located on or off the bank's premises. Its function is to receive and dispense cash and to handle routine financial transactions.

It is made to work 24 hours a day. For this purpose, plastic currency and debit cards are used while withdrawing cash from the ATM machine. The user's or customers's account number and credit limit are magnetically embedded on a strip of the tape on the back of the card, The operation mechanism is that the card is inserted into the ATM, the terminal reads and transmits the tape data to a processor which activates the accounts. According to the instructions, the details are displayed on the screen and by clicking a few keys of the keyboard, the user can direct the computer to carry out the financial transactions.

ATM is only one type of electronic fund transfer (EFT) situation, usually connected to financial computers. The banks or other financial institutions own their stations located at the important check-out counters of stores, hotels, hospitals and in rail, road and airline terminals.

ATMs are now widely used in banks enabling quick cash withdrawal. Waiting in queue to pay our electricity bills or to buy railway season tickets has nowadays become tedious and time consuming. Payment of bills on utilities and issuance of railway passes are a few additional applications that the bankers have been providing through their ATMs.

EFT in the form of ATM is a definite revolution cum cash payment of the electronic payment systems. It is a revolution that can change the pace of Indian customers and make life all that simpler. HDFC Bank has launched the operation of accepting payments for utility services such as electricity and telephone bills through ATMs. There is a network of ATMs being shared by a group of banks. It allows the customers access to services through any of these ATMs irrespective of the bank he or she holds an account in.

The individual banks in the network are proposing an arrangement with railways whereby ATMs would dispense season tickets. Under this system, a special software would ensure that the entire system is menu driven with the purchaser having to enter only an identity card number. It avoids the formation of queues. The system has potential use, and many banks in India have evinced interest and installed this system which needs substantial business.

The suburban services of the Western Railways and Central Railways together issue on an average. 70,000 season tickets per day.

Still there is a possibility in India to expand the network by installing more ATMs. The expansion requires to issue an increasing number of card bases so that the expanding network can be achieved to install more ATMs. When there are more card users, it facilitates to turn to increasing utility of the cards by upgrading it to debit facilities by installing the Point of Sale (PoS) terminals at merchant establishments. The portable post device would make it possible for a cardholder to use his ATM card for making payments. The charges would be directly debited to the customer's account through the centralized operations.

Banks have now set up ATMs at strategic locations in metro cities and they are planning the possibility of tie-ups with other bank's ATMs. Banking on the Net is only an extension of the ATM and telebanking services.

Automatic Teller Machine (ATM) at Home

Home automatic teller machines have been designed and are available for installation at homes of the PC users. A banking ATM at home is not a big-sized machine as installed in banks. This is a software that provides ATM like service from the user's computer. It has features similar to the machine kept by banks as ATM. Thus, makers are producing home ATM, home pay system and home ATM, turning the PC into an ATM. with the help of the ATM, users can get electronic account statements, pay bills, transfer funds and apply for loans. It permits users to withdraw cash from the bank account instantly by remaining at home or in office. The user who wants the benefit of electronic bill payments, there is the home pay bill package.

Banks now set up automatic teller machines at strategic locations in metro cities and is exploring the possibility of tie-ups with ATMs of other banks.

Electronic Fund Transfer (EFT)

The conventional method of payment or transfer of funds is based on paper. It involves a series of steps and nature:

- use of paper
- work
- labour
- time
- billing
- mailing
- checking
- late payment
- bouncing
- resubmitting
- cost
- error-prone
- time intensive

- unpredictable cash flow
- loss of invoices
- labour intensive
- recurring problems in case of recurring payments.
- to drive distantly located bank branches
- to stand in queue and
- check account statements and wait for these never ending minutes.

An electronic fund transfer mechanism of fund information and fund management between banks and financial institutions is done through the electronic data interchange (EDI). But this system involves only minimum amount of data interchange between two parties.

There are three major world wide electronic fund transfer networks.

They are :

- Clearing house interbank payment system (CHIPS).
- Fed wire and
- Society for world wide interbank financial tele-communication (SWIFT).

These networks transfer millions of dollars in each banking day and are capable of handling millions of messages per day.

Banks have been using EDI services widely. Banks, financial institutions and insurance brokers can use EDI to send messages to the computers of various partners.

The Reserve Bank of India has introduced the electronic fund transfer facility for customers of Indian banks. Under this facility, the customer has to provide the details of the beneficiary account at other centres. In turn, the customer will then send the particulars to the local clearing centre, which subsequently processes the transactions and will pass on the instructions to the local bank via the bank's network to credit the account of the respective beneficiaries.

Uses

They read as follows :

- The EFT stations are used.
- To verify customers' cheque at home.
- To check credit card transactions for honour.
- To transfer funds electronically from a shopper's account to a merchant's account.
- To call up a bank computer.
- To enter data through the telephone buttons.
- To transfer funds to or from an account.
- ATM machines can handle routine financial transactions 24 hours a day.
- Stores and hotels can use EFT terminals to verify that a customer's cheque is genuine.
- It facilitates cardholders to replenish the credit balance at an automatic banking machine.
- EFT facilitates 24 hours banking, 7 days a week and 365 days a year of operations.

- Offers a greater variety of services for the customers.
- Replaces expensive time consuming paper-based process of cheques.
- Increases cash flow.
- Reduces overheads.
- Immediate payment in the bank accounts.
- Complete security.
- Low cash flow.
- Recurring monthly or periodic payments are facilitated.
- Automatic plan.
- Billing and collection by using the no hassle solutions.
- EFT represents a most significant solution for e-commerce development and technology breakthrough. This revolutionary approach allows for the easiest to use e-commerce enabler on the Net.
- EFT service providers give all facilities for processing provider on network. For instance, checkfree is EFT's processing provider on networking.
- Collection of payment in time is achieved.
- The free authorization facility permits periodical payments which are made automatically.
- Wherever the bank of the customer is located, their payments can be automatically collected and deposited into the merchants' accounts.
- The customer's monthly credit and statement shows itemized payments.
- The chances of errors, frauds, lost and stolen cheques etc. are drastically reduced.
- EFT promotes prestige, establishes long relationship with customers. This customer retention rate is higher with EFT.
- Online banking offers real time interactivity from one's own desktop.

EFT system uses a computer to transfer debits and credits with the help of Electronics Pulses. These pulses are carried through wire either to a magnetic disk or tape.

Computerization in Clearing Houses

In clearing houses also, computers are employed to handle cheques, The nature of work involved in clearing operations is voluminous, repetitive, routine in nature, it is complex to clear, exchange and settle the transactions among several banks. Computers are deployed in clearing houses to speed up the process and clearing the operations quickly and efficiently which is voluminous work. Foreign clearing houses managed by the Reserve Bank in major centres like Mumbai, Kolkata, Chennai, Bangalore and New Delhi have been computerized. The new technology is used in clearing houses for the purpose of balancing of Reserve Bank's inward and outward clearing cheques. Another use is the preparation of scrolls dealing with receipts and payments transactions on account of government departments.

Thus, computerization in clearing houses initiates quick settlement of operations. There is a specially designed IT system known as the *reader sorter system*. It is powerful IBM system which facilitates cheque sorting and cuts delays in operations. This system was introduced at Delhi, Mumbai, Chennai and Kolkata. These four systems at these centres process millions of instruments per day. Thus, the new technology has potential to ensure systematic and timely balancing of clearing houses and transactions made online.

TeleBanking

Telebanking facility is another variant form of bank automation. Some banks in cities have potential and they introduced telebanking, a service where the banks get hundred of calls during the bank's working hours. Banking on telephone helps to do all usual banking transactions sitting at home/ office except deposit of amount and withdrawals. All that a customer has to do is to call up the bank wherein he is advised to press a particular number for a particular service. It works with the technology of the microprocessor. There is no need to have any software for this. It recognizes the tone signal and pulse. Telebanking or banking on phone is more popular in advanced countries.

The advantages of this system are :

- The caller can obtain information of his account as well as his credit card account.
- Thousands of calls can be processed within a short time.
- It facilitates the sending of fax through the same system.
- It gives security against unauthorised access to the customer's information.

Banking on Home Computers

A separate electronic system bank at home has been designed to facilitate the bank customer to link the bank with that of the user. Banking communication takes place over the telecommunications networks. The lines let the people to interact with their banks. The access to a bank computer takes place by way of phone or the two-way cable TV. Banking on the home computer was once considered as a scientific fiction but has now became a reality.

A home computer enables to do bank work comfortably. Personal computer, video text, modem, number, a bank computer etc. constitute the working of a bank at home service system. The computer based or aided home banking system enables the users to check balance in their accounts, transfer between accounts, track cheques, pay bills etc. Other advantages of a bank at the home system include applying for a loan, purchasing bank certificates and enquiries etc.

Electronic Money Transfer (EMT)

Transfer of money by electronic means is known as electronic money transfer. It operates by sending money to distant stations through computerized telegraphic networks. The stations are connected to the EMT networks stations. The Indian postal department has been adding more stations to the existing one for speedy money order delivery. With the EMT technology, the department is able to provide fast data text and money order delivery for the people in remote areas.

Union's Electronic Money Transfer (EMT)

The new technology permits quick money transfer of the Union by electric operations. Now it is possible to transfer money from abroad to India within a few minutes. It is one-way money transfer service. The DHL World Wide Express, a division of Air freight Limited has linked up with the western union financial service. The object is to provide one-way money transfer service from nearly 75 countries including United States, United Kingdom and Canada to India. The scheme is called western money transfer scheme. Under this scheme, both inbound and outbound money transfer services will be made possible.

Western Union's money transfer service enables customers to transfer cash within minutes to a recipient located at any city or town in 75 countries that is serviced by an agent outlet. When a sender pays the required cash, along with a service fee, to any western union agent office, the company's computerized network transmits instructions to a specified western union agent office in India, to pay out cash to the denominated recipient within a short time-with the money being paid in, the recipient can collect cash in rupees at the office of Western Union's agent in this locality.

Besides Non-Resident Indians (NRIs) remitting money to India, the money transfer service is also targeted at potential tourists, businessmen and other professionals visiting India.* They bring foreign exchange into India in a big way.

Updating Bank Savings Accounts

Usually, all business houses, employees and others may have an account in the bank's main branch or other branches and other banks. Money deposits, withdrawals from savings bank account, loans, repayments, even draft and other transactions are of common interest to operate. These transactions require periodical calculations like interests, debits and credits and reconciliation which presently are being done manually. Now however, this work is strategically handled by a computer system.

This system of updating the bank savings account by the computer is widespread in advanced countries.

Under the system, soon after filling the pay in slip, it is necessary to present it at the counter of the bank along with the passbook. The teller of the bank in turn inserts the passbook into an online transaction terminal. It is then keyed into transaction data, the details of account number, the type of transaction and the transaction amount etc. will be entered into the storage area of the processor. The computer in response retrieves the keyed saving account records and gives effect to the transaction, may be credit or debit. The account is updated with balances in the passbook as inserted in the terminal by the teller.

Computer Bank Branches

In recent years in India, like in other countries, computerization of bank branches is happening in a big way. In a major move towards improvement, some of the commercial banks with an ambitious plan have computerized their branches and some are fully computerized and some other banks partly computerized. The automation of the banking operation by means of electrification will help provide better, quicker and cheaper services to the customers.

Financial Transactions Terminals (FTT)

In addition to cashless shopping and cyber laundering, there are other types of financial transactions terminals (FTT) in general use. The best instance of device used is the electronic fund transfer (EFT). Automated teller machine is one of the examples of electronic fund transfer. In

---

* *Computers Today, August, 1994, p.17.*

banks and other financial institutions, financial transactions terminals have been designed to facilitate bank transactions and online terminals are used to handle both deposits and withdrawals of the customers.

E- Cheque

Introduction: E-cheque has been appreciated as an important facility being given in e-banking in recent years. E-commerce is greatly facilitated by issue of e-cheques. Under the traditional method of the issue of paper cheque, considerable amount of time is being spent in its preparation recording signature and fulfilling other formalities.

As a result of advancement in sophisticated information technological techniques, the issue of paper cheques has become obsolete. The issue of an electronic cheque has now become reality and widespread particularly in advanced countries. In tune with e-commerce, the trend of writing and issuing of paper cheques is a memory of the past.

Meaning: With the development in the field of the information technological techniques the issue of e-cheque is greatly facilitating and has revolutionized the banking business and financial transactions. E-cheque is created on a computer and is processed through the Net. In other words, it is essentially an electronic version of the paper cheque. The process of issue of and the nature of workflow in the issue of e-cheque is the same as the conventional paper cheque.

In the year 1998, in Singapore, the banks cleared over 600 billion worth of cheques. In the US, the banks handled more than 70 billion cheques on a regular basis.

Origin of E-cheques: There is a great practical utility for the use of e-cheques. To exploit this potential, an original e-cheque was developed by the Financial Services Technology Consortium (FSTC) in the US. It is an alliance of 65 financial service providers, universities, government and IT companies. Proved successful, there are brighter prospects for the implementation of electronic cheques on a global basis.

E-cheque is now established as the main medium of payment. It has legal support and recognition. In recent years of business moving over the Net, the e-cheque is used as means of payment they are between individuals and organisations, between businesses from one individual to another for various online services.

As the volume of business over the Net continues to rise, there are no alternate modes of financial transactions for the banks and customers to consider as no other method is flexible as e-cheque.

Features: With respect to the e-cheque, the special features are:

- Verification is digital
- Verification is automatic or manual.
- Before the cheque is issued, the payer has to submit his digital signature to the bank just like his specimen signature. The signature is verified online for security reasons.
- There will be an independent and separate organisation known as Certification Authority (CA). For instance, there is Net Trust in Singapore.
- This authority will issue in turn to the payer with a digital certificate on the tamper resistant smart card.

- The smart card has the capability to plug into a computer or point of sale terminal (PST).
- Issue of an e-cheque is possible with the help of a special electronic cheque book issued by the bank to the payer.
- A separate e-cheque software is to be used which displays an electronic cheque on the screen.
- An e-cheque has all the same features as a paper cheque.
- The payer has to sign the cheque with his digital signature.
- To sign the e-cheque, the payer then keys in a secret PIN, in addition to etc. via the graphical user interface (GUI).
- Privacy and security are ensured. There are various levels of security involved in an e-commerce transaction.
- It assures more safety and is more efficient than paper cheques. There is a facility of encryption of information for extra security.

There is an inbuilt mechanism of automatic blocking of payment if someone tries to tamper with the signature or change of information.

- As soon as the payer signs the e-cheque, all the information is transmitted to the bank for automatic checking of the signature and logging of all other details.
- Issue of an e-cheque begins by first entering a PIN and if a wrong PIN is entered, the smart card is disabled to work.

Advantage of E-cheques: There are a number of advantages emerging from the operation of e-cheque both to customers, banks and online merchants. The major advantages of e-cheque are as follows:

- Cutting overall costs
- Increasing security
- Payment system is more intelligent and flexible.
- Facilitates on-line payment.
- Supports the e-commerce revolution.
- E-cheque can also complement and co-exist with the paper cheque.
- Different account numbers are used for e-cheques and paper cheques.
- No one can forge an e-cheque by the issue of paper cheques.
- An e-cheque presentation can be synchronized with information in the bank's database to ensure that every detail is correct.
- It alarms for any altering of any discrepancies.

Magnetic Ink Character Recognition (MICR) and Cheques

For printing a text, a special ink is used, which contains practices of magnetic materials. Magnetic Ink Character Recognizor (MICR) has the capability to identify characters printed with a special ink containing particles of magnetic materials. The device is more useful in banking operations to clearly and successfully read the characters of cheques. This device cannot recognize all character styles. It recognizes perfectly, provided the characters are accurately formed.

The MICR technology requires standardization of cheques, which demands uniformity in terms of quality of paper, pattern and printing of relevant particulars of cheques like serial number, city or bank or branch on which drawn, account number, nature of transaction and the amount in magnetic ink. In respect of some particulars, they are reprinted. In respect of other particulars, a specially designed tool known as encoder is used to record account number and the amount which are encoded by the bank.

In order to clear cheques of high value of more than rupees one lakh, special clearing houses have been introduced in metropolitan cities like Mumbai, Kolkata and Chennai.

Automation of banking operations involve sophisticated information technology for gathering, processing, correlation and distribution. The electronic modes of communication and computer related technology have been greatly facilitating the information processing and distribution of these services.

Similarly, Store and Forward Telegraph (SFT) system, dedicated network of telephone services, automatic cash dispensers, national clearing intercity cheques etc. make it easier for customers to deal with these banks. The use of telecommunication for financial banks and financial institutions to obtain uptodate news on foreign currency rates from the global money markets using online worldwide information retrieval services is potentially business oriented.

E-Banking in India

Indian banks are still in the process of exploring the potentials of the Internet as a medium for the banking as the technology heading towards more business there are potential prospects of internet banking.

Banking in India today not only provides information of its services or request services such as cheque books, statements etc. with reference to a particular branch. In India, banks still do not have a single true online internet banking service available.

According to Lawrence Alphonso, corporate communications manager of Satyam infoway Ltd, a company into providing internet- based solutions for banks, "you can request for transfer of funds from your own account to another account in the same name in the same branch and may extend it to another branch (if they are networked)". That is the extent of internet banking in India.

E-banking

The biggest challenge before the Indian banking industry is that of changing their functioning and operations online with the Internet and other IT-based technology for banking.

The last few years have probably seen the most significant charges in the Indian banking environment. The liberalization of interest rate regime and the proliferation of lending as an enabling force, have made it possible for banks to come out with a host of innovative products and distribution strategies.

The recent liberalization trend and globalization has brought many changes in business practices and economic systems in the world. Consequently, the banking sector and other financial institutions are also affected by new realities following globalization.

Information technology made its presence felt in banks in India a few decades ago. But today, it is used as a potential support system. The software packages used in banks work on stand alone systems and they are not integrated.

Offering real time interactivity from our desktop, online banking helps to transact business in a greater way and so people need not necessarily worry about the security issues. E-banking is vital to any successful e-commerce, it helps to encash online business. Technology at the heart of e-commerce is a special design to today's demanding e-commerce server solutions.

In the fast changing world of dot coms, disintermediation is the order of the day. In India, the banking sector is about to change in tune with changing technology design form of financial transactions. Accordingly, all bank dealings and banking needs would be available with a click on the keyboard. If the Indian banking system hesitates to work out strategies to develop online banking and establish itself on the internet, it would find itself outside the new growth matrix.

Today, Internet banking is becoming a strategic necessity for banks. The internet has destroyed all geographical advantages enjoyed by the retail outlets calling for newer, less expensive and more customer friendly technologies. As such, online or internet banking has emerged as the ultimate answer to survival in the world order of competition and globalization. Internet banking is changing business models, it is too powerful a tool to be just another mode of banking.

This is the age of internet banking. It is time Indian banks should start offering web-based banking services to the account holders. Online banking has proved successful in the international banking sector in other countries and has revolutionized the e-commerce industry. In India also, online banking is fast emerging as favourable. Chennai based Mega Soft Limited has launched a novel e-bank designated to cater to the needs of growing consumerism in India. E-bank is a suit of online/Internet based banking publications that have been developed using emerging technologies with seamless integration and technical scalability.

The unique feature of e-bank is a risk management system with a comprehensive user-defined reporting and any time/any where bank with an interface to the ATM machine, These features enable the bank to provide information important to ensure customer's convenience and allow the bank personnel in automative functions across the branches.

Private Indian banks such as ICICI Bank, IDBI Bank and Indus Ind Bank have taken the lead to introduce internet-based banking services in India, In fact, Indus Ind was the first bank to set up a website after commercial internet became available in India in August 1995. ICICI Bank followed soon after by setting its own website in February 1996. Citi Bank and other banks also offer internet based banking services.

The Internet banking is fast gaining ground in India only in recent years.

You mention internet banking and banks offering this facility are Citi Bank, ICICI, HDFC, Global Trust Bank, HSBC, Union Bank of India, State Bank of India and Industrial Bank.

Many other banks including some non-banking financial institutions are moving towards becoming a big player in net banking.

Both private and public banks in India have already incorporated a few basic online services like e-mail and electronic data interchanges. But in order to really make difference, there needs to be integration in the banking software. Infrastructure costs like security hardware, security software and internet banking software amount to a one time cost.

Internet banking is substantially changing the face of banking in India by making it much more efficient and customer friendly, thus changing its way of functioning.

Citi Bank was the first to go online with its banking services. HSBC has invested to establish itself it with online banking, to provide its customers with full net capability. In addition, private banks like HDFC, ICICI and Global Trust Bank have taken a lead in straight online operations.

Security of Internet Banking

Like e-commerce, internet banking also is associated with security problems. These are mainly related to the following:

1. Authentication: In this, banks use the personal identification number (PIN) and a distinct customer identity number which enables customers to access their accounts with ease and send payment Instructions. When the customer is required to connect to the bank, he has to necessarily enter the PIN each time. The PIN is an authority and only the authorized persons use it. A connection to the bank is not possible unless a request is coming from an authorized customer.

The technology involves a process to verify that a person claims to be a genuine customer. In this, a number of questions may be put from a large list and the answers are compared and if these are matched with those held on the system, it means that the person is authenticated.

2. Privacy: Privacy in relation to bank transactions applies to an individual customer. It is the right of every account holder to access all financial information. The internet-based banking must ensure that only the right person can access this information in order to ensure online privacy, state-of-the art 1,024 bit RSA, SSL and RCS techniques as well as triple data encryption and standard encryption are used while connecting and communication with bank. Techniques like SSL and RCS provide integrity and security to those involved in financial transaction. The encryption system scrambles data packages sent from a computer to the server. This technique prevents people from snooping on the network connection and viewing information on transmission.

Quicken is a financial software programme that has the features of a password.

3. Integrity: Integrity with reference to internet banking on the security of data and message involves the quality of being honest and appreciating positive work ethics and sincerity in electronic transactions. These ethics include financial, legal and procedural integrity. The whole transaction must satisfy the condition of being whole and authentic. A financial message through the Net is on electronic transmission-this requires integrity for successful e-commerce. It means that the message received cannot be altered after it is put online by the sender to the destination.

4. Transaction Confirmation/Monitoring: One of the security aspects in internet banking is transaction confirmation or *monitoring*. The special feature of this technique is to display a list of instructions to be sent to the bank before it goes online and provide a record of all the completed transactions. The banks operating on the internet and the vendors have been made familiar with these special features.

5. Indentification and Password: Assigning a correct password ensures the only authorization for data access. Password is the first step on which the whole process of security is involved. The existence of a password indicates an object with a unique identity assigned to it. Further, cross checks may be imposed, if some additional measures of security are desired to ensure security of information put online by customers.

Authorization: This is the last step in the matters of security of internet-based banking. One can ensure that only a user can access the data to whom permission has been granted to access, read or alter data as the case may be. Thus, a matrix can be created to indicate which users have access to which file.

Cyber crime in internet-banking is not new in developed countries, where information networks are widespread and matured. For instance, the first computer crime was reported in 1958 in the US. This crime involved substantial and strategies alteration of the bank statements.

With the growth of computer networks and electronic communication facilities, Cyber crime (a white collar crime) has been increasing and India is no exception. Effective strategies have been developed to prevent cyber crime in a big way.

According to reliable newspaper sources, recently one of the networks in India was affected though not seriously, by an unauthorized user.

The hi-tech strategies which have been getting into the encryption consists in digitizing it in ways which could be decoded normally by the parties putting it to use. The expertise which has gone into digitized encryption is now pressed into service to financial transactions particularly in the US between banks. But still it is not fool-proof. Even this too has generated fears on grounds that it could serve the interests of the black market (under-ground) economies.

As a result of the new technology, more and more transactions have place in the underground banking networks, more money will escape traditional attempt at a taxation. As this happens, the nation — state will lose more power or be forced to impose higher taxes, forcing even more corporations into the underground economy. Internet banking provides the following facilities :

- Permits to get electronic statements in print and download format.
- Sending cheques and payment.
- Write an electronic cheque that a bank will print out and send via normal mail.
- Transfers funds between two or more accounts.

Procedure

How to get on online banking? The answer is connect net, set and go. Getting started involves the following steps:

- Filing the form as provided by the bank.
- To get a password for accessing the computer from the bank.
- A personal computer.
- A modem
- Personal finance program like quicken or money or an internet browser. The internet browsers are Netscape or Microsoft Internet Explorer.
- To navigate to the bank site.
- Type a password and do professional banking business.
- To have the encryption code on each transaction.

Programs

There are separate online banking service programs as personal finance managers. They include :

- Microsoft money and
- Intuit quicken

These programs allow customers to work off-line and dial particular numbers to complete their banking transactions online.

Components

The components of e-banking are :

- Internet/Intranet/extranet
- electronic data interchange
- electronic mail
- electronic fund transfer and
- smart card.

1. ***Internet/Intranet/Extra Net:*** Internet/Intranet/Extranet are those that use web-based technologies of graphical user interface to facilitate potential online interaction and communication.

2. ***Electronic Data Interchange (EDI):*** This is an application and an exchange of information using a standard format to structure the financial transactions of data.

3. ***Electronic Mail:*** Exchange of mail messages by way of computer systems are connected over communication networking. These are sent and received at the user's convenience.

4. ***Electronic Fund Transfer:*** Electronic fund transfer is the management of cashflow and pertains to the timing of payment made to parties with the use of electronic messages.

5. ***Smart Card:*** Smart card is a plastic credit card with a computer chip embedded into and is capable of storage data which can be retrieved by a separate reader device.

A number of IT components manufacturers launched a wide range of products and services providing solutions for banks and financial institutions in the financial sector. The products include Web, ATM, Interactive kiosks for e-commerce and internet application, Colour customized ATM, Cheque processing system, Low end cash dispensers and millennium cash dispensers (MCD)

Online retail banking services include the following :

- Saving account
- Current account
- Fixed deposits.
- Bills payments and other retail banking products and
- The surge on the demand for e-commerce related services stems from the rapid growth in the internet's penetration and fundamental change in the business paradigm.

Solutions are designed on the net-based B2B payment module for both buyers and sellers to effect online payment.

How to go on Net for Online Banking

The following steps potentially initiate online financial transactions.

1. ***Log on to a Website:*** The first step is that the customer, individual or a corporate has to go to the worldwide web and log onto a website.

2. Verification and Password: Then the website server verifies the user ID and password. In case of the first time user, it is necessary to fill in a registration form to enter a website.

3. Processing: Subsequently, the request is processed by the server via firewalls.

4. Credit Card: If the password and user ID are matched, the website allows transactions. It means asking for a credit card or for telephone number to reach for online transaction verification.

Final Approval: If a website allows online credit checking, information about the credit card is passed onto the bank, and the issuing bank for credit card verification of the account status, credit limits and its own security measures are part and parcel of processing. If everything is correct, the transaction is approved accordingly.

Advantages

The potential benefits for banks conducting their business online are manifold with decreased transaction costs and access to new customers providing substantial advantages of conducting online business. However, the uptake of internet banking within the country has been slow with only a handful of players providing internet banking services. Let us take a look at some of the benefits emerging from internet banking.

- Internet banking enables NRIs in particular to monitor their local bank accounts from abroad, transfer money to joint accounts held by them in india, send money to parents back home n India and pay school fees etc.
- The global means of banking not only provides enormous convenience but the money starts earning returns faster than the conventional method where returns were lost for the period that the draft was in transmission and clearing.
- NRIs can now transfer or invest in India in open-ended schemes using the Internet through a web address. Through e-commerce facility, an NRI Investor need not visit the bank and the entire process of investing can be done over the Net. For instance, Mumbai based prudential ICICI Asset Management Company Limited claimed to be India's first mutual fund company to launch e-commerce facilities for NRIs.
- A small business firm writing about 100 cheques a month including payroll cheque costs more per cheques in paper, postage and employee time. In contrast, most electronic bill payments software costs less cheque. Electronic bill payments is one of the key services offered by the banks.
- It offers and assures security to get electronic statements printed or downloaded, send cheques, payments and transfer funds between two or more accounts.
- Permits better, efficient and timely accurate management of funds and payments in real time.
- All financial data can be obtained at any time, 24 hours a day and 7 days per week.
- Net banking premiers offer a range of services online.
- Internet banking services provide remote banking services and facilitates information needed by online customers.
- Offers account details and statement, financial modelling tools which allow the simulation of various deposit options to arrive at an optimum combination and fund transfers between different accounts.

- Freedom and access to bank anytime and anywhere.
- Offers a range of cyber-banking options including the view of accounts, statements etc.
- Avoid to drive long distances to approach neighbourhood banks.
- No need to stand in queue for hours to complete financial transactions. This eliminates the time taken for these transactions.
- To eliminate endless paper-based bank statements, spreadsheets, bulky accounts ledgers including the use of calculators.
- With just a PC link to the bank, online banking is a potential business tool. The link allows customers access to the Net and log on the website of a particular bank.
- Its use does not cost more, which may also vary from bank to bank and the type of account holding services like checking account statements are generally free, other add on features like account transfer have a nominal surcharge. Internet banking offers the lowest transaction cost among all the conventional electronic delivery channels.
- With online presence, banks can rebuild their brand in terms of service world wide at low costs.
- Net affords the lowest transaction cost among all other electronic delivery channels.
- Internet banking helps banks reduce the workload of branches like no routine generation of statements, balance enquiry and cheque requests.
- It attracts future customers who generate potential business for the banks.
- Leverage the power of visual computers i.e. personalizing the banking experiencers.
- From the customer's perspective, online banking means greater convenience, rendering limitations of space irrelevant.
- Better fund management.
- Sites can be built up with a multi-layer security architecture comprising of firewalls and filtering routers.
- Encryption and digital certification provides customers the confidence that their financial information and the accounts are protected from unauthorized access.
- Customers can get the details of accounts and transactional details instantly.
- Transfer of funds, submitting requests and intimations like stop payments and activities are very simple and easy.
- The customer can drop his plan of going to a bank to effect his bank transactions. Instead, he can relax, press a few keys to order a draft or pay or bill. Alternately, the customer can browse through his account before taking an important financial decision.
- Having logged onto a bank's website, the customer can view his accounts, credit card and home loan balances, accrued interest fees and taxes, transaction details of each account, paying of bills, transfer funds to third party accounts, which may be nominated and open a deposit right from the terminal where the customer has established a link.
- The account holder is armed with password, can use the Net to order a cheque book, stop payment of a cheque and stop the balance and individual operations in the account and transfer funds.
- Banks can target and approach both individuals and NRIs through the Net.

- Net reduces transaction cost to a great extent. Some statistics reveal that rough estimate assuming teller at ₹ 1 per transaction put ATM transaction costs at 45p, phone banking at 35p, debits card at 20p and internet banking nearly by 10p. Moreover, in the US, investment costs are likely to reach 10m potential customers through online application at $900m against $1m through the Net. Thus, the enormity of these numbers can change the face of banking.
- Improve customer orientation.
- Lower distribution cost.
- Long term customer relations.
- Ease of banking wherever and whenever the customer wants it.
- Enhance profitability.
- Efficiency cost effective with standing competition.
- Low credit card proliferation.
- Security issues.
- Accountability.
- Attract future customers and
- Better funds management.

Limitations

Customers going for online banking prefer seeking complete satisfaction and maximum benefits particularly in India, where he has a series of questions regarding the level of security and benefits from online banking. Some of the limitations are :

- Compared to other countries, banks and financial institutions in India are still at the basic stage of publishing rather than interactive and are in a small way making their presence felt in the area of providing financial transactions. The banks are yet to gear themselves for providing complete and satisfactory online transactions and services.
- Providing complete transactions and services involving huge investments in web development that will completely integrate the website with back-end systems, including customer database and applications.
- Banks have not extended the facility of third payments whereby accountholders are in a position to make payments to pre-determined parties through the Net.
- On the other hand, banks have not launched the internet payment gateway for handling net transactions of their clients.
- The Indian banking system including non-banking financial institutions are not working towards comprehensive interactive financial services in collaboration with some international organisations like IBM, which would provide a state-of- the art local platform for online banking. This would greatly help banks to handle cross border deals in all currencies.
- Presently, banks working with centralized data have distinct edge, and no processing is done at local branches. So, information moves seamlessly across different banking channels. The lack of centralized database system is one of the main handicaps in the case of online banking.

- There is no facility for inter-bank funds transfer through the Net because the cyber laws in this regard are still not in place—hence smooth cash management is not possible.
- Business and individuals are aware that reliable transaction technology as well as management of the security and privacy perceptions of customers are the key to the success of online banking. Doubts relating to the security of money online is a serious problem. The security and privacy aspects also continue to remain a major issue especially in the case of business people. Branch connections, encryption, firewalls, digital certification, automatic sign-offs, random pop-ups and disaster recovery sites are not fully looked at to ensure that the customer's money is safe in the cyber world. A certification authority needs to be set up to verify the signature of those going for online banking. However, third parties are not very keen as business volumes are not very large.
- The infrastructural costs of providing such services are prohibitive. The heavy costs are towards the development of the back-end systems. The banks not only have to automate its front-end system which the customers interface but also the back-end systems so the bank is able to provide *robust functionality.* The main infrastructural costs are towards security software, internet banking software and security hardware which are costly. These are, however, on time costs. The recurring costs pertaining to intrastructure also account for some proportion.
- There are many banks who invest in cost-effective strategies to establish themselves in online banking- considering the risks involved in dealing with other's money.
- Lack of awareness is seen as one of the biggest road blocks for successful online banking. The problem of awareness is more than acceptance. Effective and wide media efforts in publishing internet banking need to be emphasised.
- Internet access in India is tilted towards corporate access and therefore people access the Internet more from offices than from homes. But in the U.S., access to the Net is more titled towards home use.
- Only a few organisations are using internet banking. Even among those organisations which are adopting internet banking, it is only major corporates and multinational firms having a strong trust for technology driven operations which have also accepted internet based banking system in a big way.
- Merchants, customers and general public do not have a full idea of the issues involved in online banking. Those who know, they only know that Net usage involves certain risks but accessing accounts through the web fascinates them.
- Given that matters regarding security are very serious, bankers, corporates, merchants and customers agree that privacy, authentication, integrity and non-repudiation are the four primary concerns. They worry about the lack of standards and security that is universally accepted and adopted.
- A formal governmental paper on cyber laws and the legal framework for internet banking are not formulated.
- The Reserve Bank of India (RBI) has so far not issued a policy paper covering the regulatory aspects and legal framework which are important to internet banking, to protect customers or for financial transactions over the Net and the acceptance of digital signatures.

- The banking sector also has not come out with new business models and products in the area of risk management, online insurance and loans, credit appraisals etc. to address the potential e-commerce opportunities. It requires to bring together both online sellers and buyers, guarantee and strike deals, insure transactions on the web and allow cross border instant trade to happen.
- The role of the RBI and the government is insignificant. Clearly, there is no doubt about the role of the RBI and the government in making internet banking happen and enabling Indian banks to compete with global banks. On the other hand, Indian banks are not equal in position to their counterparts in the US, UK and other Asian countries in terms of computerization. Indian banks are still behind as per as the deployment of information technology in the banking industry in India which commenced many years later compared to USA and Europe. Automation in banks have largely addressed only branch automation in a distributed environment as the conditions favourable to deployment of a state-of- the- art internet banking capability needs to be developed.
- Another road block is the cost and availability of leased lines and bandwidth is a factor which resulted in delay in online banking by Indian banks. It is neglected by the fact that international access out of India is governed in such a way which dissuades most banks to invest in net banking.
- There are two main areas of risks pertaining to banking transactions over the Net. They are preventing unauthorised transactions and maintaining integrity of customers' information about financial transactions. In the case of former's risk, it will generally be implied into the contract between a bank and its customers than in the options of any negligence on behalf of the customer and the bank will be liable for any transactions occurring on the account that have been perpetrated. As for the second area of risks, a customer's transaction history or account details are accessed by a third party. The ability to crack encryption products are commonly found. Cyber crime rates need to be declined with stategic management.
- Though banks have their presence on the Web, they are not offering accurate account servicing to the online customers considering the internet risks. To curb this, strategies need to be written to protect the security of the customers.
- Online banking needs to strengthen the roots following the cautious attitude of people towards security issues and the privacy of personal financial information. They would like to stand assured of online security of information available on the Net.
- All banks are not behind the curve in developing a customer friendly online presence.
- Online bank transactions are not popular because what most banks are offering is an e-mail version of banking, which permits to the right to e-mail with specific instructions to transfer funds and so on. Net banking facilities are not widespread and not easily available.
- Software companies in India need to work out strategies to encouragingly further net banking, No serious thought has been given to bring together bankers, financial institutions and other supporting and related organisations to harness emerging technology to exploit new growth opportunities.
- The low base of PC users in India coupled with conventional mindset and fear of electronic fund transfer needs to be monitored and changed to be with the times.
- Online banking and financial programmes face many hurdles. So; not all banks are prepared to access the Net for online banking and financial transactions.

- Low density of telephone lines and computerization of banks in India is also a bottleneck for online banking. For instance, out of 65,000 bank branches in India, only 5,000 branches are computerized.
- People do not use personal financial software because they are hesitant to enter all their detailed financial data into the computer system. Security towards this end needs to be assured by merchants.
- Many people are away from net banking on the assumption that it is more expensive than the traditional method of dealing with bank transactions. They still prefer going to the bank and undertake financial transactions following its popularty even today. Under the conventional method of banking, they feel that financial statements and accounts are more simple requiring no such high-tech banking techniques.
- It will not prove risky to the customers. The conventional banking process takes time, cost and efforts. The cost of software is higher and banks in India still have to prove their credibility. In a country like India, private banking is directed towards welfare, social banking, risk prone rural activities where e-banking may not be fully successful.

Spending time, money and efforts may not be practical and long lasting. So, it is important to be practical and analyse the needs as per the technology rather than being carried away by the buzzwords of business used today. The interest of the customers must assume an important role. Moreover, the cost of recording it, change in technology and software in terms of value and manpower are very difficult.

Conclusion

Thus, all the channels of banking will co-exist with the internet banking facilities. Right now with low PC base, lack of adequate infrastructure and internet penetration, it is going to take time and the traditional means of banking will co-exist but their importance in distribution will drastically come down as and when the market matures.

□□□

E-commerce Security

Introduction

E-commerce is still a young industry that is growing fast and has not experienced security as a high priority area. The industry in turn is a sophisticated way of doing business. The internet where e-commerce is operated, is very much an environment where networks and computers participate by playing by rules. But some unscrupulous hackers are breaking the rules to cause privacy and security problems. The industry requires an instantaneous solution to these problems caused by hackers.

Need for Security

In today's competitive computing environment, the importance of security mechanisms cannot be ignored. The mere traditional security mechanism does not seem suitable and enough. To portify e-commerce transactions, industrial strength and security solutions are made. A high performance related to high security applications are designed to support internet based e-business process. Every business has to develop the strongest security framework in the market to give business and customers a total transaction security.

Over the last one year, a majority of businesses particularly outside India, have moved to the Net. Security is essential for e-commerce and that is why more than 2,500 internet service providers and web hosting companies have contributed their expertise to make it easier than ever for small and medium sized business to secure web store fronts virtually overnight.

Security is an essential aspect for the successful infrastructure of e-commerce business strategy. What is needed is public key infrastructure solutions for secure e-commerce. Reports of breaches of customer's privacy online stores demands early concern because internet security is justified. There is potential for exposing information as a result of misconfigured e-commerce software and inadequate security.

Many online stores hosted the web individually, revealing customer name, address, credit card number and other purchasing information. Such incidents of privacy breaches maybe expected to increase as more and more businesses get connected online.

Personal information is more sensitive in nature. The inception of the web has been seen as the powerful platform for online shopping and shopping at home.

The use of the web presented a problem of security that has to be resolved before any PC initiates using the web for online shopping. The problem is that the security of any business transaction takes place on the internet. Due to the use of public networks to transmit and exchange any business data between any two users, the risk of any transaction being intercepted remains to a large extent.

The Net provides potential opportunities and benefits to the customers, suppliers and business partners. But web-based commercial transactions are susceptible to major insecurities. It is a serious personal data like nature of transaction, credit card number, bank details, name, residential address, financial matters and other personal details.

Security is important for conducting potential business on the Net. E-commerce has established itself as a potential business. The conventional security mechanism is not enough. It is necessary to look into the realistic state of security for internet business. So far, the efforts of security measures have focussed on protecting the actual transaction while neglecting the other components necessary for secure e-commerce. A realistic security problem of Net business needs to be properly understood.

It is desirable to have high performance, high security application to support internet based e-commerce process. Employing the strongest security framework gives customers' business total transaction security. Web business offers reduction in the cost of transactions, boosts productivity and gives a competitive advantage over other businesses.

If we need to be confident about the identity of persons sending an electronic message, it is essential to be sure that the message has not been tampered with and it should be kept in confidence.

Serious business crimes are also prevailing in the market with the emergence of drug traffickers, paebophiles and terrorists trying to encrypt to conceal their activities, If these activities are not checked, this will make the work of law enforcement increasingly difficult. This demands promotion and development of appropriate encryption technologies to prevent online crimes.

Inadequate security definitely hinders successful e-commerce. Unwarranted hype over the security risks of e-commerce has led to fear and analysing benefits about setting up internet business.

Accuracy, confidentiality, security, privacy of customers and employees' personal information is utmost important, which is the core of e-commerce encryption. E-commerce prefers the process of transactions over the Net which raises the issue of security and privacy pertaining to online business and information given by customers.

Security Concepts

Net business requires privacy and security. Today, there seems to be boom on e-commerce requiring a secured defence. People who are doing business through the Net are skeptical over the need for cryptography particularly indigenously designed. The rise in e-commerce has led to the need of privacy, security and a strong crypto. Public crypto is important for online application. An authentication through a digital signature is an essential feature pertaining to online security.

The combination of security and authentication will ensure that cryptography can strengthen the foundation of an e-commerce infrastructure. In recent years, the issue of encryption has gained the attention of the businessworld as e-commerce gained momentum. It is a vital aspect to render security to the business data and message transmission. E-commerce is establishing itself in India including a presence in the international business scenario and trade globally-this calls for strategies assuring online security.

E-commerce by nature of transactions requires the encryption of message transmission in order to protect national security, public safety, personal privacy and to support online commerce without interruption.

Therefore, what is required today for e-commerce is to build good strong applications that utilise tried and tested crypto techniques to ensure absolute security to the confidential business message and data and the smooth routing of contents. This is where we need solutions strong enough for global markets.

The electronic internet mechanism has been offering an unlimited and invaluable scope for e-commerce on a global canvas. But it is time to recognize and worry about security and privacy of transmission with information available on the Net. Global e-commerce necessitates to devise ways and means to lock the e-commerce message put online to be transmitted which gives scope for anyone to access these messages. As such, only the trading partners who want to communicate must have access to it and no one else. So, these trading partners must be registered online.

At the heart of the problem, in every business, there is the fear of loss of privacy, lack of security for monitoring electronic transactions from snooping, spying and capturing virtually any data transmission online and through cellular phones.

Once more and more new e-commerce data messages are kept in digital form, the protection of this data kept in electronic computer system needs greater recognition. Thus, it has given a challenge to designers, researchers, system managers, government software developers as well as users. E-commerce data and messages involve financial transactions and confidential information calling for a secured reliability. Therefore, pilfering of messages is serious threat for successful e-commerce.

Thus, in the current scenario of e-commerce, online security and privacy has become a much talked about issue. Since internet is easy to access and cheap to use, the confidence in security of messages and data online is of serious concern.

Privacy, security, integrity, confidentiality and secrecy are the various terms used in this connection. However, these words are used interchangeably and synonymously with security. No two words will have exactly the same meaning. There is some difference literally and from the technical point of view. In order to ensure protection in all these areas, it is better to have an idea about these terms. The most important e-commerce related crimes (cyber crimes), threats, lack of security and privacy are common which are mostly committed intentionally by competitors, hackers, intelligence agents and criminal corporate riders. If e-commerce related data and information, media and channels of transmission are not secured, crackers or cryptographers can easily intercept and tap the secret commercial and financial information, proving detrimental to the trust of customers who give personal information on websites of various firms.

A businessman needs data available online to be securely stored yet readily accessible by him, his customers and business partners.

Networking businesses undoubtedly can be a great equalizer, help to improve efficiency, competitiveness and productivity of various business firms. The advantage it offers in terms of productivity business, profitability and customer responsiveness are counter balanced by potential security and privacy risks. So privacy, identity and non-refutability are the three essential requirements for successful e-commerce.

Regardless of whether it is intranet, expanding intranet or virtually, the Internet, *the safety of content is critical.* To plan and build a safe e-commerce networking environment, it is necessary to understand the business value of assuring security, privacy etc. to the data available online.

Security

The term *security* with reference to the message or information put on transmission through the Net is protection from danger of data being prone to accidental or intentional. destruction, disclosure, modification or alteration in the original message before it reaches the receiver. It involves measures taken to prevent spying and attacks, which proves detrimental to the original message.

Steps involved in security may take the form of technological safeguards with strategic software and managerial procedures applied to hardware, software, networking, the Net etc.

In recent years, the use of the Net is rapidly growing, For reasons of efficiency, more and more corporate and financial institutions have started networking with both LAN and WAN to improve their efficiency. Sound and vital decisions are taken based on the information available to the decision maker through these networks. So, it is more important that an appropriate level of secrecy, security and privacy is maintained with reference to this information.

But in the process of e-commerce through networking, business people also make their messages or information insecure as these data are vulnerable to interception or corruption in many ways. Similarly, since information technology, the Internet is loaded with so many communication facilities such as voice mail, telephone, fax, e-mail etc, the privacy of a business man is at stake. There are a number of weak spots in the entire process of e-commerce transactions, some unauthorised and unscrupulous users are cashing on the weak spots and then breaking into the system to steal, alter, destroy and affect privacy of data either stored in the memory or is being transmitted. These are not difficult in the vulnerable electronic system. Communication systems such as e-mail, fax, networks server and hubs are some of the potential sources of danger. Weak spots include weak physical procedural controls, pure programming practice and weakness of the operating system.

In the present information highway and information super highways, cyber crimes related to e-commerce transactions such as data manipulation and eavesdropping intentionally or unintentionally are becoming common. If proper security measures for e-commerce through the internet are not taken, this may prove detrimental to businessmen who invest for the front global recognition via the Net.

Security means providing assurance of privacy, identity and non-refutability for e-commerce data information exchange as well as managing the security itself

With billions of rupees anticipating the change of hands regarding data across the globe, the most relevant problems have to do with the exchange of financial instruments over the worldwide network. Infact, e-commerce has far more to do with the transfer of information than with money. The growing problems of security, privacy, retaining the identity of customers and non-refutability must be solved in order to build up an effective digital commerce.

Privacy

The expression *privacy* with reference to e-commerce pertains to that aspect wherein business messages and information demand freedom from interference or detrimental public attention. It is the right of every individual to privacy. Privacy refers to security of messages and data belonging to the sender and for the use of one particular person, called the *receiver* at the destination.

Privacy purely applies to an individual. It is the right of every person involved in commerce to decide what information the sender wishes to share with another trading partner or is willing to receive from others.

Of all the issues of e-commerce via the Net, privacy is the most important one. The ability to secure digital exchange against interception, corruption, steal and alter data by third parties like riders, competitors, intelligence agents, hackers, cyberspace burglars is critical for allowing wired access to this data.

There are two methods by which online privacy is generally addressed:

Restriction of access which includes passwords, accounts and access to control lists etc. and *cryptographic services.*

Confidentiality

It involves assurances to keep the message and data secure from hackers and cyberspace burglars.

Non-refutability

It is all about being able to prove what has transpired when and between which parties. With time stamping information, the ability to prove the occurrence or absence of request and e-mail transmissions is critical in the event to re-create or refute alleged past events. Of course, the more rigorous efforts in capturing data, storing it in a secure fashion and ensuring its validity (with regular, scheduled testing of the data's recoverability and accuracy) are the more useful efforts, especially, if the records are required as legal proof.*

Survey Finding on Security

There are many people who have been the victims of cyber harassment, following easy access to the Net and web technology, which made it possible for various people to obtain or intercept certain business information that is not possible to collect through conventional means.

There are many methods by which information goes to different websites explicitly through forms, registering in pages and online contents. In addition, many websites implicitly gather personal information by using cookies and specialised software, without the knowledge of the surfing customers. This proves detrimental to the identity of the customers in terms of personal information available on the Web. As there are no restrictions on how this information can be used, cyber privacy and security have become a much debated topic all around the globe and solutions to the problem are still being addressed with the increase in e-commerce transactions and net privacy has emerged as a major issue today.

E-commerce related security woes are increasing with the risk of losing potential revenues and vital information. Security breaches or corporate espionages are commonly reported facts of security on web-based commercial transactions. Corporations conducting business through the website or ERP applications are more likely to control information available on the website by security means.

Business data are more sensitive, personal and confidential, and linking to back-end data bases is more complex, thus potentially creating more entry points for attackers. Information loss, theft of data or trade secrets, loss of revenue and low sales records are some of the consequences of unchecked net business.

Kadence, UK, a British research firm, conducted a survey on security issues by collecting information from 322 respondents. The findings of the survey revealed the following :

---

* *Anand Hafdle, Computers Today, 1-15 Sep., 1999, p. 62.*

- 56 per cent of the surveyed respondents said that information security was high priority.
- only 19 per cent have complete security policy.
- 49 per cent admitted that they do not know whether inadequate online security caused monetary loss.
- The biggest threat remains internal.
- The authorized respondents were believed to be responsible 58 per cent of the time.
- Unauthorized employees -24 per cent.
- Former employees -13 per cent.
- Hackers or terrorists expressed 13 per cent.
- Competitors accounted for 3 per cent.

In a survey of 1600 IT executive from 50 nations, 13 per cent reported some security breach or corporate espionage.

Recent Attack

The internet security is as big an issue as any other threat in the real world. It seems that nothing is secure. The American National of Standards and Technology, Carnegie, Melon's, Computer Emergency Response Team Centre and the Federal Bureau of Investigation (FBI) have been actively working on these problems. It is quite a big problem as it may insist on spending lots of money just to be prepared. Many business people, particularly in India, believe that security measures are not effective to prevent cyber crimes and that customers suspect the reliability of the Net.

Strong boundaries are needed to guard against the detail of service attacks which have a long history in cyber crime, largely because they are a relatively easy way to wreak havoc with external computers or websites. For the first time, on February 7th 2000, popular sites like Yahoo, CNN, eBay, Amazon.com, Bay.com and E-Trade exposed to weakness of the web as the security hackers disrupted these popular websites for several hours, causing loss of millions of dollars in revenue.

Their trade was paralysed by a series of Denial of Service (DoS) attacks. It is an avalanche of fake requests for information, which give a lasting blow to e-commerce. The denial of service attacks are not new. For instance, in December, 1999, electro-hippies shut the website of the World Trade Organisation (WTO). Yahoo was attacked by 50 computers stuffing its servers with the equivalent of 5 lakh typed written pages a second.

The attacks on these popular websites question the vulnerability of online business. The above cited sites have not experienced anything like this before. Yahoo and eBay have been hit by major outrages. A system can be knocked out by a distributed denial of service attacks.

The hackers shut down these websites with massive coordinated attacks on top e-commerce sites. It is an internet sabotage. Golbally, business people are sensitive about these happenings.

Hackers in the beginning of this fiscal launched a starting wave of attacks, taking hostage popular sites like Yahoo, the largest independent website, leading retailers Buy.Com, eBay, Amazon.Com and the new site CNN.Com

The Net brought customers and merchants closer together on one hand,but on the other hand, this has necessarily resulted in greater vulnerability of online business by those who have clearer motives.

But in the e-commerce industry, especially in the world of hackers, there is fear and doubt about the technology's ability to halt the hackers. Policy decisions and new enforcements need to be chalked out to protect the increasingly important e-commerce sector, that is long-term plans and broader cooperation to work out strategies to prevent cyber crimes.

Cyber Crimes

They include - snooping, impersonation, denial of services, anonymity, attacks on the network, tampering of data, burglary of confidential information, tracking usage illegally, cookies, growing online terrorists, encryption, breaches of security, corporate espionage etc. Some other crimes are intruders into confidential data, online privacy and denial of service attacks.

Reasons for Privacy Tampering

There may be many reasons of tampering privacy and security. Privacy breaches may happen mainly with smaller businesses. Some of the reasons for breaches of privacy are :

- Lack of expertise and technological sophistication.
- Improper installations of e-commerce solutions.
- Costly to hire experienced firms to prevent privacy from being tampered.
- Adopting multi-site hosting services.
- Building their own devices and using simpler commerce packages.
- Not carefully selecting firms to set up and host their e-commerce sites.
- Not getting references and enquiring about privacy and security upfront before installing a website.
- Businesses which are not having awareness of the necessity for security.

E-Commerce and Security

E-Commerce security aspects are to be examined from the following relevant processes:

- Introduction
- E-Commerce
- Security features
- Firewalls
- Proxy settings
- Proxy server
- PPT sites
- Online transmission and
- Technological terms.

Introduction

This is the following criteria :

- Security features
- Online transmission and
- Technological terms.

E-Commerce

It covers :

- Beginning
- Electronic data interchange. A faster and less expensive way of online business.

Security features

They include :

- Firewalls
- Proxy server and
- Encryption.

A *firewall* may be defined as a system or group of systems that enforces an access control policy between two networks. Firewalls perform an important function as a corporate ambassador, it blocks traffic from outside and gives summaries to administrators to ensure security among networks. Firewalls, however, are subject to certain limitation like tunneling, data-driven attack and the existence of viruses.

Proxy servers include the following areas of business like marketing, selling, payment, collections and they ensure the necessity to servers and close detrimental direct access to potential information on the Net and also restrict custom configuration with reference to the Demilitarized Zone (DMZ).

Advantages of Proxy Server

They read as follows :

- Free up internet bandwidth and
- Uses one IP address.

Disadvantages

They pertain to :

- Management of online business effectively,
- Maintenance and
- Difficulty in using the new internet tool.

Encryption

This includes :

- Private key
- Public key
- Digital signature
- Digital certificate and
- Technological terms (DES, RSA, IDEA).

PPT Sites

They are encrypted, and include the following : Signatures', Key, Senders key, Net and Sender's Public key.

Online Transmission: Under payment option, e-cash, first virtual, cyber cash and credit cash are used-these options are made functional by setting up an account, a third party account and verification. Further, with reference to additional protocol, the following are accepted in a big way :

- Secure Electronic Transactions (SET)
- Secure Socket Layer (SSL)
- Transport Layer Security (TLS)
- Secure Merchant Service (ECS) and
- 128 Bit Security.

Security for Payment: The service providers offer customers Secure Socket Layer (SSL), a protection strategy to ensure that their credit card numbers are safe and will not be intercepted by hackers while it travels over the web. E-cash, online currency, virtual money and cybercash are various new currencies, they are internet terms coined to refer to the mode of payment in various online businesses.

A great complex problem in online business is payment. Payment by credit cards involve leakage of credit card details over the Net. There are several technical and non-technical security implications whereby personal information can be intercepted *enroute* at any one of the many computers, the details may pass through between a PC user at home or office and the merchants. Scrambling transactions are circumventing security of sites.

FabMart is one of the high payment security levels. It is an exciting new online store which brings one of the world's most secure payment systems for shopping on the Net. If a customer is using the Citi Bank Suvidha card, he can submit card details and the personal identification number (PIN) directly to the bank, making the transaction more secure than any other online store.

It also ensures the same level of security available on websites, worldwide to all Master Card, visa and Diners Card holders through the SSL technology. This technology transmits all payment details in encrypted form, thus preventing any one from getting access to credit card details. So, the of need of password and user ID is imperative to access online data.

The name, address and credit card number etc. are critical in an online business. They should be encrypted, compressed, encoded and sent by e-mail. In many e-mail programs, there is a filter option to display only e-commerce orders, enquiries or both. So, it is possible to separate online setting from other e-mails, send and receive important messages and data.

Areas of Internet Security

To understand what is internet security, it is first necessary to be clear about the areas of internet security :

1. Communication Security: The communication channel through which information is transversing the Net is easily accessible to third parties. Sensitive information pertaining to credit members and other messages may be intercepted. Communication security is an important aspect because the bulk transfer of information passes through the Net. In addition to interception, the parties can modify or alter communication, questioning the very essence of online security. But today, there are a number of encryption systems available to ensure that communication is not accessible to third parties, thus securing information available online.

2. Server Security: The server is an important device that contains the commerce site which is also subject to being cracked by attacks by hackers. Server attack therefore is also an important issue to be addressed. When a server is attacked, the service may be disrupted, with information available on the server destroyed and the attackers may intercept confidential sensitive financial information like identity of the customers, the amount of purchase and the details of credit cards.

Server security solutions are also available to prevent breaching. UNIX server is usually protected by using the HT Access Protocol.

3. Transactional Security: The other aspect of online security is that of transactional security. The consequences of this security includes the non-shipment of goods by merchants, non payment for goods dispatched and fraudulent orders etc. Transactional security is also seriously addressed to and there are a number of solutions designed to insure against transactional insecurity. One such solution is *payment gateway.* This solution permits to obtain confirmation that credit card details of the user are correct and funds are available. Before shipment, the payment gateway ensures that funds are credited to the merchant account. Secure electronic transaction is a new payment protocol.

4. Security Aspects: Subsequently, security aspects are identified and grouped as under:

- Security in conventional media.
- Security in e-mail and
- Security on the Internet

All these forms should strategically address security and privacy of customers and their confidential financial information.

A brief description on the security aspects of these areas are described below.

5. Security in Conventional Media: Phones, fax or mail order business are considered to be conventional media. There is no security of information in a credit card order even in the phone, fax and mail order method. For instance, in the case of fax, anyone can grab and tamper with messages, sensitive personal financial information or credit card number. When a credit card is given to a server or a friend, no one knows what happens to it when it is out of our hands.

6. Security in e-mail: Credit card transactions are also risky when credit card information is sent or e-mailed without encryption or as plain text. Even in e-mail, the encoding number is essential as the possibility of interception of credit card numbers cannot be ruled out when they get routed through the Net to the target destination. Snooping is not possible when credit card numbers are separated into two e-mail messages, one half in each. In an Internet mechanism, the two e-mails travel by entirely different routes. When interpreted, it is not pôssible to get the two parts separated. It is a process of splitting of the e-mail and the encoded attachment.

7. Security in Internet: Today, those in business think that security problem is closely associated in e-commerce over the Net. E-Commerce is known for lack of privacy and security. These aspects have been well addressed to meet the growing needs of e-commerce. Netscape Navigator, Opera, Microsoft and Internet Explorer are the major net browsers. They include the SSL technology.

Types of Security

The security of e-commerce on the Net is available under the following two categories.

- Non-technical security systems and
- Technical security systems.

Non-Technical Security Systems: There are a number of ways which Net merchants can give users security without the use of advanced internet security technologies. The following measures address the non-technical security systems. :

- The user (client) can be given the possibiiity of placing an order without giving the credit card details.
- Internet merchants can simply contact the user by telephone to obtain the details and
- The user can print the order form and after printing it, fills out the credit card details and faxes the order to the Net merchant.

The above mentioned possibilities are indispensable to a good net merchandising. Though many sophisticated internet security technologies are available and used, still some users do not wish to store the details via the Net.

Security for E-commerce

This pertains to :

- E-Commerce transactions
- Electronic payment systems.
- Secure electronic transaction
- Merchant accounts
- Digital signature
- Secure socket layer and
- SET-based secure transactions.

In web-based commercial transactions, cyber cash or virtual cash is desirable for security.

Web Security Issues

This includes :

- Web security
- Web client server security
- Web transfer protocol security and
- Operating security web server.

Web Insecurity

This involves :

- Impersonation
- Snooping
- Denial of service attacks
- Common gateways interface
- Usage analysis
- Privacy and
- Server Logs

Web Server Security

This pertains to :

- Access control restrictions like name, password, IP address, digital certificate.
- Web traffic encryption using public key encryptography.
- Digital certificate and secure sockets.
- SSL Security.
- Firewall based networks
- Software security tools and
- Developing security management policies.

Web Client Security

This involves :

- Cookies
- Security risk
- Security holes within the web browser and
- Surfing the web anonymously.

Internet Security

This pertains to :

- Networks security
- Equipment

- Security of operations and
- Systems tools and techniques.

Some Cyber Crimes-explanation

1. *Hacking and Hackers:* Hacking is the fastest emerging and growing crime. The computer attacks are one of the fastest growing areas of crime. The continuing updated technology made it nearly impossible to keep track of the problem. Recent attacks on major commercial websites like Yahoo.Com, Amazon.Com etc. show how important it is for the industry to device strategies against growing cyber crimes. How to deal with cyber crime is one of the most crucial areas to be addressed. The need for means of ensuring iniform standards with respect to equipment and technology cannot be overemphasized. The computer equipment needs to be standardized as continually updated technology. Otherwise it will become obsolete. An effective law is necessary and tougher penalties should be imposed on cyber attackers or hackers to deter them from wreaking havoc on the Net.

The unauthorised user of the network is called a *hacker*. The hacker is able to break into encryped communications by making use of Hi tech which he has professionally and legally acquired. The hacker who breaks into communication systems means not all of which is encoded and branded by governments as an unethical electronic operaion. Bu they regard themselves as competent computer professionals and their ability to break into systems only exposes the vulnerability of the systems. Risks to security of information is always there. This directly demonstrates the need for achieving greater perfection of the same. If the skills with which these professionals have enabled themselves to break into uncoded communication systems, the chances of their being able to break into encrypted systems cannot be wholly ruled out.

2. *Cyberspace Burglary:* E-commerce via the Net is now so vulnerable and easily exposed to cyberspace burglary. This is usually done by professionals who have the ability to break into encrypted systems containing confidental data. This calls for painstaking efforts to proceed with what now belongs to the realm of *cyberspace burglary*. A cyberspace burglar is a person who enters a transmission channel illegally to steal alter, modify, destroy the message or data which is either stored or is on transmission line.

A number of cyberspace burglaries have been reported in recent years. What is needed for successful e-commerce is to build up burglar proof storage or transmission channel so that burglars cannot break into the encrypted system of data and messages. A burglar alarm is an automatic device that rings an alarm bell when a burglar enters a building. On similar lines, an electronic device may be designed to indicate when a burglar attempts to break into the encrypted system.

But the emergence of cyberspace crimes only draws attention to the vulnerability of systems facilitating e-commerce for the possibility of cracking of the passwords. If the hackers resent being labelled as burglars, it is difficult to think of another description for what they could do which includes credit card frauds, computer virus and detrimental free internet access.

Hackers, however, attribute all this to the skills which cyberspace technology has enabled them to acquire and from which encryption systems are not inviolable.

3. *Denial of Service Attack:* The attack on websites and denial of services are common on the Net. Using technologies like spoofing, broadcast and ping and denial of service attacks can be conducted on the sites. In February, 2000, the Yahoo website was knocked out by a distributed denial of service attack. The tools needed to launch these attacks secretly installed on many computer systems across the Net without the permission of the owner or knowledge.

A denial of service attack occurs when attackers bombard a web server with fake packers of information requests. When the targeted server responds, the attackers' system steps up the barrage by sending more requests. The affected website struggles to keep up with the mounting number of requests showing performance for the user or ultimately crashing the system. This proves detrimental for online businesses.

Brute force denial of service attacks have a long history in the computer underground, largely because they are a relatively easy way to wreak havoc with external computers or websites

In its common form, an attacker strategically takes over another machine or group of machines working on the web, and then program these slave machines to send streams of information at the target side. Attackers commonly insert fake addresses into these tiny steams of information making them virtually untraceable. This problem needs to be tackled to secure the information available on websites.

Compounding the risks used to launch, denial of service attacks are easily available online. Where an attack once might have required sophisticated programming knowledge and computing resources, these downloadable tools now have brought the ability to wreak havoc on unprepared websites within the range of relatively casual computer users. This proves detrimental to those investing in a big way for online presence.

How Denial of Service Attack Works

In a typical connection, the user sends in a message asking the server to authenticate it. The server returns the authentication approval to the user, who acknowledges this approval and then is allowed onto the server.

In a denial of service attack, the user sends several authentication requests to the server filling it up. All requests have false return addresses this is a clear indication of denial of service attack. So, the server can't find the user when it tries to send the authentication approval. The server waits, sometimes more than a minute, before closing the connection, When the server does close the connection, the attacker sends a new batch of forged requests and the process begins again, typing up the service indefinitely.* This is detrimental to the requests.

Security Precautions

Mark Gibbs has hinted at the following possible trouble spots in e-commerce:

- Physical access during which data might be stolen or corrupted.
- Malignant software that could deny or reduce online service.
- Network security breaches during which users running personal web servers on PCs could expose data.
- Directed attacks against known problems with operating systems and applications
- Protocol attacks during which a hacker exploits weaknesses in protocols.

He also suggested a strong security plan which hinges on the following five basic aspects :

- Limit access. The fewer people who can get physical and administrative access to servers, the better will the security be.

The New Indian Express, Feb 14, 2000.

- Use security tools available in your e-commerce products.
- Perform regular audits to verify configuration and expected usage patterns.
- Protect complex systems with simple ones. A full blown e-commerce server is complex and a firewall is relatively less so. So, protecting the former with the latter makes sense.
- Make back-ups and have a disaster recovery plan to ensure security to customers.

Intrusion Detection Systems (IDS): Intrusion Detection System (IDS) are of two types: host-based IDS and deployed like virus scanners, agents installed on all services with a management consule for reporting. Network-based IDS uses passive systems which stiff the wire to detect attack signatures among the life traffic patterns.

How to Block Denial of Service Attacks: One of the most common methods of blocking a 'denial of service' attack is to set up a filter or *sniffer* on a network before a steam of information reaches a site's web servers. The filter can look for possible derimental attacks by noticing patterns or identifiers contained in the information. If a pattern comes in frequently, the filter can be instructed to block messages containing that pattern, thus protecting servers from having their lines tied up.*

Deception

With an increase in the number of net users, the net business is booming. If free access to online marketing is allowed, it is an ideal place for deception. Online frauds and deception are thriving, it is to think and check this detrimental act of deception. Today, there are inadequate checks and controls. Many unscrupulous traders, competitors and others practice the art of deception on the Net. There is a scope for forging digital signatures. Digital photographs and graphs can be copied and maintained artfully, proving detrimental to the original photographs and graphs.

Deception on the Net is something wherein a technical track is intended to deceive formation. Identity related artifices is the most common deception practiced online. Whether deception is open-ended or closed ended, depends on the definition of dishonesty and deception. When the person on the other end is expecting you to be one person and you pretend to be somebody else, that could be called *deception.*

Intrusion

An *intrusion* is an attempt to break into or misuse a system. An intrusion may be operated either by a hacker, script kiddie or unscrupulous competitors who access information without online registration.

There are network based intrusion detection systems which monitor packets. There is a separate device known as Intrusion Detection system (IDS) which is placed on an independent machine watching all network traffic :

Its features include.

- A system integrity verifier (SIV) monitoring files and
- Log files monitors (LFM) which monitors log files of the network services.

**Ibid.*

An IDS works with one or several sensors with the capability to listen to the network traffic. These sensitive sensors are located at sensitive areas and potential net connection points. The IDS has another device known as *console* which permits to process the events and services of the Net. A console is located ideally and safely within online security parameters using graphical interface security. It can also be located anywhere else on the Net.

Bugs or Misconfiguration

Bugs or misconfiguration problems on the web server allow unauthorised remote users to :

- Steal confidential documents not intended for their eyes.
- Execute detrimental commands on the server host machine allowing them to modify the online systems security.
- Gain information about the web server's host machine that will allow them to break into the system and
- Launch denial of service attacks, rendering the machine temporarily unusable, thus affecting the online businesses in a big way.

Browser-Side Risks

Browser side risks include the following :

- Active content that crashes the browser, damages the user's system, breaches the user's privacy or merely create an annoyance and.
- The misuse of personal information knowingly or unknowingly provided by the end user.

Interception: This is interception of network data from the browser to the server or vice versa via network eavesdropping. Eavesdroppers can operate from any point on the pathway between browser and server. This is the catching of message when it is put online before it reaches the final destination.

E-commerce may be Bad for your Computer

Encouraging customers to do their shopping online without any security leads to a decline in customer loyalty and referrals to friends over the long term result in a decline in profits. That is the conclusion of a report released recently by public relations research firm, the Bristol Group.

The report called '*E-business as the Speed of Life*,' concludes that internet retailing has not extended and strengthened the retailer's relationship with existing customers. "*The key to ensuring long-term retail success*," the study says," *lies in the relationship that retailers have with their customers*."

"*As customers have told us, it is still about how we make them feel*," said Jim Barnes, Executive Vice-President of Bristol Group, which conducted the study." *Our basic online strategy must reflect our commitment to genuine relationships and not technology driven transactional encounters*."

The study surveyed about 1600 residents of Canada and the United States and found that over 60 per cent of the offline customers said that are very likely to continue to buy from the retailer, compared to only 43 percent of online customers.

** The Financial Times, 21th Feb, 2000.*

Many Women not Shopping Online

Concern about the security of online transactions is the primary obstacle keeping women from shopping online, according to recent study from Cyber Dialogue.

According to Cyber Dialogue, online security concerns appear to be stronger predictors of online purchasing than any other factor, including internet experience.

The study found that among the 24 million online women who have not purchased online, 40 percent said they are concerned about the security of the personal information that they give on sites.

"*E-commerce marketers are eager to target women because they traditionally make the majority of household purchase decisions"* said Idilcakim, an analyst for Cyber Dialogue. *"Yet based on their online shopping habits, women are reluctant to seek product information or place orders online mainly because of security concerns relating to stolen credit card transactions, personal privacy and the lack of net regulations.**

Encryption

Origin: The Encryption concept, as we are talking today in the context of e-commerce on the Internet was initially used for defense purpose for LANs. It was regarded more as a secretive, and even an arcane sub speciality of mathematics and espionage. But with the advancement in sophisticated technology, it rapidly developed into a delicate science called *cryptography.*

With new and more global information criss-crossing the boundaries through electronic networking, cryptography is now being increasingly recognized by its necessity and utility aspect.

The science of cryptography has its history of atleast 4000 years. In the old cultures like Egypt, India and Mesopotamia, which were considered as ancient cultures, have developed courses independently. The oldest evidence of cryptology is an ancient inscription. It was found carved around 1,900 BC in the main chamber of an Egyptian tomb. They are in the form of hieroglyphic symbols than ordinary symbols. It indicates as one method of cryptography transformation of the text.

Nearly more than 2,000 years ago, Julius Caesar used a simple cipher system for the purpose of concealing military information. This type of encryption can be broken and can easily be detected by trying all possible displacements till the message becomes plain and meaningful.

For instance, consider replacing the letters of alphabets in the original text by letters that are a predetermined number of places away. Thus, the plain and cipher letters may look as follows:

Plain - ABCDEFGHIJKLMNOPQRSTUVWXYZ

Cypher - FGHIJKLMNOPQRSTUVWXYZABCDE

In addition to this, there are a number of other systems developed from time to time. For instance:

- Messages may be written backwards.
- Secret messages may be written horizontally or vertically.
- Adopting special symbols for the normal letters of the alphabet.
- Dots may be used for ovals and
- Greek, Roman, Italics and alphabets of other countries may be used.

Meaning

A simple way to protect from electronic snoopers is through encryption. It is a process which involves scrambling the data or message in a complex manner. The art of scrambling the data makes it unintelligible to any one except to the intended recipient. It is a process of mathematical representation wherein an algorithm is used to transform plain text into coded equivalents for transaction or storage. It is the sure fire way to protect privacy and security of communication on the Net.

The Encryption Process may Appear as follows

Customer names, addresses and credit card numbers are processed by complex mathematical encryption algorithms to ensure that only the authorized server to which they are connected can decode the information. The strong encryption versions of the major web browsers are secure, restricting entry by unauthorised users.

The Government of United States has classified the encryption technology as :

Munition like guns and explosives.

There is restriction on the strong encryption browsers from being exported outside the USA and Canada.

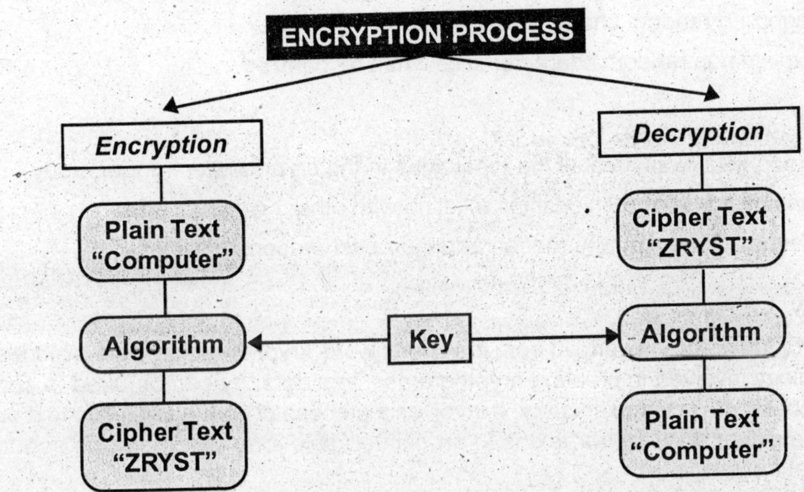

The process of transformation of the plain text into cryptogram is called encryption, enciphering or encoding. Only authorized persons who know the key will be able to get the original information.

The process of reconverting the cryptogram back into the original information is called decryption, deciphering or decoding.

In this age of communication, transmission of data does not take place only through the passage of text alone, but it includes text, audio, video, graphics, animation etc. Therefore, several crypto systems are also used for encryption. For instance :

For speech-Ciphony

For facsimile-Ciphax

For television-Civision

The need to use algorithms for present day encryption should give an indication of the specialised knowledge and training the job calls for. Encryption is one of the various security options available through which a password, account information, transactions and other formation get transmitted and is scrambled so that no one can figure out the key needed to access information on the Net. So, connection, encryption, firewalls, digital certificate, automatic sign-off, random pop-ups, disaster recovery sites are required to ensure security of business information on the Net. An independent authority will act for verification of digital certificates.

Cryptogram

Cryptogram means writing a message which appears to be meaningless to those who have no means or the key to extract the original text from the cipher text. A message written in code is called *cryptogram.*

A critical analysis and interpretation of confidential information without any previous knowledge of the system or key is known as *cryptanlaysis.* It is the science of breaking ciphers.

There are three important stages in cryptanalysis

- Arrangement and rearrangement of data to indicate non random characteristics.
- Recognizing random characteristics and
- To explain non random characteristics when recognized.

Cryptanalyst

- A person who examines all the messages in the cryptosystem under study
- Studies all possible relationships existing with other cryptosystems.
- Gathering all relevant information and their past present activities.

Cryptography

The word *cryptography* is derived from the Greek word 'kryptos' which means hidden. It is an art and methodology involved in creating cryptograms. Cryptography can be used to combat the problems of computer privacy and security. It involves a process of converting plain text or original message into the cipher text. Cipher text is in an unintelligible form which can be sent over any unsafe channel of transmission.

Crytography may be explained as a method of scrambling confidential information sending information, and then unscrambling it so that it can be read in its original form by the recipient party.

Today, there are two methods of cryptography in use. They are private key and public key.

Crytography is the artful practice of digitally scrambling a message using a secret key or keys which are used to unscramble or decrypt the messages.

The conversion of cipher text or the transmission of original information process is controlled by a 'key'. Any person who wants to access the cipher text, which is an unsafe channel of communication will need the key to be able to convert it into original information. Only authorised receivers are in possession of that key.

The application of cryptography offers effective means of providing security to information networks. Towards this end, simple and complex encryption and decryption software have been developed to protect unauthorised entry into confidential information.

All the users of internet who are in e-commerce sharing, storage and transmission channels are required to insure themselves of their privacy through the use of cryptography.

E-commerce is characterized by remote electronic operations between ad hoc trading partners. Data will be transmitted over open communication channels and in many cases, it will be temporarily stored and processed by a variety of computer systems under the control of external and often foreign parties. So, there will be no formal exchange of signed documents. In these circumstances, how can either party be assured that:

- The other party was a legitimate trading partner.
- The messages originated from that party and not an entity masquerading as the party.
- The party originating messages in an organisation had the authority to do so.
- Sensitive data exchanged was not revealed to an unauthorised third party.
- The data sent or received was not illicitly modified at source, in transit or upon receipt.
- The other party will not subsequently, and successfully, repudiate the transaction in a legal challenge*.

A public key Infrastructure (PKI) is defined *as a set of agreed upon standards.* Certification authorities, structures among multiple certification authorities, methods to discover and validation of certification paths, operational protocols, management protocols, interoperable tools and supporting legislation are some of these standards.

Cryptography has long been used to keep private data which is not to be generally shared. Many forms, implementation and strength of cryptography are available today. Regardless of what system of group is ultimately used as the global standard for supporting commerce and document interchange, the conversion of plain text into cipher text and back again is the basis of all digital security services.*

Cryptography has a proven capability to tag a document with a digital time stamp and proof of authorship. Staring a document in an encrypted form along with time stamp of creation, the identity of its author and message digest is necessary to prove that a document has not been altered. Therefore, it assures to store any document on any system.

Thus, cryptography ensures that servers, laptops and browsers can all accurately identify each other.

Again, cyptography has the capability to lay the foundation of an e-commerce infrastructure. It is one of the most used security technologies which covers activities relating to security messages, authentication, digital signature and electronic money.

---

* *Dataquest, Nov., 15, 1999, pp. 128-129.*

Types of Cipher Systems

Though there are many variations in the cipher system, but in practice, there are only two popular types of cipher systems.

Transposition Cipher Systems: Transposition is a process of causing letters of the plain text to change places. It involves rearrangement in the sequence of the letter of the plain text information. By this, it will not change their identity.

Substitution Cipher Systems: Substitution cipher system involves replacement of the plain text letters by other letters or symbols. In this, there will not be any change in their sequence.

These two cipher systems may be combined to form a *single crypto system.*

Code System

The code system involves words, letters, symbols etc. which are used for secret messages or for presenting, transmitting or recording information. It is a system of rearrangement of signals used to send messages by electronic means. It is a special form of substitution. Coding system involves replacement of words, phrases or sentences of the plain text by the arbitrarily selected equivalents, which may be other words, phrases, group of words, figures or some other combination.

There is a separate code book which may be used by the person who wants to convert his text into a code system. The code book contains the words, phrases, and sentences of the vocabulary which are listed in an orderly and systematic manner. The code book is also accompanied by their equivalent code groups. For sure security and privacy, organisations may formulate their own codes for their own use.

Cryptology

This is a method to design and unitrate the analysis of codes and ciphers.

Cipher

It is a secret writing in which a set of letters or symbols are used to represent the same to others. Ciphers are codes. Encryped message is known as the cipher text. It is an encoded message content hidden from external users.

Decipher

It is a process of converting the coded message in an understandable form.

Jumbling

The simplest way of encoding a message is the jumbling of letters and words in any message transmission. Jumbling up the information is one of the methods wherein once the data is jumbled, it cannot easily be understood. Jumbling is a process of mixing the data or message in a confused form. In a mixed collection of data, it is not possible to find meaningful content.

It is a process of scrambling. The unscrambling of the jumbled mixed message to enable them to make sense could be done quickly, slowly or laboriously, depending upon the sharpness or lack of intelligence of those who are doing it. The scrambling of data is to be very complicated if the purpose of encoding is to make the message wholly indecipherable to everyone except to the sender transmitting the message and the person receiving the message.

Asymmetric Crypto System

The term 'Asymmetric Crypto System' relates to electronic transactions in e-commerce practice. In e-commerce activities, electronic record is used which is generated, communicated, received or stored by electronic, magnetic, optical or other means. In these records, recorded, digital signatures or electronic signatures are used with the application of the asymmetic crypto system. The system is capable of generating a secure key pair. The pair consists of two keys namely private key and public key. A private key is used for creating a digital signature and public key is used to verify the digital signature.

Data Encryption Standard (DES)

These are standards of both commercial and defense applications. The production of encryption includes activities like developing and testing which are incredibly difficult and expensive.

IBM developed the data encyption standards algorithm which specified a method for encrypting 64- bit blocks to plain text into corresponding 64- bit blocks of cipher text. It employs a user specified 56 bit key. The DES is capable to double or triple encrypted data for additional security.

The mathematical presentation of plain text or algorithm uses a key. A key is made up of bits of information. They are called binary bits or digits or codes which have the value of '0' and '1'.

8 bit combinations of the keying variables are possible. The keying variable can be changed when required. The system of algorithm seems to be highly secured. Those using DES have found it a reliable standard of application.

Under this standard, operating at one try per micro second may need 2284 years to break the code.

DES is more useful in the following cases :

- In the design, generation and verification of personal identification numbers.
- DES algorithm is used in message authentication.
- DES assures a high degree of security for e-commerce threats.
- DES permits lengthening a key to 128 bits.
- DES is based on an algorithm and key. The algorithm is a complex interactive process.

Types of Bit Keys

- A 8 bit key has 256 possible values
- 40 bit encryption
- 56 bit key has 72 quadrillian combinations. The 56 bit encryption has been recognized as data encryption standard.
- 120 bit encryption and
- 128 bit encryption.

Certificate Based Security

Certificate: The word 'certificate' relates to a concept of electronic financial transaction associated with certificate authority. It governs certificate of transactions. A certificate is also called Digital ID. In a secure electronic transaction (SET), certificate is a public key that has been digitally signed by a trusted authority i.e. a financial institution, which identifies the user of the public key. The function of SET, a certificate is a public key that has been digitally signed by a trusted authority i.e. a financial institution which identifies the users of the public key. The function of SET is to use certificates to encrypt payment information.

An electronic identity certificate is used in the shopping cart in which the SSL technology was implemented in many shopping cart style sites.

The certificate acts as a signature to verify that a secure web server is from the company.

Digital certificates are a crucial part of internet trust service behind e-commece service. They combine ease of use of password based access control with security of public key cryptography.

The digital certificates issued by the Certificate Authority (CA) should be trusted by all major browsers and mail applications such as Microsoft, Netscape and other vendors.

A Certificate means a *record issued for the purpose of supporting digital signatures which purports to confirm the identity or other significant characteristics of the person who holds a particular key pin.*

Certificate Authority

A service provided by the bank in the electronic payment is called Certification Authority (CA). It digitally signs public keys sent to the bank by a web browser or the merchants' server software.

In other words, the certificate authority means *a person or an organisation that issues certificates* indicating secure transaction. The authority may follow specific practices adopted and applying them in issuing certificate. The practice is called the *certification practice statement.*

The mechanism of Secure Server Certificate (SSC) is intended to verify the customers. A company has the right to use the domain presented to the browser by the SSL secure server. The object of verification of name is to prevent a third party from accepting orders.

There are a very few global certification authorities (CAs) such as Globalsign, Thawte and Veri Sign. These CAs, after following the verification procedure, issue secure server certificates. Generally, they issue certificates following after the administrative procedure, paperwork and verification of articles of incorporation to verify the identity of the customers.

Thawte Certification: It is a world web of trust (WOT) which spans about 30 countries. The web of trust is the first free, global trusted personal certificate system. It can be used for secure e-mail with Netscape, Microsoft and Mail clients. The WOT is a unique community driven certification system based on ID validation. Its unique feature is that is a bottom-up certificate authority compared to the traditional top down CA system.

Thawte was started in the year 1995. It is now the second largest internet certification authority worldwide. It has its offices both in the United States and South Africa with representation in many countries. Thawte certification provides certificates for signing and encrypting e-mail. Today in digital certification services, it is a global provider of digital certificate products, services and solutions that create security, privacy and authentication in e-commerce.

Thawte offers a wide range of certificate solutions that encompasses the following :

Internet Security- Software distribution

Entrant Security

E-mail security and

Enterprise PKI requirements

Thawte's certificates are recognized and trusted by the majority of e-mail clients on the Net. Thawte is a global certificate authority that has issued SSL certificates to nearly 40 percent of the world's active internet e-commerce web servers. It has also issued thousands of certificates for secure e-mail. Its web site address is http :// www. thawte.com.

The following types of products and services are offered by Thawte :

1. Web Server Certificate: It issues trusted SSL web server certificate which are used to secure and authenticate websites ensuring secure e-commerce across the Net.

2. Chained CA Programme: This product and service is meant for those organisations that need complete control of the certificate issuing process. Thawte is a specialised authority which offers trust delegation or cross certification.

3. Developer Certificate: It also issues certificates for developers. They can use these certificates to sign their Java or Active-x software for distribution across the Net. These certificates are compatible with Microsoft Authentic code specification and Netscape code signing.

4. Personal Certificate: Individuals can also use digital certificates for web authentication as well as e-mail signing on the e-mail encryption. This facility is available in the case of web browsing and e-mail clients using Microsoft, Netscape and other vendors. The system of personal certificates permits individuals to manage their own certificates.

5. Globalsign Certification: Globalsign is the leading European trusted network of certification authorities which signs and manages digital certificates. It offers certification authorities products and services which enable individuals and organisations to secure personal and business transactions taking place across communication networks like internet and intranet through the use of digital certificates.

The web site address is http :// www. glowsign.net/prod/personalsign/index.html.

6. Verisign Certification: Verisign is also a digital certificate provider (DCP). It is one of the leading providers of digital authentication products and services. Versign offers a free trial digital ID for use to positively identify and receive encrypted messages from business assoiciates, friends and online services when we use secure e-mail.

The web site address is : http : // www.verisign.com/client/index.html

Like Thawte, Verisign is also the certificate authority rendering digital certificate services.

Certification Authority — A Trustee: A certification authority (CA) is a person or organisation created to facilitate electronic. transmission for secure e-commerce. It has been considered and treated as a trustee. It is formed to manage the affairs of the authority for the benefit and confidence of the parties. It is an office of trust like a bank or an insurance company. It is a trustee in a real sense of the word, because it is not vested with the ownership of the trust. So, a CA acts as trustworthy system in giving secure services.

A trustworthy system means computer hardware, software and procedures that:

- Are reasonably secure from intrusion and misuse.
- Provide a reasonable level of availability, reliability and correct operation.
- Are reasonably suited to performing their intended functions and
- Adhere to generally accepted security procedures.

Ec Builder Solution

The Ec Builder multi-active software provides a security solution by means of a certificate. X 509 offers certificate-based security to ensure personal data security and credit card information cannot be available to anybody else while in transit across the Net.

The certificate serves as an electronic credential over the Net for individuals and computer services (web sites). These certificates are used in the same way as birth certificate, the passports or driver's license to validate the indentity of the individual for website access, communication and e-commerce.

An individual wishing to send an encrypted message applies for a digital certificate from a certificate authority who subsequently issues an encrypted digital certificate containing the applicant's public key and variety of other information pertaining to his identification. The authority makes its own public key readily available through print publicity or perhaps on the Net.

The recipient of an encrypted message uses the CA's public key to decode the digital certificates attached to the message, verifies it as issued by the authority and then obtains the sender's public key and identification related information held within the certificate. With this information, the recipient can send an encrypted reply. The most widely used standard certificate is OS X.509 technology standard for defined digital certificates. This standard for digital certificate binds the identity of a person or organisation to our electronic identification key. The digital certificate contains information about its owner, its issuer and expiry date, stamp and information for verifying the integrity of the certificate that can be useful for digital IDS, digital signatures and electronic fingerprints.

Digital Certificate

A digital certificate is an electronic certificate. The basic requirement for successful e-commerce is to ensure integrity of online transactions to the customers. It means that the security solutions must assure the following :

- To verify authenticity of the information on the website.
- To secure the submission of confidential customer information and
- To prevent from denying any transaction by either of the party.

Digital certificate plays a major role in securing online customer's financial transactions. X.509 is the popular digital certificate. The purpose of a digital certificate is to serve as an electronic substitute for a sealed envelope or signature when sending messages across the Net. Its features include :

- The digital ID decides in browsers only or e-mail software
- Permits to sign digitally and encrypt e-mail and
- Client certificate ensures integrity of shoppers' information.

What is a Client Certificate

Obtaining a client certificate is necessary to ensure integrity of the shopper's sensitive personal financial information.

The certificate is used for two purposes : encrypting and verifying.

A private key is used to decrypt sensitive financial information of the shopper, which is usually sent by e-mail. The credit card is secured by it. Thus, client certificate is used for the encrypting purpose. Similarly, the client certificate is also used for enabling the shoppers to verify the authenticity of a supplier.

There are digital certificates issue providers such as Verisign, Thawte and Globalsign which have been dealt with earlier.

Digital Signature and Electronic Signature

Signature denotes a person's name written by himself. Where the law or the procedure requires a signature of a person, it is to be written. It is a method used to identify a person and to indicate that person's approval of the information mentioned in the document.

A digital signature has become common practice in e-commerce. It is an electronic signature consisting of a transformation of an electronic record using asymmetric cryptosystem. It has a hash function, so that the person having the initial untransformed electronic record and the signer's public key can accurately determine:

- Whether the transformation was created using the private key that corresponds to the signer's public key and
- Whether the initial electronic record has been altered since the transformation was made.

The expression 'electronic signature' is also popular in use. An electronic signature means any letters, characters or other symbols in digital form attached to or logically associated with an electronic record. Such a signature is executed or adopted with the intention of authenticating or approving the electronic record.

On the other hand, an electronic record means a record generated, communicated, received or stored by electronic, magnetic, optional or other means in an information system. It also includes records for transmission from one information system to another system. A party in the electronic transaction of online business signed or signature to any electronic record means any symbol methodology or procedure employed or adopted, by a person with the intention of authenticating a record, including electronic or digital methods.

A digital signature is to be verified. To verify digital signature means to determine accurately whether :

- The digital signature is created using the private key in relation to the public key and
- The record is not altered since the creation of a digital signature.

How to Ensure Secure Electronic Signature

Privacy, security or authentication is to ensure the signature by following these security procedures. The procedure involves the following two steps :

- Verification of a particular electronic record relating to a specific person and
- Detecting error in the communication, content or storage of an electronic document from a specific point.

A prescribed security procedure of a commercially reasonable security procedure is generally agreed mutually by the parties involved and whether they are followed or applied.

A signature can be considered as a secure electronic signature when it is:

- unique to the person using it.
- capable of identifying such a person.
- created in a manner under the sole control of the person using it and
- is linked to the electronic record to which it relates. It means there is a change in the record, then the electronic signature will become invalid.

Message Digest: A *message digest* is a fixed length digital with signature of a variable length data stream. It is a highly secure version of the venerable check sum unique value. The authentication through a digital signature is possible by putting the message through a computation which produces a unique value called a *message digest*. This unique value of the message digest is encrypted with a private key and then appended to the message.

When the message is received at the destination, the receiving person at the end performs the same computation on the message to obtain the digest. So, the process of decrypting the digital signature using the public key makes it possible to compare the two and ascertain the orign of the message and that it has not been altered.

E-Commerce Security Solutions

Introduction

E-business pace setters have to prevent unauthorised access and open the new media effectively to the customers and trading partners but closed strongly to intruders, It may be called *e-business paradox.* Businesses evolving e-transactions must be opened and closed at the same time. It means open to sharing information with trading partners and customers and closed to hackers, mall contents and other intruders. Creating IT- security culture and infrastructure that straddles this fine line can mark the difference between an e-business, page setters and a laggard security is the foundation of everything.

If businesses that use the Net for mechants cannot convince their customers and partners that their information is secure, then the whole idea of e-commerce is at risk. There is no question that e-business is big business. IT security is becoming top priority. IT-based aspects like network security, technologies, products and services, e-commerce, software enterprise, resource planning applications and other strategic areas are to be addressed.

There is a wider than ever assortment of tools that go beyond standard firewalls and user password. As the business world is thinking about Information technology security which gets more sophisticated, so do the products. Some tools such as digital certificate and intrusion detection system show some particular promise. Security is a key enabler of e-business and under the same time, business has to understand that security is not a paranoia.

Security conscious business must invariably give insight into the tactics and long-term business strategies. IT security permeates every fact of business by using a wide range of assortment assets.

The IT-based infrastructure, products and services may include a software suit from internet security systems that collects and integrates data from multiple points in the organisation and from other security tools such as firewalls, intrusion and vulnerability detection systems. Multiple internal and external firewalls are more secure. The strategy should be to use encryption for all external communication like e-mail TCP/IP. It is need to build security tools for all the hardware and software platforms and adopt authentication tokens to strengthen the security of internet offerings and PC - based fund transfer services.

In addition to them, various other products and services may include single sign on access control software, virus scanners for multiple platforms and lock down checks to prevent hardware thefts. It is a matter of concern that security and privacy touches all aspects and IT including keeping the infrastructure running making new product purchases and granting access to certain applications.

Internet, digital signature, cryptography, web security etc. are frequently asked questions. It is the common question from the customers that how do I know I am secure. Therefore, the Herculean challenge for e-commerce is ensuring that the global transactions are secure. There are many agencies, people, government agencies, companies and competitors etc. who are capable of intercepting transmission overseas. Protecting overseas transmission encryption will become particularly important in developing e-commerce exponentially.

In order to protect data and information, the asset system must encrypt absolutely and everything when it is put on transmission with the strongest encryption. It is utmost important that businesses take a holistic approach to security and develop all security solutions as an integral part of every application. The technique of encryption is the mature part of all sensitive web transactions. Digital certificate will work effectively over years to come. Information technology security is primarily important particularly in the financial matters because privacy is placed on personal monetary matters. It is the security that enables businesses to happen.

Solutions Providers

The following is the brief description of services and service providers.

Synto Net

It is an expert advantage for e-business. Its services include the following :

1. ***Network Serving:*** Network consulting and value service provides with a single easy to access service for networking needs.

2. ***Server and Security:*** SyntoNet provides server and security solutions. Appropriate security arrangements of this technology allow businesses to confidently use services and methods of working which enable the extension of business, without worrying about exposing it to additional risks. It provides a secure server and remote access solutions to effective firewalls. It has a feature of adoption of major new security architecture like virtual networking and public information.

3. ***Intranet:*** The design of the internal network is highly skilled and is a technical marvel which provides appropriate performance and resilience for any modern business. These are complex networking servers and application technology. In all aspects of Internet, Synto Net has designed LAN and WAN integration and the implementation of complex enterprise wide services such as e-mail and the world wide web.

4. Remote Access System: E-commerce access and secure control over the business data is essential. It is designed to suit all travelling employees or teleworkers to access intranet network services.

5. Internet and E-service: Internet presents enormous opportunities for the simultaneous expansion of business. It provides unique added value and reduced transaction cost when communicating with customers, suppliers and business partners.

E-Locking Technique

The Information security company provides public key infrastructure (PKI) based digital signature products and services. E-locking technologies offer strategies for assuring potential e-business. They offer two types of protection like products and services.

E-Locking Products

The products assuring e-business are as follows.

1. Assured Officer: One of the e-locking product technologies is assured office. It provides trusted security to business documents straight from the desktop, using PKI-based digital signature and encryption. The assured office product integrates right into the window environment to providing digital signing capabilities and security to any file format.

2. Assured Website: Another product of e-locking technology is the assured website. The product gives assurance to the end user by digitally signing the web contents on site. Another feature of assured website is that it helps the web master apply digital signature to HTML pages and the images within them to provide assurance to information on the web

3. Assured PKI: It is a product relating to infrastructures and is an easy to use public key inrfrastrucutre. The product will run over MS Certificate Server and MS Crypto API, adding value to it. It extends a simple GUI for issuing and managing digital certificates within the organisation thus eliminating the complexity of developing the PKI infrastructure.

4. Assured Transaction SDKs: E-locking technology extends solutions to assured transactions. They are a family of software development kits. They are designed to help systems integrator and software developers integrate essential elements of trusted security within business processes or applications. They help to provide PKI based digital signature, encryption and policies.

E-Locking Services

1. Security Risk Assessment: One of the e-locking technologies towards security service is in the form of steps taken for safety and security. Security risk assessment solution includes external vulnerability tests for organisations to help them access the level of risk they face from unauthorised intrusion into the internal or external business processes.

2. PKI Consulting: E-locking service by way of public key infrastructure consulting service helps an organisation to define its PKI developed needs and methods depending on various factors such as organizational structure, its infrastructure including the personal and the business application of PKI.

3. C A Houses: Digital signature is crucial for the success of online business including PKI developed digital signature capabilities which are essential but extremely complex to develop within the business environment. This task deters many organisations from implementing it. E-lock technologies help organisations that want to use assured office or assured web site products deploy PKI providing a certificate houses service. By this, the organisations will have PKI based digital signature and encryption implemented within their business process.

4. Customization and Integration: E-Lock devices provide customization of its SDKs and PKI, adding value to the existing process by creating a secure environment which is vital for e-business to be secured. E-locking customization and integration services provide a total security solution for organisations that want to implement digital signature and encryption technology within the business process.

PKI 2.1 assured PKI service as a critical foundation for more secure electronic commerce, providing the means to ensure authenticated, private and non-reputable transactions and communication. E-lock technologies provide various tool kits and SDKs to provide digital and encrypting facilities to application. It also provides digital signing capabilities for various HTML forms.

Netscape Security Solutions

New security and user management solutions ExtraNet and e-commerce is provided by NetScape. There is a netscape directory for secure e-commerce, a new integrated directory and security internet software solutions for companies building e-commerce oriented applications to complete the net economy.

The US department of commerce has recently granted verisign Inc, which is an expanded license to issue 128 bit server digital certificates to a much broader range of sites. Now online merchants, banks, healthcare and insurance companies and organisations including subsidiaries of US corporations can use 128 bit server certificates to enable strong encryption for all customers who either use the domestic encrypt version of the latest leading browser.

The following are some important US security organisations :

- Social Security Administration.
- National Security Agency.
- Information Security
- National Security
- ADT Security Services Canada, Inc.
- First security Bank
- NT Security and
- Forum of Incident Response and Security Team (FIRST).

Pryzone E-commerce Software Security Internet Transactions

Areas of Internet Security

Following areas of internet security have been identified :

- Communication security.
- Server security and
- Transaction security.

Security Solutions: Pryzone E-commerce software security solutions include three areas of internet security mentioned above. They are discussed in detail below:

Communication Security: Security in the transfer of information put over the Net is a prime security issue. Every user must ensure that personal and sensitive financial information such as credit card details cannot be intercepted. Such interception can give rise to the following issues :

Credit Card Details: Third parties may obtain credit card details for use from elsewhere.

Modification: Third parties may modify the communication messages, for example, have the goods shipped to a different address.

Confidentiality: Third parties may obtain confidential commercial information with regard to online financial transactions. For example,the identity of customers and the amount purchased of a particular product or service may be tampered with by the third parties.

It is technically possible to obtain a credit card information interactively from the internet in a similar manner in bugging a phone. Communications security issues and dangers are to be addressed on a priority basis.

There are a number of encryption systems designed which are in use at present to ensure information transversing the internet is not accessible to the third parties. The most commonly used security technique is the secure socket layer (SSL).

Server Security: Server attack is also one common type of security problem. It also equally deserves to be addressed specifically. A server contains many e-commerce sites which need to be strongly protected from being cracked. Lack of server security may lead to the following consequences :

- Possibility that third parties can obtain confidential commercial information with regard to transactions that have taken place, for example, identity of customers is disclosed and the amount of purchase of a particular product,

Some other instances are :

- That the server may be disrupted
- That the information held on the server can be destroyed and
- In case of integrated internet/intranet, the users can breach the firewalls.

Information held on a server is generally protected by using the Access Protocol. The infomation is inaccessible to the ordinary users. The update and administration of the site remains entirely separate from the public system. Thus, the information can be accessed only by the persons responsible for maintaining the site.

The following measures may be adopted :

- The merchant should back up the information held on the server regularly to an offline machine or to tape. In this way, the disaster can be quickly overcome.
- The merchant should ensure that the server holds no unnecessary infomation such as customer list or sales records.

By following both technical and non-technical measures, such dangers can be avoided to some extent. In this way, unlikely events that the server security is breached can be prevented from occuring. The possible damage can be quickly repaired preventing chances of considerable information being made available to the attackers.

Transaction Security

If there is no security for the transactions, it may give rise to the following :

- The third parties may impersonate a user / card holder to send spurious or fraudulent orders.
- That the dispatched goods may not be paid for and
- That the merchant may take the payment but may not ship the goods.

There are a number of electronic devices and systems currently available to solve the issue of transactional security. The solutions for these purposes are often referred to as payment gateways. This involves an e-commerce system sending a request to an outside source to obtain confirmation that the credit card details of the issuers are correct and that the funds are available.

As soon as the goods are shipped, the e-commerce system sends a further request to the payment gateway for the funds to be credited to the merchant account. In this way, the merchant's concern and the acquirer's concern are largely solved. Data cash is also a measure. It is such a payment gateway and contains full description of the data cash system.

Secure Electronic Transaction (SET) is a new payment protocol which may be expected to become more popular in the days to come. SET can be considered as an application, it is rather a protocol that software developers will use in developing the payment gateway.

PKI

It will change the face of online security, as such understanding of PKI is necessary. It addresses the role of strong authentication in securing the electronic business environment and building a foundation necessary to establish trusted secure electronic communication over the Net. E-security is essential for e-business and e-commerce.

The application of IT world wide has become more and more complex, placing increasing demand on resources. Encryption and authentication technologies are installed and are in use on a global basis.

Sierras Internet Solutions Inc

Its headquarters are located at San Francisco. It is one of the leading unified access management solutions for global 2000 corporations. The salient features of the company's product include delivering improved security and lower administration costs.

The above features are addressed through its Unified Security Management Model, ie. the Unified Access Management.

The Sierras Internet Solutions provide integrated suit of products and a full range of critical security services which are required for :

- Web applications
- Access control

- Single sign on
- Authentication
- Auditing
- Business rules and
- Delegated administration.

Clear trust products are designed for 24/7 security™ and emphasises enterprise scalability by leveraging the industry's only corba based security architecture.

The potential customers of Sierras Internet Solutions Inc. include :

- Bank of America
- Wells Fargo Bank
- General Electric
- Raytheon
- Fujit Go
- Ascent
- Silicon Graphics and
- Pacific Bell.

Clear Trust Secure Control™

It is an integrated web security management solutions, providing the following secure control services :

- Single sign - on
- Native LDAP suport
- Fine grain access control
- Authentication
- Authorization
- Auditing
- Business rules and
- Delggated administration for web-based applications.

The service is designed to provide the industry's most scalable and manageable online security.

Other Security Features

They include :

- By using clear trust secure control, organisations can build a secure global entrance by allowing partners and suppliers to securely access web applications.
- Clear trust enables organisations to provide fine grained access control to data and application for hundreds or thousands and even millions of users.

- It can also be used on the Net to protect online applications from misuse and inappropriate access and
- Its suit on intergity, security and management of product enhances and complements both networks and system level security.

It is ideal for the following levels of security :

- Electronic commerce security
- Extranet security
- Intranet security
- Web security and
- Supply chain security.

Securant Technologies

The organisation Securant Technologies Inc was established in 1994. Its main activity pertained to developing security of e-commerce. The company is the leading developer of software solutions that provide a solid integrated security infrastructure for e-commerce. The software of this solution provider enables the companies to easily manage a cohesive security policy required when developing secure electronic commerce applications on the Web or in an enterprise. The company's software facilitates the company to easily move their business online to create new revenue opportunities and improve their work efficiency. The company provides means for companies to adminster for environments scalability and reliability as and when required.

Unified Access Management (UAM)

In order to efficiently manage and administer security in the age of Net business, a new and integrated approach to policy managment cannot be ignored.

Unified Access Management is securant's platform for effective success and for managing enterprise security polices for today's electronic commerce infrastructure.

The basic features and benefits of UAM are as follows:

1. Integration: The UAM integrates existing IT infrastructure resources and applications to leverage investment in corporate data directories, public key infrastructure authentication systems and extends these components into enterprise security policies.

2. Unification: The platform of UAM unifies all aspects of security policy. The security policy may include :

- Access control
- Authentication
- Delegated administration
- Auditing
- Suspicious activity and
- Monitoring response.

3. Delivery: The UAM platform is designed to deliver security services cosnsistently across the enterprise, regardless of platform and technologies by using modular extension and an easily accessible user interface.

Clear Trust the Infrastructure for Secured Commerce: Securant's technologies and infrastructure solutions are designed for global 2000 organisations in the world and in a wide range of industries including :

- Financial services
- Manufacturing
- Telecommunications
- Healthcare and
- Government.

Securant's products are built on scalable UAM platforms and designed to provide tightly integrated functionality. They deliver extensible and flexible information that can easily be deployed as a company migrates to an electronic commerce model.

Clear Trust delivers an ingtegrated suit of security management products for a complete range of web and enterprise security services. Such services may include :

- Access control
- Authentication
- Authorization
- Auditing
- Delegated administration
- Single sign on
- Business tools enforcement
- Threat detection and
- Response.

Other Features

They include :

- The clear trust of Securant's technologies provide a packaged solution for heterogeneous web and enterprise environment.
- It effectively integrates the existing IT infrastructure.
- It seamlessly extends reserves into web and enterprise applications.
- It provides off the shelf integration with leading infrastructure technologies such as web server, LDAP directories, application servers, authentication systems, public key infrastructure (PKI),PKI-based digital certificates, database and applications development tools.

Its security solution is highly scalable and provides a reliable security servicing platform that can support environments with tens of millions of users performing daily transactions on a large basis.

Clear Trust Secure Control

In an integrated and policy based access management solutions, the software provides the following :

- Authentication
- Access control
- Auditing and
- Delegated administration service for web based and enterprise applications.

It enables simplified management applications requiring multiple levels of access control and is accessed by a large user base.

Security Check Points: A security check point is a testimonial service which the customer and the shopper enter into the e-commerce service. The security check post is used when the user changes certain pieces of the buyer's information. It is an additional layer of security.

RSA Data Security

RSA Data Security Inc. is the global brand name for cryptography with potential encryption and authentication. It offers customized security solutions built with the world's best encryption technology. The company is the most trusted name for electronic security, helping organisations to build a secure trusted foundation for e-business through these factors i.e. authentication, encryption and public key management systems.

The company provides the security needs of e-business and brings trust to the emerging oneline economy. By providing technologies, the RSA helps organisations to conduct e-business with confidence, that is using the RSA security technology in a big way or securing e-commerce and communication.

The following are some of the features and operations of RSA data security :

- *Enterprise Board Room :* It is a suitable solution and product that will meet enterprise security concerns and make networks secure. It is necessary to prioritise enterprise security issues.
- *RSA Secured:* It is concerned with user authentication. It provides solutions which are centralized, strong two factor authentication services for enterprise network and appending systems.
- *RSA Keon Application Security :* RSA Keon is a PKI-based application security solution. It helps in making sure enterprise application as safe.
- *E-Commerce Security :* It has software components that secure electronic data. It meets the customer's need for secure application.
- *RSA-B-SAFE :* It is one of the trusted e-security components. It provides a wide variety of security development kits that allows software and hardware developers to incorporate encryption technologies.
- *RSA-FAQ :* This frequently asked question about cryptography covers crypto law, digital certificates, algorithms etc.
- *Keon™ Certificate Server :* RSA security introduces the keon certificate server, a public infrastructure key. It offers services that can help organisations world wide, enable them to make potential business on the Net and take advantage of e-commerce.

RSA's encryption technology is embedded in Microsoft Windows, Netscape, Navigator Intuits, Quickens, Lotus, Notes.

Computer Security Institute (CSI) : In the light of the growing importance of privacy and security, an autonomous and independent voluntary organisation has been started particularly in other countries.One such organisation is the Computer Security Institute (CSI). It is the world's leading membership based organisation established in 1974. It is dedicated to serving and training computer network professionals on information technology.

Its activities include :

- Providing education and advocating the critical importance of protecting information assets.
- Encryption technique, intrusion managment, firewalls awareness etc.
- It undertakes publication activities like ALERT newsletter and other periodicals.
- Conducts surveys on security issues such as computer crimes and information security assessment.
- Conducts seminars on topics like internet security, Windows NT security, network security risk analysis, awareness etc. and
- Conduct classes to teach on the subject to meet the special needs of organisations.

Problems

They read as follows :

- The concept of encryption has not been given much importance even though much advancement made in electronics and information technology has revolutionised e-commerce.
- People in India do not feel serious to develop indigenous software. But the growth of e-commerce will spur the domestic market for encryption software.
- It is evident presently that efforts are focussed on the application side more and the encryption area is not considered as application technology. It is required that the country work out strategies and develop its own encryption software.
- Encryption is considered as munition
- The cipher text (key) may be cracked due to the lack of application oriented encryption software.
- Export of encryption software through the Net violates free speech protection.
- Lack of monitoring mechanisms on all internet service providers to check all traffic through its servers.
- Relying on imported encryption software leads to dangers. A foreign code may be cracked.
- Since there is no profitable market for encryption software, entrepreneurs are not coming forward which is a must for successful e-commerce.
- Internet service providers generally give assurance on reliability and optionally guranteed bandwidth but may be little provisions for privacy assurance.
- Even protocol schemes such as SET, SMIME, SSL and SHTTP have a common short coming, because each protocol addresses only a portion of the general need for secure communication.

- The response of the IT industry to making encryption technology is sluggish at the moment though e-commerce gains momentum.
- Restrictions unfavourable infavourable cyber laws and their inadequacy are not encouraging manufacturers and exporters of the technology as one of the primary e-commerce solutions.
- Lack of indigenous cryptography greatly slowed the velocity of international business and trade and delayed the adoption of e-commerce internationally.
- What is therefore important is to build one's own system to ensure security, privacy and the routing of content.
- Indian IT industry is therefore advised to make and deliver security solutions strong enough for the global electronic market.
- Government is not taking adequate steps to identify the ways and means of meeting law enforcement requirements while promoting the growth of e-commerce.
- Many people resist to establish online business, because it uses language that is alien to many businesses.
- Fear of stopping credit cards with payment not being made and the system failing over.
- Reputed internet providers are not being employed by the users, in highlighting risks to information avialable on the Net.
- The merchants are not to rent space on a server or to run their own server. Many users are at present renting virtual server space on American machines simply because they are cheaper both in space and bandwidth.
- Serious criminals, drug traffickers, pedophiles and terrorists are turning to encryption. If unchecked, this will make the law of enforcement increasingly difficult. Attackers, burglare, snoopers, breachers etc. are commonly found. They are all *hackers*.
- The other major constraint is verification of digital certificates. Such certificate verification is not set up in India to verify the signature. But now the third parties are not very keen as volumes are not very large.

The infrastructural costs of providing such services are quite high. The heavy costs are in the development of the back-end systems. It is not only neccessary to automate its front end systems which the customer interfaces with but also the back-end systems so as to provide robust functionality. The main infrastructural costs are for :

- Security software
- Internet banking software and
- Security hardware.

Suggestions

The security of e-commerce through the Net involves our attention on various issues in developing e-commerce related information and security systems to protect online data and other information being stored or transmitted. It is always desirable for each organisation to develop its own security mechanism based on various levels of secrecy to be maintained.

Allowing or restricting access of information to various people requires greater attention. At each level, confidentiality, integrity and authenticity have to be checked. In addition to physicial damage, electromagnetic interference, viruses, worms and other areas that need security include multiple levels of access, files media,channel operating systems, node to node local and wide area networks.

Therefore, no encryption technique is completely secure in all cases and cannot be uniformly applied. For instance, a 40 bit key code can be cracked by trying a million combinations with the help of a super computer. On the other hand, for fool proof security, it is always desirable to use a 128 bit code.

The interest of the e-commerce community especially through the Net is in seeking access to encrypted communications so as to ensure that there are no commercial riders, competitors, crime and acts of violation of individual rights. There is no absolute assurance, intelligence agents and riders would not break into a secret system. This threat would become greater if hackers, riders, criminals and other cyberspace burglary could further perfect it to make it unbreakable for e-commerce also.

Every organisation must think about the systems of their own that will be possible when the network itself provides security instead of having several services to each application individually and Internet-based collaborative e-commerce culture is compelling in its own right.

An effective and successful use of any e-commerce data security technology can be measured both in terms of the efficiency uitility which it brings to the organisation and the extent to which it enhances the existing global market and creates newer and more profitable ones.

When a business house is clever enough to design for its use, it will be the first to reap the benefits of the security infrastructure in the coming years.

An interesting feature of encrypting and decrypting technology is that the identity, privacy, security of the sender and the receiver or both should be assured.

Though the industry response to encryption issues has not shown much interest for the movement, it would increase once the emerging e-commerce gains momentum, rendering transmission security as a vital aspect.

Security Precautions in E-Commerce

Many business people and merchants on the Web think that security concerns might prevent e-commerce transactions over the Net. But actually, these e-commerce transactions are well secured on the Net. The key element lies in the perception and proper understanding of security and privacy of transactions on the Internet.

This topic is designed to have some insight into the security aspects of financial transactions. The security issues have been well addressed here as well. Business people need not worry about security pertaining to online transaction. The problem of security in case of transactions over the internet is not so special in e-commerce. As a matter of fact, there is no guarantee of security of information even in traditional media of transmission of messages. So, security issues exist in any medium in any commercial transaction.

There are many conventional ways of doing things, but still people perceive these kinds of transactions are safe, because they have been in practice for years. People trust that nothing will be done with information on transmission.

The following precautions are suggested for the security of personal financial information and other messages put on the Net. Following measures will definitely help the parties for successful e-commerce over the Net :

- It is always better not to provide a credit card number to an internet merchant who is not running his shopping page on a secure server.
- It is always desirable to send the credit card number through e-mail address irrespective of presence on the Net or on online service.
- It is always secure to give the credit card number without checking them out first.
- It is always good and secure to use the service of Better Business Bureau (BBB) or the internet fraud watch. Its web site address is http://www.fraud.org.
- It is always better to make sure that whenever credit card information is asked, the URL (Universal Resource Location) or internet location starts with :

  https : //

  In https - 's' stands for secure.

  So, when SSL protocol is in use, the internet location will start with https ://, instead of just http://.
- NetsCape 4.0 and Microsoft Internet Explorer are the two popular browsing softwares. It is always desirable to make sure that the browser also gives an indication when using the SSL. NetsCape indicates locked padlock and the Microsoft Internet Explorer displays a lock on the status bar, when SSL is encrypting information and
- Make sure that internet merchants are running a potential SSL. Merchants may have a special security section on their sites. Alternatively, the merchants may even highlight this security feature on their home pages.

Role of the Web Master

The single most important step that a web-master can take to increase a site's security is to create and ensure a written security policy. This security policy should succintly layout the organisation's policies with regard to :

- Who is allowed to use the system.
- When they are allowed to use it.
- What they are allowed to do.
- Procedure for granting access to the system.
- Procedure for revoking access.
- What constitutes acceptable use of the system.
- Remote and local login methods.
- Systems monitoring procedures and
- Protocol for responding to and suspending security breaches.

Security Devices

Security devices are used to implement security procedures for verification, detecting error or alteration. They are possible with the help of security devices mentioned below :

- Use of algorithms
- Codes
- lentifying words or numbers
- Encryption
- Answer back
- Acknowledgement procedures, and
- Similar security devices.

Public Key Infrastructure (PKI)

Public key infrastructure is the principal tool to establish a trusted path for electronic transactions. It guards against a variety of possible assaults like unauthorised disclosure of sensitive information, data alteration which damages the contents of a transaction or 'spoofing', creating illegitimate sites which mimic real businesses to steal credit card information. The classic protection technique involves the use of public key and private key cryptography. A key pair is generated for each business. The private key is installed on the server of a particular business and no one can access it. The matching public key of business is freely distributed as its Server ID. Customers will use the Server ID to encrypt communications sent to that particular site and the owner of that site only holds the matching private key.

Private Key and Public Key: The cryptographic method to provide security to e-commerce involves the key method. There are two key systems in security :

- Private key (symmetric key) cryptosystem and
- Public key (asymmetric key) cryptosystem.

Private Key: In this kind of security, the encryption and decryption keys are similar. To make it difficult to encode the key, and even using a powerful computer, it should be of a very high order. Implementaion of these keys is possible by Application of Specific Intergrated Circuits (ASIC) chips, wherein field programmable gate arrays are added on the chords.

Public Key: By nature, public key has essentially two keys. One key is used for encipherment and the other for decipherment. The key used for encipherment should be confidential. The code cannot be cracked by the decipherer unless he knows the key used by the encipherer. In such a case, in this system, the encipherment key may even be published like a telephone directory. The fact is that even with the algorithm for description, it is impossible to find the deciphering key.

Therefore, only the user who has his own secret decipherment key will be able to decipher the cryptogram addressed to him.

In recent years, effective algorithms have been developed for practising public key cryptography. This key can provide the following utilities :

- Authentication
- Access control
- Confidentiality
- Flow of information
- Integrity and
- Non-repudiation.

Working of Keys: In electronic transactions, the asymmetric cryptosystem is followed. The system is capable of generating a secure key pair. The pair consists of two keys: private key and public key.

A private key is used for creating a digital signature and the public key is used to verify this signature. A private key is a mathematically related public key having the proprietary. A private key is a key of a key pair. Similarly, public key is also the key of a key pair.

A secure certificate is issued by the Certification Authority. The subscriber identified in the certificate assumes a duty to exercise reasonable care to control the private key corresponding to the public key. He should prevent from its disclosure to a person not authorised to create a digital signature.

Public key cryptosystems are designed around the possession of both the private and public keys.

They are built by each entity, wishing to engage in secure electronic transactions and communication.

- Consider these points below :
  - A public key is known to everyone.
  - A private key is known only to the owner or creditor.
  - Algorithm is used to generate these keys.
  - Either of the key is used to encrypt a message.
  - The other corresponding key in the key pair will be able to decrypt it.

Public key cryptosystems are used to provide both the services of confidentiality and authentication.

- For instance, X is sending a confidential message to Y.
- X encrypts the message using y's widely known public key.
- Y receives message from X as encrypted, Y decrypts using X' s private key.
- A private key should be carefully protected.
- The public keys are made known to whoever wants it.

When a public key cryptosystem is in operation, the secret private key is not shared with anyone. A public key is not kept secret, as no purpose is served. The public key as a matter of fact should be made available to anyone who wants to engage in secure electronic transactions and communication with the owner of the corresponidng private key.

The Certification Authority issues public keys in the form of certificates.

Authentication: Authentication is the *process of verifying identity so that one entity can be sure that another entity is who it claims to be.* A public key cryptology is used to verify indentity of the entity.

Example: The following is an example which illustrates public key cryptology to verify identity.

Suppose X wants to authenticate Y. Y has a pair of keys, one public and one private. Y discloses to X his public key. X then generates a random messages and sends it to Y.

Random Message: Y uses hsis private key to encrypt the message and returns the encrypted version to X.

X receives this message and encrypts it, using Y's previously publicised public key. He compares the decrypted message with the one he orignally sent to Y; if they match, he knows that he is talking to Y. An imposter presumably would not know Y's private key and would therefore be unable to properly encrypt the random message for X to check.

RSA public key cryptography is widely used for authentication and encryption in the computer industry.

Public key encryption is a techinque that uses a pair of asymmetric keys for both encryption and decryption. Each pair of keys consist of a public key and private key. A public key is made public by distributing it widely.

The data that is encrypted with the public key can be decrypted only with the private key. Conversely, data encrypted with the private key can be decrypted only with the public key. This asymmetry is the property that makes public key cryptography so useful.

The private key is never distributed, it is always kept secret.

The key means that something has been encrypted or decrypted using either of the keys.

Privacy Enhanced E-Mail: With data or message put on transmission channel, communication security is of crucial importance as the entire channel over which information flows must be made secure. In case of e-mail, privacy enhanced electronic mailling (PEM) provides both encryption and authentication of mails.

Pretty Good Privacy (PGP): PGP is fast becoming popular as it offers encryption for privacy. But it does not protect authentication. Present encrypting programs are known as Pretty Good Privacy (PGP), which involves the use of 'clipper chips' designed to ensure legitimate secrecy. The clipper chip is a US government built encryption device developed by National Security Agency (NSA). It has a classified encryption algorithm.

Digital Signature Algorithm: For electronic funds transfer, software distribution and other applications which require data integrity, assurance and data origin authentication, a digital signature algorithm (DSA) has been recommended in the US as a standard. The DSA authenticates the integrity of the signed data and identity of the person who signs it. As said earlier, there is a greater awareness of the need for security protocols among the users in developed countries. In India, the awareness for security protocols is growing. The expected explosion of information networks only makes it imperative to address the issue of security on a priority basis. (P. Sekar, The Hindu).

Firewalls

Firewalls are an electronic device that blocks all traffic, then selectively allows only a few well selected items. A fence around the network is simply a firewall. There may be some well selected gates. The function of a firewall is to restirict access to the destinated points by growing non registered users.

Sometimes, security holes are left open accidentally. In these cases, firewalls need to be administered carefully. It is a preventive measure. It gives rules that allows specific types of traffic to go through the firewalls.

These are like doors in a house which restricts the entry of intruders. Any private network connected to an external link like the Internet needs a firewall which will allow friendly access and repel unfriendly ones. The worry is that will one be able to tell one from the other? That is one reason as to why the firewall is always supplemented by other security devices. A new firewall product tailored for personal computer users has just been released. 'Norton Internet Security' provides protection from hackers for networks and comes bundled with the 'Norton Antivirus'.

Firewalls are also security devices which are called as *access control filters*. These devices are put on the routers, proxies and gateway posts. The filters on routers work at the network level. Those on proxies operate at the application level. A variant and expensive alternative known as *'hybrid firewalls'* are available in the market. The sender and the recipient of the message will need to have the key for scrambling and unscrambling of the message. The levels which have gone into making encryption are very much a fortress to the eavesdropper.

Drawbacks: It has no capability of detecting anyone trying to break in. For instance, digging a hole underneath it.

- It does not know if the person coming through the gate is allowed in.
- It is not a dynamic defence mechanism of security.
- Firewalls are incapable to recognise any attack against the network.
- It restricts access only to the web server. When the web server itself is hacked, it cannot protect the server.
- Firewalls can only watch on the boundary of a network and not beyond it. Most of the problems related to insecurity arise from inside the network.
- Firewalls of the network see nothing going on inside.
- It watches only the traffic which passes between the internal link and the Net.
- Firewalls cannot sense the network traffic and cannot process the events of the Internet.
- There is no protection from firewalls at several sensitive areas and net connection points.

There are some secure internet and e-commerce protocols which have been evolved and implemented to increase the security of transactions on the Net. Three of such leading protocols are the Secure Socket Layer (SSL), Secure Electronic Transactions (SET) and Super Hypertext Transfer Protocol.

In order to exchange information over the Internet in a secured manner, Netscape designed Netscape Navigator and server products.

The SSL was developed by the Netscape considering the following three important points :

- The ability to secure (encrypt, authenticate and provide data integrity), TCP/IP connection using TCP/IP application level protection. Such protocols include HTTP, Gopher, FTP, Telnet, S-HTTP and others.
- Simplicity with reference to the fact that it can be easily used and verified and
- Suitability.

The SSL will be the most popular way of encrypting information to be transmitted along with the Net.

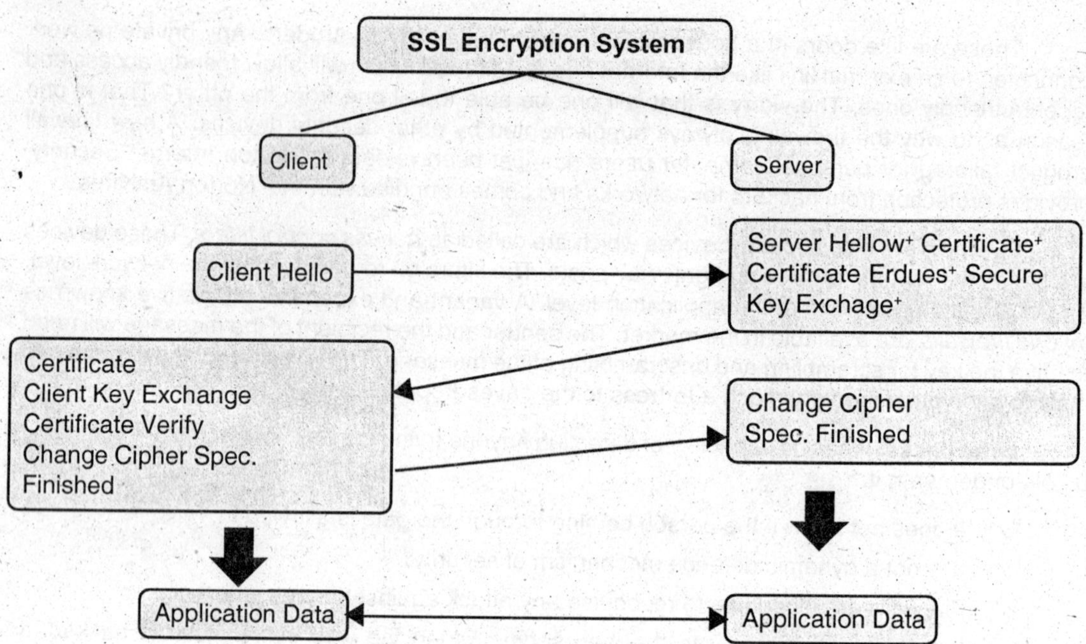

Secure Socket Layer (SSL)

This is a security device developed by Netscape Communications. It is currently the most widely accepted method for performing secure transactions on the Web. It is supported by most web servers and clients including Netscape Navigator and Microsoft Internet Explorer.

The SSL protocol provides several additional features that make it possible for use in e-commerce transactions. Here privacy is ensured through encryption while authentication is assured through the digital certificate. Although the information can still be intercepted by a third party, they will be unable to read them as they have no access to the encryption key. Authentication is provided through digital certificates, which provides the basis for secure e-transaction, enabling the participants in a transaction to quickly and easily verify the identity of the participants. Essentially, SSL is a secure key encryption nested with the public encryption, which is authenticated through the use of certificates.

SSL uses a level of encryption like the secure code to scramble the transmission between the buyer and the merchant. It facilitates that anyone attempting to intercept the message will be unable to read it. SSL is a widespread tool which is the best available means of securing e-commerce transaction over the Net.

There is a growing acceptance of SSL for secure credit card transactions. Booming e-commerce brings along new concerns regarding transaction security. The possible way out is standard data exchange protocol like SSL and SET.

Netscape Navigator, Microsoft Internet Explorer and Opera etc. are major internet browsers. They have included the SSL technology to secure web transactions. The SSL technology implemented in many shopping cart style sites uses electronic identity cetificates.

The SSL is the most widely used mechanism to provide full security and privacy for electronic transactions over the Net. It encrypts technically all communication between the server on the Net and the customer's computer, thus providing complete security. SSL includes protocol and maintains the security and integrity of the transmission channel by using encryption and message authentication code. So, it enables an order in a protected environment, protecting it from being seen by anyone else except the merchant for whom the message is intended.

The SSL server's function is to encrypt data as it travels between the browsers and the servers. A secure server is essential for any online store. Protection of credit infrormation in transit is doubful completely without SSL. There are chances that anybody may intercept the personal financial information put on vulnerable transit via the internet, thus proving to be a potential risk factor for the online victim whose functional information has been tampered with.

Netscape has designed and specified a protocol for providing data security layers between application protocols such as HTTP,Telnet, NNTP or FTP and TCP/ IP. This security protocol card provides :

- Data encryption
- Server authentication
- Message integity and
- Optional client authentication for TCP/IP connection.

SSL is an open proprietary protocol. It has been submitted to the W3 Consortium (W3C) working group on security for consideration as a standard security approach for world wide web browsers and servers.

The Secure Electronic Transfer (SET) is a protocol and an open industry standard developed for the secure transmission of payment information over the Net and other electronic networks.

Secure Electronic Transaction (SET)

The security mechanism of SSL is a low encryption standard, which led to the designing of a powerful new standard called the Secure Electronic Transaction (SET). Its draft specification of the standard was published in 1998 which was introduced jointly by credit card majors such as Visa and Master Card.

The primary object of SET is to help credit card members and those seeking transaction information prior to being sent over the Internet.

SET is a single technical standard for safeguarding the payment card for purchases made over the Net. The year 1996 witnessed a new turn in the security front. Visa International and Master Card International along with others made it open. In the year 1997, Secure Electronic Transaction (SETCO) was formed to implement the SET specifications.

SET uses 128 bit encryption for credit card numbers worldwide. It is possible to receive confidential, financial and other information from buyers and sellers, only if banks will need to build SET into their server.

In a SET transaction, the information is private between two SETs of parties. They are :

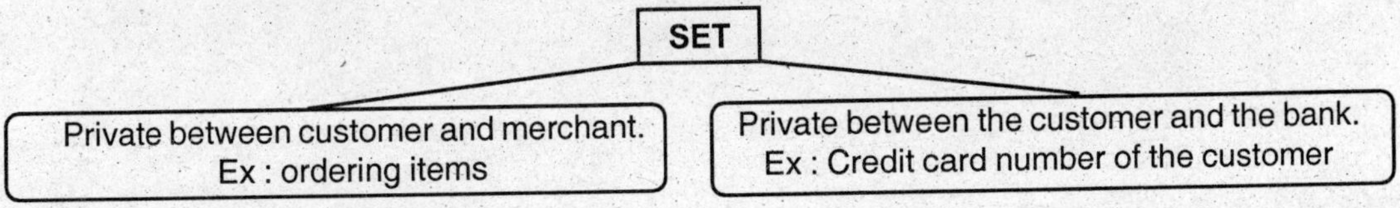

SET

Private between customer and merchant.
Ex : ordering items

Private between the customer and the bank.
Ex : Credit card number of the customer

A bank has its own public key and the merchant has his own public key. Information important for the bank is encrypted using the bank's public key while information for the merchant is encrypted by using the merchant's public key. Thus, it means that the merchant has no access to the credit and details, so there is no scope for fraud and the fraud is effectively eliminated. Besides, both the sets of information are digitally encrypted.

SET uses the public key encryption to provide confidentiality of payment information and ensures payment integrity. SET authenticates all parties involved in the payment process including the card holder, merchant and the acquiring bank to ensure that they are legitimate entities prior to the transactions.

Visa and Master Card have jointly developed the secure, cost effective bank card transactions over the Net. SET emphasises on the protocol for purchasing products and services electronically, requesting authorization of payment and requesting credentials i.e. certificates. It is designed with the objective of ensuring confidence in secure electronic transaction over the Net to boost e-commerce.

Advantages of SET

- It prevents payments from being altered.
- Confirms the identity of the seller.
- Confirms the validity of the purchasers' card.
- The standard uses digital signature, encryption and cryptographic signature.
- SET allows for the merchant's identity to be authenticated through digital certificates.
- It is not possible to use stolen credit cards through digital certificates.
- The merchant has no access to the customer's credit card number, thus another source of online fraud is eliminated.
- In the US, about 99 percent of the transactions are done over the SSL.

Complexity and cost of the set system are the two disadvantages of the SET.

Set Logo

It is yet another concept of secure transactions which displays on the shopping mall- thus proving to be an assurance that the merchant is using software that has successfully completed the SET software certification test. One should not forget to check out and complete the SET transactions.

Super Hypertext Transfer Protocol (SHTTP)

It is an open standard designed by Enterprises Integration Technologies in 1994. As a secure enhancing device, it provides general purpose transaction security services which are necessary for security in e-commerce applications like transaction confidentiality, authentication, message integrity on the Net and the non-reputability of origin. It supports end to end secure transactions by incorporating cryptographic enhancements to online messaging at the application level.

❑❑❑

E-business Communication

Introduction

In the age of instant global communication, information is considered as wealth and wide access to it is necessary. To strategically mention, the keys to such a source lie in the application of information retrieval techniques which have contributed substantially towards the emergence of new communication technologies. But the use of the word 'new' is not appropriate because technologies are not new, but remarkable developments have taken place pertaining to their application for communication. They are now available for mass consumption. These technologies have been defined as "*the acquisition, processing and dissemination of information by means of a micro-electronic system incorporating computers and telecommunications.*"*

Importance of E-technology in E-business Communication

The new technologies are those based on the silicon chip, the laser, fibre optics and the set of technologies known as electronic technology. Over the last two decades, remarkable developments have taken place in the field of communication technology, constituting an important and inevitable component of both written and oral communication media network. The corporate sector in India has also realised the potentialities and value added elements of new technologies for instant transmission of information. Many corporations, financial institutions, banks, non-banking financial institutions, production and service corporations have made significant strides in the application of communication technologies. The installation and application of national and international connections and the scope of corporate information transmission based on mechanical communication media has been further enhanced.

However, the limitations of old technologies in communication cannot be overemphasised. They have been practised in all organisations, whether private or public over a fairly long time. The availability of communication technologies calls for an early switch over to new communication technologies. The change, considering the availability, is indispensable which would not only enable the management to solve the problems relating to the qualitative improvement of transmission of messages, but also provide access to all. It may be more appropriate to mention that new communication devices serve as an aid for instant transmission of information, accuracy etc. and not as a replacement to the human element.

New technologies, both in written and verbal media, have a potential role in distance communication which has emerged as an important channel for external communication. Different technologies like telephone, teleprinter, telex, short circuit TV, Video cassette, dictaphone and many other telecommunication devices have been used in India for distance communication.

---

* *Gillman, J. A., Information Technology and School Resource Centre, (London Council for Education Technology)*

Modern communication technologies have the potential to bypass several stages and sequences in the process of development encounters in earlier decades.*

The use of new communication technology can tackle some of the basic problems like accuracy, cost, speed, quality and quantity in the light of the existing wide corporate business operations. The predominant methods of communication in many organisations have been through old and manual methods involving cost, time, lack of accuracy and the inability to shoulder the growing quantity of messages. So, the search for alternative methods became imperative in modern complex business organisations, where communication has to expand over a vast geographical territory-both in India and internationally.

Overscoring the traditional media, radio, television, computer, audio and video cassette, videotext, telephones and many mechanical devices have been successfully used as a means of communication in many organisations. They have also assigned management in decision making quickly and in discharging many managerial functions like planning, control, direction, motivation etc.

For all times, the business world must adopt new technologies for instant and effective communication to serve the community at large—this is taken as a social responsibility, it will be difficult to survive in the competitive conditions. In the light of the recent developments in telecommunication services, the corporate enterprises should use their potential to expand their area of operations.

Assumptions

The assumptions behind the communication technologies are as follows :

- *Equality :* New media can achieve equality in the provisions of communication reaching, particularly with reference to the geographical location.
- *Quantity :* It can lead to cover the quantity of population to whom the messages must reach. Mass media helps substantially in this direction.
- *Quality :* New technologies help to bring an improvement in the quality of the subject matter to be transferred. Accuracy in the quantity message load can be better handled by the new technology.
- *Economics :* It can help to reduce the cost of communication in terms of quantity information and quality of data.

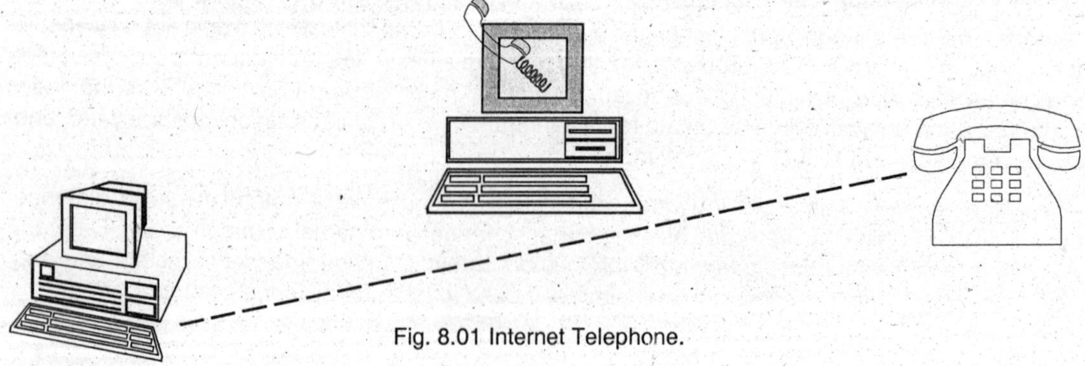

Fig. 8.01 Internet Telephone.

* *Natonal Policy on Education, 1986, Government of India, Ministry of Human Resource Development, p.22.*

E-business Conferencing

Routine and extraordinary meetings, group discussions, training conferences, workshops etc. are some of the essential activities undertaken in any organization to work out strategies to implement business activities on efficient and effective lines to survive in the competitive global environment. In these activities, concepts like brainstorming, sharing and exchange of ideas and problem solving techniques are closely associated. Sometimes, they may involve situations of geographically dispersed groups of people. It permits for real time meetings with people geographically scattered including the dispersed group of people.

Every organization has the following alternative techniques for meeting people who are out of town on business work :

- Audio-conferencing (tele-conferencing)
- Document-conferencing
- Computer-based conferencing and
- Video-conferencing

Audio Conferencing

In every business organization, there are some special categories of working people who are out on field work-they are called '*out of town*' people. These categories include executives, sales representatives, surveyors, dealers, outworkers, customers, doctors, engineers and others. Some of them are geographically scattered all over a region, state, country or even internationally.

A formal meeting scheduled with people gone out of town on field work is necessary for exchanging information, review of performance, quick-decision making and problem solving etc. The audio conferencing enables them to participate in formal meetings and discuss strategies to ensure good business.

The audio conferenceing technique is more appropriate to a particular group of people to meet frequently wherever they are geographically scattered and whatsoever is the physical distance between them. It is known for an effective communication mechanism from anywhere to anywhere and anytime communication across the globe. Status positions, monitoring of sales orders etc. can be exchanged and transmitted instantly. It is the audio-conferencing which is an effective and efficient means of electronic communication for interactive exchange, reporting about a project status, checking its progress, performance evaluation, instant decision making and discussing strategies for immediate problem solving which tend to crop up.

The day-to-day business activities and organizational problems, which otherwise used to be solved under conventional system in the early days by taking considerable amount of time, resulted in delayed decision-making and belated problem solving. As a new device, audio conferencing can be used to solve problems quickly, monitoring the progress and status and subsequently take instant decisions. The audio conferencing mechanism is designed only for voice transmission but it can be supported by e-mail documents which can be used during audio conferencing. Another important aspect to be known about this conferencing is that this mechanism and technology was first available only in the conference room but is now available on desktop machines also.

Document Conferencing

Document conferencing is also called 'audiographic' conferencing. This technology allows people to participate and meet by involving with their personal computers and telephone lines. Under this system, the mechanism of telephone lines connects the participants. Document conferencing is an effective means of communication technology which allows participants to share audio information and data stored in their personal computers.

Two important operational devices employed in this system are telecommunications and personal computers. One of the advantages of document conferencing is that it alloows people the facility of online editing of a document by several participating people in the conference. The second advantage is that this technology is more practical in the field of education. It can be used to extend the boundaries of the classroom of educational institutions and stretch out into the community. The word '*document*' in document conferencing may include a text, graphics, audio and video clippings.

Teleconferencing

The Concept: In this type of conferencing, discussions pertaining to direct communication between the participants is carried out via the public telephone system. It is an arrangement which facilitates speakers to communicate with each other in different localities using public telephone links. Participants of the conference located in different geographical distance areas can discuss issues by using their terminals that are linked together via the telecommunications network.

This concept helps them to communicate with voice and text in a big way. It is an electronic linking of geographically distanced people who are participating at the same time. Under this system, they are participating in discussions through the telecommunications system. It uses a two-way voice or text communication. Under this system, the participants can interact over distance in real time.

Meetings are Business: Meetings are the lifeblood of every business, whether one is exchanging information, reviewing performance, checking progress, making presentations or discussing strategies to boost businesses. There is often no substitute for audio telephone conversation but meetings can be difficult to arrange and expensive, especially when long distance travel is involved. In this case, teleconferencing proves beneficial.

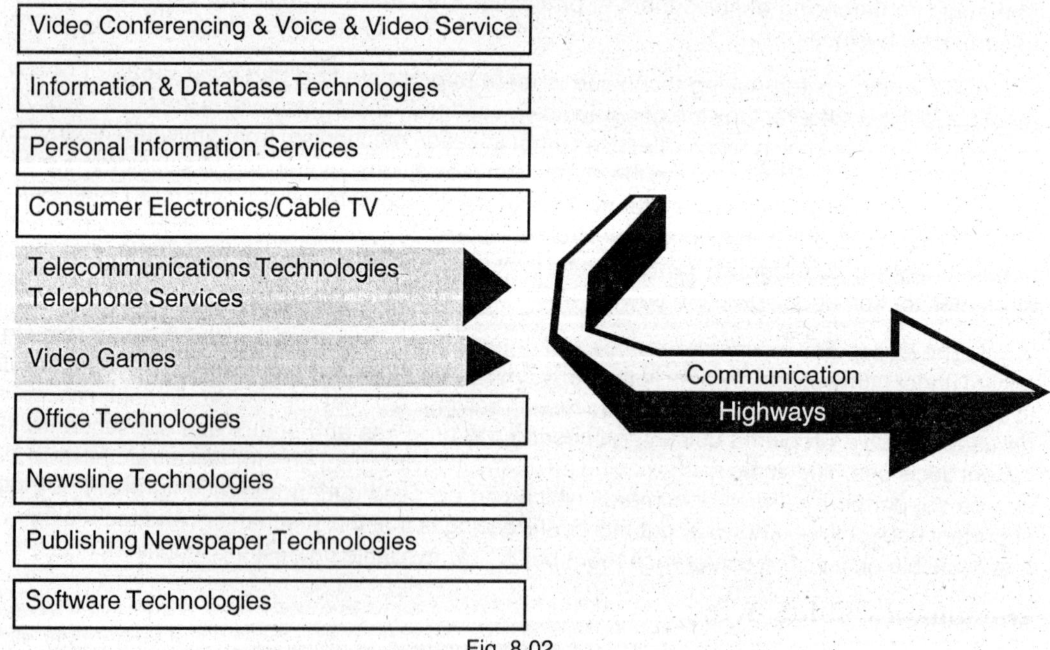

Fig. 8.02

Development of Telecommunication Technologies and Strategic Views: This is however an alternative which not only cuts cost and reduces major time on travel, but also lets one arrange meetings without the usual strategic dealings. The best alternative is *teleconferencing.*

In recent years, business organizations have started using the teleconferencing method to conduct business meetings with the concerned executives including customers, dealers etc. who are geographically scattered all over a region. For instance, a firm having a chain of branch offices, offers a network for teleconferencing service. The members or participants can go to their local branch, participate and interact in discussions with the other branches. It may be mentioned that an alternative to computer conferencing is teleconferencing which is an oral communication through a medium but without the presence of persons.

Participants in the teleconferencing can use facsimile devices and electronic blackboard which reproduces chalk impression on distance television monitors, picture phone meeting services and other communicating techniques which transmits opinions, facts, feelings, figures etc. over a wide distance in real time. This system passes papers back and forth to one another as they talk, argue, debate, exchange and interact on important points to ensure good business.

This development of telecommunication resulted in electronic meetings (T.V., Radio Internet) time on travel and business trips. It helps in face-to face conversation with the people at distant locations. The American Telephone and Telegraph (AT&T) Company operates picture phone meeting services, by linking all conference facilities that are part of the picture phone meeting services operated by the company. They are located in Atlanta, Boston in Chicago, Dallas, Los Angels, New York City, San Francisco, Philadelphia, Pittsburgh and Washington.

Sophisticated technologies in satellite communication have also been developed and expanded the range of possibilities for meetings, conferences and lectures. Under the system, it operates satellite teleconferencing which is a program of simultaneous sessions in several places or at distance locations which are linked electronically with speakers shown on screen television equipment. Thus, it facilitates the speaker to travel and spend less time by online participation.

Advantages of Teleconferencing

The saving of travel time and the cost of meetings is reduced and boarding for the participants can more than offset the cost of using the electronic technology of teleconferencing. Many organizations have been using this technology to hold national press conferences to answer reporter's questions. The participants can ask questions, seeking clarifications and get answers simultaneously in two-way communication with the speakers. Thus, this medium is being increasingly used by many organisations to initiate instant communication and gain potential business.

Teleconferencing offers the following advantages to the users and participants :

- Time of the participants is saved
- Cost and energy are saved
- Travel to distant places is avoided
- No monotony or fatigue and
- The tedious work of arranging and providing facilities for business meetings etc. are avoided.

Limitations of Teleconferencing

In teleconferencing, it is necessary that all the participants be present or be online at the same time. The system uses audio equipment primarily for communication. The requirements of all the participants to be online at the same time often poses problems. Under computerized teleconferencing, it is not necessary for all the participants to be online at their terminals or personal computers at the same time.

Computer-Based Conferencing

Features and Working: The electronic mail/message system (EMMS) electronically is a device which can be used to store and deliver messages which otherwise would be sent over telephone lines. The EMMS system is capable of performing a number of functions, among them computerized conferencing is one. Computer-based teleconferencing permits the facility wherein conference dialogues can be stored in computers. A participant can sit at a terminal or personal computer at a convenient time and call up any conversation not seen, make comments if any and reply to questions at his discretion.

The special feature of this system is that many participants can speak at the same time. Thousands of people at different geographical areas can use the system. The system requires that each participant is expected to have access to the computer terminal connected to the conference network. The participant can sit at the terminal or personal computer at the convenient time and call up any conversation and respond to any message.

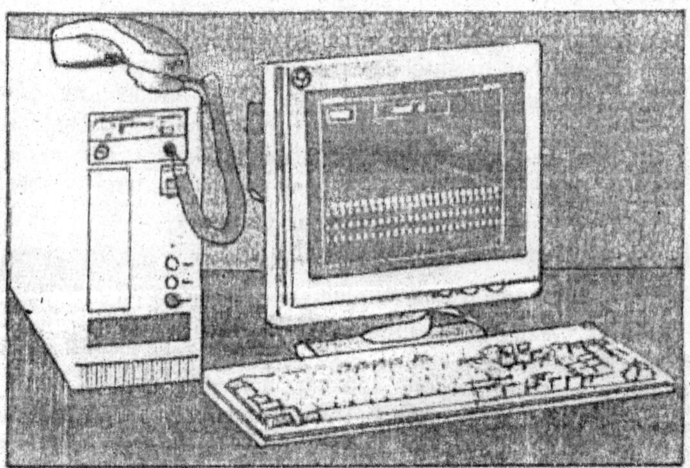

Fig. 8.03 Computer-based telecommunications

There is a database facility in the system possessing a large number of text messages. The conversation or message is entered by a member participant of the computer conference who can directly write his conversation, messages and comments which will be stored in the computer.

In, developed countries, computer-based conferencing is being increasingly used. There are many computer-conferencing networks developed for providing this service. For instance, the Informedia Corporation of Palo Acto, USA provides two computer conference facilities known as Planet and Notepad. Similarly, the New Jersey Institute of Technology, USA, offers conference services on their network known as the Electronic Information Exchange System.

In order to use this service, any member or participant of a group has to dial the local access telephone number which couples the telephone to a terminal. All the group members can share a file. Under these systems, the subscribers are grouped categorically according to their specific topic of interest such as technology, economics etc. A subscriber who is interested in many topics may join more than one group. Group members may belong to corporations, governments, educational institutions and other groups like hospitals, local authorities and non-profit organisations.

Advantages of Computer-based Conferencing

This system offers a number of advantages. A few of them are as follows :

- A lot of time of the participants is saved.
- A person can sit at the terminal according to his convenient time.
- It avoids extensive travel and stay as is seen in the case of conferences.
- It saves money and energy of a group of participants.
- They can attend other important works at the same time.
- It maintains permanent history of all conference discussions.
- The discussions are recorded and stored in a computer.
- It permits repeated access to any message or conversation each participant has already seen.
- When operated, it displaces all the conference entries which have not been seen and
- A person can directly read and write at a convenient time.

Thus, government and business organizations and educational institutions etc. can use computer conferencing profitably to conduct periodic meetings, transmission of various business ideas, opinions and facts etc.

Video Conferencing

Business Communication Tool: Video conferencing is a new business communication tool which helps corporates to manage the business environment and its key challenges economically. Meetings are the lifeblood of every business and organising them is difficult and expensive especially when long distance travel is involved. Electronic video conferencing is an alternative that cuts out the cost and time spent on travel besides arranging for these meetings without usual delays. The service is one of the business tools and many organizations experienced and gained its benefits. Conferencing of this type has become an essential ingredient in communications mix, playing a more major role in the overall communications strategy adopted by corporates.

Face-to-face Contact: There is no substitute for face-to-face conferencing for exchanging information, reviewing performance, checking the progress of the project and making a presentation. This is a potential online business strategy.

Global Communication: Video conferencing allows people in different locations to communicate face-to-face. It is almost like being in the same room even though the participants might be located miles apart. By looking at combined monitor\camera units a few feet in front, one feels as if his colleagues are sitting on the other side of the table. Without thinking about it, one enters into a natural conversation, picking up the nuances of body languages and facial expressions which are so crucial to personal communication. And thanks to the open sound system, everyone can forward their piece of massage without having to worry about cutting someone else off.

Video conferencing may sound complicated, but it is not so. Anyone who can handle the remote control of a television can master the technique of this facility within a few minutes.

Running Meetings as Normal: The video-conferencing services are designed to make life straightfroward and natural, besides enabling instant and strategic communication. One can use a flip chart or the electronic white board, show overhead slides and transparencies, study plans and documents and look at objects in detail. One can play videotapes and display PC graphics, see and hear what is going on and speak whenever they want to. One of the few things that cannot be done is to pass the coffee pot across the table, to his colleagues, otherwise the rule is carry on as normal. This technology is appreciated by both private and public business organisations in a big way.

Fig. 8.04 Video Conterencing Media.

Applications and uses of Video Conferencing in Business

1. Executive Communication: It helps to inform internal and external audience of a company's strategy, plan of action etc. Executive communications are greatly facilitated by video conferencing. It creates a greater impact on the audience compared to presentations on paper.

2. Privacy: Under this technology, conference proceedings are conducted with absolute privacy. The service assures secrecy of conferencing only among the participants. Once the meeting is ready to start, the operators leave the room, allowing the meeting to proceed under conditions of total confidentiality.

3. Sales Presentation: One of the primary objects of video conferencing is to avoid travel and get and do potential business. Video conferencing is a new business communication tool and business activities can be carried on across the table and across the world. This technique can be applied to sales presentation to offer sales proposals from remote locations without any travel.

4. Meetings: As a new business tool, it permits to run meetings as normal and makes life straightforward and natural. Video conferencing is one of those modern business tools which facilitates to conduct meetings face to face while the participants are far apart or geographically dispersed. It tends to produce highly efficient meetings among the staff and divisional managers. E-conferencing increases the frequency and effectiveness of communications among groups whose members are in differnent geographical locations. It enhances communication between the headquarters and field locations of various offices.

5. Product Reviews: This technology is more useful to deliver products to market at a faster rate. It also permits in product development and achieve coordination more closely in functional organizations involved in a new product development.

6. Project Management: The user can enjoy all the benefits of in person meetings. In product management, video conferencing facilitates enhanced information exchange while the members of the group remain far apart. It helps to manage products and business more effectively.

7. Training-Education: For every large business organization, video conferencing is a new business communications service device which cuts on the expenditures incurred by various organisations. The alternative to this cumbersome training is video conferencing. This facility enables online business seminars, workshops, conferences and lectures.

8. Inter and Intra Meetings: Video conferencing allows to conduct inter and intra meetings, by conveying information to internal and external audiences with more impact than paper presentation. This system streamlines communication between dispersed suppliers, distributors, customers and employees.

9. Remote Consultation: As a new business communication tool, video- conferencing provides expertise to individuals or project teams in remote locations without the need for travel. This is a fast tool for potential business.

10. Market Research: Market research is the lifeblood of every business. Video conferencing is used for market research\focus group studies. It solicits inputs from more groups considerably in less time besides obtaining the meaningful qualitative information usually associated with an 'inperson' face-to-face session using a cost effective face-to-face solution.

Fig. 8.05 Global View

11. Market Preparation: The application of video conferencing and its use is that it has the ability to make inperson meetings more effective. It gives an opportunity to have a face to face review of important items before and after meetings.

Types of Video Conferencing

Based on speed, there are three broad categories of video conferencing :

1. Low Speed: Low speed video-conferencing gives a good quality picture. It is most useful for smaller meetings of three to four people on each side.

2. High Speed: In this choice of video- conferencing, it is possible to involve six to eight people in meetings each side. In this also, best quality video- conferencing is achieved using strategic network allocations.

3. Very High Speed: This is a highly sophisticated service provided through the IBS carrier. VSNL in India offers the three options for video- conferencing mentioned below :

System

The video conferencing systems include a monitor, camera, audio system, video codec, document camera and network interface.

Electronic White Board

The video conferencing system can support electronic white boards.

Video Cassette Recorder (VCR)

The system permits to connect a VCR into the system to both play and record meetings.

PC Graphic

The transmission of PC graphics is another option available with the video conferencing system.

Multi-PointConferencing Unit (MCU)

The multi-point conference unit is an advanced switching system which enables video-conferencing meetings to be conducted upto four locations simultaneously. It is capable of supporting upto two simultaneous multi-point conferencing schedules and point to point connections.

VSNL, Mumbai Video conferencing studio is provided with the multi-point conference unit which permits simultaneous video conferences from New Delhi, Chennai and Kolkata in addition to Mumbai. Some high power video conferencing systems allows upto six conference participants to be viewed at the same time on two by side monitors.

Outgoing pictures are transmitted by using two single sensor colour cameras, which allow the images of six participants to be displayed via the split screen facility or alternatively the three participant images as viewed by either camera. The images are transmitted to the remote locations. Incoming pictures from the remote locations are viewed on two colour monitors mounted side by side. One monitor is reserved for the incoming pictures while the second monitor displays the local requested image.

There are two low profile microphones and two bulletin loud speakers. In order to facilitate private conversations to take place during conference time, there is a mute facility. The device of volume control enables incoming sound to be set at a comfortable level.

There is a separate device system equipped with a standby mode which enables both sound and vision to be switched off temporarily to provide full privacy during a transmission.

As a new tool, the MCU enables interactive conversation to take place with the help of full duplex open sound at wide band frequencies. There is a facility for use with facsimile machine and electronic white board which are general data communication applications, as there are auxiliary data ports for usage.

The system with various devices allows users to integrate video, voice and data traffic.

In addition to real time moving pictures in full colour, the codec can handle important document transmissions.

During online meetings, the video is switched either by voice or by manual selection. Control by the chairman of the meeting is also available.

Video Conferencing Systems

1. *Studio-Based:* Traditional video conferencing is typically very plush and boardroom surroundings come with considerable concerntration on room lighting and acoustics. Usually, it is a dedicated satellite or leased line communication.

2. *Roll About:* The first move to mobility is enabled by diad-up communication. Practically, considerations such as the weight of the equipment and fear of damaging it have limited movement in practice. It uses multiple ISNO lines on dial-up or switched service basis.

3. *Desktop:* It comes in two forms :

- A compact dedicated video conferencing system and
- A plug in option for an existing PC.

Though core standards exist, there is much jockeying for prominent market positions in the area of data exchange, annotation, whiteboards, computer conferencing etc. Two digital telephone lines are used.

4. *Video-telephony:* This service has been promised for so long but has not delivered. Now, merging with the desktop market, this has been made possible and it usually uses single digital telephone lines.

5. *Multi-Media:* This tends to overlap with desktop video conferencing. Multimedia concentrates on creation, storage and reply to online queries rather than deal with interactive meetings.

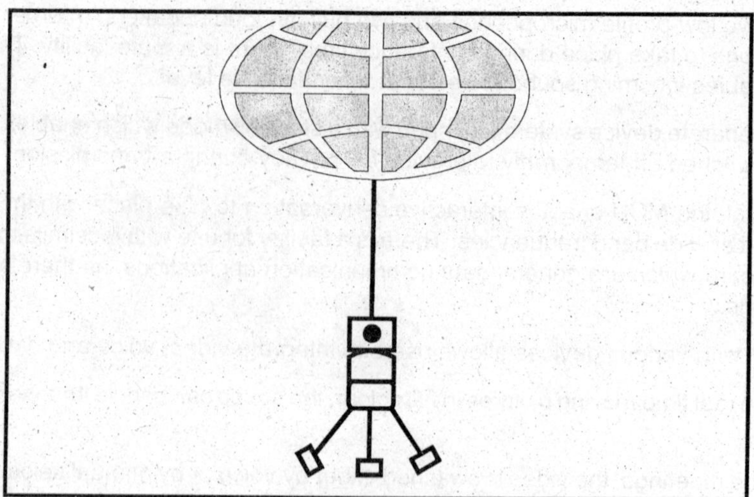

Fig. 8.06 Operating the System.

Advantages of Video-Conferencing

One can observe many advantages in video conferencing. A few of them are as follows :

- Presentation of equipment or products to overseas customers, colleagues, employees etc.
- Management and administrative meetings are conducted more economically and instantly.
- Engineering and technical discussions are more effective as they are 'in person' discussions, are cost-effective and face-to-face.
- Business negotiations are contracts and signing of other documentation works are greatly facilitated.
- The key advantage is getting down to business and the user will enjoy all the benefits of in person meetings.
- Video conferencing enhances the decision making process. Managers and other key people in different parts of the world can confer at short notice instantly and more frequently.
- The systems help to make more timely and sound decisions by sharing information more effectively and efficiently.
- It helps to interact instantly and respond more quickly to customers and react faster to market changes.
- More informed decisions can be made by exchanging pertinent information during the decision-making process. The device helps to convey oral, written and electronic documentation for review in an effective way.
- Participatory (involved) decisions can be made by including all appropriate or concerned people in meetings without incurring additional travel costs.
- It also saves from certain trips which need not necessarily be made, saves time, minimizes productivity losses due to travel, streamlines project development time and reduces information turnaround time. This ensures potential business.

- Face-to-face interaction is more effective and faster and improves communication between people.
- It helps to enhance company operations by boosting employee satisfaction through greater involvement and participation in decision-making.
- Video conferencing decreases the negative effects of geographically dispersed organizations and promotes unified corporate image and impression.
- It is easiest to use and work with the remote control for a television set.
- It's easier to master the techniques of video conferencing within few minutes.
- It is cost-effective. For instance, bringing in three participants from Chicago for a meeting in India may cost around ₹ 3.5 lakh, when all travel and accommodation charges are taken into account. In addition, potential time is lost in travelling and the subsequent fatigue. Video conferencing link to Chicago may cost around ₹ 60,000 an hour for both end charges.

Videsh Sanchar Nigam and Video-conferencing

In India, Videsh Sanchar Limited (VSNL) has four public video conferencing centres, which are located at Mumbai, New Delhi, Kolkata and Chennai. There are more than 450 public video conferencing centres in cities throughout. Europe, North America, the far East and Pacific Rim. In addition, thousands of companies around the world now have their own inhouse video conferencing facility centres.

The centre at VSNL allows upto seven conference participants to be viewed at the same time on two side by side monitors. Control of the system is by means of the infra-red control key pad. Outgoing pictures are transmitted using the two signal sensor colour CCD cameras, which allow the image of six participants to be displaced via the split screen facility or alternatively, the participants as viewed by either camera. The 10- inch confidence monitor displays the image currently being transmitted to the remote location. Incoming pictures from the remote locations are viewed on 27 inch colour monitors mounted side by side.

With either the graphics recall or preview, facilities are selected and one monitor is reserved for the incoming pictures while the second monitor displays the local requested image. This simultaneous display allows for continuity to be maintained throughout the conference.

The system includes two profile microphones and two built-in loudspeakers. A mute facility is provided to enable private conversations to take place during a conference, including a volume control device which enables incoming sounds to be set at comfortable levels.

The status display informs participants about the current mode of operations and the overall system status. The VSNL systems are equipped with a standby mode. This feature enables both sound and vision to be switched off temporarily to provide full privacy during a transaction. The system supports auxiliary video interfaces such as display station, camera and VCRs with selection via the infrared control key board. Full duplex open sound at wide band frequencies enables interactive conversation to take place.

E-mail in E-commerce

The basic factor in e-commerce is to have an e-mail account. It is a modern electronic medium which is the easiest, simplest and the cheapest way of online communication. Telephone and fax are no doubt most commonly used in conventional businesses, but in case of business over the Net, e-mail is the most promising link between corporates, business partners and the society at large.

According to some research studies, 97 percent of the estimated 110 million people world wide who access the Net, use e-mail. A full 90 percent of them check it at least once a week and two-thirds use it daily. As against internet users, 84 percent stated that they could not survive without e-mail and 56 percent have more than one e-mail account.

Practically speaking, in reality, the number of people who have access to e-mail are more than the world wide web. Similarly, according to some study estimates, e-mail use is infact growing faster than the web use. The advancement in sophisticated communication technology, which has become so pervasive in recent years, clearly indicates that no business is complete without an e-mail address. Besides, this gives the business a global presence.

The New York Catholic Bishop has even proclaimed that "*If Jesus were walking the earth today, he would have an e-mail address.*"

For effective and successful e-commerce, e-mail has many uses. The customers will use the e-mail for :

- Enquiries (information retrieval),
- Orders,
- Correspondence and
- Status etc.

Therefore, an e-mail address proves beneficial to every business to maintain contact with their clients and customers, twenty four hours a day, seven days a week and 365 days a year.

In other countries, there are free web-based e-mail services. There are also free nets in some selected places like libraries and other public places, where one can get free e-mail accounts. Today, many business firms and clients are using e-mails which are more cost effective to run businesses and this is like having a pay phone.

It can also be connected directly from home or office using a modem. An e-mail account can be obtained from the Internet Service Provider. In India, the Videsh Sanchar Nigam Limited (VSNL) is the service provider for the Net. This is the best source of online communication.

In order to accommodate certain contingencies, a permanent e-mail address can be obtained. In the following circumstances, a permanent e-mail address is more useful :

- Change of e-mail address in future
- When there are many addresses
- Using different e-mail addresses at different times and
- When an e-mail address is hard and complex to remember.

Under the above instances and to facilitate business communication without interruption, an e-mail forward service such as ***POBOX*** can be availed of. It provides a permanent e-mail address.

---

* *Ibid.*

When information or messages are sent to it, it redirects the same to any other specified e-mail address. It can also help to safely put the permanent forwarding service. E-mail addresses are now being printed on :

- Business cards
- Visiting cards
- Flyers
- Letterheads
- Packings
- Invoices
- Bills
- Vouchers and
- Corresponding documents etc.

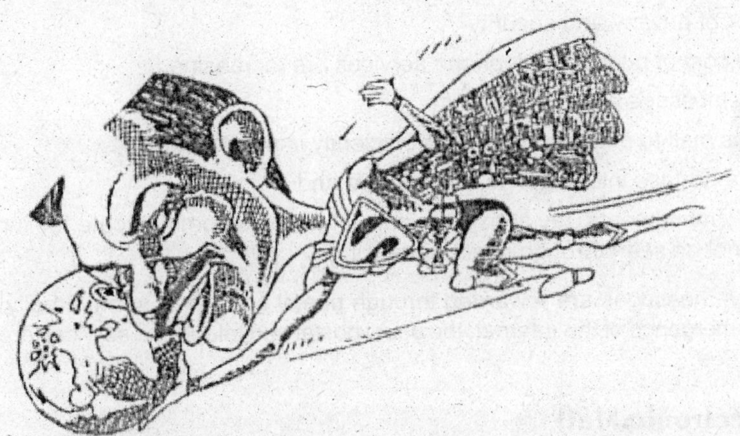

Fig. 8.07 Global E-mail Postman

Thus, an e-mail address has become a part of potential business identity like telephone numbers, fax numbers and mailing addresses.

It is the business practice particularly in case of large organizations to check e-mails every day. E-mail accountholders having more customers may check their mail twice or more in a day to quick response time. Normally, people online are also accustomed to contact customers by e-mail rather than by telephone.

On the Net, e-mail is voice, which has become invariably essential for being able to do e-commerce on sound business lines.

Like regular mail, e-mail is only done via, computers. It is a fast way to communicate on and via the Net. If you know someone's e-mail address, you can get a message within minutes, anywhere across the globe.

Problems of Conventional Mail Services

Conventional communication of written messages is by post and oral messages are by telephones. These two are administered by the post office and telegraph office. The postal department was separated and the telegraph work has been taken over by the telecommunication department. Postal department is an important department of the Government of India which has established a wide network throughout the country. But with the recent strikes throughout India, online communication via e-mail has proved a 'boon' in a big way. The conventional communication of post and telephone are associated with a number of practical problems. They are :

- The conventional services are relatively slow.
- Delay in delivery.
- Often messages get lost in transit
- The services are known for their inefficiency.
- The telephone requires the messages to the recipient to be available.
- Lack of interest by the recipient to receive calls.
- Frustrating game of telephone tag.
- Lack of privacy and security
- The cost of post and telephone services are increasing.
- Low message handling capacity.
- Mass mail to multiple addresses efficiently is not possible.
- Face- to-face interaction is not possible and
- Body movements, facial expressions, which also communicate feelings and attitudes cannot be seen through teleconferencing.

Presently, messages are fowarded through postal service or sent verbally over telephone lines. With the emergence of the Internet, the usual postal and telephone services are being sidelined to a certain degree.

Need for Electronic Mail

Exchange of business information between partners has been traditionally carried out either through paper documents or delivery by sending mail or messenger services. With the growing business, the use of conventional mail by postal, telephone conversation and face to face meetings are found to be inefficient and ineffective for smooth functioning of any business. Modern competitive business environment requires efficient exchange of information instantly, accurately and capable of handling heavy load of the messages. The e-mail system seeks to replace exchange of information by delivery of paper reports, samples, other postal mail services, telephone conversation and face to face meeting. In addition, these services are associated with high costs. The conventional services include courier services and speed posts by the Indian postal authorities.

In order to overcome the problems of conventional services, the Electronic Mail Message System (EMMS) emerged which is also called Computer Mail Message System (CMMS), electronic mail, global electronic mail service or simply e-mail.

The concept of electronic mail has been designed in response to the limitations in the conventional message delivery systems. E-mail performs many functions like message distribution service, transmission of documents and pictures and computerized conferences.

By whatever name it is called, it is a potential network that can store, transmit and deliver messages by electronic means. Because it has several advantages and overcoming the problems in the case of usual postal services, EMMS has gained much popularity in most of the advanced countries. Using telephone for message transmission does not ensure that the message reaches the recipient. The presence of the recipient and willingness to take and interpret the call in the same sense are the problems associated with it. The EMMS network has been developed with a view to solve some of the problems in the existing message distribution system.

The new concept or network facilitates the transmission of large message loads or information at high speed. Many devices like telephone lines and hook-up devices etc are used to connect distant locations. An Electronic Computer Originating Mail (E-Com) is the postal service system available in the Us. Under electronic means, the terminal or personal computer to the customer transmits messages with high speed, quickly economically and accurately. The computer or the receiving post office records the message of which is printed on the paper. The printed message is then delivered to the addressee. The advantages of this network are that it saves typing time, addressing the message to the concerned person and mailing cost.

E-mail is currently the most popular communication medium with millions of users worldwide. The main reason for the popularity of this medium is due to the fact that it transcends time, distance and more importantly, political boundaries. It brookes no authority to control or censorship perceiving to the data which is received and sent as it is .

The earliest form of e-mail was the telegraph. During the 1990s, telegraph lines spanned continents, dramatically reducing the time taken for information to pass between towns, cities and countries. The earliest form of telegraph needed someone at either end of the line to code and decode messages manually. This was a time consuming process..

This was later replaced by rapid tele-technology. Telephone and telegraph systems developed in parallel lines during the later half of the nineteenth century. In the later part of the 20th century. e-mail technology which has come to replace the earlier technology brought in some innovative changes. E-mail is the most popular communication tool today in all levels of business.

Electronic mail offers three types of services. They are mentioned below:

- The transmission of short text- that is sending messages directly to the recipient.
- The communication between users of fully formatted documents including graphics and spreadsheets.

The above two services are mainly used in the reference sections of high level academic libraries.

The third service is the use of standard forms for communication between corporations for specific applications such as ordering books in the acquisition section and sending reminders against the missing of journals in the periodical section etc.

E-mail is the most widely used application of computer networking today. It allows to keep in touch with the day-to-day happenings instantly in one's business profession and in day-to-day activities. Thus, e-mail has become a part of our daily routine. Today, there are tens of millions of people with e-mail addresses. It is estimated that there are about 40 million people registrered online who use e-mail for instant communication.

Meaning and Nature

The term electronic mail is a generic word used to describe any form of communication sent electronically, be it a short message or a complete document.

The abbreviation e-mail stands for electronic mail. It is also called Electronic Mail Message System or EMMS. In order words, it is popularly known as electronic message delivery system or electronic document distribution. The system uses electronic means, devices and tools to capture, store, transmit and deliver messages in the least possible time.

It is the electronic means of transmitting textual materials from one place to another place at any time throughout the globe. It is a paperless electronic means for capturing transmission and delivering of information, electronically sending and receiving pieces of messages, mail or documents. It is a form of electronic document distribution or communication.

Thus, e-mail means an electronic transfer of information pertaining to business documents etc. Therefore, this online mechanism is designed mainly for sending and receiving electronic pieces of text. In the present world of the wonders of electronics and information technology, e-mail is considered to be the first experience in terms of exposure to the field of data communication and networking. An electronic signal system allows thousands of users exchanging lakhs of messages everyday.

E-mail simply means sending messages and receiving back electronically to individuals or group of individuals in an inter and intra-office environment. The electronic system permits the users instant exchange of electronic messages across the world. In electronic frontier, e-mail is a widespread and popular way of communication. It is based on time and location, it is independent and at the same time, a non-interactive mode, designed to exchange information for the events which require wider distribution of complex information. It is easier to store and retrieve text in e-mails.

Until recently, the true potential of electronic mail messaging was limited by its proprietary nature, it meant different services to different users who were unable to communicate with each other earlier. But with the designing of messaging standards and their acceptance as the global standards for electronic mail, the final barriers to the effective use of e-mail have been removed, enabling all users to communicate with each other in a better and faster way.

The development in the field of telecommunications have come a long way in making the world a global village. India is also a part of this miniaturized scenario. It may be admitted that e-mail came to India rather late. E-mail, as it is popularly known, is the first value added service to become operational in the services sector. As a part of the liberalization drive in India, it has been thrown open for potential private participation. Presently, a few companies are offering the services which have been given licenses to operate.

In India, the e-mail service started in 1986, with initiation of Education and Research in Computer Networks Project (ERNET) and UNDP. Subsequently, ERNET started a small network of its own, reaching out to colleges, research labs and commercial organizations to acknowledge its research work in a big way.

The e-mail is a system of transmission of messages electronically, providing personal messaging and computer file transfer, which supports the rapid transfer of information and quest for increased competitiveness. To connect to a e-mail box, one needs to use a PC, a telephone home connection and a modem link. The messages are prepared on a computer and transmitted using telephone circuits. Messages are processed across various computer gateways till they reach the electronic mail box at the destination. In case the receiver is not available due to the change of address, the message is re-routed, re-transmitted or is bounced back to the sender. This ensures safety of the messages which has been acknowledged by the recipient himself. In addition to sending messages back and forth, the other uses that can be obtained from the messaging infrastructure include :

- Multimedia mail
- Database access
- Document storing
- Fax routing
- Scheduling
- Workflow
- Deviation support and
- Task automation information routing etc.

Today, companies are using a number of tools to help business information and communication needs. These may include personal computers, word processors, courier delivery services, facsimile machines, telex services and more. Unfortunateky, most systems fall short of the requirements in terms of benefits like speed, convenience, confidentiality, security and load handling capacity. E-mail offers a perfect combination of these all at fraction of the cost of traditional delivery methods.

Information captured and efficiently transmitted is the key to success. In today's competitive world, organizations both large and small, need to respond quickly to opportunities, threats and needs of their customers. Hence, efficient methods of communication are imperative. The electronic messaging system is changing the way organizations and individuals do business. A simple and fast way for individuals to communicate has involved into a vital business and personal communication tool both for global and domestic messaging. Most of the corporate organizations are accepting office automation systems. LAN, WAN, Internet and personal computers today face challenges of establishing better communications among these systems, both internally and with outside business partners.

Electronic Mail Box

Under this system, each user is allowed an electronic mail box. The user can scan a list of the messages in the mail box by operating a suitable command. Display of the text message, sending a message to the recipient and so forth are the features of the electronic mail box. The message so sent is stored or resides in the mail box until it is read by the recipient. So under the e-mail system, it is not necessary to be present before the computer when the message is mailed. The mail can be forwarded or stored for delayed delivery. As the message is stored in the electronic mail box,the recipient can read the message at his convenient time, not necessarily be present before the computer when the message is mailed.

An internet account includes an electronic mail box in which a message is received on the Net and the host computer where it is stored. When the user logins on his internet account, he has to check his mail box.

The UCB Mail, Elm, Pine etc.are some of the mail programs which exist on the Net. The programs are user friendly. The e-mail on the Net permits the user to be in direct touch with his friends and colleagues. The e-mail user needs to have a friend , a researcher or anybody for obtaining a copy of the selected papers.

Mailing List

A significant feature about the e-mail is that the user can be in touch with a group of people who share his interests. The subject of interest may be very wide like research, games etc. It is a way for the people to share this interest and establish and maintain contact with the subscribers. A group of people who are interested to share and exchange messages and maintain contact are called as mailing list or simply list. They are nothing but mailing lists of the members' e-mail address. The user can subscribe to any of such lists. Accordingly, the user can receive copies of all the mail sent to the list. On the other hand, the user can also send mail to all the subscribers of the mailing lists.

List Administrator: The e-mail mechanism provides an opportunity to become a list subscriber by contacting the list's administrators with a request to be added to the list. There are two types of list administrators. They are hardware and computer program (called list servers.)

There are several lists who will accept different online subscriptions and one can join any number of lists. Accordingly, there will be plenty of mail in the user's electronic mail box.

Moderated List: When the user has joined any list, the problem is that lots of mail may be added in his mail box accompanied with a scope to wind up with lots of mail in the mail box. When the user has subscribed several active lists, his mail box may receive, store and contain hundreds of messages every day.

The e-mail mechanism permits to limit the users's subscription to a limited list. The moderator is a human person who screens the user's incoming mail and redistributes only a selected portion to the list.

Unmoderated List: It is opposite to the moderated list which undertakes the work to pass mechanically along all the mail. There is a facility for the user to withdraw from a particular list, unsubsribing from it. For this, one must approach the administrator for unsubscription.

E-mail Pieces

E-mail, according to its features, has three pieces. They are :

Envelope: It is used by the message transfer agent for delivery to the recipient.

Headers: It is meant for user agents like receiver, message ID, frame, data, reply etc.

The Body: It is the content or text of the message from the sender to the recipient.

Mechanical Infrastructure

To set up an e-mail service system, the following equipments are required:

- PC-AT/XT with peripherals
- ACU/MODEM with error correction facility.
- Telephone lines with STD facility.
- Port
- Printer and
- A communication software package.

E-mail Address

In the case of e-mail, the address is in the form of a line like @ symbol followed by the location of the user's computer. The last letters of the e-mail address indicates the country's name For example.

uk	United Kingdom
jp	Japan
no	Norway
ve	Venezuela
aq	Antartica
in	India
au	Australia
at	Austria
ca	Canada
fi	Finland
fr	France
de	Germany
il	Israel
it	Italy
kr	Korea
es	Spain
se	Sweden
tw	Taiwan
ch	Swizerland and so on.

Letter Codes

In addition to e-mail address codes indicating the name of the country, there are other letter codes indicating the type and nature of the destination. For instance :

mil	:	Military
org	:	Organization
gov	:	Governmental
co	:	Commercial Organization

Features of electronic mail services

As the name suggests, e-mail has some special features comparable with those of conventional services. However, the following are some of the special features of gateway e-mail services:

1. Mail- Box: There is a distinct electronic post box known as mail box for each subscriber, which is accessible by a computer terminal. There is a separate subscriber number called the account number which is like telephone number and a password. The account can be opened anywhere and he can log in the gateway e-mail services from anywhere.

2. Investment: Installing e-mail service on the computer requires no additional investments. If the perspective user has already a PC and modem or telex or fax, there is no additional investment required for accessing through the gateway.

3. Computerized Service: The electronic mailing system has the facility of the computerized way of preparing and editing the text to be forwarded. The message heading is displayed on a computer screen as soon as the message is entered into the system.

4. Handling Capacity: Data handling capacity of gateway as per the standards include text, binary, telex, fax and videotex.

5. World-wide Twenty-four Hours Services: A salient feature of e-mail is that services are available globally round the clock. The subscriber can send and receive messages to any part of the world at any time. He has his own discretion in terms of using time .

6. Address and Text: The information to be transmitted consists of two parts-the address of the sender and the receiver and the body of the message, i.e. the text.

The mailing system performs functions like choice of messages to be read, displaying, saving, forwarding, replying and other computerized functions.

7. Multi-Media: Gateway e-mail service has the feature of multimedia messaging. The user of this service can send his messages to e-mail, telex or fax subscribers domestically or internationally.

8. Postal Service: The service supports domestic postal deliveries of e-mail and fax messages. Deliveries in Gateway e-mail node cities is arranged through courier, while in other cities by post.

9. Access and Compatibility: There is no problem of incompatibility associated with terminals. The gateway is easily compatible with various terminals and networks. There are multiple access options. The user can access gateway through PSTN, GPSS, I-Net, RABMN, HUNET etc.

10. Pricing: The pricing mechanism of e-mail service is transaction based pricing. It permits the user to estimate and track the user's messaging costs with invoice details. This method provides valuable usage and billing information that identifies all users and indicates monthly charges including the number and type of messages sent.

11. Cost Effective: The cost factor cannot be ignored while going for the e-mail service. There are no additional expenses as well as recurring maintenance costs. The service is cost effective and all business messages can be delivered at a cost much less than the cost of the courier service. Since the text documents are created off-line, the user has to pay only for the transmision cost but not its input.

12. Connivent: The e-mail to be used must be convenient both to the sender and the receiver, The experiences indicate that the system is most convenient. The user can pre-compose messages off-line, send them from anywhere in India or abroad from a PC to any subscriber possessing e-mail account on any major public e-mail system in the world or telex fax number.

13. Simple to Send: Simplicity of electronic mail services feature does not exist in the case of conventional postal services. The purpose of message transmission is clear and simple. The system is very simple to understand operate and use. Sending a message to someone internationally is as simple as making a local telephone call.

14. Security: The e-mail facility assures the user security of messages at all times. There is no direct access to internal systems of the organization. But it allows individuals outside the organization to exchange messages with employees without granting them direct access to the facility.

15. Accuracy: The error-free transmission and receiving of information are indispensable for effective e-mail services. The correctness is assured from electronic mail. The error is human but not so with electronic mail. The correspondence is picture perfect using the built in word processor and as a result, it is error-free.

16. Paperless Office: E-mail helps to realize the benefits of a fully automated office. There will be no paperwork involved for business correspondence and communication.

17. Express Delivery: The system has a facility of express delivery options to send urgent business messages to potental clients and business firms including customers accessing the Net.

18. Mass-Mail: Mass mail efficiency is assured by the system. Under this, the user can correspond to several hundred addresses, enabling him to target mailings to customers, suppliers, employees and others directly from the PC.

19. Auto-System: E-mail facilitates auto reply or auto forwarding. The user can set his account for auto reply of messages or auto forwarding to someone else in the organization while travelling. This ensures communication on regular basis.

20. Other Features: The user can get delivery or non-delivery notifications for the message sent. It provides access to other domestic e-mail services and proprietary local e-mail systems. Private mail systems use public packet switching systems in which both the sender and the receiver should possess a computer which does the work of effectively assembling message transmissions etc.

Applications and Uses of E-mail

They read as follows :

- It has merit of speed, economy and efficiency.
- It can be used to access out of town libraries.
- Exporters can transfer trade documents to their foreign partners.
- Customs office can send memos to and fro.
- Journalists can send their copies across.
- Lawyers, doctors, consultants and government departments can just use it to keep in touch with each other.
- Traditional postal services do not guarantee security of delivery, delays and loss of mail, causes inconvenience and confusion. Postal Services are quite unreliable and known for delay.
- E-mail can be used to transmit computer programmes, spreadsheets and images in machine readable form.
- It permits to avoid duplicate data entry.
- E-mail is error free.
- From the cost point of view, e-mail works out to be much cheaper and convenient.

- It allows to send prepared documents and graphics to the recipient.
- It is simple and easy to transmit information and query for answers to questions.
- It gives the users the benefit to receive, respond to a file and discard incoming messages quickly.
- Handles lakhs of messages everyday.
- Ensures reliable delivery of messages.
- Provides a smooth migration from the old e-mail system to a new LAN-based e-mail system.
- Remote e-mail users can work off the network as easily as when he is connected.
- There is a facility for the sender to restrict delivery of messages to authorised readers by way of password.
- In e-mail system, the mail can be forwarded, stored for delayed delivery and sent anywhere at a particular phone number.
- Telex messages can be provided as an integral part of the e-mail facility.
- It permits to deliver copies of a message to all individuals listed in a certain file.
- It also permits merging of one data file with a particular message.
- It eliminates the option of speaking to the respondent in person, the message is stored and the user can read the message at his convenient time.
- Delivery of message can be confirmed.
- Instantly or within a few minutes, the message transmitted reaches the recipient. Paper cost is also saved.
- The enterprise wide connectivtity allows users to communicate with the people on different e-mail systems and on remote work relations. It connects the feature to compose and send messages easily.
- All the subscribers in the mailing list can get copies of messages automatically.
- The electronic delivery systems inlcude features like composing messages, text editing, message filing, retrieval, content processing, accounting, billing, security of data etc.

Electronic Mail Services provide the following

1. Electronic Mail: The global electronic mail services enable the user to exchange electronic messages and binary files with any e-mail subscriber or any of the major domestic international public e-mail systems.

2. Telex: Telex despatch is another service of gateway e-mail, allowing the user to send and receive telexes from the privacy of his own computer terminal and can communicate with over 1.7 million telex subscribers around the globe.

3. Fax: Fax despatch is yet another communication service of e-mail. Gateway e-mail service allows the user to send fax messages from his computer terminal to more than 4.2 million fax machines the world over.

4. Accuracy: The error-free transmission and receiving of information are indispensable for effective e-mail service. The correctness is assured from electronic mail. The correspondence is picture perfect, using the built in word processor and as a result error-free.

5. Postal Dispatch: Postal dispatch is a a client feature and service of global electronic mail service, made possible with gateway e-mail service. The system supports domestic postal deliveries or e-mail including fax messages. Deliveries of post in gateway e-mail nodes is arranged through courier while in other cities by post under the certificate of posting (UPC).

6. Directorty Services: Under the gateway e-mail service, subscribers' directory of information can be accessed online.

Videsh Sanchar Nigam and Global Messaging Service

The Videsh Sanchar Nigam Limited (VSNL), a Government of India enterprise, has introduced GEMS-400 device, a global messaging service to provide international telecommunication service. It is foremost in this service which connects islands of electronic mail, making them accessible to the individual PC user. GEMS-400 is a global electronic communication service which connects 'island' of electronic mail, making them accessible to the individual PC users. It also provides India's existing proprietary electronic mail systems.

The VSNL in 1991 started operating its GEMS-400 service to act as a gateway for international mail from India. In addition to its services in India today, there are about ten companies offering this and many more are expected to come up in the near future using the e-mail facility in India. The list of e-mail subscribers has been increasing considerably. NICNET Dataline and Research Techonologies, Business India Information Technology and Datapro are some of the companies rendering the services to the internet savvy population.

Coverage: GEMS is India's premier e-mail service, a potential communication gateway to global messaging and store and forward service. The gateway has formed a host of strong alliances with public and private electronic mail networks around the world. These effective partnership provide all the multiple delivery and handling options of corporate needs. One can access GEMS-400 from more than 79 countries through Public Switched Packet (PSPDS). It is now interconnected to over 34 international e-mail networks. Connectivity is also provided to over 20 million e-mail subscribers on Internet Network. Data Networks subscribers on INTERNET work under the e-mail system the user can communicate directly with over 1.7 million telex subscribers world over. There are more than 4.2 million fax machines or fax machine world over. It is possible to access to over 20 million e-mail subscribers on INTERNET at domestic gateway E-mail service.

It provides users to simultaneously log on for more than 500 users. It has a busy hour's message handling capacity of more than 60,000 messages per hour. Peak busy hours system response time is less than 2 seconds. Gateway has the capacity to deliver more than 95 per cent urgent messages within 45 minutes.

Hybrid Mail Service in India

The Hybrid Mail Service was introduced in India for the first time in January 1995 by the Department of Posts. The service envisages that a message brought to that post office manually can be transmitted electronically to another post office for delivery through the postman to the premises of the customers. This service facilitates to deliver messages to the destination within 12 hours.

A customer will have the option of presenting the materials-either the manuscript, typed form or on a floppy. After the message is recorded on the computer, the system will automatically calculate the service charges to initiate early delivery of these messages.

Hybrid mail service is now available in many advanced countries. But in India, it was for the first time introduced initially in a network comprising of Delhi, Mumbai, Bangalore, Chennai, Patna, Lucknow and Shimla.

Advantages of E-mail

1. Increased Productivity: E-mail is a powerful way to enhance productivity without making additional investment in the hardware.

2. Anywhere, Anytime: The users of E-mail can reach effectively customers, branch offices, distributors, vendors, suppliers, project teams and sales offices anywhere and at anytime, by utilizing existing office equipment and communication software efficiently.

3. Virtual Communication: The powerful e-mail system of communication transforms internal business systems into a virtual communication network.

4. Immediate Connection: India's premier e-mail service messaging system gives immediate worldwide connectivity even to dissimilar systems. There is no problem of incompatibility.

5. Access: It offers facility of easy access using our own installed PCs and office automation systems or LANS.

6. Access to Domestic E-mail: Another great advantage is that it provides access to Domestic E-mail services and Proprietary Local E-mail systems.

7. Worldwide Connectivity: Under the e-mail system, it is easy to send information around the world. E-mail is a gateway to global messaging and communication through it results in convenience, speed, confidentiality and economy. Besides, it is easy to send information around the world. One can access from more than 79 countries through the Public Switched Packet Data Networks (PSPDN).

8. Sending Message as normal: The great advantage is that the user can send electronic mail, fax messages, telex messages and postal messages without leaving their desks. It permits to turn equipment already installed into a global messaging system. The system puts a new world of messaging capabilities and services at the user's finger tips.

9. Better Business Communication: Using e-mail for business means better communication because it offers valuable benefits of speed, convenience, impact and control. This concept covers very little cost compared to conventional message delivery methods.

10. Speedy Business Communication: For successful business, business communication should be fast and with speed. E-mail ensures speedy business communication and in turn carrying business effectively, efficiently and profitably. Under conventional business, communication systems are not compatible today's with growing needs, They create barriers to achieving business goals. Postal communication system are not compatible today with growing business needs. They create barriers to achieving business goals. Postal communication systems as evidently known, keeps us waiting for days or even weeks. Other problems are that overnight couriers are expensive, even traditional telex and fax is known for speed but costly, All these problems can be solved with global messaging system via computers which are fast, cost effective and easy to use.

11. New Kind of Business Tool: India's gateway e-mail is a new kind of business tool which facilitates to explore new unique uses. This new business tool does following special works :

- Distributes hot mail leads to the concern's sales force in an instant.
- Receive ordering information more quickly and effectively than by regular mail or phone.
- Distributes reports to key people as soon as they are ready.
- Send price changes and product announcement to remote offices quickly and
- Expedite communications with dealers and distributors by eliminating paper backlogs and jammed phone lines.

12. Reporting: Practice and research revealed that e-mail helps to expedite and steamline business reporting. The problem of delays and inefficiencies in business reporting system can cripple the effectiveness of communication. Electronic mail replaces crude and conventional report delivery and distribution. A reporting may be internal and external to the business house. Distribution is facilitated because of stored lists of key recipients. Yet another advantage of electronic delivery is that delivery time is less, thus proving beneficial to business.

13. Responsiveness: Electronic mail improves the responsiveness to market conditions. It facilitates to improve responsiveness by revising price change in marketing programmes instantly. Time factor or timing the marketing and understanding its potential and selling the product are very important factors. Timely information given accurately to dealers, distibutors and sales force is very crucial, otherwise it results in the loss of business. Electronic mail networks are a powerful tool to any business-both domestic and external-to implement in marketing programmes with greater accuracy. Pre-empting competitivenes with a change in marketing practice before they can react and improve responsiveness by revising price changes and marketing programms instantly are the twin benefits to business.

14. Coordination of Sales Efforts: Sales force spends a major portion of their time in their sales efforts on the roads. Their main communication tool is to contact by phone their regional offices, head offices, customers etc. They have to heavily depend on telephone calls. Communicating by telephone is an endless game of tag and makes an endless frustrating game out of tracking down leads and following up sales calls. Another serious problem of telephone is misplaced late delivery, forgetfulness or undelivered information, which results in losing of customers and loss of sales. The use of e-mail can avoid these problems by eliminating telephone tag, sending and receiving messages at the user's convenience, linking sales and team members together including international representations.

15. Public Relations Programmes: In the fields of broadcast, press releases, financial updates and other corporate communications, e-mail ensures better communication because in these fields, things that are important include speed, convenience, accuracy and effectiveness. In addition,electronic mail can improve the efficency and effectiveness of the corporate public relations programmes. It is possible to expedite and streamline copy reivews and approvals can be expedited by circulating instant messages.

16. Simplicity: Information to clients precisely is essential to any business. The simptification of client's communication instantly helps to make decisions. As such, maintaining close contact with clients is a priortity now-a days in any business. Simplicity greatly aids appointment confirmation, request for information and follow-up reports can be exchanged with greater efficiency by using strategic instant messages.

17. Large Group Meetings: E-mail facilitates planning and execution of large group meetings such as seminars, conventions, symposia and conferences etc. Organizing such meetings involves a great deal of time and efforts to manage the success of any firm. Arrangements must be synchronized and effectively coordinated among a variety of diverse groups in different locations, hostels, hotels exhibitions, the media etc.There are always the problems of events being postponed and last minute announcements. Electronic mail offers great scope to make these jobs easier and more effective. There is flexibility in both electronic distribution of messages including print form.

18. Others

- The order entry system under the e-mail package helps in serving instant messatges as electronic purchase orders confirmations and maintaining inventory levels.
- Any where -anytime facility should reach customers, branch offices, distributors, vendors, suppliers and the project team.
- E-mail is more useful to large business organisations.
- In particular, it is more useful to travelling businessmen.
- The system operates day and night regularly and helps to pick-up messages left for the receiver.
- Electronic mail box allows access by using a portable personal computer and modem.
- It permits that messages can be sent to other electronic mail boxes.
- Messages concerning the office, business, marketing and other activities can be sent by e-mail.
- A business house subscribing to various electronic mail boxes can obtain useful information about other subscribers together with their mail box numbers.
- There are a number of private electronic mail systems.

E-mail Working at a Glance

They are :

- All that one needs for using e-mail is a PC.
- A telephone connection and a modem link.
- Subscriber's Mail account.
- Terminal located in customer's premises anywhere in india.
- Handles text,binary, teletext and fax videotex.
- Converts text, graphics programmed letterheads, logo signature and post script attachment.
- Gives world wide connectivity to international e-mail networks and millions of e-mail subscribers on the Internet.
- Fax viewing facility for received faxes on PC screen.
- Supports CC Mail, MS Mail, Vines Mail, Quick Mail, WP office, Netware Mail, Unix Mail, and SMTP Internet mail.
- Devices needed to access a Gateway e-mail are PC, telex, fax, machine, terminal, communiaction software and a modem.
- To obtain permission for connecting modem fax from Department of Telecommunication after paying necessary license fee.

- Selecting a password.
- GEMS can be accessed using maxware, mail max-400 and remote user agent (RUA) and
- Gateway to e-mail and store and forward fax service is a communication gateway to global messaging.

Snail Mail

For those used to instantaneous delivery of electronic mail, snail mail is the term used for the more traditional pace of the US Postal service.

List Servers or Mailing List

This is an e-mail discussion group. There are thousands of List servers or mailing lists to which you can *"subscribe"* to participate in online discussions that arrive in your e-mail each day.

Eudora

This is a widely used graphical e-mail program that allows you to receive, read and send electronic messages to people around the world. It is a potential method of global communication. A pager is portable and compact one-way wireless communication device that allows to receive messages by the user who is on the move. Pagers are ideal for contracting field staff like office boys, customer service personnel, maintenance engineers, salespeople, doctors, consultants, courier boys, delivery boys etc.

A person on the move carries the pager, with a distinct identification number. To contact such persons, you call a designated telephone number, the service provider for that pager, give the message and the pager identification number to the operator. The operator keys in the message into a paging computer and the message is transmitted as a leading signal over the air. The designated pager receives the radio signals extracting the message from it and informs the recipient.

Pager

A pager is a one-way wireless message receiving device, enabling a person to receive complete messages and allowing to act upon them. Pager keeps the person constantly in touch. Paging service is very simple. The person calls up the paging company and gives the operator the pager number and the message. Almost instantly, the pager alerts to press the red button and get the message, which is received instantly.

History of Paging

The beginning of the paging industry can be traced back to the first land-mobile radio systems pioneered by the Detroit Police Depatment, US, as early as 1921, when the concept of one-way information broadcasting was introduced. The 1930s witnessed the armed forces in US using powerful transmitters to broadcast voice messages from a stationary location (base station) to a mobile unit. From the voice brodcast service, paging evolved into a digital service with addressing whereby messages can be addressed to specific pages. In India, the paging facility appeared way back in 1982 during the Asian Games. But it was not a success. Liberalisation saw pages coming in a big way for communication.

Need for Paging Facility

Today, we are spending a lot of time travelling for business purposes to attend assignments etc. It is known that the conventional devices cannot keep us in touch with clients' firms while we are on the move. Some research studies found that 65% of the senior executives and businessmen interviewed in a 8-city survey felt the need for a mobile communication device. Paging service companies get licence to cover more cities and one can also use the pager across wider geographical areas.

Fig. 8.08 A-hand-held Pager

It is an internal oral communication system useful when executives move from one section to another section. Under the electronic paging system, each executive is given a number. It is a telecommunication facility. In recent years, satallite link is being used substantially as sophisticated communication technology in the highly specialised age of informaion and communication. A satellite link at the national level and globally serves an important purpose. Satellite links are being used and applied for meteorological purposes, research, defence, exploration etc.

In the United States, there is the national paging facility. Paging is a telecommunication device which helps to seek or summon the required personnel. The purpose of the paging facility is to establish contact between the organisation and the personnel working away from the organisation, either localized or far away from the organisation. A message or a code is transmitted by the communicator to the person who is required, which serves as an indication to the person to establish contact with the organisation. For this purpose,the persons carry a separate device known as beeper which receives the signals of the message transmitted. This paging facility proves beneficial in contracting the personnel with the help of the beeper wherever they are.

Thus, the system ensures maintaining contact with the personnel. In some organisations or professions, the personnel will be moving from one place to another by virtuse of their position to discharge their duties. For instance, doctors, police, travelling executives, defence and other industrial supervisors etc. are frequently on the move and the paging facility proves beneficial. According to the size of the organisation and nature of activities where personnel are working, paging facilities can be localised or extended to far flung areas. The Mahanagar Telephone Nigam Limited (MTNL), New Delhi, has started providing localised paging facilities to organisations in the Union territory of

Delhi. Paging facility can be operated either by using the telephone exchange for the purpose of transmission or through satellite links.

Types of Paging Services

- *Individual Paging :* By this, one can page to subscribers whenever they are.
- *Anytime Paging :* One can page any subscriber twenty four hours a day and 365 days a year.
- *Auto paging:* Auto paging facilitates one to page any subscriber automatically by dialing a given number.
- *Group Paging :* Group paging helps to page a group of people at the same time by dialing a number. The group is given a pager number. The common message to be conveyed is transmitted by the group pager. Within seconds,all the members of the group will receive the same message, whatever the time, wherever they are. Thus, all this makes instant communication the norm. So, paging helps in the potential world of communication.

Paging Receivers

There are many types of paging receivers offered by different pager manufacturers. They are :

1. Tone Receiver: This is the first and simplest paging receiver facilitated with four to eight different audible tone patterns to alert the bearer.

2. Numeric Pager: The numeric pager has a display of typically 12 or 24 digits, whereby the caller can send a telephone number that he wishes the bearer to contact. The pager is able to store these numeric messages in memory. Only numerals are flashed.

3. Alphanumeric: This type of pager displays 16,32 or 80 characters. Charters or messages ranging between 500 and 5000 can be stored in the memory, In case of alphanumericals (alphabet + numerals), an alphabetic message can be flashed.

- Multiplicity paging
- Calling line identification
- Mobile telephone answer
- Personalised service and
- Secretarial service.

Service Providers

There are many service providers and users have the options to choose a service provider. In the paging technology presently, there are two kinds of paging techniques available in India. They are Post Office Code Standard Adivisory Group (POCSAG) and FM RDC Radio Data Service.

The FM-RDC paging is offered on AIR's FM transmission infrastructure.

The signal quality and the ability of the pager to receive the message depends upon the service provider and in the kind of infrastructure in terms of transmitters, power of transmitters, topology of the city, telephone links etc.

Present Position

There are about 2,70,000 paging subscribers in India and more than 80 % constitutes of users like traders, doctors, entrepreneurs etc. and the remaining 20% are from the corporate segment.

New Value Added Service

There are many value added services available to the subscribers by the service providers. The following are a few value added services :

- Paging in Indian languages like Hindi, Telugu, Gujarati etc.
- Online foreign exchange quotes.
- Online stock exchange quotes.
- Interface with e-mail to get short messages directly to the user's pager
- Interface with the cellular source to screen incoming calls.
- Interface with systems or equipments to monitor its health and report status by sending alarms to the maintenance engineer's pager.

There are two requirements to fulfil for availing paging services. They are a paging device or pager and a paging service provider.

Radio Paging Services

Radio paging services belong to the same technological family of mobile telephone service. This service has been introduced in India in Delhi and Mumbai. It has been decided to franchise these services to private parties. Initially, it was decided that cities with a population of one million or above or having a telephone capacity of more than 25,000 lines will be covered. On this criteria, the service will be introduced in the following urban areas: Delhi, Mumbai, Kolkata, Chennai, Ahmedabad, Bangalore, Hyderabad, Pune, Kanpur, Nagpur, Lucknow, Surat, Jaipur, Ernakulam, Coimbatore, Vadodra, Indore, Patna, Madurai, Bhopal, Varanasi, Ludhiana,Vishakapatnam, Chandigarh, Rajkot, Trivandrum and Amristar. In Phase II, it has been proposed to cover all territorial circles other than the 27 cities.

Recent developments in telecommunication are as follows:

- There are two personal mobile satelite communication services.
- Portable mobile data.
- A brief case telephone.
- Satellite paging, a global paging service to pocket-size data receivers.
- Global hand-held phone.

Radio paging services would provide alert signals, emergency calls, valuable information etc. The service will be highly useful for medical professions, business executives, commercial applications and emergency services in most of the urban and rural areas. For the operating services, All India Radio appoints licencees / operations at selected centres where AIR has FM transmitters. FM Radio broadcast technology has an advantageous feature to initiate potential communication.

Radio Paging in India

In the communication service, India has made another landmark in recent years. Radio paging based on modern sophisticated communication technology was introduced in India for the first time on January 1995 in New Delhi through the All India Radio. The use of this technology in India is for the first time through the Government bradcasting department.

The radio paging service has the facility to provide alert signals, emergency calls and valuable information etc. This service will be more useful for sales persons, sales representatives, medical professionals, business managers, calls for emergency services etc. The proposal was made to operate radio paging services in 13 cities in India by the end of March 1995, including Tirupathi in Andhra Pradesh. For this purpose, All India Radio had decided to appoint licensees or operators. The subscribers have to send their data or messages to the control room. The persons to whom the messages have to be transmitted will have a separate device called *receivers.* The receivers will give signals in turn as soon as messages are transmitted by the control room. Information can be observed on the alloted liquid display of the receiver.

The radio-paging broadcast technology has an advantageous feature. The vacant space of a radio in its allotted. frequency band permits to inject additional signals in the form of data on sub-carriers. The data or information can conveniently be utilised to disseminate value - added services like public utility information and educational information etc. This service is in addition to the main programme like stereophonic and monophonic. When the radio is used in the broadcast channel, it is called RDS whose primary application is radio paging.

All India Radio (AIR) has announced the availability of FM-based paging services, making it the first public broadcaster in Asia adopting paging techniques for public information services using the FM band.

Radio Paging Mechanism

The features of this mechanism are :

- The person sending the message calls the paging service office with the number of the pager and gvies the messages.
- The operator who takes the call enters the page number and the message into the computer terminal.
- A paging computer encodes the message in Post Office Code Standardisation Advisory Group (POCSAG) Protocol.
- A roof top antenna beams out the message using ultra high frequeny (UHF) waves in the 425 MHZ bandwidth.
- Roof top antenna or drop station relays the message to the pager through very high frequency (VHF) waves, using the unique bandwidth for that company.
- Recognising its unique number, the alphanumeric paper picks up the signals, decodes it to digital form and flashes it on the screen using letters and
- In case the target pager is a numerical one, it receives and displays numerical messages-only usually a number has to be called back.

Global Page Service

The world's first global personal pager is now under development to be operated via satellite system, wherein the pager will be able to receive messages of upto 64 characters in length. It is compact, light weight and pocket portable, with signal strength indicators, saves on power and has sufficient memory to store messages. Services have options like tone, numeric/alphanumeric message reception, call designation based on priority, protection against message loss and value added applications like market update, weather services and news.

Novel Uses of Pager

When you are on the move, you as a user can join the paging business community which widens coverage and reach. Some of the novel uses are as follows :

1. *E-mail Alerts:* The user can send and receive mail from his personal e-mail ID. Moreover, the page automatically alerts you whenever an e-mail arrives, thus saving valuable time and money. The user gets information on the Net when the Net gets in touch with him.

2. *Send a Page:* Welcome to one click paging. You can page a message to any other pager from the service provider's site in utmost privacy and click on it any time and in any way. The message gets there.

3. *Virtual Secretary:* This enables the user to enter all important dates, events and appointments on the web site of the service provider and the cyber secretary will send the user a reminder on his pager, enabling him to concentrate on his business and the virtual secretary helps the user to stay on schedule for business.

4. *Travel Mail:* When travelling outside your city, your pager message will be delivered to your e-mail account which can be accessed from anywhere in the world.

5. *Business Directory:* This is a dynamic, web-enabled business exchange that enables the user to identify perspective trading partners across over a hundred product categories. For instance, Max Page with www.indiamarket. com helps locate the suppliers needed for your business, identify a prospective client and more so get *the site and get on with business.* *

Fax or Facsimile (Transmission of Documents and Pictures)

Like messages, pictures can be transmitted by using a special machine known as facsimile machine or fax machine. Under the electronic mail message system, an original document containing photographs, maps, charts and other drawings are transmitted by placing and the sending facsimile machine. The computer-based facsimile systems are more useful in modern offices. This machine scans documents containing pictures and the receiving system reproduces the scanned picture or image.

Fax is a short form of facsimile, a public service device which has been more popular in recent years and as such, its use and importance has grown beyond expectation. It can be used for transmitting pictures,diagrams, images from place to place within a few minutes from anywhere to anywhere. A fax terminal appears like a small desktop electro-static photocopier, which scans and prints pictures, images, diagrams etc. on the same principle of the photocopier.

---

* *Sudhir Chowdhary, Computers Today, 16-30, June 2000, p.65.*

Fax has the facility of both transmitting and receiving documents. Some makers of fax machines include the facility of automatic dialing, multiple polling, call reservation and tranmission of documents of various standard sizes. This public service has grown in importance because images, pictures and diagrams can be transmitted from one place to another destination with terminals connected to a standard telephone line.

Transmission of documents and pictures instantly is now possible to any distant place electronically through a special computer related machine called the Facsimile. A document or picture to be transmitted is to be placed in a separate sending fax machine. At the destination, there will be another machine called *the receiving fax* device So, there's a communication link up beween sending and receiving machines.

The function of the sending fax machine is to scan the document or a page and picture, while the receiving device produces the scanned document, picture or any image on the document. The transmission may be a picture or a text, using the process is the receiveing device to produce a duplicate page or facsimile of the original document placed in a sending facsimile. There are low speed and high speed fax services. It looks like a photocopy of a xerox machine which reproduces the duplicate copy of an original document. The facsimile system enables a precise reproduction of the original document.

The afference between xerox machine and a fax machine and their processes is that fax facilitates the transmision of documents and pictures to any distant place including other countries within a few seconds. Thus, fax is one of the automatic machines which forms part of service institutions like universities etc. So, the Xerox machine reproduces a duplicate copy at a stationary place, but cannot transmit to other places.

Though the use of fax machines has been there, but in recent years, efforts are being made to improve the working system by way of enhancing transmission speed and reduction in the cost of transmission speed. So, the facsimile system is designed to facilitate the user to transmit and receive documents and pictures.

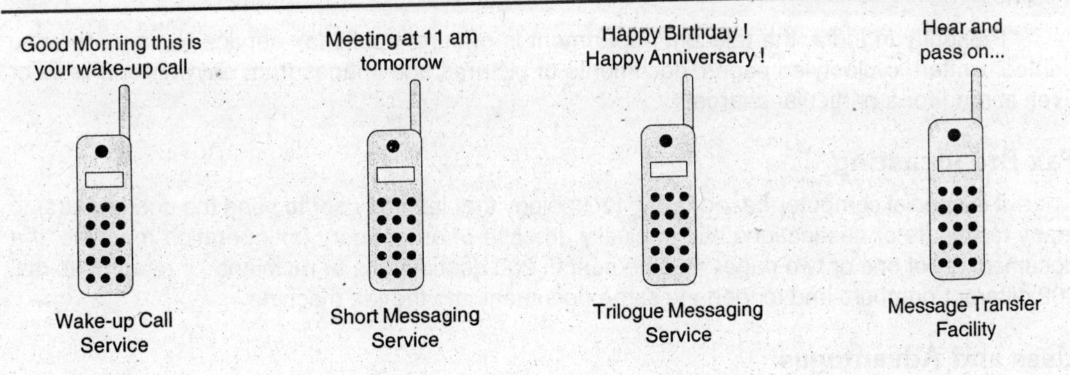

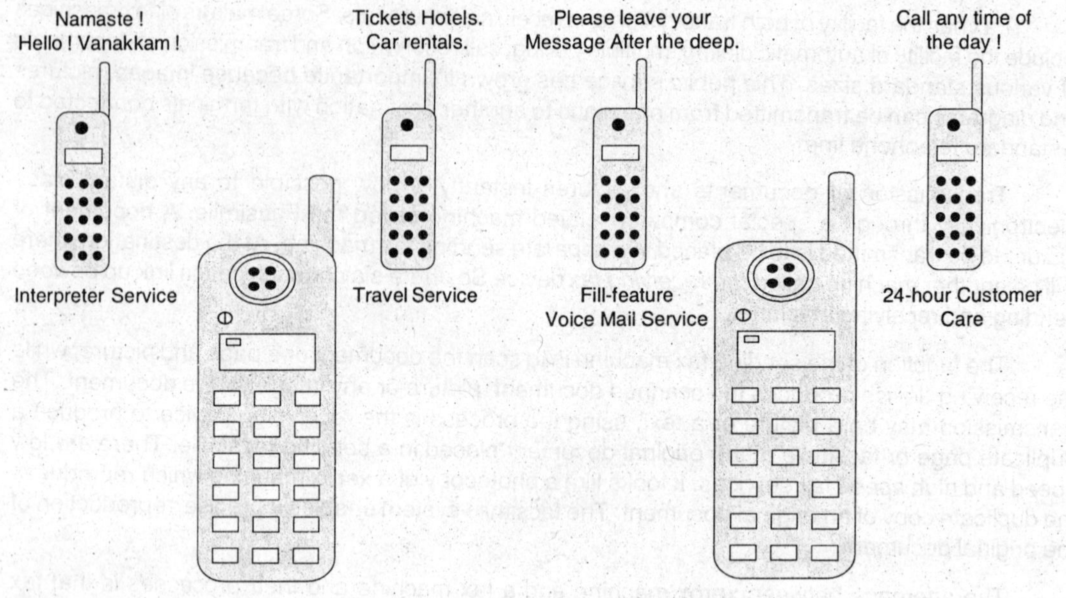

Fig. 8.9 Some designs of fax machines

Both the machines use the method of synchronized scanning at the sending or transmitter and receiving or receiver device ends. The original document inserted into the sending facsimile machine pertains placement of documents around a drum inside the facsimile machine. The transmitter or sending machine scans the data line by line. It is more fascinating to note how documents or pictures are transmitted at the receiving end. While scanning line by line, the resultng electrical signals are transmitted over the telecommunication link to distant receiving stations. The duplication can be either on a paper or document.

There are two forms of facsimile systems analog and digital-faster than analog systems.

The process is a sort of electronic mail message service.

Presently in India, the telecom department is offering public fax service to users to send printed, written, cyclostyled pages, documents or pictures and images from anywhere in India or even abroad for a particular charge.

Fax Broadcasting

It is special computer-based faxing technology that lets the user to send the document(s) to many recipients or destinations automatically. In case of an ordinary fax operation machine, if a document (s) of one or two pages is to be sent to 200 destinations or recipients, it repuires to dial 200 different numbers and to feed the same document into the fax machine.

Uses and Advantages

Fax broadcasting benefits the following business situations:

1. Stock Market: For fast and information delivery of time sensitive and essential information like share prices, quotes and company results.

2. Sales: To communicate price changes, specsheet revisions, product introductions etc. immediately to all dealers and company offices.

3. Business Communication: Transmitting documents (like memos, circulars, requests for proposals or invoices) to branch offices, company representatives or vendors in diverse locations quickly and efficiently.

4. Advertising and Marketing: Distributing time-sensitive information like press releases, special offers and focussed marketing campaigns to a large aduience.

Crisis Communications: Where immediate dissemination of information can help save lives and prevent injury. (drug recall or defective product alert, for instance). This is more of a social service.

Mobile and Cellular Telephone

The word *Cellular* is derived from a cell or area created around an antenna to transmit and receive telephone messages. A cellular telephone makes it possible for the user to have two-way telephone conversation from a car. The user of a cellular telephone has to dial and receive any call from a car or from any mobile location to another car with such a phone at a stationary location within or outside the city.

In order to provide city wide coverage, it is necessary that the antennas and cells should be repeated at many places in the city. The cells are interconnected for uninterrupted communication from a moving vehicle. The whole system of operation and communication is linked to the telephone exchange of the telecommunication authority. This facilitates the user to talk to any other user in the same city. The user can also make STD/ISD calls from moving vehicles. There are many cellular technologies which have become both popular and standardized.

The Pan European digital mobile telephone standard is specified by the European Telecommunications Standards Institute. This specified standard has been adopted by many countries.

It has three elements:

- Mobile Stations (MS)
- Radio Based Station System (RBSS) and
- Mobile Service Switching Centres (MSSC).

The Centres are associated with the Home Location Register (HLR) and Vistors' Location Register (VLR).

The digital cellular and radio mobile system will be accessed through the existing Public Switched Telephone Network (PSTN).

A cellular phone is a wireless communication medium which uses limited frequencies to a system of transmitters set up in a honeycomb pattern. The use of radio waves as communication link eliminates the use of wires and ensures a reliable high quality voice and data communication whether at home, enroute to office or just about anywhere in the city or the adjoining suburbs.

With the number of cell phones touching a million, Indians have been networked into a new lifestyle. The cell phone has become an integral part of the urban landscape and poised to benefit upwardly mobile urban Indians. The era of the cell phone has dawned in India. The urge among urban Indians to converse while moving has become an essential norm quickly cascading from the lofty heights of governmental and the corporate front to professionals, traders, housewives, school children and criminals even.

It has become popular because it satisfies the need to communicate in an instant. The capability to communicate just in time is a basic benefit that the users have just begun to exploit. There are many handset models for the user to choose from.These cellular models have inbuilt facilities like wake-up call service, short messaging, trilogna messaging, message transfer facility, fax interpreter service, full feature voice fax mail service, 24-hour customer care etc. to attract users. The trend is the expanding cellular connectivity which benefits people constantly on the move. The use of cell phones has increased, resulting in the concept of a mobile office, though it turns out to be costly. But most people use cell phones for a short time to pass on an emergency message.

Fig 8.10 Mobile Phone

A new innovative value service which provides the widest coverage and clearest signals, helps people cross boundaries through this type of communication. It has developed as a global link system, making the cell phone from a basic communication device to one of total utility whether at office or at home.

Advantages

- Some important political figures etc. regularly carry two cell phones.
- The user can discuss with colleagues in legal profession, the academia, consultants, doctors not through the switch board but over the cell.
- To talk to people who are at wedding parties, conferences, meetings, watching a cricket match or a movie.
- School going children are armed with cell phones that are programmed to connect at the path of a single button home, father's or mother 's cell phone or some other alarm point. Cell phone is really a handset and it is an angel in crisis and emergency.
- Doctors can make it a point to leave their mobile numbers with patients, nurses, and others- a timely call can be made to save life, treat or cure patients, whether they are in hospital or home or shopping or busy with other engagements, driving or taking a walk. It is lot more than an emergency kit. The cell phone can be used to get information pertaining to price of products and place, buy or sell orders. The problems of delay in giving or acceping offers leading to significant price changes can be solved.
- It has become common in crowded metropolitan markets where shopkeepers move about with mobile phones to check on the discount rates offered by the suppliers. The urban youth has also taken to the cell for instant communication besides being a status symbol. The cell-phone toting sales people call up markets,local representatives, friends and homes, various appointments, shifts in appointments, if the train is running late, accidents etc.
- Outworkers can be connected by their staff, where there is no fixed phone within a few kilometres.

Advancement in Information Technology has introduced a wide range of high quality devices tailored to help the user to get the most out of it whole. With the technology moving ahead so rapidly, it is important that the mobile phone of today's choice is also future prepared. Most of the mobile phones available today are a generation ahead, employing the very latest in technology, and are emerging as personal accessories that should have great looks as well as great performance. Spectialists and accessories designers sebsequently emerged in desiging new telephone connections and sent their cash boxes ringing.

The cellular phone can be used for mobile communication for a mass market. It is really innovative and dramatic for expansion in the marketing technology today. In a country where developed and underdeveloped markets exist, there is a greater scope for new potential mobile subscribers to join the line. The terrestrial and satellite based mobile communication systems allow potential users, buyers and sellers to contact either ways, make calls from any point on the earth using the multipurpose handset. The set can be used either in home, in office or outside. In this respect, Japan has made an headway by introducing for the first time the Personal Handy Phone. It is an inexpensive, light weighted handset that operates as a cordless telephone.

The satellite-based systems provide inexpensive world wide personal communication. Cellular phones, paging services and trunking services consititute three of mobile phones. Cellular phones have appeared in a big way recently in the conuntry. The mobile telephone service in India has begun on a limited scale. For the first time, it has been introduced in Delhi by the Government owned Mahanagar Telephone Limited in the early 1980s. Radio paging services and cellular phones both to the same technology family of mobile services including satellite and cordless phones. In advanced countries, the mobile telephone services had been inroduced much earlier.

To mention, the first Korean mobile telephone service began in 1960s itself with a three cellular system called Mobile Telephone Service (MTS) which served a very limited area of coverage of the SEOUL metropolitan areas, Later, the service area expanded to cover all cities and major highways, resulting in its expansion.

Teleprinter

The Teleprinter is a specialized type of typewriter, a telegraphic system by which messages are sent out at one place and received at another place in printed form. Typing is connected to a telephone line and the messages typed at one place transmits electrical signals over the wire and the message is simultaneously reproduced, printed at a distance place by the machine. It is used as private circuit or through the post-office telex service system. The post office gives teleprinters on rent to form a part of the private telecommunications.

A teleprinter is made up of a keyboard for data entry and a built in-printer to record typed inputs and produce computer process output.

Portable Teleprinter

There are many small and portable teleprinters mostly used by :

- Salespersons
- Newspaper Reporters
- Engineers
- Doctors and
- Lawyers and others on mobility.

A travelling sales representative can use the teleprinter for sending sales information and quantity particulars to the head office over the telephone either for knowing the stock positions, placing orders etc. A portable teleprinter can be carried by them wherever they go. A sales representative can link the terminal to a customer's telephone and dial into a company's computer system. It is possible to obtain immediate information on the terminal printer. Similarly, lawyers, press reporters etc can also carry this teleprinter.

Small portable teleprinters have been used substantially in recent years mostly by sales persons, engineers, reporters, managers, medical professionals and others, who are always on move on their duties. For instance, the sales representatives can send sales orders to the head office. The terminal can be attached to the telephone and transmit information to the computer system by the company. It is the most convenient, easy and time saving device to ascertain stock availability and the order of the customers can be booked instantly.

If there is no stock, it is an alarming signal for the production manager to produce quickly according to time schedule. Thus, the teleprinters facilitate to communicate from any remote location to the company's computer by the sales representative. moving in the field. The battery operated portable terminals are also available which can be placed on the palm of the hand used to send information of sales to the computer. The small battery operated terminals have limited capacity to receive essential data.

Telecommuting

Telecommuting refers to employee's work which is either done at home or on the computer linking to the office. In advanced countries, telecommuting is the most popular method of communication between home and office. With the help of a computer, people are benefitting from various services like booking orders over the phone, processing,filling forms and analysing information. Forecasters predicted that 10 to 20 milion people could be telecommuting by the year 2000. Telecommuting in India is at present not widely and popularly used, and it may in the years to come.

Teletype

An electronic system of transmitting information is in typewritten form. It is in operations pertaining to various public relations activites, newswire as well as by the Associated Press and United Press International. It is a mechanical device of a telegraph system of transmitting messages by means of a typewriter keyboard. Each key of a keyboard produces coded signals which are simultaneously printed at the receiving end called the teleprinter. Teletypes relate to message transmission by teleprinter or teletype. A teletype is also called teletypewritter or telex, which provides automatic communication through the printed words between subscribers having telex facilities.

Future of the Printed Word

Will the printed word survive the onslaught of electronic invasion. There are skeptics who believe that there is no future for the printed word produced in the traditional way for over 500 years. They predict that there will be a worldwide paper shortage in the next century and printing of books will be extremely costly and electronic publishing of both books and newspapers will be very much cheaper. Though the actual events based on the experience of the past may disapprove this belief, it is still anyone's guess.

Some damage has already been done by displacing the printed word in several areas.

Here are some of these :

Microform publication or micro publishing and micro libraries are the dreams of the future which may completely displace the printed book. The dream is of a potential library, housed in a catalogue cabinet. The 'microfiche book' is a development that has come to stay and the computer output of microfiche has enlarged its shape. As an indication of the space saving capacity of micro publications, a library in the UK contains some 58,000 pages of data on 880 microfiches each, 105 x 148 mm., filed in cabinet 7 inches by the printed issues. However, where continuous updating of information is essential such as in legal, professional practice and financial compilation, microform publication has become an established and competitively priced medium. Synoptic publishing and simultaneous publishing are two recent developments in periodical and learned journal publishing using microfiche.

Photo Typesetter and the Printed Word

Though the entry of electronics has vastly changed the printing machinery processes and techniques in a general way, the greatest impact is in the area of typesetting only. Infact, photo typesetters have not only revolutionised the typesetting process but changed the very structure of the printing industry as such.

With the introduction of photo-typesetters of the first generation in the beginning of the 50s, we have come to the further generation of photo-typesetters in the beginning of the 80s. These are the electronic marvels which are very highly sophisticated and capable of things beyond the common man's comprehension. Many factors outside the printing industry have played a dominant role in bringing out these third and fourth generation photo-typesetters. They include computers, microcomputers, lasers, digitization of information, screen-based technology including television and telecommunication.

What is a photo typesetter? To define it in simple language, *photo-typesetters are machines which produce images on photographic film or paper as negative or positive in the design required for the printed page.* They have suitable devices to store the characters, to select and expose them in the required size, form and measure on film or paper.

The first generation machines (1946-50) were just the replica of the hot metal mechines and the operation was mechanical. The second generation machines help negative film of characters, in a disk or drum and use the optical system such as zoom lens or torrent lens to vary the type and size. They were partly mechanical and partly electronic. The third generation machines are wholly electronic and use cathode ray tube (CRT) for the projection of characters. The characters are digitised and stored in magnetic disks. They can be electronically enlarged, reduced, slanted and emboldened. Digitization also provides the potential of producing pictures as well as text.

The fourth generation typesetter machines use lasers for imaging and its revolution is 1000 dots per inch and output speed of about 1000 newspaper lines per minute can be achieved.

Today, we have a proliferation of these phototypesetters that are manufactured with a system and modular approach to enable a buyer to install a simple system according to his present needs and expand it periodically to suit his growing needs. The direct entry photosetter is the simplest of these machines and it is being manufactured in India with foreign collaboration. Then we have the online systems, offline systems and page make-up systems.

The common feature of all photo typesetting machines is the input system to capture the author's words in the form of digital data, which can be manipulated and fed into a phototype setter to produce the printed word. Keyboards are still the principal means of capturing the text, which are based on the Qwerty standard typewriter lay-out, with a number of additional functional and command keys besides the usual alphabet, punctuation marks and numerals. In the offline systems, the keyboards which are attached to the central computer directly or indirectly, are termed as the *front end system.*

Most of the systems were developed initially for use in newspapers as they have been mainly responsible for taking the initiative in changing over the new technology. Today, photo-typesetters have become the mainstay of the general printers too.

The Printed Word and the Electronic Invasion

It was the invention of the 'movable type' cast in mould, using an alloy of lead-tin-antimony, by Gutenburg, a German, in 1554, who created a revolution in the medium and introduced the term 'printed word' which led to the fight against illiteracy and superstition and in spreading knowledge in a big way.

The traditional method of printing termed the letterpress, started by Gutenburg, using the metal type through the printed message remained almost unaltered for over 500 years. Any subsequent changes that were introduced in the methods or techniques of composing were only in the mechanisation and automation of the type-setting process but not in the basic process of printing by the letterpress method. With the spread of books, journals and newspapers in the western contries after the industrial revolution, which required faster typesetting and printing, mechanisation of the typesetting process became neccessary. From hand composing, an entirely manual process of setting individual types, the transition was to mechanical compostion, that is setting types with the help of machines.

Several inventors came into this field of typesetting machines between 1820 and 1889 but many of them could not stand the test of time. Only two machines-Linotype (1886) and Monotype (1887), both American, survived the test for fully automatic text setting. With several improvements made constantly, they were serving the printers, particularly the newspaper printer all over the world setting types in all the languages in use. But with the invasion of the electronics in the field of media during the 50s, these hot metal typesetting machines have become completely outmoded and in the advanced countries, they have been entirely displaced by computerised photo typesetting machines. This technological revolution in the form of photo typsetting has taken place in India also.

Let us examine briefly the electronic revolution in the field of communication and its impact on the printed word. After World War II, there has been enormous growth in the amount of recorded information, especially in science and technology, which is often referred to as 'Information Explosion'. This created the need for information storage and retrieval systems vastly different from the traditional method of the printed book which was too slow to keep pace with the information explosion.

One of the effects of the expanded quantity of information is the emphasis on specialisation. There is so much to know about so many things that nobody can encompass everything known in a particular area of study. Therefore, one tries to segment the field, learn it in brief or outline first and concentrate on a sub-field in detail, which is specialisation. As information of every major field increases enormously and the areas of specialisation widen in greater proportion, the traditional methods of storing information in printed books becomes uneconomical, making the process laborious and time consuming.

Thus, arose the need for a new way of processing information at a fast pace, which will also permit subsequent locations of study and infomation retrieval as quickly as possible. This was how electronics came into the field of information processing. Though originally, the systems were developed with scientific and technical communication specifically in mind, they were further developed to accomodate the transfer of other kinds of scholarly and professional information. It is a new technology and a technological revolution which is related to electronics and computers. A whole range of new methods and techniques have been developed over the past a few years for each segment of our communication system through the printed word.

Though initially these changes were more technological than conceptual, the sweeping technological changes started encourgaing new conepts and new modes of communcation. Some of new methods and techniques are listed below:

- Electronic document creation and editing which includes word processing and computerised text editing.
- Photo-typesetting with direct entry, online and offline computerised systems.
- New imaging and reprographic techniques such as electronic printing, microform publication and laser electrographic printing.

- Electronic communication including e-mail, e-publication and electronic journals and
- New recording storage and retrieval systems like holographic storage, bubble memories and so on.

What is the impact of these electronic media on the printed word and what changes have they introduced in the traditional method of making the printed products? The first of these has been to alter the nature of the basic product. In traditional printing technology, the printed word was the one and only product. But with the introduction of computers and electronic media, the fundamental product was now a database. It was no longer the printed word but a precise and compact record which could be used with considerable flexibility of various applications including that of the printed product.

The first impact is then the development of an electronic literature, a term used very slackly. The new technology makes possible ways of presenting information that were previoudy not paid attention to, creating enormous user searchable bibliographic and numeric databases stored in the interactive computer systems as well as electronic message systems. Publications such as dictionaries, telephone directories and trade journals can now be revised, updated, sub-divided and raised with a degree of flexibility never before known and only the computers make all this practical in a faster and efficient way.

It is also now possible for the text or databases created on a word processor or computer in one location to be transmitted electronically to a compatible device in another location simply through the conventional telephone lines. An author, for example, can sit at home, use his word processor to create a machine readable record in the form of magnetic disc, transfer the text-data to the printing press through the telephone lines and the printer and by using an interface, can transfer these data to the photo-typesetter which produces the author's copy in the form of final page proofs. By this means, the publishers and the typesetting operator are eliminated and the author directly produces the printed word and the pritnter carries out only the plate making and printing in the press.

Farewell Gutenburg

John Gutenberg was the man who assembled the world's first press to use movable types of characters to print matter.

He is considered as the father of the printing industry. It has a long history from hand composing to today's elecronically generated type faces. The sojourn started with unotype, monotype machines and reached the latest photo optical system, typesetters, image setters and digital printing, The latest is the computerised page make-up which is used widely.

Publishing is now reduced to desk top publishing (DTP). The basic workhouse of computer based publishing is still the personal computer. Electronic publishing is becoming more popularly emerging as a revotution not just confined to the printing industry alone, now it is possible for any one to own a printing press and schedule the publication to suit him without running around for matter. This has been made possible through online communication. Computer-based printing has eliminated problems and drawbacks associated with classical printing. A new printing technology has finally replaced the age old classical printing like individual type, hand composing by the electronic printing devices. Desk top publishing has greatly facilitated text entry, file management, proofing, image editing, scanning and typesetting etc.

The impact of electronics on modern life is best seen in the field of composing and printing where the scene has shifted from hazardous metal composition rooms to air-conditioned computerised and congenial page make-up environment. There has been a spectacular development in the area of publishing and packaging. The dissemination of information to the reader also has undergone a sea change. Though developments have taken place at an unbelievable speed, there has been a great dearth of books about the printing industry. Biswanath Chakravarthy has been congratulated on his painstaking efforts in bringing out an authoritative and easy-to-understand handbook on printing and packaging.

Global Mobile Communication

An important dimension of communication services is the global mobile communication services through satellites designed to provide communication services to a particular group of individuals. The international telecommunications network has been providing invaluable, reliable and multicommuncation services for people both in India and abroad. But still there are some crucial areas which require satellite communication services for commercial, distress and safety applications at sea, in the air and on land.

Users of Mobile Communication

Global mobile satellite communications services assure providing reliable services to people who are on move either within the city or on assignments to other places. These are made available by INMARSAT which include both global and domestic value- added mobile satellite communication services.

The informational needs of these people are quite different. A distinct mobile communication through satellite has been developed towards this end.

Establishment of INMARSAT

In order to provide global mobile communication, a separate and specialised orgainsation was constituted. It is an acronym which stands for International Maritime Satellite Organisation. It was set up in the year 1979 with its headquarters in London. In 1995, there were 79 member countries in it. It is an internationally owned co-operative orgainisation. India is not only a member in it, but has a credit for being the founder member of INMARSAT. On behalf of India, the Videsh Sanchar Nigam Limited (VSNL) is a signatory to this organisation.

Objectives of INMARSAT

It is the task of the organisation to fulfil the following objectives :

- To provide a comprehensive range of services to meet the needs of a vast range of users for commercial distress and safety applications at sea, in the air and on land.
- To provide world wide mobile satellite communications for maritime, aeronautical and land mobile users.
- To provide direct dial telephone, telex, facsimile. e-mail and data communications between mobile users.
- Render support service.
- To serve the world connected to international public switched network and
- To provide value added two way message communications between subscribers and people on the move.

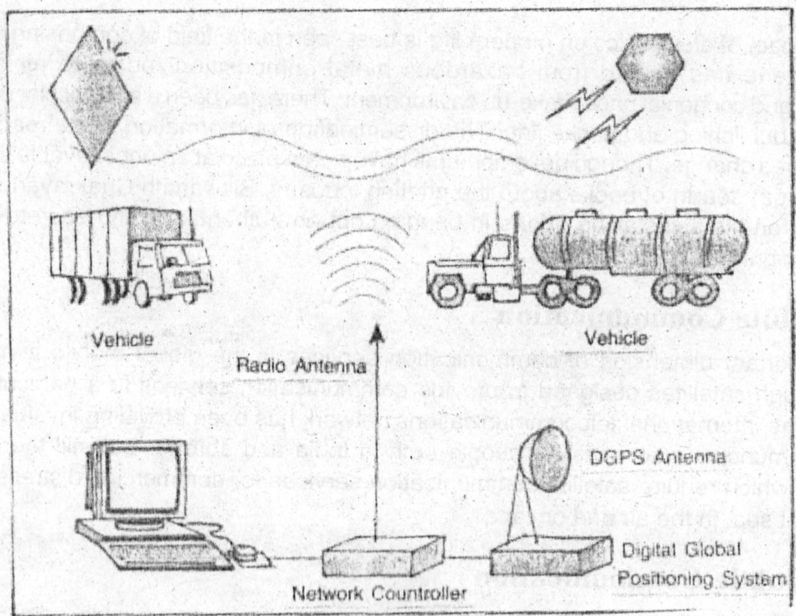

Fig, 8.11 Satellite - based Vehicle Tracker.

The three essential components of the Inmasat system are :

- The Inmarsat space segment. The satellites and their ground support facilities.
- The land earth stations (LES) which provide an interface between the space segment and the national and international fixed telecommunications networks and
- The Mobile Earth Station (MES) and the satellite communication terminals located on ship, truck etc.

Services of Inmarsat

The mobile communication services offered by the Inmarsat have been classified into the following types : A,C,B, M and P,

A profile of services under these groups are presented briefly below.

Inmarsat-A Service

Inmarsat-A system forms the backbone of the organisation's global mobile satellite communication networks as there were nearly about 7,626 land based and over 17,823 maritime Inmarsat - A. It enables to take anywhere satellite phone, telex, data, facsimile, electronic mail or photo services in the world, where local network or terrestrial communications are unavailable or unreliable. In order to meet special communication requirements of the users, different terminal options are available like multichannel systems which are able to handle two, four or six voice calls simultaneously ensuring high speed data transmission etc.

Inmarsat-A is transportable and a flexible communication tool which can be used for a variety of applications, for instance, from sites of natural catastrophes. The terminal is also used for more general communication from remote sites like mineral exploration sites, construction sites, rural areas, news broadcast, surveyors and explorers.

Inmarsat Service

Inmarsat offers one way, simplex high speed data (HSD) or two way duplex high speed data (DHSD) facility for a data rate of 56 kbps and or 64 kbps. The following are high data communication applications :

1. File Transfer: Inmarsat high speed file transfer service is more useful for high volume data communication users like seismic vessels, research vessels and offshore platforms. A file can be transferred from a ship to the head office of the ship at a very high speed.

2. Store and Forward Video: The techinque is used for data transmission. It stores and forwards video material at 56 or 64 kbps. The received material is error free, as it has a device of error detection.

3. High Quality Audio Transmission: The device is used to provide a high broadcast quality voice transmission from ship-to-shore or shore-to ship. It is more useful to the maritime community, mainly used by land to sea reporters and staff on the ship. It proves beneficial for land to sea contact and vice versa.

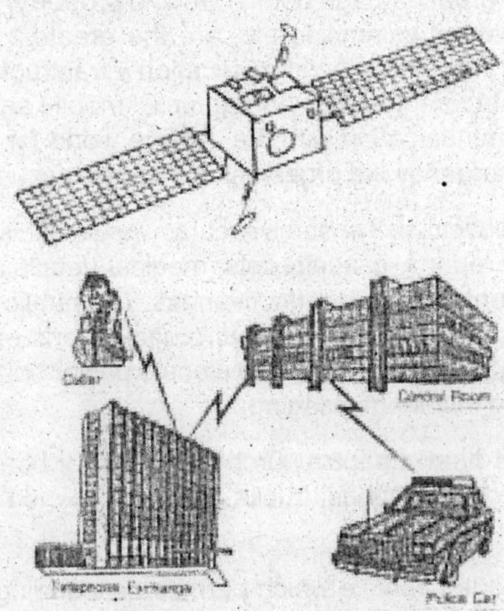

Fig. 8.12

4. Multi-Media Communications: It is used for advanced communication services such as video conferencing and digital video phones.

5. Multi Plexed Channels: It is used for several simultaneous digitized voice, fax and medium speed data calls. It is highly useful for passenger ships and reduces communication costs.

Inmarsat -'C'

This system is an important one. It is a sophisticated packet data communication system which uses a small, low cost mobile earth station which can be conveniently installed in any size of vehicle, truck, car, bus, train, ship, yacht, fishing boat or at remote data monitoring and control sites or carried in a briefcase by an individual, making it a portable facility. The special feature of the system is that it provides two way messaging and data communication. It is a highly flexible system that can support a broad range of messages only and transmit only services also. The system is primarily a two way message communcation between mobile terminals, maritime, vehicular and personal and fixed communication networks. Following are the several uses of this system :

1. Transport: Mobile communication is the first reliable communication for people who are constantly using transportation. The system can easily be mounted on any vehicle / vessel to provide instant communication between the driver and the base. It provides accurate position reports to the base or transport vessel operator on call or at fixed time intervals. It is more economical as it reduces telephone bills, minimises empty loads, ensures greater productivity and safer journeys.

2. Business Travellers: Until recently, the international telecommunications network has been unable to provide reliable communication facilities for national and international business travellers. But the Inmarsat has how designed a unique briefcase-sized version, enabling staff travelling to areas with unreliable telecommunications to contact their offices, customers, databases or other user groups in the field. It has the capacity of messaging upto 32,000 characters at one time.

Disaster Communication Remote Area Reporting: A disaster is an extremely unfortunate event or happening that causes great damage both to life and property. For instance, earthquakes, floods, hurricanes and other natural calamities etc. are the greatest disasters occuring. These natural disasters may leave the potential telecommunication infrastructure in ruins. In such cases, it is necessary to communicate to remote areas. Inmarsat 'C' mobile satellite communications can be used to establish instant communication with the outside world for local authorities to resune rescue services and involve emergency aid organisations in the rescue programme.

The system is more useful because it ensures accuracy and reliability of hard copy information. Useful information like damage reports, casualty lists, medical details and instruction etc. can be communicated effectively, efficiently with cost effectiveness. The public switched network makes it easy for field workers to contact various international organisations or offices directly. It can be operated from self contained batteries, solar, thermo electric power sources and it has the feature of lower power consumption and instant messaging.

4. FleetNet ™: The word 'fleet' means a number of ships or boats, under one command or sailing together. It includes a group of buses, trucks, taxis etc. owned by one person or persons travelling together.

Fleetnet ™ is the value added service which permits descending of a message to virtually unlimited number of predesignated mobile terminals simultaneously. This service is one of the most convenient for information subscription services, distributing new stock exchange reports, sporting results, weather analysis, road and port information. In the field of commerce, any organisation can become a fleetnet ™ service provider.

5. SafetyNet ™: The flexibility feature of Inmarsat-C can support yet another value added service for its growing number of users. It provides safety information. SafetyNet ™ has been specifically designed for the distribution of maritime safety information. Information relating to safety aspects is more important for the use of hydrographic, meteorolological, coast guards and search and rescue coordination authorities. Its object is similar to FleetNet ™ . Its additional feature is that it is capable of being able to target messages mobilise in or approaching specific geographical regions such as the area around a hazard or a rescue operation.

Maritime Distress and Safety System

There is another service called Global Maritime Distress and Safety System (GMDSS). When the ships are on board or at sea, many things may go wrong or certain unexpected happenings may warrant fast communicatin for maritime safety. GMDSS is specifically designed for fast communication and maritime safety information. Under this, every In marsat earth station is fitted

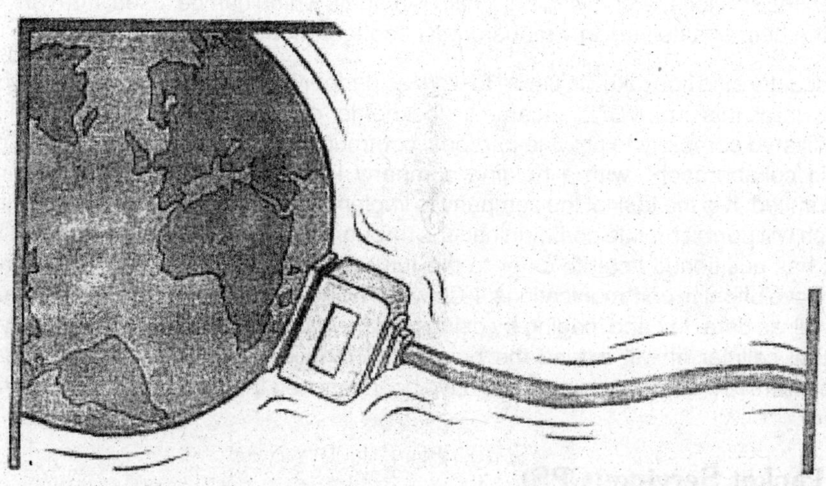

Fig. 8.13 World Connectivity

with a special alert mechanism to handle emergency situations. The system is operated by pressing a single distress button or a special abbreviated dialing code which connects automatically to a rescue coordination centre (RCC) for action. These centres are responsible for dealing with any emergency situation. So, satellite communication is a cornerstone of GMDSS which requires communication for ships operating in almost all parts of the world except in the extreme polar regions.

Monitoring Central Acquisition: Remote monitoring, control and data collection is another Inmarsat-C service. This is more useful for all Supervisory Control and Data Acquisition Applications (SCADA).

Inmarsat-M and Inmarsat-B

The Inmarsat- M system is a compact and portable satelite teminal, which supports voice, fax and data while Inmarsat- B is digital version of Inmarsat-A.

Handheld Phone (Inmarsat 'P')

The twenty first century India's electronic satellite communication equipment is *Inmarsat 'P'* services which can be used from anywhere to anywhere on the globe, using a novel handheld mobile terminal. It is global personal communication system under the sponsorship of Inmarsat. The Inmarsat 'P' system, as it is named, has been envisaged to provide global mobile communication through a handheld telephone service.

This service was expected to be available for use by the end of 1999. It is a global capital intensive verture in which VSNL has been actively participating to set up gateway facilities as well as satellite access network in India.

The advent of the handheld satellite phone will be the realisation of one of mankind's ultimate dreams, that is the ability to communicate instantly and effectively globally.

The 21st century will witness a number of operators taking to the global personal communications services, employing handheld terminals which can be used from anywhere in the world with the help of satellites in various orbital configurations.

The country also has taken initiative to work as partner in major global personal communication services. Towards this end, VSNL became a stockholder of the Inmarsat consortium. Inmarsat has set up an affiliated company to provide personal communications services by the use of handheld telphones in collaboration with a holding company known as I-com Global Communications (Holdings) Limited. It is the task of the company to implement the global handheld satellite telephone system which will permit mobile communications through a handheld phone anywhere in the world. Thus, India has positioned itself to cater to the future personal mobile services market which is expected to revolutionise communications. I-Co will provide a unique, low cost global satellite phone service as well as data, fax and paging by using handheld pocket sized terminals. Fully compatible with terrestrial cellular, it will extend the benefits of mobile communications to everyone from business travellers to those who could never have been reached through conventional communication infrastructure.

Concert Packet Service (CPS)

It is a globally managed data network service that provides a suit of seamless data network solutions on a global basis. The CPS provides extensive geographic coverage, protocol, conventions,

Fig. 8.14 Satellite Constellation

comprehensive security and substantial cost saving. The service acts as one with a national platform available for business corporations to transfer data over a single value added network and reliably. The system works alongside to PCs to meet all business communication requirements.

The service is most suitable to meet business requirements for global data networking. The advent of village globalisation and liberalisation means that major business organisations need communication on a global basis. Every busienss organisation irrespective of their sizes, whether private or public or whether profit or non-profit organisations, have been adjusting towards global changes. In other words, if they do not adjust, it means the loss of competitive advantage, business opportunites and substantial profits.

Following globalisation of the market, market protentials are expanding and the cost of supporting a traditional private network has been increasing. It is more beneficial for a corporate organisation to seek strategies/jobs to delegate all or part of the management of private communication networks. This relieves the concerns of communication networks- as such they can concentrate more on their main business activities. Systems have been developed rapidly on a global scale to manage their business and grow in the potential global market.

Features of the CPS

1. Security: The network offers security for protection against misuse of data, accidental loss or deliberate fraud.

2. Access Control: The access control facility of CPS provides an extra protection because user identity is checked by way of user names and passwords, reducing frauds subsequently.

3. User Groups: Under this service, closed user groups are formed, which in turn assures to effectively create one's own virtual private network with CPS. The formation of closed user groups restricts the number of people and locations which are allowed access to specific hosts or sites.

4. Monitoring: As referred above, security is assured following monitoring of the network performance round the clock.

5. Confidentiality: The facility of inter-nodal protocol helps data transmission over CPs to be automatically protected. There is no scope for individual user's data, and it is virtually unintelligible to anyone trying to break in and steal the data.

6. Billing and Audit: Bills are itemised to provide a very accurate audit trial for all usages on the PC.

7. Site Security: The system has arrangements for site security or physical security by means of security teams and an alarm system.

Types of Services

The services which are being provided by the CPS are broadly classified into the following three types.

- Accessing concert packet services.
- Enhanced global connection services and
- Basic global connection.

Coverage

Concert- packet service offers connections to over 115 countries end-to-end service in over 40 countries and gateway access to a further 171 networks. Global coverage access is available thorugh over 4700 nodes in more than 115 countries and cities world wide accompanied with facility for expansion and network enhancement.

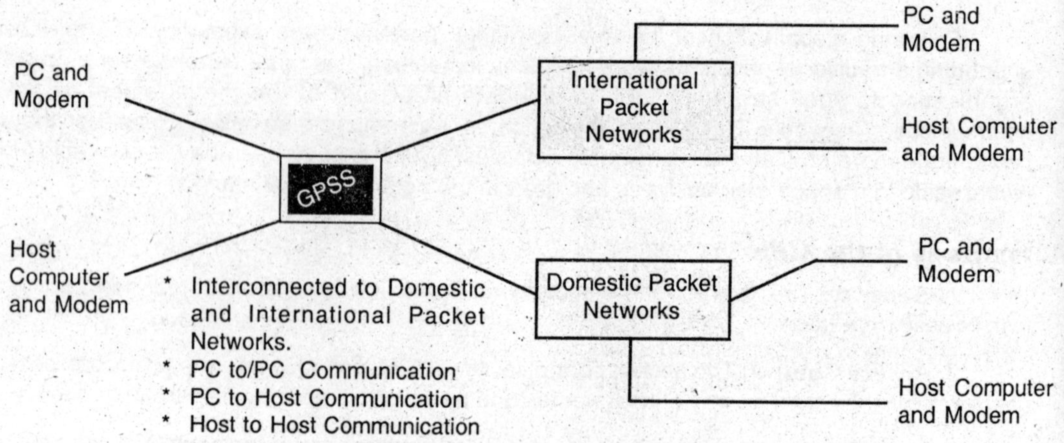

Fig. 8.15 Gateway Packet Switched Service

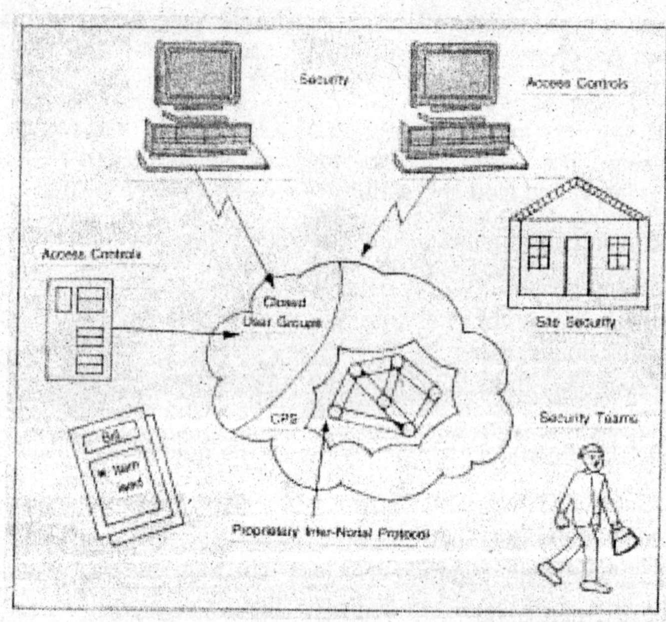

Fig. 8.16 Proprietary Inter-Nodal Protocol.

VSNL and CPS

Concert packet services are available in India through a partnership between the Videsh Sanchar Nigam Limited (VSNL) and British Telecommunications, which is one of the three largest international telecommunications carriers in the world and the largest in Europe. VSNL is India's highway to the world which has undertaken the task to provide and maintain external communications facility to Indian customers.

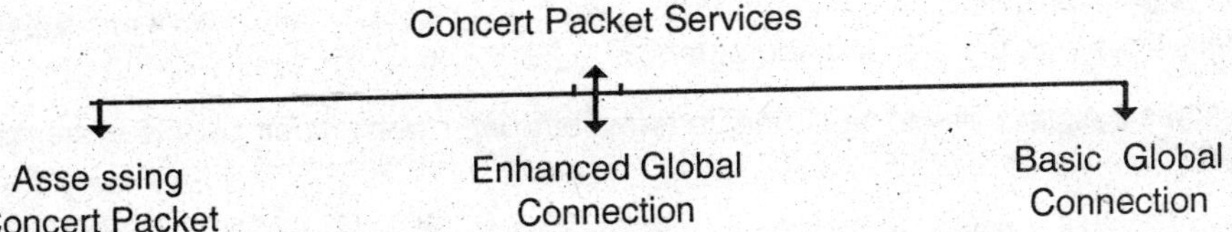

Gateway Packet Switched Service (GPSS)

The Gateway Packet Switched Service, popularly called in usage as GPSS,is yet another electronic gateway for the world of data communications. The system facilitates to simultaneously communicate with more than one terminal equipment. It is India's gateway to the international public switched packet data networks (PSPDN) in over 80 countries. The system communicates data fastly, efficiently and is cost-effective. The gateway facilitates a new business organisation world wide enabling access by remote customer database and or time sharing computer system connected with packet switched service network.

Packet swithcing exchange at Mumbai, New Delhi and Kolkata are inter-conncected through high speed links to major international data networks. The Remote Area Business Message Network (RABMN) is a data network of Department of Telecommunications exclusively developed for communications from remote locations of India which is also interconnected to GPSS based at Mumbai.

Packet

Concept and Meaning: *A packet is a block of data whose maximum length is fixed.* Like a postal letter, the packet of information is sent from one place to another. The sender's data is divided into blocks of data called *packets* and each packet contains particulars like address along with the header and control information for routing purposes.

The packets are then routed individually via the most efficient path from the point of origination to their destination,where they are reassembled into their correct order.

Packet Switching

A packet switched network is designed to meet the specific needs of the subscriber requiring:

- Terminal - to - terminal link
- Terminal - to - host link and
- Host - to - host data communication.

A packet - switched network is a group of interconnected packet switches which routes packets from the sender to the receiver. Both the sender and the receiver require an access line to the closed network access point.

Packet Assembler / Disassembler (PAD)

It is a device of GPSS which converts data to be sent into packets, then transmits them over the network to another PAD at its destination, where it is converted back to its original format.

Features of Packet Switched Service

There is no problem of incompatibility with the switched packet service. It supports a variety of access links with the existing computers.

It has the capability to work and communicate with many incompatible systems and terminal devices.

- With the help of virtual circuits, the service uses communication facilities more efficiently than traditional circuits switching.
- Both public and private networks instantly reach hosts over the international packet switched networks.
- The fixed costs associated for its utility are relatively less.
- Data security facility is also available in the system through alternate network paths to be reassemled securely at the receiving location.
- Billing, track, data time, length, origin, destination etc are easy to understand and operate.
- It offers online real time connection at speed upto 64 kbps.
- The service provides two-way access to the network depending upon the user's requirements.
- GPSS helps to obtain service of GEDIS i.e. import and export transactions which are paperless.
- One can communicate worldwide at the application level.
- The electronic mail service is also availble through the packet switched service.
- Easy Net system can also be accessed through the GPSS according to procedures.
- The Consultative Committee for International Telegraphy and Telephones (CCITT) established communication standards which ensures that devices and data networks communicate effectively with each other.
- It provides for inherent error detection and corrections for the rapid exchange of error free data.

Uses and Applications

1. *Interactive:* The system greatly facilitates interactive transmission such as travel reservations, credit checks and the point of the sale system.

2. *Databases:* It is most suitable for accessing information from databases as well as the resulting information search and retrieval cost down.

3. *Time Sharing:* In addition to databases, some computers provide time sharing services for data processing and software development.

4. *Link:* The packet service serves as a link between the subscriber's terminal and the computer.

5. *Multi-national Corporations:* The packet switched service greatly helps multinational corporations to communicate with their headquarters and regional offices around the world for the purpose of transfer of management information, access the corporate's host computers for electronic mail and data processing .

6. Network Integration: The special application of the gateway packet service is network integration, i.e. it permits the integration of different types of terminals, PCS and host computers with it.

7. Electronic Order Exchange: Packet switching for the world of data communication is ideal for electronic order exchange. As it is connected to the network, it accurately transmits and receives information, orders, invoices, payment, availability and shipping.

8. Information Provider: What is needed in the present expanded worldwide market is to have easier access to information. It is information being provided to business parties that enhances the goodwill of a concern. Global packet switched service provides international access to the concern's market awareness. So, investment in this system proves rewarding in terms of sales and profits. The vendors can provide computerised services to the users to generate potential business for themselves.

Universal Connect Data and Global Business

The Scenario: In the information savvy society, modern businesses are becoming increasingly dependent upon the speedy and frequent movement of trade and the market for transaction based information. Globally, the need for high speed pathways for global business is being strategically felt. The liberalisation of the communication policy, deregulations, delicensing and freedom for foreign investment in the last decades witnessed globalisation of businesss and growing interdependence in the world's economy.

These factors and various other developments in the sophisticated electronic information prove that the lifeline of all successful corporate business is their communication network. Accordingly, every corporation, its branches and multinational corporations should possess efficient and effective power to communicate with speed and ease without compromising on quality.

In the light of these developments, what a business world requires is an effective communication technology giving the assurance that what is desired to commumnicate and information communicated has reached its destination with least cost and with minimum time loss. This would prove an asset which every corporation at the national and international level ought to have. Every business organisation wants to stay ahead in the business world that is driven by severe competition. Such circumstances demand to have an efficient telecommunication network which is imperative for any business to flourish.

The traditional media of communication has proved absolute both in terms of operations cost and management efficiency. It has been the experience of many business organizations, both domestic and multinational corporations. In the days of information evolution, the business world has been increasingly experiencing the ill-effects of obsolete technology. The home grown or patchwork systems of communication have proved outdated in view of the emerging new information technology.

What the business world needs today is solutions that are integrated, flexible and user friendly, enabling quality time to be utilised in the core business of the organisation. These are necessary in order to stay abreast of new technology which as a matter of fact have become essential.

Gratifying Global Media Global Business

The need to unite the world through communication cannot be ignored. A universal connectivity is to be established as the *lifeline* of any successful global business. Accordingly, for the need to form a global telemedia,an autonomous body was felt.

Arrival of TeleMedia International

TeleMedia International (TMI) Limited is a wholly owned subsidiary of Telecom Italia S.P.A. It was established in the year 1982 to provide value added telecommunications to multinational corporations. In the field of telecom services, it is the first of its kind to provide reliability, experience and customer satisfaction. It has been rendering highest quality services to its users.

It is a private digital network with 78 points of service with an extensive network. TM1 is managed by a team of highly specialised dedicated experts. It has global recognition.

TMI now offers communication solutions to multinational organizations in the following major ways :

- Value added services
- Customised solutions
- Big cost saving
- Connectivity
- Flexibility
- Creativity
- Guarantee of services
- Convenience
- Quality
- Reliablility
- Economy and the world of other benefits to the global customers.

TMI thus provides universal connect which is an international data transmission service.

VSNL AND TMI

The universal connect to unite the world through communication, which is a perfect solution to multinational organizations is now available in India, in association with VSNL. The Videsh Sanchar Nigam (VSNL), a Government of India enterprise which covers international telcommunication needs four international telecom gateway at Mumbai, New Delhi, Chennai and Kolkatta, it has been responsible for providing and maintaining international communication facilities to its Indian customers and has fully and computerised telephone telex and telegraph switching exchanges, both with satellite and cable circuits and computerised telephone. Thus today, VSNL is India's highway to the world. Accordingly, TMI Universal Data Network is available now in India in association with VSNL for global multinational businesses.

Global Business Connect Packages

TMI has designed universal data network as universal connect data. The package of network includes two most advanced telecommunication data services in the world universal connect datafast (frame relay).

These two data services have been designed to satisfy the needs of the most complex business requirements.

A brief descriptin of these two data services is given below:

Universal Connect Data

This package is the lifeline of global business organisations for successful business. Multinational organisations have large volume of data transmission. Universal connect data is the most suitable for data transmission. It is one of the most advanced telecommunications data services in the world designed to satisfy the needs of the most complex global business requirements. The package transmits voluminous data at relatively lower speeds (9.6 kbps to 64 kbps) requiring mostly interactive applications such as :

- Financial Data Processing
- Low Speed LAN (Local Area Network) interconnections.
- Electronic Mail (E- mail) and
- Electronic Data Interchange (EDI).

The package offers international connectivity for substantial data transfer.

User Groups

The package is now being availed by different cross sections of the business world. As it is one of the most popular and reliable protocols in the world, its users would come from a gamut of sectors. For example, Credit, Finance, Banking, Insurance, Airlines, Travel Agencies, Manufacturers, Publishing Companies, Hotels etc.

Services

The universal connect data offers many benefits plus enhanced and superior technology at no extra cost. It ensures massive cost savings in the annual expenditure of the user. The user has to pay only for one local leased circuit for each destination of their network in order to connect to the nearest TMI centre. However, the package offers the following advantages:

- Reliable packet data transfer protocols with automatic error rectification
- Opportunity of alternative re-routing back-up
- Connectivity Public Switched Data and
- Choice between flat-rate and traffic volume dependent prices (unlimited or limited traffic options).

Universal Connect Datafast

Universal Connect Datafast is another package which is one of the most advanced telecommunications data services in the world. It is designed to meet needs of most complex global business requirements. It is a communication interface designed for international data transmission applications at relatively high speeds. The capacity of speed may range from 64 kbps, onwards for multinational organisations utilsing LAN based information systems. It uses both interactive and non-interactive applications such as:

- File Transfer
- Database Transfer
- Electronic Mail
- Electronic Data Interchange and
- Image Transfer etc.

Any multinational organisation or in general any organisation with an aim to keep ahead of competition needs to maintain universal connection for data transfer between businesses world wide. It is the reliable and cost effective solution to international business communities world wide. The user can access service through a local point digital circuit connecting the customer's premises to the nearet TMI node centre.

Features

Unviersal connect data has distinct features offering superior solutions. It may include the following :

- Highly reliable protocol that 'frames' all data in well protected 'packets' to avoid error and data loss.
- Simple, fast and cost effective network configuration.
- Optimisation of traffic handling and provides low transit delay.
- Burst traffic handling for sudden increase in traffic.
- Adoptive dynamic re-routing, with virtually no service failure occurences.
- Interactive response which supports data, voice and graphic applications.
- Interconnection with packet and circuit data networks well connected worldwide and,
- Universal connect datafast is based on the latest technology of Virtual Private Network which allows for a more efficient configuration and offers more saving in comparison with the traditional private networks using international leased circuits.

TMI- Worldwide Service

Telemedia International Limited has been rendering valuable telecommunication services and value added solutions to solve most of the problems of multinational corporations. The system helps both in terms of cost including management efficiency. Its worldwide services are integrated, flexible and user friendly, enabling quality time to be utilised in the core businesses of organisations.

The following are the worldwide serivices of TMI:

Outsourcing

Outsourcing means delegation to external specialised companies or outsourcing compaines. Outsourcing usually represents a class separate from networking, it is separate because in addition to private circuits, they include several products and services for all customers who wish to outsource i.e. delegate to external specialised companies. It may be globally or partially the activites relating to design, implementiation and management of their global, regional or local private networks. This service includes :

- Project management
- Technical support
- Equipment housing
- Round the clock network management and
- One stop shopping.

Network Service: In the worldwide service of the TMI, private network as well as public services are included. It supports the existing private network. Network services have been designed and tailored to enhance the user's existing private network or to interconnect to public services. As such, this service enables the user to transmit :

- Data to telex devices
- Facsimile machines
- Host computers and
- Other high speed terminals.

Network sevices includes private and virtual digital network (4.8 kbps), local area network / wide area network, internet working, network and facility management and outsourcing.

Value Added Fax: Store and forward fax service is the forefront in providing the latest international telecommuniction services. Value added fax service of the TMI is based on store and forward technology which offers a reliable international service for companies who want to send messages by fax to one or more destinations around the world. The features of this service include:

- Broadcasting of the fax message to multiple destinations.
- Insertion of cover page
- Speed code (use of short dial number)
- Automatic interception and management by TMI operators
- Automatic retry at programmed intervals in the events of interrupted transmission and
- Regular report on delivery status, cancellation notification and activity report (on request).

Video Communication Video communication service or video conferencing allows people in different locations to meet face to face far apart, across the table and across the world. It enables inter-office communication without having to travel. It has the potential to play a major role in the overall communication strategy of an organisation. It is ideal for big companies which have global operational branches. Multinational corporations having branches worldwide can conveniently communicate face to face without leaving the office. Services of this type include :

- The option of holding video conference meeting using TMI's network equipment and
- The option of having "ad-hoc" video conferencing using TMI's premises and equipment.

Messaging Services

In the light of interdependence in the world's economy, it has become evident that the lifeline of all successful corporations is their communication set-up. Any global service which enables organisations to communicate with speed and ease without compromising on quality enable them to reach their destination with minimum time loss and cost is an asset which multinational corporations ought to have. The TMI, with its modern sophisticated technology system, has been rendering efficient messaging services to ensure accurate and timely delivery of business messages. Messaging services of TMI offer a wide variety of domestic and international messaging services including fax and telex, combined with its high technology hardware and sophisticated systems.

Intelsat Business Service (BS)

Intelsat Business Service (BS) is a totally integrated digital service designed to accommodate the full range of business communications on point to point basis viz. data communication, voice communication, video conferencing, high speed facsimile, CAD/CAM, electronic funds transfer etc.

However, data transmission represents the largest business application of IBS on the Intelsat system. IBS offers a wide range of data rates, from 64 kbps or mulitples of 64 kbps upto 8.448 mbps to provide all forms of non-switched service to end users. IBS provides private communications direct to the end user via a small and medium size antenna located in cities or at end user premises. IBS is used extensively by the financial community for applications such as electronic fund transfer, cash management operations etc. Inter-computer transfer involving corporate star networks is an efficient and promising application of IBS. IBS provides an attractive alternative using quicky installed low cost wide band data communication links, avoiding last mile local extrension problems. IBS may not be connected to the public switched telephone network. The direct satellite link will be provided on a point to point basis.

Videotex

Videotex is the international name for the system originally designated to view data but also often to mean the broadcast service, generally known as teletex. Sometimes, the term 'broadcast' is used for teletex.[1]

A remarkable development in the electronic media, among others is the videotex technology which increases the capacity of the television set to function like a computer terminal and retrieve information and graphics from a remote database. A videotex system would be very useful in disseminating general information about courses and programmes available through distance education.[2]

Word processors and text processors have made text editing much less cumbersome to provide and ensure easy availability of simpler text versions to suit the competent individual learner. Electronic publishing could be videotex-based. Videotex system comprises a telephone, a television set for monitoring a computerised database, a keyboard controller and a modem unit. 'Modem' is an acronym for a modulating-demodulating device because it converts a digital square wave signal that cannot be processed by a telephone into an analogue signal that can be easily processed by it. It also provides for reverse function i.e. conversion from the analogue into the digital form. Videotex systems, a variant form of the videotext, has been designed to perform the function of transmission and receiving electronically transmitted messages. It has the capacity to store a large amount of graphic and alphanumerical information. Telephones and other channels can be used for receiving customer's request for stored information and forwards the retrieved information electronically to the customers. It is thus an interactive and graphic service. The use of videotext home information

---

1. Studies in Distance Education, Association of Indian Universities, 1998, P.106.
2. Antoni, Learning At a Distance, A World Perspective, p. 290.

networks has become more popular in recent years. The following figure represents a schematic diagram of the videotext systThe listener / viewer operates the key controller and oral inormation is available through the modem over the telephone and its visual counterpart is flashed on the TV screen. The telephone and modem allow for a two-way interactive system wherein the listener / viewer can also ask questions, seek clarifications or get supplementary information.

Prestel (Great Britain, Antipoe (France), Captain (Japan) and Telidon (Canada) are good examples of successful videotex systems. Among these, Prestel was the first to become a world videotex service of the succesful videotex system in 1979. Teletex, on the other hand, provides a one-way facility for getting information. The listener/viewer, however, cannot seek additional information. Videotex is relatively faster and provides easier access to and a more fruilful use of computer database, thus holding greater promise for the Indian Open Learning System (IOLS).

Videotex is a transmission device system, which uses a TV set to display text. It helps to use computer-based information service. Teletext and view data are the two kinds of video systems.

Thus, Videotex is an electronic device of sophisticated commumnication technology, which greatly helps as it provides new opportunities for communication with the general public. Here, the viewer is directly connected to a central computer by way of the home terminal, permitting the viewer to call upon or send information, making a two-way commumnication system.

Videotape

It is a recording tape carrying pictures and sound, used to record programmes in pictures and sound using videotape. Videotape is a powerful alternative to conventional printing which has literally taken over the entertainment world from the Indian cinema. Videotape stores magnetic signals for the simultaneous and subsequent retrieval of the visual and the audio information components. Lectures by experts, demonstration of processes, techniques and field trips and inaccessible remote regions could be recorded on videotape for subsequent use. TV series like 'Secrets of the Sea' and 'The Living Planet illustrate the numerous possibilities of IOLs as well as FLS. Video disks have not been as popular as videotape despite their obvious advantage. Compared to video tape, videodisk represents the largest/densest storage medium in existence. It is very durable and because of the nature of the system, (free from wear), its radial format provides almost instant access to any one of the 55,000 clear, sharp and rock steady images instead of having to wind foot after foot of video tape.[1]

Compared to the videotape, videodisk recording is less cumbersome, though its front end cost is much higher. It is almost thrice as cheap as videotape in the long run[2]. Videotape, as potential technology, removes the constraint of viewing TV programs at a fixed time.

These tapes are like films and have the same impact as the film. The audience for a film is larger than videotape, but tapes are being seen on a televison screen. The audience for videotape is smaller such as family, friends etc. Films are costly to make while videotapes are cheaper to make. Tapes are, however, subject to editing, but no need to be processed. There are large companies which have their own video studios to produce programs.

---

1. *Grove Michael, The interactive Video Disk in education and technology, London, as reported in Studies in Distance Education, Association of India Universities, 1984, p. 97.*
2. *Zorkoczy, P. Information Technology, An Introduction, London, Croom Helm, 1982.*

Datel

Datel is a service for standard point to point transmission. Datel has different numbers mainly Datel - 200, Datel -600. Datel -1200 etc. The number of Datel indicates corresponding transmission speed in bits per second (bps). Datel works with higher speed upto 48,000 bps with wide band circuits with the facility of both public and privately leased lines which can be suitably used by all orgainsations having considerable quantity of data to be transmitted.

Prestal

Prestal is a device of terminal used as a computer-based information service available over the telephone lines. It is viewed as a technology which is internationally known as videotape. Both public and privately operated view data systems are available. Prestal is a public view data service in British Telegrams. The working of this system is that the view data terminals are plugged into standard telephone sockets. It has the advantage of various business applications and may provide lakhs of frames of information which is a screen size page of information. Information like money market, stock exchange, insurance, agricultural market,travel information etc.are more useful to the business and this can be viewed through the view data. The rent and cell charges are to be paid by the users for the page viewed. It is a coslty method to view for a few minutes.

Message Distribution Services

The message distribution system has a separate storage mail box wherein messages can be transmitted at any time of the day. It is not necessary to have the presence of the receiver of the message. Even if the receiver is present, there is no need to disturb his present work to receive the message. The message is conveniently stored in a storage mail box. As a result, the receiver can read the message by retrieving the message in a storage mail box. The facility is there for both spoken message or text.

It is an electronic process of converting voice into digital pulses. In case of keyed text, the teleprinter is used for entering and receiving keyed messages. The advantage of e-mail is that messages can be received and sent at any time. The message distribution system greatly helps people who are located over wide geographical areas to have instant communications of both receiving and sending messages.

The voice is transmitted by a separate device called the input device which does the work of converting human language into machine language. A human voice or speech is converted into electrical signals by the device of telephone or microphone. The storage of a computer has a dictionary. The human speech in electrical signals are to be transmitted to a computer for comparison.

Teletext

Teletext is an electronic device of communication which operates with communication technology. This technique of communication offers a limited or narrow choice of information and services. The messages are transmitted and delivered by the conventional television signals and decoded by a device attached to a television set. Teletext is one way link like the television.

In the UK, this technology has been developed under a variety of trade names since 1979. For instance, Knight Ridder Newspaper and AT&T developed a video system as Viewtron. The system combines a space age technology with a television set and telephone lines. Since 1983, this system began operating in the USA, South Florida. Taft Broadcasting, USA, developed the one-way teletext system. These two systems have been meeting the needs of information in a big way.

Teletext refers to the transmission of text on usual television channels. The system displays text on the TV set. The British Broadcasting Corporation (BBC) and Independent Television (ITV) render pages of information when requested by the viewer. The Teletext system is more popular in the British region. On switching the key pad within a few seconds, the required page appears on the screen. The system covers many specific topics like stock markéts, consumer prices, financial matters, weather information, economics. technology etc.

It enables television broadcasting authorities to broadcast digital data which takes place by inserting it into the normal television signal, using special equipment located at their stations. The decoder of any TV set equipment can on the viewer's request work to suppress the normal program picture display and pick out the digital information from the broadcast signal and display it on its screen as the fixed page of letters and numbers.

Broadcasting TV singals is not completely occupied with picture information. Picture information is sent as a series of still pictures with a gap of about two thousands of a second duration between stills. This gap is called as vertical blanking interval. It is used to transmit data without disturbing the preceding and following picture information.

Various levels of information are available through teletext. Currently, pages containing information like news, sports, finance, weather, rail and delay status, TV and cinema program timings, city engagements, tourist services etc. are available. The information on the above categories and others is sent to the broadcasting authority studio by the supplier agencies by facsimile, voice, hotline or data line. In the former two cases, it is entered into the teletext controlling computer and in the latter, it enters the computer directly.

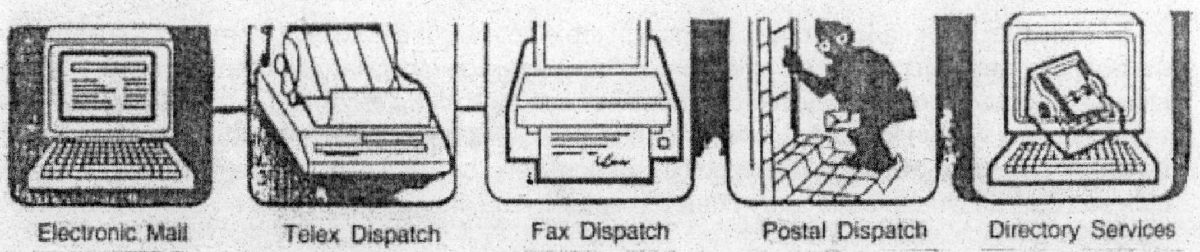

Fig. 8.17

The nucleus or the heart of teletext transmission system is a piece of equipment called the multi-plexer. The device has one video input and one or more data input. One of the functions of the multi-plexer is to output the same video signal with the data inserted in video compatible form into a few previously empty lines of the vertical blanking period. The second function is to split the physical television channel into a number of logical data channels.

The intelligence and control of the teletext transmission system is provided by the computer which also performs other teletext service management functions such as arching of pages and actually broadcast holding of predesignated pages for editiorial authorization before broadcast for providing libraries etc.

Viewdata

Viewdata is another type of videotex system. It is a computer-based information system. The network operates by linking viewdata terminals to a central computer through telephone lines in the case of teletext, and on request by the viewer, the page appears on the screen and the printer. Originally, information is transmitted on pages.

Difference between Teletext and Viewdata

Viewdata and teletext are the important and useful devices generally confused by non-technical peple. It is important for us to look at the differences between these two devices. One therefore, should not get confuse viewdata with teletext. Both are computer based information and technologies. Both have some features common to each other.

The operating features of the teletext is that the frames of information are transmitted along with television signals. It is possible only when a television set is fitted with a teletext adapter. The adapter is capable of viewcoding the signals and display these frames.

Video-Cassettes

The technology is available and is gaining importance all over the world. The materials used for radio and television can be supplied in the form of video cassettes. The video cassettes can be stored. |n view of the limitations of television, increasing use is being made of video cassettes.

Videodisc

Videodisc is yet another development in the electronic media which increases the capacity of the television set. Videodisc is a system similar to the long conventional television set. It has enormous storage capacity. The glossary of technical terms is related to the recording video information on the videodisc as a system for record, which enables it to be replayed. However, such a system can also be used to record digital data. Such discs can hold very large amount of information, although the data can only be written once and in order to amend data, it has to be rewritten on the blank part of the disc.

The optical disc has more enormous storage capacity of 1,08,000 tracks and 54,000 on each side. The - Encyclopaedia Britannica can be stored on a single disc with room to spare. They are powerful alternatives to conventional printing.

❑❑❑

Some e-mail Addresses

ADDRESSES	ORGANISATIONS
it cot @vsnl.com	Industrial and Technical Consultancy Organisation of Tamil Nadu.
in vitro @bgl.vsnl.net.in	In Vitro International
geaed @ md4.vsnl.net.in	Gea Energy Systems (India) Limited
reach@midcindia.com	Maharashtra Industrial Development Corporation
sales@adityagroup.com	Aditya Promoters Pvt. Ltd.
svl-narayana@satyam.com	Satyam Computer Services Ltd.
ssg@corp.cmc.net.in	CMC Ltd.
raj-saraf@zenith-india.com	Zenith Computers Ltd.
info@compuageindia.com	Compuage Electronics Pvt.Ltd.
info@amkette.com	Allied Electronics & Magnetics
wikky@sai.cii.ernet,in	Confederation of Indian Industry
mktgft-sa.itindia.com	L&T Information Technology Ltd.
bdps@bdpsindia.com	ECIL-BDPS Computer Education
rkapoor@summitindia.com	Summit Data Products Ltd.
vshah@novell.com	Novell Software Development (I) Pvt.Ltd.
nai@godrejpacific.com	Godrej Pacific Technology Ltd.
pansari@bom2.vsnl.net.in	Rashi Peripherals Pvt.Ltd.
dds@cal.vsnl.net.in	Digital Data Systems
recovery@nde.vsnl.net.in	Stellar Information Systems P.Ltd.
vsi@viewsonic.com.tw	View Sonic, USA.
unistal@unistal.com	Unistal Systems Pvt.Ltd.
recruit@kanbay.com	Kanbay Software (India) pvt.Ltd.
info@3dvsystems.com	3DV Systems Israel.
atrpltd@gias-bgol.vsnl.net.in	Telematics 199, Banglore.
ganeshn@aptech.ac.in	Aptech Ltd.
bombay@lipidata.com	Lipi Data Systems Ltd.
rarora@giasbmol.vsnl.net.in.	Datapro Infoworld Ltd.
info@vsoft.stph.net	Visualsoft (India)Ltd.
biz@teil.soft.net	Tata Elxsi (India) Ltd.
Kieand@mahindrabt.com	Mahindra-British Telecom Ltd.
anil.laud@boml.siemens.com.in	Siemens Information System Ltd.